CINEMATIC GUERRILLAS

Cinematic Guerrillas

Propaganda, Projectionists, and Audiences in Socialist China

Jie Li

Columbia University Press   New York

Columbia University Press
Publishers Since 1893
New York   Chichester, West Sussex
cup.columbia.edu
Copyright © 2023 Columbia University Press
All rights reserved

Library of Congress Cataloging-in-Publication Data
Names: Li, Jie, 1979– author.
Title: Cinematic guerrillas : propaganda, projectionists, and audiences in socialist China / Jie Li.
Description: New York : Columbia University Press, [2023] | Includes bibliographical references and index.
Identifiers: LCCN 2023008240 (print) | LCCN 2023008241 (ebook) | ISBN 9780231206266 (hardback) | ISBN 9780231206273 (trade paperback) | ISBN 9780231556392 (ebook)
Subjects: LCSH: Motion pictures—China—History—20th century. | Motion pictures—Political aspects—China.
Classification: LCC PN1993.5.C4 L4694 2023 (print) | LCC PN1993.5.C4 (ebook) | DDC 791.430951—dc23/eng/20230607
LC record available at https://lccn.loc.gov/2023008240
LC ebook record available at https://lccn.loc.gov/2023008241

Cover design: Elliott S. Cairns
Cover image: Xin Liliang, "Rural Projectionist," Shanghai People's Art Press (1966)

To Liselotte and Daniel

Contents

Acknowledgments   ix

INTRODUCTION
Revolutionary Spirit Mediumship   1

PART ONE Projectionists as Media Infrastructure

CHAPTER ONE
Cinematic Nation-Building: Media Networks and
Spiritual Battlegrounds   41

CHAPTER TWO
Mobile Projectionists and the Things They Carried   66

CHAPTER THREE
The Three Sisters Movie Team: Projecting Models,
Model Projectionists, and Female Projectionists   91

CHAPTER FOUR
The Cost of Spiritual Food: A Ritual Economy of Rural Cinema   121

PART TWO Audiences as Creative Agents

CHAPTER FIVE
The Hot Noise of Open-Air Cinema   145

CHAPTER SIX
Guerrilla Cinema and Guerrilla Reception   163

CHAPTER SEVEN
Transcultural Guerrillas: The Reception of Foreign Films in
Socialist China   193

CHAPTER EIGHT
Poisonous Weeds and Censorship as Exorcism   215

Epilogue   241

Appendix: Interviews   251
Notes   265
Index   323

Acknowledgments

More than a decade in the making, this book owes a tremendous debt of gratitude to many individuals who offered their generous help and engaged me in generative conversations. My first thanks go to the projectionists and audience members who shared their cinematic experiences, archives, images, jokes, plights, and insights, taking my academic research questions on imaginative flights and bringing them back down to earth. The seeds of this book were planted when I worked at the Long Bow Group on a documentary film and website about the Chinese Cultural Revolution. I thank Carma Hinton, Richard Gordon, Geremie Barmé, Hua Dong, and the late Nora Chang for showing me the art and ethics of oral history as well as the power and limits of audiovisual propaganda. Meanwhile, conversations with my extended family in China and their circle of old classmates, comrades, and neighbors made me realize how cinematic enchantment had much to do with the exhibition and reception context as well as the creative agency of audiences. I am grateful to Chen Qiuping, Li Rong, Lou Weihua, Lu Guoguang, Pan Hengsheng, Qin Guangren, and Zhu Xueqin for early interviews that helped me formulate research questions. Special thanks go to Ma Lin for organizing a focus group of former sent-down youths to answer a detailed questionnaire and to discuss their cinemagoing memories. Professor Feng Xiaocai of East China Normal University helped organize several collaborative field trips to rural Zhejiang, Hubei, Hebei, and Northeast provinces with his curious and capable students. For making local contacts, interpreting between Mandarin and dialects, and taking notes at interviews, I thank Cui Longhao, Feng Lin, Gong Wei, Gong Wenya, Lin Qi, Lin Ruyi, Qin Yuan, Sheng Chaicai, Shi Xiankui, and Wang Yufei. I am especially grateful to Li Bingbing, Lyu Hongyun, and Wang Sisi for undertaking multiple fieldtrips, excavating rich archival materials, and asking generative and incisive questions. Xin Zhou kindly introduced me to his grandmother, who served as a factory projectionist for several decades. I also wish to give special acknowledgment to Peng Hai for independently collecting fifteen invaluable oral histories from Ningxia.

Research for this book took me to many libraries and archives. It was in the stacks of the Chinese University of Hong Kong Library that I first discovered a treasure trove of local film gazetteers that prompted my search of similar sources on used bookstore websites. With the kind assistance of librarians, I made serendipitous findings at the Changchun Library, Harbin Library, the National Library of China in Beijing, Shanghai Library, Shenyang Library, Tokyo's National Diet Library, and the Library of Modern History at Taipei's Academia Sinica. I am also grateful to the patient help of staff at the Beijing Municipal Archives, Heilongjiang Provincial Archives, Hubei Provincial Archives, Shanghai Municipal Archives, Shenyang Municipal Archives, Zhejiang Provincial Library, as well as various prefectural- and county-level archives in Zhejiang, Hubei, Hebei, and the Northeast provinces. At the Harvard-Yenching Library, Xiao-he Ma, Sharon Yang, and Adrianne Gren have always been amazingly resourceful and responsive to my many requests. Nancy Hearst of the Fairbank Center library helped me locate some rare and unique historical sources.

The writing of this book took place in Princeton, Cambridge, Taipei, and Speyer. At the Princeton Society of Fellows, Mary Harper, Susan Naquin, Jerome Silbergeld, and Susan Stewart were some early interlocutors while this project was at a gestational stage. Since joining Harvard's Department of East Asian Languages and Civilizations and Program in Film and Visual Studies, I have received ongoing support and inspiration from my colleagues: Ryuichi Abe, David Atherton, Peter Bol, Guiliana Bruno, Chan Yong Bu, Carter Eckert, Mark Elliott, Andrew

Gordon, Helen Hardacre, David Howell, Wilt Idema, Wesley Jacobsen, Tom Kelly, Sun Joo Kim, Hisa Kuriyama, Wai-yee Li, Jennifer Liu, Melissa McCormick, Si Nae Park, Michael Puett, Eric Rentschler, James Robson, Michael Szonyi, Karen Thornber, Xiaofei Tian, David Wang, Tomiko Yoda, and Alex Zahlten. I am lucky to have the unwavering support of departmental administrators Gustavo Espada, Alison Howe, Susan Kashiwa, and John Park. Hisa Kuriyama, Michael Puett, and Karen Thornber invited me to present my research at the department, the Fairbank Center, and the Harvard Asia Center. David Wang, Wai-yee Li, and Alex Zahlten each read the entire manuscript and gave invaluable feedback on its structure and key arguments. This book further benefited from the insights and research assistance of graduate students at Harvard, especially Peng Hai and Tim Shao-hung Teng, as well as Menglan Chen, Alina Scotti, Huanruo Wang, and Shaowen Zhang.

Various talks that turned into book chapters elicited thought-provoking responses that helped to refine, refocus, and redefine key ideas. I thank the organizers of and participants in the Permanent Seminar of the History of Film Theories at the University of Michigan (2011), the workshop on Maoist micropolitics at East China Normal University (2013), the East Asian Cinema Workshop at Princeton (2014), the workshop on "Chinese and Sinophone Cinemas" at the University of Washington (2015), the conference "Shadow History—Archive and Intermediality in Chinese Cinema" at Berkeley (2017), the symposium "Beyond the Film: Interdisciplinary Approaches to Movie Audiences and Their Environments" at Washington University, St. Louis (2018), the workshop series "Material Culture in Mao's China" at King's College London (2018) and Yale (2019), the conference "Thinking the Ecological in Media Studies" at Columbia (2019), the conference "Histories of Tacit Cinematic Knowledge" at Goethe University Frankfurt (2020), the workshop "Revolutionary Experiences Compared: Russia and China Under Communist Rule" (2021), and the workshop "Global South Cinemas During the Cold War" at Concordia University (2022). I gave additional presentations of work in progress at Academia Sinica, Buffalo, Communication University of China, Duke, Freiburg, McGill, NYU, Oxford, Peking University, Stanford, UC Santa Barbara, Wellesley, Yale, and Zhejiang University. For their kind invitations and incisive interlocutions, I thank Jennifer Altehenger, Yomi Braester, Eileen Cheng-yin Chow, Steven

Chung, Xinyu Dong, Feng Xiaocai, Aaron Gerow, Vinzenz Hediger, Lena Henningsen, Margaret Hillenbrand, Denise Ho, Erin Huang, Jin Jin, Andrew Jones, Brian Larkin, Haiyan Lee, Diane Lewis, Li Daoxin, Xiaoning Lu, Rana Mitter, Debashree Mukherjee, Markus Nornes, Peng Hsiao-yen, Franz Pritchard, Ying Qian, Elena Razlogova, Carlos Rojas, Masha Salazkina, Tanya Shilina-Conte, Mingwei Song, Weijie Song, Jing Tsu, Xiaojue Wang, Lingjia Xu, and Mayfair Yang. The book also benefited from the thoughtful feedback of discussants and audiences, especially Francesco Casetti, Robert Chi, Harriet Evans, Jacob Eyferth, Yuriko Furuhata, Karl Gerth, Tom Gunning, Barbara Mittler, William Paul, Elizabeth J. Perry, John Durham Peters, Robert Weller, Bhaskar Sakar, Michael Schoenhals, Xiaobing Tang, Emily Wilcox, Jiwei Xiao, and the late Rudolf Wagner and Yingjin Zhang.

Many friends and colleagues generously took the time to read the manuscript at various stages. For their insightful and constructive suggestions on selected chapters, I thank Jennifer Altehenger, Geremie Barmé, Yomi Braester, Luca Caminati, Tarryn Chun, Carter Eckert, Harriet Evans, Poshek Fu, Denise Ho, Xuelei Huang, Mei Li Inouye, Yan Liu, Stephen Smith, Shengqing Wu, and Man-Fung Yip. I am especially grateful to Weihong Bao, Chris Berry, Gail Hershatter, Brian Larkin, Laikwan Pang, Alexander Zahlten, and Zhang Zhen for taking part in my book manuscript workshop in 2021. Their illuminating, detailed, and candid discussion of the manuscript gave me a roadmap of revision that improved this book immensely. I am also grateful to Nancy Hearst for checking my sources and doing meticulous first-round copyediting. At Columbia University Press, my heartfelt thanks go to Christine Dunbar for her steadfast support and judicious guidance from the proposal to the review to the revision stages. Three anonymous readers provided detailed comments and productive suggestions. I am also grateful to Anita O'Brien for the last round of copyediting, to Mary Mortensen for making the index, and to Christian Winting and Susan Pensak for shepherding the book through production.

Earlier iterations of some parts of this book appeared as "Gained in Translation: The Reception of Foreign Cinema in Mao's China," *Journal of Chinese Cinemas* 13, no. 1 (2019): 61–75, also reprinted in *Cold War and Asian Cinemas*, edited by Poshek Fu and Man-Fung Yip (New York: Routledge, 2020); "Cinematic Guerrillas in Mao's China," *Screen* 61, no. 2 (2020): 207–29; "The Hot Noise of Open-Air Cinema," *Grey Room* 81 (2020): 6–35, also reprinted in *Sensing China: Modern Transformations of Sensory Culture*, edited by Xuelei Huang and Shengqing Wu (New York: Routledge, 2022); and "Mobile Projectionists and the Things They Carried," in *Material Contradictions in Mao's China*, edited by Jennifer Altehenger and Denise Y. Ho (Seattle: University of Washington Press, 2022). I thank the editors and reviewers of all these journals and edited volumes for their comments and suggestions. The research and writing of this book received support from the Chiang Ching-kuo Foundation Scholar Grant, the Dean's Competitive Grant for Promising Scholarship, the Fairbank Center for Chinese Studies, the Harvard Asia Center, and the Harvard China Fund.

My grandparents Li Baoren, Wang Zhengwen, Yao Zhanghua, and Zhu Yuehua sparked my initial interest in China's revolutionary century. As former cultural workers and propaganda artists under state socialism, my mother Wang Yaqing and father Li Bin inspired and anchored my historical research through vivid and nuanced accounts of their youth. From early contacts with interviewees to scanning images and securing permissions, my parents have remained tireless and faithful champions of my work. I completed the first complete manuscript draft under the roof of my wonderful parents-in-law, Anne-Dore and Klaus Koss, who helped teach and care for our children throughout the pandemic lockdown. Anton and Renate showed me how to see and listen to the world afresh. Liselotte waited until I submitted the manuscript to the press before her joyous leap into this world. This book is dedicated to her and to Daniel, whose love and companionship have been the greatest blessing of my life.

CINEMATIC GUERRILLAS

INTRODUCTION

Revolutionary Spirit Mediumship

The Chinese revolution was a media revolution. From 1949 to 1983 the film exhibition network in the People's Republic developed from fewer than 600 movie theaters to some 162,000 projection units.[1] Most were mobile movie teams that conducted open-air screenings in the countryside. To areas without electricity, they brought not only films on celluloid but also power generators, lantern slideshows, gramophone records, propaganda posters, live performances, and the hustle and bustle of mass participation. Alongside the growth of radio broadcasting into 100 million wired loudspeakers, the film exhibition network projected and amplified the party-state's visions and voices to the most peripheral corners of the country. How did the "hot noise" of cinema and other media solder a scattered population into revolutionary masses, transforming their perceptions of space and time, past and future? Did mobile projectionists and their diverse practices reinforce or undermine propaganda? How did grassroots audiences sense and make sense of cinema as film texts, media technology, and social experience? In what ways might the study of film exhibition and reception in socialist China intervene in global histories and theories of film and media?

As an entry point into these questions, let us consider a children's film, *The Heroic Little Guerrillas* (英雄小八路) (1961). In 1958, when the Chinese People's Liberation Army (PLA) sought to "liberate" Taiwan from the Nationalist Party (KMT) by shelling islands in the Taiwan Strait, a group of primary school students, inspired by war films about anti-Japanese guerrilla heroes, helped the troops do laundry, deliver water, hide cannons, repair telephone cables, and catch spies. Their feats were written into a play that was adapted into a film.[2] In the climactic ending, an enemy bomb blows up the PLA telephone cable. As a result, the headquarters cannot issue an order to fire back. In a quick-witted response, five "little guerrillas" hold hands and grab onto the two ends of the broken cable to let the current pass through their bodies (figure 0.1). Thanks to their conduction of electricity, the KMT flag on the other shore falls, and the film closes on a triumphant note with their song, "We Are the Heirs of Communism." This song later became "The Song of the Young Pioneers of China," taught to all schoolchildren as they put on their red scarves, a corner of the red national flag "colored red by the blood of revolutionary martyrs."

The origin, climax, and afterlife of *The Heroic Little Guerrillas* allegorize the power, mechanism, and legacy of mass media in Mao Zedong's

FIGURE 0.1 Human bodies as extensions of media infrastructure in the film *The Heroic Little Guerrillas* (1958).

China and beyond. Onscreen guerrillas inspired emulation by the audiences in real life, which in turn inspired an idealized model representation onscreen. The brave, resourceful, and self-sacrificial spirit of the guerrilla was meant to circulate like currents of electricity and blood across various media, including film, theater, song, and the people. Setting aside its scientific implausibility, the scene of children holding hands to connect a broken wire suggests the integral role of human agents in the Chinese media infrastructure: if the Communist Party did not have enough cables to provide electricity to the entire country, then people, especially youths with hot blood coursing through their arteries, would step in as conduits of the revolution. Such was the mediating role of mobile projectionists—also cinematic guerrillas—whose bodies wired the nation with audiovisual propaganda to electrify their audiences. If media theorist Marshall McLuhan defined media technologies as "the extensions of man," Maoist guerrilla-inspired ideology and practice turned human beings into flexible extensions of media technology.[3] The Mao era, then, was not only an age of mass media but also an age of masses *as* media.[4]

At the levels of media infrastructure, filmic representation, exhibition practice, and audience reception, an ethos of the guerrilla enshrouded cinema in socialist China. *Cinematic guerrillas* refer to human nodes in Maoist propaganda networks; guerrilla fighters celebrated in revolutionary films; mobile projectionists who brought cinema and other media to the Chinese masses; and audience members who employed guerrilla cinemagoing and reception tactics that subverted propaganda goals. Blurring the lines between soldiers and civilians, guerrillas onscreen and guerrilla projectionists were recruited from the masses and mobilized the masses for political campaigns with militant urgency. Meanwhile, with improvisation and ingenuity, they imparted guerrilla tactics to guerrilla audiences who not only supported but also challenged state hegemony. Thus a multivalent concept of cinematic guerrillas gives nuance to and fleshes out the power and limit of propaganda as well as the mobility, heterogeneity, and creativity of audiences in the circulation and reception of audiovisual media.

Alongside cinematic guerrillas, this book reconsiders Maoist propaganda in terms of its *revolutionary spirit mediumship*, encompassing three dimensions: media propagation of the revolutionary spirit (革命精神); mediating acts performed by human bodies; and media reception enmeshed with grassroots religiosities. Like missionaries and ritual specialists, many projectionists saw themselves as messengers of the party and disseminators of the revolutionary spirit, preaching communist ideology and battling so-called feudal superstitions with centrally produced films, records, and slides as well as local dialects and performance genres. Their audiences attended film events like temple festivals and formed mass congregations to communicate with past spirits and to envision future paradises. As the aforementioned "heroic little guerrillas" acquire revolutionary spirit from cinema, their handholding not only physically connects a broken cable but also enacts a spiritual communion through a sacred hymn.

Revolutionary spirit mediumship can be further illustrated through the film *The Everlasting Radio Signals* (永不消逝的电波) (1958), which opens with a shot of Yan'an's pagoda, the symbol of the Chinese revolution, emanating waves as if it were a radio tower. Its protagonist is a Communist agent sent from Yan'an to Shanghai to maintain an underground radiotelegraphic station that collects intelligence and disseminates propaganda in Japanese- and later KMT-controlled Shanghai. The hero eventually sacrifices his life, and the film ends with the superimposition of his transparent image ecstatically tapping out telegrams onto the clouds and onto documentary footage of Shanghai's liberation (figure. 0.2). The intersection of technology and spirituality, of media and "mediums," has precedents in American Spiritualism of the nineteenth century.[5] We see a similar intersection in this visual overlay of the

FIGURE 0.2 Revolutionary spirit mediumship in the film *The Everlasting Radio Signals* (1958).

human medium and technological media, of the guerrilla fighter's face and radiating wireless waves in the clouds, that suggests spiritual transfiguration: revolutionary martyrs are like angels hovering over history, inscribing prophesies of the future that will turn into glorious and sacred histories. Meanwhile, audiences watching guerrilla war films were expected to undergo a metamorphosis from receivers to transmitters of the revolutionary spirit—in a moving and exhilarating process akin to spiritual possession by the Holy Ghost.

THEORIZING CINEMATIC GUERRILLAS

Where might we find Chinese media theory? Who were some major Chinese media theorists? Building on pioneering scholarship that traces critical genealogies of Chinese media theory from the late Qing to the Republican eras,[6] I propose to excavate latent film and media theoretical discourses in the People's Republic from the writings and speeches of Communist Party leaders, from the film texts and periodicals, as well as from oral histories with grassroots projectionists and audiences. As much as treating these sources as raw materials for empirical analysis, I tease out their underlying thought and put them into conversations with theories produced in a Euro-American intellectual genealogy.

We can find the foundations of a guerrilla media theory in Mao Zedong's influential treatises on guerrilla warfare, which not only guided the CCP's military battles against the Japanese and the Nationalists in the 1930s and 1940s but also informed political and cultural governance from the socialist era to the new millennium.[7] The Chinese term for "guerrilla," 游击, literally means to "roam and hit." According to Mao, "guerrilla strategy must be based primarily on alertness, mobility, and attack. It must be adjusted to the enemy situation, the terrain, the existing lines of communication, the relative strengths, the weather, and the situation of the people."[8] More intriguingly, Mao explained guerrilla methods via the parable of a fisherman and his nets, with Confucian, Daoist, and Biblical resonances:

> The leader must be like a fisherman, who, with his nets, is able both to cast them and to pull them out in awareness of the depth of the water, the strength of the current, or the presence of any

obstructions that may foul them. As the fisherman controls his nets through the lead ropes, so the guerrilla leader maintains contact with and control over his units. As the fisherman must change his position, so must the guerrilla commander. Dispersion, concentration, constant change of position—it is in these ways that guerrillas employ their strength.[9]

This passage brings together the flexibility of the guerrilla with the pliability of the net, local improvisation with central organization, suggesting that piecemeal skirmishes must be woven into a unified network. For Mao, the first step in the guerrilla struggle was to "agitate and organize the people" through propaganda, or *xuanchuan* (宣传), a term first used in the third-century *Records of the Three Kingdoms* (三国志) to mean the dissemination of military skills.[10] On an organizational chart, Mao prescribed a "mobile propaganda unit" (流动宣传队) for every guerrilla company.[11] While being woven into guerrilla networks, propaganda officers aimed to capture the people inside ideological nets—agitating and uniting audiences into the masses, out of which more guerrillas could be recruited. Extending the fisherman's net conceit, Mao likened guerrilla troops to fish and the people to water, an analogy he reprised after 1949, such as when he told CCP cadres to "swim" amid the masses.[12]

Whether applied to military, political, or cultural governance, guerrilla networks were woven out of mobile human agents who further recruited supporters from the grassroots. Unlike industrialized modern warfare, guerrilla warfare "can be conducted in any terrain, in any climate, in swamps, in mountains, in farmed fields. Its basic element is human, and man is more complex than any of his machines."[13] When advanced technologies were absent or scarce, human eyes, ears, hands, and feet served propaganda and mobilization, communication, and surveillance, thereby casting an ideological and organizational net over a vast territory with poor infrastructure. Mao wrote as early as 1927 of the human mediation of propaganda: "Political slogans have grown wings, they have found their way to the young, the middle-aged and the old, to the women and children in countless villages, they have penetrated into their minds and are on their lips."[14] The masses were the revolution's agents and subjects as well as its means and ends, mediators and milieus. Not merely addressed by mass media, the masses themselves constituted a media network.

How did cinema figure in this guerrilla media network? Early twentieth-century Marxists from Vladimir Lenin to Walter Benjamin theorized film as a revolutionary new medium for the masses.[15] Yet before the 1950s and beyond metropolitan centers, the Chinese populace were not proletarian workers undergoing the shock of industrial modernity but rather a mostly illiterate peasantry outside the reach of modern communication technologies. While the KMT and the Japanese occupation held sporadic mobile screenings in rural areas in the 1930s and 1940s,[16] the CCP cultivated a film group (电影团) in their Yan'an base area—their first film camera was donated by the Dutch filmmaker Joris Ivens in 1938—and in 1940 Premier Zhou Enlai brought a 16mm projector back from the Soviet Union and taught the Yan'an projection team its usage (see figure 0.3).[17]

Amid wartime austerity, Communist guerrillas maximized and militarized whatever media technologies they had. The foreword to the inaugural issue of *Photography Net* (摄影网), a magazine intended to train guerrilla photographers, declared: "In Chinese history, outside of

FIGURE 0.3 *Zhou Enlai Shows Films*. Illustrations by Shen Yaoyi, *Lianhuan huabao*, no. 2 (2012).

liberated areas, few have used cameras as revolutionary weapons." Like other guerrilla weapons, cameras were often expropriated from enemy troops or even "exchanged with blood or lives."[18] The Chinese Communist Party (CCP) also developed a wireless radio station, Yan'an Xinhua Radio, to disseminate propaganda beyond their base areas. More than electrified media technologies, however, the Chinese guerrillas relied on a human-constituted propaganda infrastructure, especially "literature and arts work groups" (文工团), a service corps of writers, artists, and performers using storytelling, drama, reportage, New Year's prints, and folk songs to win over hearts and minds.[19] These low-tech, folksy, embodied yet mobile messengers of the revolution were the cultural counterpart of guerrilla warfare.[20]

As the Communists established control over the country, guerrilla warfare ceased to be a lived reality but rather became a mythology transmitted through mass media and applied to political campaigns and everyday life. In guerrilla war films, to be discussed in chapter 6, charismatic heroes and undercover agents with limited resources and ingenious bricolage led the masses to victory against their better-equipped enemies. Widely and repeatedly screened to peasants, workers, soldiers, and students from the 1950s onward, these "red classics" were also remediated through televisual broadcasts and drama remakes since the 1980s to have a formative and formidable impact on the memories of multiple generations. Such onscreen guerrillas kept alive and reinvented war memories, helping to militarize discourse, labor, social organization, and everyday life even when there was no open military engagement on the battlefield. Yet besides serving socialist and patriotic education, guerrilla discourses and tactics also retained the potential for resistance against the state's hegemonic propaganda.

Besides onscreen guerrillas, cinematic guerrillas also refer to mobile projectionists, who carried cinema to the vast countryside that was mostly off the power grid. A mobile movie team typically had three to four members, sharing tasks such as generating electricity, projecting films, and conducting live performances, publicity, and logistics. Mobile projectionists transported heavy machinery and personal baggage on wheelbarrows, pack animals, shoulder poles, or simply their shoulders. They traveled by foot, on bicycles, horse carts, tractors, jeeps, and boats, breaking ice over frozen lakes, building bridges, and repairing roads along the way (see figures 0.4, 0.5, and 0.6). They set up open-air screenings on threshing fields, pastures, forests and deserts, construction projects and battlefields. Appropriating military metaphors, official publications called projectionists "vanguards on the cultural front" who "hack through brambles and thorns" in order to "spread the seeds of socialist thought to the broadest masses of people."[21] They likened projectors and films to "guns and bullets" that help to "occupy the thought front" in the vast countryside.[22] Projectionist itineraries were called "battle lines," while expansion of the projection network into the mountains and hinterlands was described as the "wiping out of blank spots."[23] While opening up "virginal lands" that did not yet know cinema, they also likened hanging silver screens to hoisting flags in territorial conquests.[24] Rural audiences who had previously encountered Communist troops likened movie teams to "Eighth Route Army soldiers" or the "Red Army," since they ate, lived, and labored with the masses.[25] Moreover, projectionists supplemented the "advanced weapon" of cinema with low-tech propaganda methods like clapper-talk and slideshows. As their voices and bodies extended the machines, the projectionists not only transmitted but also embodied the guerrilla spirit.

Studies of early cinema and nontheatrical exhibitions have moved beyond a psychoanalytic conception of spectatorship and of apparatus theory based on classical Hollywood cinema.[26] Even more than media archaeologies of machines and devices, hardware and software, the embodied practices of Chinese mobile projectionists transformed films from standard, industrial, and centrally distributed products into localized rituals and live performances, which could both enhance and diminish the "ideological effect of the cinematographic apparatus."[27] While making propaganda, projectionists had to juggle political priorities with economic sustainability, a central concern of chapter 4. Whereas the authorities decreed the screening of socialist education films on class struggle and agricultural production, rural audiences preferred traditional opera films and action-packed war movies. Even with popular films, it was not easy to sell tickets or collect fees from an impoverished and dispersed populace. With few state subsidies, projectionists resorted to guerrilla tactics, including deception, trickery, and subterfuge, sometimes making a travesty of the propaganda messages they were meant to convey. In different times and places, guerrilla

FIGURE 0.4 Projectionists on the road on the covers of *Film Projection* magazine from the 1950s.

FIGURE 0.5 Projectionists conducting multimedia propaganda on the covers of *Film Projection* magazine from the 1950s.

FIGURE 0.6 Woodcut image of projectionist performing clapper talk with a slideshow, by Wu Qingxun and You Jingu. First published in *Mass Cinema*, nos. 2 and 3 (1965).

projectionists could be faithful missionaries or cynical charlatans, and their guerrilla practices could range between self-sacrifice to serve the people to feasting at the expense of villagers.

Besides onscreen guerrillas and mobile projectionists, film audiences could also be cinematic guerrillas. Crisscrossing the thin line between emulation and mockery, sacrifice and subterfuge, imitating guerrillas could mean performing revolutionary action off screen—such as working harder—or putting up a show that concealed their true thoughts and feelings. Whether out of conviction or pretense, revolutionary performance (表现) translated into not only affect but also action, serving collective rituals and labor mobilization. As much as ideological interpellation, Maoist cinema physically congregated audiences to participate in mass campaigns. Meanwhile, audiences treated cinema as respite from discipline and surveillance, as an excuse for carnival, feasting, romance, and scuffle. The double-edged nature of guerrilla audiences thus complicates understandings of media audiences as either passive or active, docile or resistant.[28]

Given infrastructural poverty, grassroots audiences often took arduous paths to get to the movies, climbing hills and fording streams, such that their filmgoing memories focused more on the *going* than on the film. Even urban audiences practiced guerrilla tactics of sneaking into ticketed or restricted screenings, for example by scaling walls, climbing windows, or arriving early and hiding until dark. Projectionists and local cadres enhanced the policing of those spaces, turning auditoriums and courtyards into fortresses, such that the siege of cinema sometimes could lead to real casualties. Besides guerrilla cinemagoing tactics, or everyday spatial practices along the theorization of Michel de Certeau, audiences also adopted guerrilla reception tactics, closer to what John Fiske, quoting Umberto Eco, called "semiotic guerrilla warfare," or media consumers' resistance to the hegemonic messages of media texts.[29] Audiences bored with socialist cinema's predictable heroes and didactic messages might harbor secret admiration and desire for more idiosyncratic villains and their milieu.[30] Some "reactionary" rural audiences even openly rejected socialist education films that challenged traditional morality and lacked entertainment value. Audiences of war films might be less inspired than horrified by the violence onscreen, while "antisuperstition" films and slideshows could reinforce rather than undermine indigenous religiosity.[31]

Despite alternative readings of propaganda texts, audiences still had to perform correct responses in public. Tibetan historian Tsering Shakya gave an extreme example of such "hidden transcripts" vs. "public transcripts," with reference to the film *Serf* (农奴) (1963) (see figure 6.6).[32] "Everyone in Tibet was supposed to watch the film and cry; in those days if you did not cry, you risked being accused of harboring sympathy with the feudal landlords. So my mother and her friends would put tiger-balm under their eyes to make them water."[33] Guerrilla audiences grew during the Cultural Revolution, when few films were produced but projection teams proliferated to disseminate the revolutionary model works.[34] Yet, as historian Paul Clark put it, repetition of the works, with their relentless posturing, gave rise to "popular grumbling and private derision. A certain tone in singing a model opera aria, or a certain flick of the head in exaggerated parody of a central hero, could provide an outlet for a largely unspoken but shared sense of the ridiculous."[35] The exhibition and reception context introduced extrinsic new meanings and sensations to films, sometimes changing the genre and tone of films from heroic martyrology into kitschy comedy, from propaganda into carnival. In sum, although revolutionary media set out to "mold the Socialist subject," onscreen guerrillas and guerrilla projectionists trained guerrilla subjects in guerrilla tactics that could both support and subvert propaganda goals.[36]

While Chinese guerrilla projectionists were showing films about guerrilla heroes, Latin American filmmakers explicitly called for a "guerrilla cinema" in their famous manifesto "Toward a Third Cinema" (1970). Inspired by Maoist theory, Fernando Solanas and Octavio Getino considered the camera "the inexhaustible expropriator of image-weapons; the projector, a gun that can shoot 24 frames per second." Their manifesto focused on guerrilla *filmmaking*, whereby "a revolutionary film group is in the same situation as a guerrilla unit," but the authors also mentioned film projection as an occasion to create the masses, to "offer an effective pretext for gathering an audience," to "provoke with each showing ... a liberated space, *a decolonized territory* ... a kind of political event, which, according to Fanon, could be 'a liturgical act, a privileged occasion for human beings to hear and be heard.'"[37] Chinese revolutionary cinema was such a liturgical act, but liberation also had the potential to turn into oppression, and giving voice could easily turn into ventriloquism.

What, then, of a Chinese "guerrilla cinema"? The editors of the collection *Rethinking Third Cinema* consider China to be the "biggest definitional problem" in the studies of "Third Cinema" that largely leaves Maoist cinema off its historical trajectory and global map.[38] Maoist cinema was defined against both the "First Cinema" of Hollywood-type commercial entertainment and the "Second Cinema" of European auteurs. Like the "Third Cinema" elsewhere, the goals of Chinese revolutionary cinema were to "mobilize, agitate, and politicize" the masses. Yet, unlike other militant or anticolonial cinemas, Maoist cinema was not *oppositional* to a hegemonic "System" but rather state-sponsored at the levels of production, distribution, and exhibition. Instead of a cinema of resistance that "prepares the terrain for the revolution to become reality," Maoist cinema aimed to perpetuate a "continuous revolution," even after the revolutionary party became the ruling party.[39] The projectionists' guerrilla practices were integrated into a politically centralized network, and their "liberation" and "decolonization" of landscapes and mindscapes became new forms of oppression, which in turn gave rise to guerrilla reception tactics.

Maoist cinematic guerrillas connect "militant cinema" of the global 1960s with scholarship on war films, theoretical ruminations on the military use of film technology, and studies of "cinema's military industrial complex."[40] In *War and Cinema*, media theorist Paul Virilio discussed the parallel technologies of warfare and cinema in terms of the "logistics of perception." With a focus on mediated vision, Virilio argued that military strategy has been dominated by the struggle between visibility and invisibility, surveillance and camouflage.[41] Expanding beyond cinema to other media technologies like the searchlight and the radio, Friedrich Kittler showed how war served as a motor for media's evolution and "spread out in layers of psychophysical mobilization—a permanent drill experienced by many as an ongoing thrill."[42] Focusing on modern industrial warfare in which technology displaced or trained humans, Virilio and Kittler did not mention low-tech guerrilla warfare where humans replaced machines. Yet insofar as Chinese guerrilla cinema militarized their audiences' ways of seeing and feeling, it became logistical media that prepared the population for war—after all, the original meaning of logistics was the art of assembling and supplying armies.[43] Besides human ingenuity, flexibility, and bricolage of scarce resources on challenging terrains, the Maoist cinematic guerrilla—as both propaganda and propagandist—is a militant figure who helped to militarize the civilian population even in peacetime. As the logic and logistics of guerrilla warfare permeated political movements and everyday life, the cinematic militarization of the masses also became a revolutionary spiritual crusade.

REVOLUTIONARY SPIRIT MEDIUMSHIP

层层梯田像石阶，羊肠道九弯十八拐，
绕过十里桃花林，放映队来到咱山村。
谷场搭起土戏台，槐树下扯起白布一块，
贫下中农大伯前头坐，孩子们爬上谷堆还叫矮。
《白毛女》不知看了多少遍！摸胸口，阶级仇恨常在；
今晚又看《大寨之路》，一派革命豪情满心怀。
"学大寨，赶大寨…"，土戏台变成誓师台，
电影映毕人不散，议论着：把大寨的精神搬进来。
　　—叶庆瑞，"贫下中农看电影"

Layers of terraced field like stone steps,
Mountain paths with coils and turns
Bypassing ten li of peach blossom forests
The projection team comes to our village

Build a mud stage on the threshing field
Pull up a white cloth under the locust tree
Poor and lower-middle peasant uncles sit in front
While children climb on the grain hill

How often we've watched *The White-Haired Girl*
Touching my chest, class hatred is ever present

Tonight we watch *The Path to Dazhai*
Heroic revolutionary passion fills my heart

Learn from Dazhai, catch up with Dazhai,
The mud stage turns into a vowing stage
After the movie the crowd does not dissipate
We discuss how to bring over the Dazhai spirit
—Ye Qingrui, "Poor and Lower-Middle Peasants Watch Movies"

Published in *Dazhong dianying* (大众电影) (Mass cinema) in 1965, this poem by a projectionist provides a vivid and idealized description, and prescription, of Maoist rural film exhibition and reception: the makeshift theaters of an open-air screening, the congregation of a community, the emotional response of audiences, and finally, cinema's ritual efficacy and transformative impact. The first stanza references fifth-century poet Tao Yuanming's (陶渊明) utopian fable "Peach Blossom Spring" (桃花源记), in which a fisherman chances on an idyllic village that has escaped centuries of dynastic conflict and change. Like the fisherman, the movie team takes a circuitous path through the mountains and forests into a poor and remote village. The films they show conjure up old ghosts for class struggle and project utopian visions of a communist paradise.[44] The cinematic event here becomes an exorcist ritual and a virtual pilgrimage. As the films (re)fill their hearts with class hatred and revolutionary passion, this congregation of film audiences turns into ritual participants as the "mud stage turns into a vowing stage." If the fisherman in the classical tale is ever thwarted on his path back to Peach Blossom Spring, the mobile projection team would show these peasants the path to a communist utopia.

Complementing the three dimensions of "cinematic guerrillas" as filmic representation, exhibition practice, and audience reception, a second major conceptual framework of this book is propaganda as *revolutionary spirit mediumship*, parsed into three interrelated dimensions: media propagation of the revolutionary spirit; mediating acts or *mediumship* by human bodies; and media reception enmeshed with grassroots religiosities. With cinema and other media as ritual paraphernalia, mobile projectionists mediated communions with revolutionary martyrs, divined communist futures, and exorcized class enemies. Revolutionary spirit mediumship theorizes propaganda as proselytization, mediation as mediumship, and reception as ritual participation.

In his essay "That Holy Word, Revolution" (1994), the Nobel Peace laureate Liu Xiaobo reflected on the sacred righteousness connoted by the Chinese word *geming* (革命) over the course of the twentieth century to mean "devotion, sacrifice, daring, fearlessness, idealism, and romantic feelings. It implies longevity and flourishing vitality."[45] Indeed, after the 1911 Revolution separated the state from cosmic power, the Nationalists and Communists replaced ancient rituals associated with the Mandate of Heaven with new ceremonies of popular sovereignty.[46] In 1921 President Sun Yat-sen elaborated on the significance of a "revolutionary spiritual education" (革命的精神教育) in a speech that became the title and preface for a Whampoa Military Academy textbook in 1929.[47] Sun Yat-sen's proclamation and later KMT slogan—"To make revolution, we must uproot hearts-and-minds" (革命先革心)—was indebted to Christianity and suggested the redemptive fervor of religious conversion. At the grassroots level, this revolution of the spirit attacked various numinous powers condemned as "superstition" (迷信)—defined against both the secular state and the Protestant-informed category of "religion" (宗教).[48]

During the Second Sino-Japanese War, while Generalissimo Chiang Kai-shek launched a National Spiritual Mobilization Movement (国民精神总动员运动), Mao celebrated the militant guerrilla spirit of resistance, struggle, and hard work, calling for the people's "spiritual emancipation" (精神解放) from the "spiritual yoke of the reactionary ruling classes" (精神上的桎梏).[49] In the socialist era, the revolutionary spirit—invoked in writing, films, and social practices—came to include values such as "selflessness, sacrifice, courage, discipline, honesty, and frugality."[50] All are connected to a voluntaristic ideology "in which spirit and will played a strong role in actualizing the series of leaps toward communism."[51] Meanwhile, the category of "superstition" expanded to include Christianity, Buddhism, and Islam as well as "feudalism," "imperialism," and "revisionism," eventually becoming a shorthand for anything that contravened a communist faith, as defined by the party-state.[52] The 1920s call for a revolution of hearts and minds developed by the 1960s into "a revolution exploding in the depths of the soul" (灵魂深处爆发革命). This revolution of the spirit was reprised in 1980s campaigns to eliminate "spiritual pollution" (精神污染). As the CCP celebrated its one hundredth birthday in 2021, the Propaganda Department enshrined the "first batch of great spirits in the spiritual pedigree of the Chinese Communists" (中国共产党人的精神谱系第一批伟大精神) from 1921 to 1949 with a focus on "fighting bravely without fear of sacrifice," "overcoming difficulties with hard work," and "relying on the masses for victory."[53]

Whereas the party-defined revolutionary spirit was often militantly atheist, its propagation through mass media and reception at the grassroots took on quasi-religious overtones. Later chapters will analogize film reels to holy scriptures or Buddhist "precious scrolls," film images to sacred icons or miraculous visions, film screenings to ritual performances in auditoriums literally called "ritual halls" (礼堂), projectionists to ritual specialists, and audiences to faithful assemblies or virtual pilgrims to sacred sites projected onscreen. I shall discuss cinematic liturgies led by projectionists before, during, and after film screenings. The magic of the film apparatus, communal sing-along and call-and-response, localized live performances, slideshows, amplified speeches, and choices of location all contributed to a sacred atmosphere akin to both the "hot noise" of Chinese popular religion and the congregational worship of Christian churches.

A spiritual framing of propaganda harkens back to the word's Latin etymological origins, referring to the Vatican's *Sacra Congregatio de Propaganda Fide*, an administrative body established in 1622 to spread the Catholic faith.[54] Twentieth-century Chinese usage of the term *xuanchuan* was quite close to how "propaganda" was understood in early modern Europe: "to propagate what one believes to be true."[55] Like the Catholic Church, the CCP built up a vast propaganda system "comprising not only the media but cadre training, universities, research institutes, and cultural organs," with the explicit role to transform the heart and soul of the masses through education (教化).[56] The parallel is more than accidental: because many early Chinese revolutionaries attended mission schools, the institutions they set up adopted Christian normative models that included the idea of a missionary corps.[57]

With "revolutionary spirit mediumship," I am not arguing that Maoism was a religion. More than drawing equivalence, the preposition *as* draws analogies (how revolutionary acts *resembled* religious practices) and traces substitutions (how Maoist rituals and pieties *replaced* prior religiosities).[58] Attending not only to ideological creeds but also to

Introduction   19

ritual forms, spaces, and practices, I ask how revolutionary culture borrowed from and transformed traditional religiosities while creating new political religiosities.[59] An early generation of China scholars pointed to the quasi-religious qualities of the Chinese revolution, from its embrace of what Robert Jay Lifton called "a secular utopia through images closely related to the spiritual conquest of death" to Maurice Meisner's observation of the Mao cult's "infusion with traditional religious symbolism."[60] Richard Madsen referred to Mao Zedong Thought counselors as "ministers of Maoist ritual" who preached via parables and choral singing during the Socialist Education Movement, whereas Elizabeth Perry compared the Cultural Revolution to a religious revival "led by a messiah seeking to purify and preserve his true faith against the dual dangers of complacency and heresy."[61] Chinese New Year prints and European religious paintings both influenced communist propaganda art, such that Mao's image took on the religious aura of the Kitchen God and Christian prophets.[62] Other scholars have provided astute analyses of pilgrimages to revolutionary holy sites, the transformation of Mao's mangoes into sacred relics, and the demonological paradigm underlying struggles against class enemies.[63]

Beyond analogies between revolution and religion, this book theorizes *mediation* as *mediumship*. Media scholars have studied not just representations of religion in media or instrumental uses of media by religion, but also how media, like religious practice, "can focus and collect spiritual energies, foster communities or zones of like-mindedness, store and transmit culture, and unfold the data of the divine."[64] A more capacious understanding of media includes "substances such as incense or herbs, sacrificial animals, icons, sacred books, holy stones and rivers, and finally, the human body, which lends itself to being possessed by a spirit."[65] Along these lines, I consider projectionists ritual specialists, media technologies ritual paraphernalia, and film screenings ritual events. Examining the roles multimedia propaganda teams played in the CCP's revolutionary spiritual crusade can unsettle conventional wisdoms about what cinema and media are and what they do. I propose, in short:

1. Cinema was constituted not only by machines, but also by human bodies.
2. Cinema had not only exhibition value but also cult value.

3. Cinema was not only science but also magic.
4. Cinema was not only representational but also congregational—a logistical medium that mobilized the masses.
5. Cinema circulated standardized film texts, but their exhibition and reception had extensive local variations.
6. Cinema operated through not only a capitalist market economy or a socialist planned economy but also a ritual economy of sacrifice.

In sum: *cinematic mediumship* calls attention to embodiment, ritual, enchantment, congregation, locality, and sacrifice.

As much as propagation of the revolutionary spirit, mediumship highlights the role of human embodiment in Maoist media networks, recalling the cross-fertilizations of new media technologies and spiritualist movements in the nineteenth century. As media philosopher John Durham Peters put it, "mediums, thanks to such abilities as clairvoyance and clairaudience, resembled media, with their ability to transport sights and sounds from afar."[66] Film historian Weihong Bao examined a similar convergence of media and medium in early twentieth-century China, suggesting that the human body became a vibrating medium due to "technologically produced receptivity" as well as a "conduit to political action and agency."[67] Media scholar Xiao Liu studied 1980s "information fantasies" with a focus on the "cybernetic body" capable of extrasensory powers and information processing.[68] Whereas understandings of the human body as a receptive medium held niche appeal during the Republican and postsocialist eras, the embodied networking of the revolutionary spirit was a collective national project during the Mao era. The voices and gestures of projectionists, of the heroes in films, of local cadres and models, and of audiences joined to perform revolutionary spirit mediumship.

In his influential essay "The Work of Art in the Age of Mechanical Reproducibility" (1936), cultural theorist Walter Benjamin polarized the cult value of artwork and its exhibition value, arguing that "technological reproducibility emancipates the work of art from its parasitic subservience to ritual." Photography and film were the primary technologies of reproduction that made this historical transition from cult value to exhibition value, leading to a "withering of the aura."[69] In the ritualistic exhibition of Maoist cinema, however, cult value and exhibition value coalesced. Moreover, the sacred aura of communism thrived rather than withered through the technological reproduction of the cinematic altar that illuminated Mao and models, martyrs and miracles, and utopian futures and demonic pasts during village nights without electric light. Indeed, outside of major metropolises, the earliest and most frequent screenings in many rural counties took place inside or on the grounds of temples, shrines, or churches.[70] As cinema replaced ritual opera, ancestral worship, and church services, it coalesced with Maoist mass rallies, parades, and struggle sessions. As much as the mass reproduction of indexical images, cinema electrified the revolutionary masses: attracting a scattered audience with both new technological magic and more familiar "hot noise" associated with temple festivals, inducting them into the Mao cult, converting them into a pious congregation, and exposing class enemies as demons to be purged. I synthesize the revolutionary spirit mediumship of Maoist cinema with the keywords *magic, cult, conversion,* and *exorcism*.

Many mobile projectionists described how their first-time audiences apprehended the magic of cinema through the lens of their indigenous religiosity. A Shaanxi projectionist recalled how, after watching the antisuperstition film *Gods and Ghosts Are Inefficacious* (神鬼不灵) (1950), audiences mistook the movie team for the shaman (巫婆) in the film.[71] For those villagers, projectionists resembled spirit mediums who used ritual instruments to "manage relations with the ever-present unseen world, whether for purposes of exorcism, clairvoyance, or sorcery."[72] Even though spectacular forms of shamanism were suppressed after 1949, as historian Steve Smith discovered, multifarious spirit mediums, numbering more than one hundred per county in many provinces, remained the largest group of ritual specialists during the Mao era, so the masses readily combined "magico-religious elements with secular elements from the Party's own discourse."[73] Whereas spirit mediums and cult deities helped solve the worshippers' problems through efficacious response (灵应), communist propagandists had to show how "gods and ghosts are inefficacious" (不灵).[74] Alternatively, as a famous Mao quotation put it, "class struggle is efficacious at every grab" (阶级斗争，一抓就灵), a dictum illustrated by socialist education films in which the ghost or the problem plaguing a community turns out to be a sabotaging class enemy.

Beyond the content and message of antisuperstition films, Mao-era projectionists launched spiritual crusades against grassroots religiosity by showcasing the greater miracle of science and technology. A Qinghai projectionist paraphrased the bewilderment of Tibetan nomads: "How can a hanging white cloth envelop thousands of troops? How can a high-mounted wooden box speak in so many voices? How can that 'lon lon' sounding power generator (Tibetans call it 'mother' of electricity) draw lightning from the sky?" To these questions the projectionist adds his commentary: "All this is truly mysterious and unfathomable for people who worship gods and spirits without scientific knowledge."[75] Such reports of indigenous first contacts with audiovisual media are curiously reminiscent of anthropological studies of colonial introductions of modern technology to the colonized "primitives." Michael Taussig noted "the white man's fascination with Other's fascination with white man's magic," such as cameras and gramophones, and argued that this reflects the West's own obsession with "the mysterious underbelly of the technology."[76] Brian Larkin described British colonizers' efforts to showcase modern infrastructure "as evidence of the supremacy of European technological civilization." Through such displays of the "colonial sublime," cinema became inextricable from "the spectacle and bombast of government ritual."[77]

As anticolonial revolutionaries, the Chinese Communists also used cinema to provoke feelings of the sublime for a socialist modernity and to enhance Mao's personality cult, as will be discussed in chapter 1. Projectionists often mentioned Mao's appearance in newsreels as the greatest attraction for audiences, who applauded, took off their caps, or shouted "Long Live Chairman Mao!" Some allegedly asked the projectionists to slow down to "let Chairman Mao stay a bit longer!" Those who saw Mao onscreen would tell fellow villagers: "Chairman Mao came out to talk to me!"[78] For an audience exposed to film for the first time, newsreels of national leaders helped establish a quasi-direct rapport between the rulers and the ruled.[79] The cinematic cult of Mao reached its climax with newsreel documentaries of Mao's meetings with Red Guards on Tiananmen Square, re-creating the mass rallies and parades around the country. Villagers welcomed celluloid Mao with processions of gongs and drums they used for local cult deities, turning cinema into a cult object *through* its mass exhibition.[80]

Besides enhancing the Mao cult, cinema also bore witness (见证) to revolutionary miracles so as to *convert* audiences to a communist faith. In the 1950s cinema as "socialist distant horizon education" (社会主义远景教育) promoted rural collectivization by showing Soviet collective farms tilled by tractors (figure 0.7).[81] Cinema reportedly convinced skeptics of new agricultural and engineering techniques, from high-yielding experimental fields to backyard steel furnaces to water conservancy projects.[82] Screenings of films commemorating Communist martyrs baptized audiences with the heroic spirit of the revolutionary forefathers so that many labor collectives came to be named after such patron saints. Resonating with the logic of the Holy Communion, the blood of martyrs consecrated today's liberation and inspired audiences to make sacrifices for a better future.

Finally, Maoist cinema enacted spirit mediumship through its exorcism of class enemies. From land reform to the Cultural Revolution, films portraying the "hell" of the Old Society were coordinated with public tribunals and struggle sessions against "counterrevolutionaries," whereby audiences identifying with the films' victims "spoke bitterness"

FIGURE 0.7 Socialist distant horizon education. *Tractor Comes to Our Village*, woodcut by Wu Desheng, Zhang Heming, and Zhuang Ping, first published in *Film Projection* magazine, no. 10 (1956).

(诉苦) and indicted their victimizers. Cinema took on the shamanistic quality of ritual opera that staged hell at temple festivals and incorporated ordinary villagers into ritual performances.[83] Indeed, villagers not only preferred opera films but also called mobile projectionists "makers of electric shadow opera" (做电影戏的) or "three people staging an opera" (三人一台戏).[84] As mobile projectionists hoisted film screens in front of opera stages, cinema became a part of what historian David Johnson called the "ritual-operatic performance complex," in which "real priests performed on stage in certain operas, and actors sometimes performed real exorcisms for villagers." Like opera, cinema provided scripts for ritual performances "through which villagers interacted with the Powers, natural and divine, nameless and named, malevolent and benign, that they believed had a certain degree of control over their fates."[85]

Public responses to films were often performative, sometimes concealing true feelings to enact the correct emotions of joy, rage, and sadness. Even if audiences did not *feel* moved, they often had to *act as if* they were. Is this then the failure of cinematic shamanism? Or is it actually the very proof of its efficacy? The authors of *Ritual and Its Consequences* argued that ritual efficacy depends on its creation of an "as if" world rather than an "as is" world. In the illusory subjunctive world where ritual performers live "as if," the notion of sincerity or an authentic self is not central.[86] For film reception in Maoist China, what mattered was not the authenticity of feelings but rather the participation in collective rituals.

Following the communist crusade against indigenous spiritualities, Mao and the Mao era became incorporated into the syncretic, diverse, and complex religious landscape of post-Mao China. Ethnographies of Chinese popular religion in the postsocialist period have noted the posthumous cult of Mao at temple festivals and in villager homes.[87] According to Emily Ng, some spirit mediums in Henan claimed to "walk the Chairman's path," understood Mao's antireligious campaigns as a divine intervention, and considered the end of his reign as marking not "a return of *religion* but a return of *spirits*."[88] Erik Mueggler showed how a Yi community in Yunnan remembered the socialist era as an "age of wild ghosts" and worked to exorcize the troubled spirits of those who met traumatic ends during the Great Leap famine and the Cultural Revolution.[89] If the revolutionary spirit was to replace mediumship in the Mao era, spirit mediumship readily subsumed revolution into its spectral narratives and practices.

WHAT, WHEN, WHERE, AND WHO WAS CINEMA?

Film scholars have distilled the big questions of film studies into three: "What is cinema?" "When is cinema?" and "Where is cinema?"[90] The foundational question "What is cinema?" interrogates the medium's aesthetic identity, character, and materiality, whereas growing interest in cinema's social dimensions also historicized and pluralized the question into "What has cinema been understood to be and by whom?"[91] Zhang Zhen and Emilie Yeh interrogated the early Chinese names of cinema and their cultural connotations.[92] Asking "What was cinema in modern China?," Weihong Bao argued that cinema in the Republican era was "an affective medium" capable of "resonance," "transparency," and "agitation."

What was cinema in socialist China? I asked this question not only of myself as a scholar, but also of grassroots audiences and projectionists as well as cultural bureaucrats and censors. Their answers ranged from "the most popular weapon" and "spiritual food" to "spiritual opium," from "commodity" and "welfare" to "tax burden," from "sacred ritual" to "electric shadow opera," and from "hot noise" to "our only legitimate nightlife." Synthesizing their answers, I argue that Maoist cinema was a guerrilla media network woven of human agents who performed revolutionary spirit mediumship. Grounded in prescriptive theories from above and lived experiences from below, we shall explore cinema's material and spatial, bodily and social, quasi-militaristic and quasi-religious aspects. The various chapters will parse cinema's diverse meanings for revolution and nation-building (chapter 1), for different generations of projectionists (chapters 2–4), for rural and urban audiences (chapters 5–7), and for the purge of class enemies (chapter 8). Their answers draw out some further corollary questions: What was cinema for? What did cinema want? What did cinema do? What did cinema cost?

New approaches to "What is/was cinema?" have implications for the temporal question "When is/was cinema?" Film studies underwent a historical turn with early cinema research and New Cinema History, focusing less on film texts and filmmakers than on circulation and consumption.⁹³ Whereas Euro-American historiographies associate film's growth with capitalist commodity and urban modernity, the popularization of cinema among China's rural masses was inseparable from the Communist revolution, presenting a radically nonsynchronous instance of what Brian Larkin called "different genealogies for the emergence of cinema."⁹⁴ To reiterate Zhang Zhen's question: "How 'early'—or how 'late'—was early Chinese cinema?"⁹⁵ Was cinema still new and young in rural China by the 1950s and 1960s, when the medium was considered past its prime in the West?

Exhibition and reception complicate the *when* of historiographies of Chinese cinema clustered around various "golden ages," such as Shanghai cinema of the 1930s and 1940s or the Fifth and Sixth Generations of the 1980s and 1990s. Although the "missing years" of the Mao era have received growing scholarly attention, "rewriting film histories" still focuses on the canonization of films and filmmakers.⁹⁶ If we track the generations of not filmmakers but exhibitors, we arrive at an alternative periodization of film history, whereby the Cultural Revolution decade would no longer be a "cultural desert" but rather a period of unprecedented growth of screenings and audiences. This historicized approach builds on Chenshu Zhou's monograph *Cinema Off Screen: Moviegoing in Socialist China* (2021), which uses official accounts and popular anecdotes about open-air screenings to challenge classical Western apparatus theory.⁹⁷ Drawing on a vaster and more diverse body of archival sources, interviews, and ethnographic fieldwork, *Cinematic Guerrillas* takes as its premise the radical heterogeneity of "socialist China" and seeks to account for the differences made by generations, gender, economics, ethnicity, and political campaigns. Whereas *Cinema Off Screen* foregrounds the playful, nostalgic, and apolitical aspects of moviegoing, *Cinematic Guerrillas* investigates the cost and impact of cinematic propaganda, its mediation of revolutionary processes, and audience responses to influential films over time.

"Where is cinema?" concerns media platforms, screens, and physical sites of audiovisual consumption.⁹⁸ This question was asked mainly of metropolitan China in the early twentieth century, from the first film screenings in Shanghai's teahouses and public gardens and Hong Kong's YMCAs to Harbin's "first movie theater on Chinese territory."⁹⁹

Coming from and oriented toward the countryside, the Communist state revolutionized the geographical distribution and social space of cinema. This book explores the national film-exhibition network, traces the heterogeneous itineraries of mobile projectionists, and analyzes the multisensory environments of open-air cinema. Understanding how film screenings intersected with other political, social, or ritual practices in the same spaces—ranging from temple festivals to regional opera, ancestral worship, mass rallies, and struggle sessions—will illuminate cinema's place and meaning in local contexts. On a larger scale, this study maps Maoist cinema in a global film historiography, from "Third Cinema" to socialist cosmopolitanism.[100]

Explorations of "what," "when," and "where" cinema was in socialist China all point to my fourth and most important question: *Who* was cinema? Although auteur studies were at the foundation of film scholarship, far less attention has been paid to the *people* who showed and went to cinema. How did the bodies, gestures, labor, and performances of projectionists enable, adapt, localize, and diversify an industrialized, standardized mass cultural product at the grassroots? How did historical audiences receive, experience, participate in, transform, and remember cinema as texts, events, and rituals? The question of *who* involves both individual biographies and collective identities. Instead of universal human subjects, projectionists and audiences were highly differentiated by generation, gender, and geography; ethnic, economic, and educational backgrounds; as well as aesthetic talent, training, and taste. This book strives to give a sense of this diversity and unevenness of cinematic careers and access, experiences and practices. I will also tease out how cinema was embedded in local cultures and communities. Who were projectionists to the central and local governments, to themselves, and to their grassroots audiences? The party's missionaries and messengers, low-ranking officials, peddlers, tax collectors, labor models, technicians, magicians, entertainers, artists, state employees who received a salary, bohemians on the road, or (un)desirable marriage partners? I also ask the same questions of "who" and "to whom" of audiences: Were they a dispersed populace to be united, a benighted peasantry to be enlightened, a paying clientele to be enticed, an unruly mob to be tamed, a revolutionary labor force to be unleashed, or a guerrilla army to be conscripted?

RECENTERING THE HUMAN IN MEDIA STUDIES

With the conceptual frameworks of *cinematic guerrillas* and *revolutionary spirit mediumship*, this book seeks to recenter the human body and spirit in media studies. Foundational media theorist Friedrich Kittler famously called to "exorcize the human spirit from the humanities."[101] Recent media studies have shifted focus away from texts and authors to technologies and infrastructures that form "the material substrate of culture."[102] Inspired by media archaeological and ecological approaches, the present study situates cinema in a broader media environment and devotes less attention to formal analysis than it does to mediating processes.[103] More than hardware and software, however, I focus on the corporeality, voice, subjectivity, agency, labor, energy, creativity, and diversity of projectionists and audiences.

Projectionists used *xuanchuan*, the Chinese term for propaganda, as a verb rather than as a noun, thus reorienting our understanding of propaganda from a collection of texts to a constellation of acts. Moreover, *xuanchuan* in Maoist projectionist lingo refers to all activities *beyond* film projection to communicate government directives, mobilize for local priorities, and enhance the attraction and comprehensibility of film for the local population. As multimedia propaganda troupes, projectionists carried not only film projectors and prints, generators and screens, but also lantern slides, radios, gramophones, microphones, loudspeakers, posters, and pamphlets. Conjoining electrified technologies and mass media products with their minds and bodies, hands and voices, projectionists researched, interviewed, wrote, calligraphed, painted, sang, and choreographed live performances before, during, and after screenings. Their electrified mediation and embodied mediumship of propaganda also mobilized the voices and bodies of their audiences to "speak bitterness" about haunting pasts and vow sacrifice for a utopian future, to raise fists and shout slogans in leadership cults and struggle sessions, and to work extended hours under electrified lights and loudspeakers. Thus more than nonhuman technical apparatuses, this study foregrounds media networks' human agents and human impact.

By recentering the human spirit in media studies, I am not simply advocating a return to traditional humanities with their great authors and masterpieces. Instead, I highlight human constitution and agency in media infrastructures and mediating processes, thereby focusing on messengers and audiences. Instead of rejecting hermeneutics altogether, I study the extra-filmic meanings of cinema for the people involved in its circulation and reception, from the party leadership and censors to the exhibition sector and the grassroots populace. Building on media histories of portable projectors, I examine the careers and practices of mobile projectionists.[104] Extending media archaeologies of the magic lantern, I also examine lanternists as artists, performers, bricoleurs, creative teams, and ritual specialists.[105] Besides studying the materiality of screens as optical devices, I examine projectionists' treatments of the screen both as a banner to wage revolutionary conquests and as the blank sheet of the Chinese countryside to inscribe utopian visions.[106] Inspired by histories and theories of cinema as an ecology of energy relations, I study the human energies and labor power that went into and were mobilized by film exhibition.[107] Conversing with environmental approaches to media, I examine how open-air cinema—alongside slideshows, posters, exhibitions, sound amplification, and collective singing—not only transformed the visual and acoustic environment of the countryside but also altered the physical environment as the masses moved mountains, dug reservoirs, and battled pests following cinematic models. Projectionists themselves suggested that projection did not stop at the two-dimensional screen but rather emanated further into the atmosphere to create a "new climate" (新气象) with transformative impact on the people, land, and agricultural output. Projecting revolutionary spirit onto the human psyche and the atmosphere, Maoist cinema was meant not only to be a representational medium but also a climate-changing technology, tasked with not only "engineering the human soul" but also with agricultural engineering and geoengineering.

Rather than universal theorizations of embodied film experiences, the cinematic memories excavated here belong to heterogeneous, historical, and grassroots folks quite different from this book's academic readership.[108] Yet the austerity of their material worlds belies the multiplicity of their lived experiences and the ingenious ways they enriched the meanings of films that may in retrospect seem boring and formulaic. To assert such creative human agency, this book asks not only

"What does cinema/media do to people?" but also "What do people do with and to cinema/media?"[109]

GUERRILLA RESEARCH METHODS

While focusing on cinematic guerrillas, the research process for this book also adopted guerrilla methodologies, characterized by mobile and versatile fieldwork of "going to the people" as well as an agility and openness to changing perspectives, circumstantial discoveries, and local knowledge. Such methods also led to a shift of research focus from elite production to grassroots dissemination, from propaganda works to the work of propagation. Thus this book approaches propaganda not only as centralized, standardized, and mass-reproduced cultural artifacts but also as mobile, variable, and often participatory acts.[110]

To explore people's diverse interactions with projected propaganda, I draw on a cornucopia of historical sources, ethnographic fieldwork, and oral-history interviews. Projectionists across China contributed detailed reports about exhibition practices and audience responses to government archives and to various film periodicals (see figures 0.4 and 0.5).[111] Compiled from the 1980s to the early 2000s, provincial film histories and gazetteers reprinted archival documents and collect reminiscences by former projectionists. Official publications describe and prescribe ideal audiences and desired responses, but capacious and fine-grained readings can reveal the infrastructural, financial, technical, and aesthetic issues that projectionists faced, with inexorable tensions between political priority, economic sustainability, geographic coverage, and audience taste.[112] This book also reconstructs film exhibition and reception from below through a vast archive of *memory texts*—memoirs, blogs, oral histories, and even fictional works grounded in lived experiences—from more than twenty provinces.[113] Composed from the 1980s onward, reminiscences are often colored more by nostalgia than by censorship, but they still provide thick descriptions of the material conditions and diverse meanings of cinema. As Jacqueline Stewart argued in her study of African American film culture, even literary fiction can help "bridge the gaps between 'spectator' as textual point of address and 'viewer' as empirical unit." Adopting Stewart's "kaleidoscopic approach," I let the various sources "address, contradict, and illuminate each other."[114] My methodology is also indebted to Yuri Tsivian's notion of "cultural reception," consisting of "active, creative, interventionist, or even aggressive" responses to cinema.[115]

Between 2012 and 2019 I conducted and commissioned oral-history interviews with more than sixty former projectionists and more than one hundred audience members (see appendix). My guerrilla media archaeology began by "digging where I stand"—an excavation of the cinematic memories of my family members and their friends: what films they watched, where, when, and with whom.[116] More than the suturing of spectators to the films' narrative illusions, their film experiences were stitched into a larger social and historical fabric. Growing up in cities but sent to different parts of the country during the Cultural Revolution, my parents' Red Guard generation experienced cinema in urban and rural settings, some from the perspectives of both projectionists and audiences, so they could speak to school-organized trips to movie palaces built in Republican Shanghai as well as to open-air screenings in the "Great Northern Wilderness."

To expand beyond the sent-down youth demographic, I took five sets of field trips to rural Zhejiang, Hubei, Hebei, and the Northeast provinces in collaboration with Professor Feng Xiaocai and graduate students of East China Normal University who worked on their own research projects. Apart from visiting local archives, we also scoured physical and virtual flea markets for paper remnants related to film exhibition. Drawing on their local contacts, graduate student research assistants helped me find grassroots projectionists and audiences, translate between Mandarin and local dialects, and take notes at interviews. Several research assistants also conducted interviews on my behalf using a questionnaire I had prepared in advance. We found former and current projectionists through the county-level "film company" (电影公司), often headed by a "manager" (经理) who had begun working as a mobile projectionist after the Cultural Revolution. The offices of such managers were usually located inside or next to the county's "old" movie theater, built in the early 1980s and able to accommodate about a thousand people, though none of the six theaters I visited was still showing films. Instead, they either lay fallow awaiting demolition or had been renovated into commercial spaces such as supermarkets or shopping malls that sometimes also included cinema multiplexes. The rent for such "golden real estate" in the city centers often subsidized the pensions of projectionist retirees living in work-unit housing built during the same "golden age" of film exhibition.

County-level film company managers held the keys to major archival, material, and embodied legacies of socialist cinema, such as the memorial hall devoted to the "Three Sisters Movie Team" explored in chapter 3, projectionist account books in a semidemolished county cinema that inspired me to study the economics of rural cinema in chapter 4, as well as itinerary planning, personnel files, censorship instructions, old movie posters, film prints, and projectors in dusty storage rooms. The managers connected us to former projectionists, often by convening them for a meeting and a meal. My research assistants and I then followed up by interviewing individuals who also kept personal archives consisting of old notebooks, certificates, photo albums, and projectors. Some even performed clapper-talks or pantomimed animated slideshows as demonstration.

Beyond oral-history interviews, guerrilla fieldwork for this book included mobile participant observation following active projectionists and chatting with their audiences. At first we asked about the reception of specific films with titles, posters, and clips as memory aids, but sometimes their nonanswers offered greater insights, such as the popular notion of moviegoing as "hot noise" explored in chapter 5. I also learned to pay attention to "noises," such as interjections by a former projectionist's wife who could not remember watching a single film because she always had to host relatives who came to watch movies. Beyond the earthy words of interviewees and onlookers, I sought tacit knowledge from their body language and cinema's spatial configurations and material relics. In tracking down the past and present of film-screening locations from cities and counties to townships and villages, I found that even open-air locations had historical and geographical specificities, whereas the palimpsestic ruins of indoor spaces often transformed the meanings of the films screened within. At the village level, the question of *where* often boiled down to *who*. The former or current projectionist was the human embodiment of the cinematic medium, a social being—-e.g., a sister-in-law's cousin's neighbor—who could be located through a few cell-phone calls.

From the unreliability of propaganda to the unreliability of memory, each source required skeptical interrogation. Nevertheless, this book "pays attention to oral narratives in the light of the written record, and vice versa."[117] My patchwork and cross-examination between sources seeks not only to weave together a highly textured media history of the Chinese revolution but also to unveil coalescences and tensions between prescriptive theory and guerrilla practice, political imperative and economic survival, idealized representation and lived experiences.

THE CHAPTERS

The first part of the book focuses on projectionists: their networks and missions, training and careers, material paraphernalia and live performances, generational and gendered experiences, as well as entrepreneurial and economic practices. The second part is devoted to audience reception: cinema's open-air environment, creative responses to propaganda films, the extrinsic meanings of foreign films, and intoxication by cinematic "poisonous weeds" (毒草). From chapter to chapter and occasionally within chapters, perspectives shift from a bird's-eye view to a worm's-eye view, from central government policies to local grassroots experiences, from aspirational models to everyday dilemmas, from exhibition to reception, from mass mobilization to subversive pleasures.

Chapter 1 traces the Chinese revolution in, of, and through audiovisual media that extended the reach of the state over a vast territory and heterogeneous population. The first section explores how the party's human-powered media infrastructure networked the immense Chinese countryside without electrification, relying instead on the labor and talent of radio receptionists, film projectionists, propaganda performers, and other cultural workers. The next sections analyze cinematic nation-building, from how film exhibition practices contributed to Mao's personality cult to the industrialization and militarization of the populace. The last part focuses on mobile cinema's conquest of "spiritual battlegrounds" from covering vast geographic terrains with poor transportation infrastructure to the occupation of a rural community's ritual spaces.

Moving from the projection network to the projection unit, chapter 2 focuses on the recruitment and training, everyday work practices and subjective experiences of itinerant movie teams. Instead of chronicling generations of directors, I propose rewriting Chinese film history by tracking its generations of projectionists based on available accounts of their heterogeneous backgrounds and career trajectories. Unpacking the movie team's baggage, we start with the heavy technical assemblage of generators, projectors, screens, and film reels; move on to the lightweight technologies of bamboo clappers and lantern slides that helped to localize propaganda; and finally consider the weight of projectionists' bodies by focusing on their clothing, food, shelter, and transportation. This chapter theorizes cinema as a physical and spirit medium by exploring the human and material constitutions of Maoist media infrastructure.

Chapter 3 zooms in onto the nationally renowned "Three Sisters Movie Team" to discuss model projection, model projectionists, and female projectionists, thereby exploring the relationship between propaganda and reality from several angles. Proposing a methodological shift from representations to projections, I argue that Maoist projectionists projected radiant models that emitted the revolutionary spirit into both the human psyche and the physical environment. As the nation's most propagated movie team famous for its propaganda work, the stardom of the Three Sisters Movie Team grew in a larger Maoist media ecology and attention economy. This chapter chronicles their rise and fall through a juxtaposition of published propaganda against fieldwork findings. The last section draws on nine oral-history interviews with "ordinary" women projectionists who have little claim to fame, to examine the omissions of model narratives and the role of gender in film projection careers.

Chapter 4 studies the economic practices of movie teams in the socialist period. What did cinema cost, how was it paid for, and who paid? Beyond ideological indoctrination, how was cinema understood in economic terms—as commodity, welfare, or taxation? What if we saw projectionists less as self-sacrificial model workers than as *homo economicus* looking after their own interests? This chapter begins with movie teams' charging methods during rural collectivization through bartering, child labor, deceptive advertising, and price discrimination. It goes on to discuss "cinematic extraction" and "villagebusters" from the Great Leap Forward to the Socialist Education Movement. The final section analyzes the red, gray, and golden economy of commune-run movie teams in the 1970s. The conclusion reconsiders the socialist cultural economy as a Maoist ritual economy.

Turning from projectionists to audiences, Chapter 5 parses the sensorium of open-air cinema into "extra-filmic" sights, sounds, smells, taste, and touch. Drawing on scholarship in Chinese popular religion and theatre, I theorize such visual, aural, olfactory, gustatory, and haptic experiences at the cinema as "hot noise," a jarringly literal translation of *renao* (热闹) that interrogates the sources and effects of heat and noise. Emanating from the apparatus, the audience, or the atmosphere, the hot noise of open-air cinema included heat and cold, wind and rain, moon and mosquitoes, snacks and feasts, shoes and roads, hand shadows and stomping feet, screens and seating, power generators and loudspeakers. As festive occasions for spectacle, noise, commensality, intimacy, and nightlife against a backdrop of poverty, hardship, and dreariness, open-air cinema brought together revolutionary congregations, yet its hot noise also dwarfed and drowned out the films' propaganda messages.

Chapter 6 argues that guerrilla films projected by guerrilla projectionists trained guerrilla audiences in guerrilla techniques that could both support and undermine propaganda goals. Guerrilla war films inspired childhood mimicry of heroic battles, conscripted laborers for infrastructure construction, and prepared audiences for ever greater sacrifices. Yet the same films also taught audiences guerrilla tactics like the "sparrow tactic," whose weaponization of noise had off-screen resonances in mass movements from the Four Pests Campaign in 1958 to the Red Guard Movement of 1966–1968. Meanwhile, revolutionary spy thrillers fostered participatory surveillance against "internal enemies" while also allowing guerrilla audiences to indulge in forbidden pleasures. Finally, "revolutionary horror and redemption" were meant to inspire audiences to "recall bitterness" and denounce class enemies, but even tears could be performative camouflage of the audience's true feelings.

Chapter 7 studies the Chinese memories of popular Soviet, North Korean, Albanian, and Indian cinema screened during and around the Cultural Revolution decade. As films crossed borders to meet with mass audiences for whom they were never intended, the radically different exhibition and reception contexts generated heteroglossic *extra-filmic meanings*. The encounter of foreign guerrillas onscreen and socialist China's guerrilla audiences often unleashed a creative transculturation process involving unintended cognitive and affective responses and transmedial aesthetic afterlives. Studying foreign cinema's reception in Mao's China broadens the field of "Chinese cinema studies" to include "cinema in China" with all its cosmopolitan connections, revises our assessment of the Cultural Revolution, and invites us to reconsider today's Chinese media ecology in light of its socialist past.

Chapter 8 analyzes the exhibition and reception of "poisonous weed films" meant to expose "ox-demons and snake-spirits" before and during the Cultural Revolution. Relating these Chinese terms to the Greek word *pharmakon*—denoting at once remedy, poison, and scapegoat—I argue that a pharmacological and demonological discourse undergirded Maoist mass movements, in which the stage and the screen became the most symptomatic sites of ills and cures, haunting and exorcism, pollution and hygiene. Under Jiang Qing's leadership, participatory rituals of film criticism functioned as incantatory shamanism to cleanse the revolutionary air of demonic pestilences. The "public exposure" of dozens of films was meant to enhance the audience's "political sense of smell" and to increase its "intellectual immunity," yet this mass campaign of cinematic vaccination often had the unintended effect of (re)infecting the audiences.

The epilogue traces the legacies of cinematic guerrillas and Maoist propaganda as spirit mediumship from the 1980s to the new millennium. Drawing on ethnographic fieldwork and interviews from 2015 to 2019, it discusses the postsocialist plight and ongoing petition movement of film projectionists as well as the state's renewed uses of audiovisual media and rural film screenings to stage spiritual competitions with indigenous and imported religiosities.

PART ONE

Projectionists as
Media Infrastructure

CHAPTER ONE

Cinematic Nation-Building

Media Networks and Spiritual Battlegrounds

我们带着人民的热望,来自祖国四面八方。
人民电影新的天地,要我们勇敢去拓荒。
同学们,同学们!努力学习,紧密团结,
掌握技术,改造思想,为工农兵服务的意志坚强如钢,
把人民的丰功伟绩英雄形像带到部队农村和工厂。
宣扬新民主主义的文化,传播毛泽东伟大思想,
提高劳动热情,建设强大国防。
毛主席胜利的红旗,永远永远永远永远永远
在祖国的遍地河山高扬。
— 南京放映训练班班歌 (1950)

With fervent hopes of the people, we hail from far and near
The virgin land of people's cinema, awaits us pioneers.
Classmates, classmates! Let us study hard and tightly unite,
Master our techniques, reform our thoughts
Our will to serve the workers, peasants, and soldiers is like steel.
Bring the People's great achievements and heroic images
To the army, countryside, and factory.
Propagate the culture of New Democracy,
Disseminate the greatness of Mao Zedong Thought,
Heighten their enthusiasm for labor,
Construct a powerful national defense.

The victorious red flags of Chairman Mao will forever and ever and ever
Flutter over the rivers and mountains of the Motherland!
—Class Anthem of Projectionist Trainees, Nanjing (1950)

放映机,嘿!就是枪,战斗红旗飘扬在四面八方。
放革命电影,学英雄榜样。挂起银幕,摆开战场。
要革命文化占领思想阵地,把歪风邪气一扫光。
让先进红花遍地开,革命豪情变作米粮。
—六十年代中山电影幻灯宣传队之歌

A projector, hey! is a gun, while red battle flags flutter far and near.
Show revolutionary films, emulate heroic models.
Hoist up the screen, set the battlefield.
Let revolutionary culture occupy the thought front,
And sweep away all evil winds and noxious influences.
Let advanced red flowers bloom everywhere,
And transform revolutionary spirit into rice and grain.
—Song of the Zhongshan Film and Slide Propaganda Team (1960s)

放映机就是我们的武器, 银幕就是我们的战场。
片盘卷起五洲风云, 镜头映出一轮红太阳,
扬声器发出震天的巨响, 时代的凯歌四海回荡。
电源线来自北京城哟, 四面八方放射出灿烂的光芒。
喇叭线连着亚非拉哟, 胜利的凯歌天天唱。
我们是红色放映战士, 世界革命心里装,
宣传马列主义、毛泽东思想,是我们神圣的职责...
—张希廖,"红色放映员战歌"(1972)

The projector is our weapon, the screen is our battlefield
The film reel rolls up the storm of five continents,
    the lens reflects a red sun
The loudspeaker emits a thundering roar,
    the hymn of our era reverberates in the four seas.
Our electric cable comes from the city of Beijing,
    radiating brilliant light everywhere

> Our speaker cable links Asia, Africa, and Latin America,
>   singing a triumphal hymn every day
> We are red projection soldiers, holding world revolution in our hearts
> Our sacred mission is to propagate Marxism-Leninism and Mao Zedong Thought...
>
> —Zhang Xiliao, "Battle Hymn of Red Projectionists" (1972)

The utopian dreams and violent upheavals of twentieth-century China could not have reached their massive scale without the mass media that conjured into being the revolutionary masses. In this sense, the Chinese revolution was also a *media revolution*. This media revolution was not only a revolution *in* media content but also a revolution *of* media infrastructure and a revolution *through* media mobilization. As the party altered media content, revolution was a set of symbols, narratives, and myths that saturated public culture and shaped understandings of the past, present, and future. As the party established new media infrastructure, revolution was a set of technologies that extended the people's vision and hearing, augmented their perceptions of space and time, and connected the government to the people, the elite to the grassroots, and the center to the periphery. As the party used media to mobilize the masses, revolution was a set of actions to realize utopian visions or to upend the status quo—as Mao famously put it, "an act of violence by which one class overthrows another."[1] In short, media content *represented* revolution; media infrastructure *amplified* revolution; and media mobilization *made* revolution.

Certainly, media symbols, technologies, and praxis have played important roles in social and political movements throughout history. Yet the Chinese Communist Revolution stands out for its systematic orchestration of audiovisual media to unite a dispersed, heterogeneous, and mostly illiterate populace traditionally beyond the reach of the imperial state. Although cinema and audio broadcasting were past their prime by the mid-twentieth century in North America and Europe, they were still novel technologies for the majority of the Chinese rural populace. Many associated audiovisual media with the mythological figures of "Thousand-Mile Eye" (千里眼) and "Fair-Wind Ear" (顺风耳).[2] Bringing sights and sounds from afar, cinema and radio revolutionized the rural sensorium and facilitated a new national imaginary. The grassroots reception of these scarce technologies as sublime and miraculous further lent legitimacy, charisma, and aura to the revolutionary regime.

The Maoist media revolution was also a guerrilla media revolution. Just as Mao's army had limited industrial weapons and resorted to guerrilla tactics to fight against the Japanese and the KMT, the new regime supplemented its meager cache of modern electronic media technologies with low-tech propaganda techniques that relied on human voices and gestures, body and spirit. Extending the available media infrastructure, mobile propagandists wove a human media network that consistently deployed a guerrilla military discourse and symbolic repertoire to drum up the revolutionary spirit of the audiences. Cinema and radio were not only representational but also logistical media that "arrange people and property into time and space" and "form the grid in which messages are sent."[3]

This chapter examines cinematic nation-building through guerrilla media networks. I begin with an overview of the growth of the media infrastructure and cultural institutions in the early socialist decades. Connecting cinema, radio, live performances, exhibitions, and other cultural activities, this guerrilla media revolution relied on vertical national directives and horizontal local initiatives, fixed planning and flexible improvisations, and above all the organization of human agents. With special attention to the cinematic cult of Mao, the next section argues that Maoist cinema's revolutionary potential lay with its capacity to congregate, industrialize, and militarize the masses. As the guerrilla revolution became a "continuous revolution," the last section on "spiritual battlegrounds" focuses on guerrilla territorial discourse at macro and micro levels, from covering vast geographic terrains to occupying a rural community's public spaces.

WEAVING HUMAN MEDIA NETWORKS

As laid out in the introduction, Mao's theory of guerrilla warfare not only guided Communist battles against the Japanese and the Nationalists in the 1930s and 1940s but also informed the political and cultural governance of the People's Republic. As political scientists Sebastian Heilmann and Elizabeth Perry argued, China's long revolution gave rise to a "guerrilla-style policy-making" with "tactics for managing sudden change and uncertainty." Beyond the "combination of centralized leadership and intensive popular mobilization," this guerrilla governance style is defined by continuous improvisation and allows for "entrepreneurial, experimentalist, opportunistic, and ruthless policy makers' at the grassroots."⁴ On the cultural front, I propose *guerrilla media network*—constituted by versatile human guerrillas and multimedia propaganda techniques—as a defining characteristic of the Chinese Communist media infrastructure from the 1930s to the 1970s. Closely related to the term for CCP organization, *zuzhi* (组织), which literally means to "group and weave," the concept of network (*wang* 网, literally "web" or "net")—suggesting elastic and enmeshed guerrilla tactics aimed at capturing the enemy and the masses—became shorthand for the party's growing and sprawling bureaucracy.

After 1949 the CCP took over and monopolized mass media from earlier regimes and private ownership to communicate ideology and policy, yet reaching the vast countryside off the power grid proved challenging.⁵ For example, in 1950 there was an estimated total of only one million radio sets in China, mostly in bourgeois urban households. To make the most of the available technology, the party-state wove a nationwide radio reception network (广播收音网) by designating "radio receptionists" (广播收音员) in factories, schools, and army units. Radio receptionists not only organized collective listening sessions but also transcribed, mimeographed, and distributed broadcast content through school pupils to peripheral villages. These would then be copied onto blackboard bulletin boards or orally transmitted via "rooftop broadcasting" (屋顶广播), whereby village criers used homemade megaphones to relay messages from on high.⁶ Until the widespread establishment of wired broadcasting networks in the 1960s and 1970s, radio receptionists and rooftop broadcasting demonstrated the centrality of human bodies in the Chinese propaganda infrastructure.

While transforming radio from a bourgeois luxury into a propaganda loudspeaker, the new regime also revolutionized cinema from a capitalist commodity into a form of socialist welfare, from "spiritual opium" to "spiritual food."⁷ Modeled after the Soviet Union, the Chinese film-exhibition network relied on mobile projectionists to bring revolutionary culture to the nation's peripheries.⁸ Lenin's praise of film as "the most important art" in 1922 would later appear in many Chinese commune offices and workers' clubs, often alongside a Stalin quote: "Cinema in the hands of Soviet power constitutes an enormous and invaluable force."[9] Less acknowledged than the Soviet influence were KMT and Japanese colonial practices of mobile film propaganda. The KMT-sponsored *Chinese Cinema Yearbook* of 1934 called for a "national projection network" of 16mm films, and the Jiangsu Provincial Mass Education Center began conducting mobile screenings in 1935. During the Second Sino-Japanese War, the KMT sponsored more mobile projection units to screen anti-Japanese propaganda films in the hinterland.[10] Meanwhile in Manchuria, the Japanese colonial regime sponsored film production and mobile exhibitions to propagate the "new nation" of Manchukuo and to educate its citizens in hygiene, farming, military conscription, and civic participation.[11]

A key figure who synthesized Soviet, KMT, and Japanese theories and practices of mobile cinema for the CCP's film-exhibition network was Yuan Muzhi (袁牧之), the celebrated director of two Shanghai film classics, *City Scenes* (都市风光) (1934) and *Street Angels* (马路天使) (1937). In 1938 Yuan partook in discussions of a "national defense cinema" in Wuhan and helped found the Yan'an Film Group, with production and projection units. In 1940 he took the negatives of the documentary *Yan'an and the Eighth Route Army* (延安与八路军) to the USSR for development, yet all the footage got lost with the Soviet entry into World War II. At the end of the war, the party sent Yuan and actress Chen Bo'er (陈波儿) to take over the film industry in Manchuria from the Japanese colonial regime. The pair transformed what remained of the Manchurian Motion Picture Association to the Northeast Film Studio (东北电影制片厂), which later became known as the "cinema's cradle for a New China." In 1949 Yuan became New China's first Film Bureau chief and applied the Northeast template to create a nationwide film-exhibition network that extended the influence of cinema far beyond "bourgeois" moviegoers in metropolitan centers.[12]

Under the CCP, the film-exhibition network expanded from fewer than 600 movie theaters nationwide to more than 12,500 projection units by 1958 and to some 162,000 by 1983.[13] At the provincial level, the number of movie teams often grew from single or double digits in about 1950 to about 300 in the mid-1960s to the thousands by the late 1970s.

While workers' trade unions and PLA propaganda departments had their own exhibition networks, the cultural bureaucracy (文教系统) managed most urban movie theaters and rural mobile teams, which were in turn divided into state-run teams (国办队) and commune-run teams (社办队). It was often the latter that made cinema a more regular event at the village level from the mid-1970s to the mid-1980s.[14]

Like a fisherman who regularly checked and repaired his net, the government refined its media network over time to reach broader audiences. A directive in 1953 to strengthen film exhibition and distribution prioritized industrial and mining districts over the countryside.[15] When projection units failed to complete their quota of screenings, the Film Bureau admonished them to adapt to local conditions and the needs of different audiences.[16] Weaving networks required not only flexibility but also fixity: advanced planning of itineraries for where and when films were to be screened (for an example, see figure 1.1).[17] A prefectural film history spelled out the step-by-step process of weaving: set up a projection point at a populous area every few miles, link the dots into

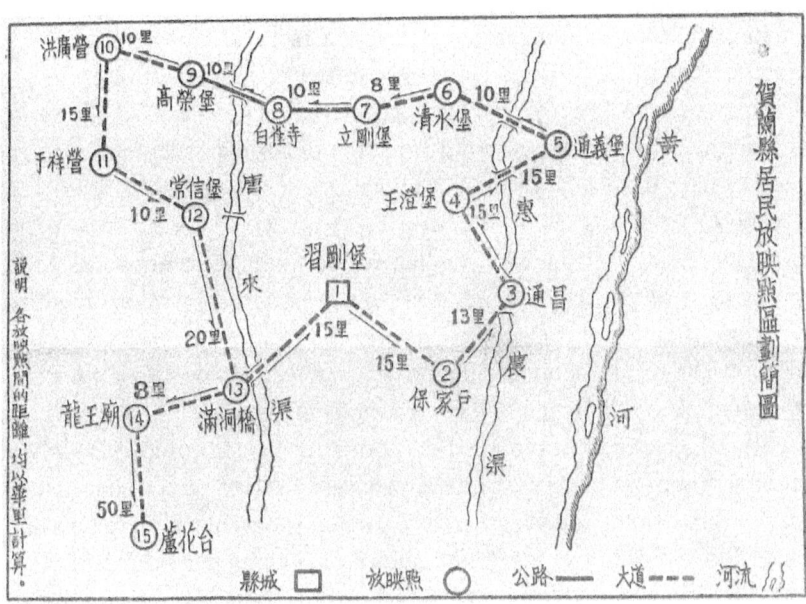

FIGURE 1.1 Itinerary map of mobile projection at the county level in Ningxia Province. *Film Projection*, no. 2 (1954).

Cinematic Nation-Building   47

lines and areas, and merge crisscrossing itineraries to consolidate the exhibition network.[18] This network also included local activists, cultural cadres, schoolteachers, and students who helped with publicity and logistics.

The film projection network developed in tandem with other cultural and media networks. When electrified technologies were still scarce, network-building consisted largely of the recruitment, training, and organization of people. A directive in 1951 to establish a nationwide "propaganda network" (宣传网) designated individuals in every school, factory, and work unit as "propagandists" (宣传员).[19] A vast network of itinerant drama troupes spearheaded propaganda in the countryside during land reform and other campaigns.[20] In 1955 the Cultural Ministry called for the construction of rural cultural networks (文化网) that included not only cinema and radio but also lantern slides, book distribution, exhibitions, performance troupes, and newspaper reading groups. Salaried employees of county cultural centers (文化馆) and township cultural stations (文化站) toured the villages with multimedia propaganda. One former cultural worker recalled teaching revolutionary songs to villagers line by line and revolutionary dances move by move.[21] Village amateur cultural organizations flourished in rural clubs (农村俱乐部), amateur drama and dance troupes, and newspaper reading groups.[22] A song from the Great Leap Forward praised: "The People's Commune is almighty, a thousand-year-old iron tree blossoms, with radio broadcasts twice a day and movies sent home at night" (人民公社力量大，千年铁树开了花，一天两次听广播，晚上电影送到家).[23]

In constructing new cultural institutions and media networks, local governments drew on local human resources, such as by reforming itinerant traditional storytellers into "people's performers" or "red propagandists."[24] The resulting human media network was highly interconnected, intermedial, and hierarchical. For example, professional theater troupes mentored amateur troupes and held competitions to promote the cross-fertilization of repertoires. Cultural workers adapted revolutionary narratives into drama, music, visual art, lantern slides, blackboard newspapers, and exhibitions. Whereas radio and cinema remediated fiction and opera, local and itinerant performers drew their repertoire of songs, stories, and characters from audiovisual and print media. Traveling from village to village, these mobile cultural guerrillas engaged in socialist "transmedia storytelling" and brought revolutionary culture to rural public spaces that used to host temple festivals.[25]

Extending propaganda into peripheral areas previously beyond the reach of the imperial state, these propaganda networks connected and subordinated folk artists under the party's leadership, giving them a grander purpose while taking away their autonomy. Guerrilla media networks updated what historian Prasenjit Duara called the "cultural nexus of power," woven out of various marketing, kinship, irrigation, and temple networks. The imperial state tapped into this interconnected web of local elites and their symbolic resources to reach into village communities.[26] While banning, defunding, and destroying many marketing, lineage, and religious institutions and networks, the CCP also rechanneled their human, cultural, and spatial resources to disseminate revolutionary symbols, stage revolutionary rituals, and effect revolutionary change at the grassroots. Joining modern audiovisual technologies with older cultural forms, the CCP's guerrilla media network linked not only propagandists but also their audiences into a national community.

SOCIALIST DISTANT HORIZON EDUCATION

Within the party's guerrilla media network, the film-exhibition network received the most sustained investment over the course of three decades. What made cinema "the most important art" for the CCP? What was it that cinema was supposed to *do* for the Chinese revolution? In 1950 the Film Bureau held a training session for more than 1,800 new projectionists in Nanjing. With representatives from every province, the army, the workers' union, and various ethnic groups, the trainees would return to form mobile projection units and to seed an exponential growth of the projection network.[27] As quoted in the first epigraph for this chapter, their class song spells out cinema's nation-building mission. Beginning with the agricultural metaphor of land reclamation, the song moves on to the industrial analogy of steel and ends with the military mandate of national defense. While peasants, workers, and soldiers turned into cinema's representational subjects and target audiences, cinema was to mirror and unite them as a nation. Going beyond filmic visualizations of the nation's "imagined community,"[28] mobile projectionists also served as the soldiers, missionaries, and messengers of the revolution. By raising film screens as battle flags of Mao Zedong Thought, they aimed to conquer and transform both the spiritual and physical landscape of the nation through mass mobilization.

In the 1950s film magazines often referred to cinema as "socialist distant-horizon education" to promote industrial productivity and rural collectivization.[29] They published exemplary audience responses: "As soon as these projectionist girls turn on a machine, they bring over to us the Soviet Union: tractors plow the fields, horses run, people jump: I hope I can live to see socialism in China."[30] (see figure 0.7). After seeing how workers used machines to turn a quagmire into farmland and dig a well in quicksand, villagers in Jiangsu reportedly exclaimed: "The working class is so powerful. They are our big brothers!"[31] Another projectionist report from Shanxi quoted a local cadre: "Watching film gave me confidence in propaganda; now I have capital to back up my talk.[32] Whereas film theorist André Bazin traced the ontology of the photographic image to the mummy complex to embalm the dead, Chinese socialist cinema was to serve as a clairvoyant crystal ball that helped audiences "look afar" into a utopian future and to connect their individual interests with the collective good.[33]

Looking back on the first decade of the People's Republic, Vice Chief of the Film Bureau Chen Huangmei (陈荒煤) spelled out three aspects of cinema's "mass character" (群众性): ability to connect the vast masses; audiovisual engagement of the people's vision and hearing; and variety of genres appealing to diverse interests. He called cinema "the most popular, widespread, and influential weapon" (最有群众性的，最能普及的，对群众影响最大的一种武器) as well as a "complex spiritual production" (复杂的精神生产) capable of "infecting" (感染) the audience's emotions, rousing their revolutionary passion, and thereby increasing their productivity.[34] Cinema would ideally forge their audiences into a revolutionary mass by appealing to their senses and emotions as well as by networking and uniting them across differences. Whereas Walter Benjamin famously valorized film's revolutionary potential to mobilize the proletariat,[35] Maoist cinematic governance was to contribute to the proletarianization of the Chinese peasantry by industrializing and militarizing their labor. Abetting this process was the cinematic cult of Mao, frequently cited as cinema's most important attraction in projectionist reports from the 1950s to the 1970s.

THE CINEMATIC CULT OF MAO

One of cinema's core missions was to exalt Chairman Mao, to enhance his sacred aura, and to project his light into peripheral territories. A rural movie team in Guizhou put it this way:

> When the masses learned that a film had Chairman Mao's image, they were so excited they began dancing to celebrate the joyous event. A seventy-some-year-old man of Tong ethnicity ran with a torch to shout out the news to nearby villages: "Chairman Mao is coming! Everyone go look!" The glad tidings of "Chairman Mao is coming" soon spread so that thousands of people hurried over.... A blind old man who heard the news asked his son to carry him through the mountains. He said: "I cannot see Chairman Mao, but I want to hear his voice."
>
> When Chairman Mao appeared in *The Great Unity of Chinese Ethnicities*, the site was filled with the sound of applause and shouting of "Long Live!" The masses lit firecrackers to welcome Chairman Mao such that smoke blurred their vision. Women shed tears of joy. When Chairman Mao's image passed, the masses anxiously shouted: "Comrade! Show slowly! We haven't gotten a clear look yet!" So our comrades had to rewind and replay that part. When the audience saw how their representatives shook hands with Mao and were welcomed everywhere [in Beijing], they understood: their disunity with the Han before Liberation resulted entirely from the discord of Chiang Kai-shek's bandits. They felt that Chairman Mao illuminated them like the sun.[36]

Highlighting the women, the elderly, and disabled persons, this is one of many patronizing reports on the cinematic enlightenment of "backward" audiences and the cinematic governance of a formerly ungovernable, fragmented, and hostile populace, now rendered benign as singing and dancing ethnic minorities under Mao's radiance.[37] Published in *Film Projection* (电影放映) magazine, such reports were less reliable accounts of audience reaction than model scripts for other projectionists to ventriloquize the rural masses as communist converts through leader worship. The conceit of "Mao as sun" permeated cultural production

Cinematic Nation-Building

from the 1940s to the 1970s, finding a synthesis in the song "East Is Red," illustrated with posters and choreographies that feature the people as "sunflowers." Besides symbolism, Mao's cinematic image literally illuminated the dark night of the countryside. In "the most enchanting film of the time," Mao turned into a "media effect," for accounts of the "radiation of his brilliance" suggest "the ethereal yet ubiquitous powers of mass media itself."[38] This compels us to consider the mediation of the Mao cult and the cult value of mass media.

Studies of Mao's personality cult have focused on the CCP's symbolic production, but little has been said of its dissemination and amplification through audiovisual media.[39] Cinema not only mass-reproduced Mao's image and voice but also congregated the masses for rituals of worship. Responding to projectionist reports, the Film Bureau mandated production of extra copies of newsreels that included Mao's image.[40] Contra Walter Benjamin's thesis on the withering of the aura with mechanical reproducibility, cinema enhanced Mao's sacred aura and multiplied the altar of his personality cult. Every screening of his moving image enabled a divine political figure to descend from his heavenly court onto the earth to meet with the people.[41] In 1958 the newsreel *Our Leaders Work with Us* (领袖和我们同劳动), showing Mao digging at the Ming Tombs Reservoir, was met with an enthusiastic reception: "Chairman Mao took time out of his busy schedule to participate in labor—we must make more iron!" Or "Even Chairman Mao is laboring—the idlers among us ought to be ashamed!"[42] As a quasi-labor model, Mao's cinematic image aligned him with the peasants, workers, and soldiers, while the occasion of film screening connected the masses with the leader, peripheries with the center.

Even when Mao did not appear on film, villagers sent out gong-and-drum processions to welcome "Chairman Mao's movie team" or "honored guests dispatched by Chairman Mao."[43] While staging a vicarious encounter with the great leader, cinema was also the culmination of technological wonders that inspired sublime feelings of awe for the party. Treating cinema as oracle and fulfillment of socialist modernity, projectionist report often quote elderly villagers: "Chairman Mao keeps his word: he said the countryside will have electric light, telephones, and loudspeakers." "Only under Chairman Mao's rule could an old man like me watch a movie."[44] Projectionists considered the very arrival of a movie team in the countryside a form of political influence, since "the rural masses naturally associate cinema with the benevolence of the party and Chairman Mao," regardless of what films they showed.[45] Maoist projectionists intuitively understood media theorist Marshall McLuhan's dictum that "the medium is the message" or the "mass age."[46]

The cinematic cult of Mao reached its climax with unprecedentedly numerous screenings of newsreel documentaries of Mao's meetings with Red Guards on Tiananmen Square in 1966. The first, featuring the August 18 rally, was shown to some one hundred million people in the first month after its release. Six more films documented the remaining seven rallies, plus one celebrating the third successful explosion of the atom bomb as the triumph of Mao Zedong Thought.[47] Projectionist interviewees in Zhejiang and Hubei recalled having to show such "red treasure films" (红宝片) for months to cover all the villages on their circuits. Every village welcomed the movie team with a procession ordinarily used to honor local cult deities at temple festivals, and the village chief personally carried the film print with red ribbons and a Mao portrait from its last projection site.[48] *Guangxi Film Gazetteer* reported similar ritual parades of "red treasure films," with the masses lining the roads to welcome their arrival. Although landlords, rich peasants, counterrevolutionaries, bad elements, and Rightists were banned from these screenings, the revolutionary masses reportedly brought their "loyal, boundless, proletariat feelings." Failing to attend invited criticism or worse troubles, so audience numbers rose to a new height.[49]

Retrospective accounts suggest a highly varied reception of these Mao rally films. Former Red Guards I interviewed in Shanghai recalled attending school-organized screenings of these films and mirroring the enthusiasm of Red Guards onscreen. In Harbin, photographer Li Zhensheng captured an audience of students applauding and shouting "Long Live Chairman Mao" every time his image appeared (see figures 1.2 and 1.3). Some were inspired by the first rally film to travel to Beijing to participate in a later rally. As workers in a Shanghai factory, my grandparents received free tickets but had no time to attend, so they gave a ticket to my great-grandmother, an illiterate rural woman who happened to be visiting Shanghai. After seeing the film, she criticized Mao's nonchalant greeting of the young people's enthusiasm, which my adolescent mother found "counterrevolutionary." Villager interviewees enjoyed

FIGURES 1.2 AND 1.3 At a screening of the first Tiananmen Red Guard rally film in Harbin in September 1966, an audience of students applaud and shout "Long live Chairman Mao" each time his image appears onscreen. Photographs by Li Zhensheng. Contact Press Images.

those newsreels as vicarious travel to the capital and often puzzled over who was who on the Tiananmen rostrum. In rural Hubei, the wife of a mobile projectionist best remembered "Chairman Mao's pretty wife." In Ningxia, a villager vividly recalled seeing Lin Biao shoulder to shoulder next to Mao: "He had on a bright green uniform, red insignia, and a wide grin. When Mao clapped, Lin would also clap and we audiences clapped too. A villager once said Lin Biao was a 'smiling tiger' who looked like a traitor. Someone reported this comment and got him executed as a counterrevolutionary. After Lin Biao really turned out to be a traitor, the villager was rehabilitated and his family received ten thousand yuan

FIGURES 1.2 AND 1.3 (continued)

in compensation."⁵⁰ If Lin Biao engineered the Mao cult yet turned against the Chairman a few years later, the audiences learned from his costumes and expressions to play their parts as a devout congregation regardless of the truth of their feelings. After all, failure to perform a correct response had grave and violent consequences.

CINEMATIC INDUSTRIALIZATION AND MILITARIZATION

Besides "socialist distant horizon education" and promotion of the Mao cult, cinematic nation-building also consisted of the industrialization and militarization of the populace. Beginning in the 1950s, workers' cultural palaces and workers' clubs mushroomed in industrial districts. Often attached to factories, these recreational spaces had multiple compartments and functions as cinemas, classrooms, theaters, basketball courts, cafeterias, and bathhouses.[51] As Chenshu Zhou observed, relocating film exhibition into mixed-function clubs helped clear the commercial and imperialist legacy of moviegoing as a bourgeois activity, instead blending propaganda and entertainment, politics and leisure.[52]

For the All-China Federation of Trade Unions, cinema's mission was "communist education for workers and their families to raise their socialist consciousness, enrich their cultural lives, and inspire their enthusiasm for labor."[53] A former union projectionist for the Suzhou Steel Factory recalled how her first screenings were open-air and attracted not only workers and their families but also nearby peasants in the suburbs. In 1958 her factory built a giant Soviet-style movie palace with 1,900 seats, ceiling fans, and a fancy audience lounge decorated with posters, albeit without a grand façade since the cinema had no local competition. Adapting the cinema's showtimes to the factory schedule, she often showed films after midnight for workers on "middle shifts." Attending to their fatigue, she decided to skip all propaganda newsreels and slideshows except for those made by and featuring steelworkers—after all, workers needed relaxation after intensive labor.[54] The daughter of a trade union activist at a Shanghai silk factory recalled her late father's film propaganda and liaison work as prepurchasing tickets from the local cinema for the convenience of his coworkers. A cinephile who in 1935 took a day off from work to join the funeral procession for the actress Ruan Lingyu, he chose films based on moving stories and dramatic performances instead of political imperatives.[55]

Besides serving industrial workers in factories, movie teams were dispatched to infrastructural construction sites to express solicitude (慰问) to short-term workers.[56] Several villager interviewees recalled their earliest film-viewing experiences as rewards for digging reservoirs, whereas projectionist interviewees recalled screenings at public projects to raucous, unruly young men temporarily recruited from different villages.[57] While documentary films trained a mostly agricultural work force in Taylorist industrial time discipline, as film scholar Ying Qian has argued, an equally important genre used to mobilize workers' labor was the revolutionary war film (see chapter 6).[58] In this sense, Maoist cinema did even more to *militarize* than to *industrialize* the Chinese masses, instilling in them a wartime logic of emergency and sacrifice in the absence of war. Mobile movie teams set up their screens in the midst of the fields so that "the bustling scene of agricultural labor off screen mirrored the heated battles onscreen."[59] After watching war films, audiences would be asked to emulate the protagonists' "heroic spirit," their perseverance in the face of adversity, and their readiness to sacrifice for the nation. Quotes from audiences modeled ideal responses: "When drinking water, forget not the well-diggers / valor and glory go to the Red Army / who shed blood and gave their lives for posterity / how could we not leap forward?"[60]

In its conscription of labor, cinematic mobilization often began with showing films to grassroots cadres tasked with further transmitting the revolutionary spirit like military orders. When one commune was slow with the spring planting and fertilizer collection, the party committee organized an emergency meeting of production brigade leaders and asked the movie team to screen *On the Long March* (万水千山) (1959). After the film, some asked: "When will we have a meeting?" The party secretary replied: "The film *was* the meeting. Follow the spirit of the Long March to accumulate fertilizer." The cadres allegedly returned to their respective brigades and finished their targeted production in only a few days. At the rank-and-file level, cinematic militarization aimed to accelerate peasant productivity through the formation of "shock battalions" (突击队) named after the heroes or heroines of revolutionary films (see figure 1.4).[61] Also promoted during the Soviet Union's First Five-Year Plan starting in 1929, shock work, as cultural theorist Susan Buck-Morss pointed out, was unlike Taylorism's standardizing rhythms. Instead, it was "executed in rushes, or 'storms,' by teams of workers." Accelerating productivity "through extra human effort *without* machines," shock workers "bore the brunt of the attack on their own bodies," entailing "physical sacrifice and exhaustion for the sake of the collective goal."[62] In the Maoist context, shock work was also a new form of guerrilla warfare.

Since cinema was meant to strengthen the fighting spirit, PLA soldiers, whether stationed in the cities or in the countryside, had the most frequent access to movies free of charge. Already by the mid-1950s, 75 percent of all soldiers could watch at least four films per month.[63] Rural interviewees with moviegoing memories that reach as far back as

(盛平插图)

FIGURE 1.4 An agricultural production group named after the heroine of *The Red Detachment of Women*. *Mass Cinema*, no. 6 (1964).

the 1950s often lived close to army bases. Even when urban cinemas were closed during the Cultural Revolution, the PLA showed films in open air or in auditoriums, so that children from military courtyards often brandished their movie tickets as status symbols.[64] Inspired by war films to join the PLA, one former soldier recalled the army's biweekly moviegoing ritual: march in rank-and-file to the drilling ground, sit down in unison on folding stools, and maintain an upright posture throughout the screening. There was often an obligatory prelude of a singing competition (拉歌) to see which battalion could sing the loudest.[65] Indeed, collective singing was a routine part of the army's cinemagoing ritual from the 1950s onward, such that projectionists taught soldiers new songs at every screening (see figure 1.5). Some army units even made their soldiers carry weapons and blankets as if they were about to depart for war,[66] so that moviegoing became a part of military training.

Cinema as military discipline applied increasingly to the general audience from the mid-1960s to the 1970s. Following Mao's slogans to

58 *Projectionists as Media Infrastructure*

FIGURE 1.5 Illustrations from film magazines showing how soldiers and general film audiences learned revolutionary songs before screenings. *Left*: woodcut from *Film Projection*, no. 11 (1964); *right*: drawing from *Mass Cinema*, no. 2–3 (1965).

"make everyone a soldier" (全民皆兵) and to "Learn from the PLA," all projectionists were to both embody and disseminate their military spirit.[67] The PLA was emulated not only for its martial strength but also for its moral authority and its association with "revolutionary purity—with combined psychic and material power."[68] During the Cultural Revolution, paramilitary organizations governed the social lives of many students and cadres. Sent-down youths of "construction and production corps" and other farm-garrison systems in the borderlands wore military uniforms and called themselves "corps soldiers" (兵团战士).[69] In sum, while prioritizing workers and soldiers as the audience, movie teams also contributed to the industrialization and militarization of the body and spirit of the population at large.

SPIRITUAL BATTLEGROUNDS

Military conquest, protracted warfare, and continuous revolution pervaded discourse on Maoist media networks.[70] In 1950s China, war was not a mere metaphor but rather a recent memory, if not an ongoing reality: coming to power after the Second Sino-Japanese War and the Civil War, the CCP sent one million troops to Korea, was ever preparing to "liberate" Taiwan, and suppressed the Tibet uprising in 1959. Projection teams accompanied the PLA to various battlefronts and vowed to "raise

Cinematic Nation-Building 59

the screen wherever the red flag is raised."[71] During the Great Leap Forward, Mao elaborated on the flag conceit for all revolutionary endeavors: "Hoist the red flag and find the wind direction. If you do not hoist the flag, others will. On a big mountain or small hill, on the field, hoist it wherever there is no flag and uproot the white flag wherever it is found."[72] Projectionists thus vowed to "stick the red flag of communist thought in factories, mines, and the countryside,"[73] to "occupy ideological territory" (占领思想阵地), and to "vanquish blank spots" (消灭空白点). Geographically, "blank spots" often mapped onto mountainous regions and so-called *laoshaobian* (老少边) areas: former revolutionary bases, ethnic minority territories, and border regions. Projectionists testified to cinema's efficacy in promoting national unity and convincing non-Han peoples to send their children to government schools. There were concerted efforts to translate films into minority languages and to cultivate ethnic projectionists.[74] Still, these areas fell out of the network most of the time and retained their "art of not being governed."[75] In the vast Qinghai Province, with its challenging climate and nomadic population, even though every county had its own movie team by 1956, projectionists showed films only near county seats. With hilly terrain and linguistic diversity, the southern provinces of Yunnan and Guangxi brought cinema regularly to peripheral regions only by the late 1970s.[76]

Besides geographic coverage, every screening location was considered a spiritual battleground. Since Christian missionaries used new visual technologies to proselytize and win converts, churches were often among the earliest local sponsors for film and slide projections in the countryside, whereas itinerant entrepreneurs projected films and slideshows at temple festivals.[77] After 1949 many rural film exhibitions still took place inside or in front of spaces of worship, from ancestral halls to temples devoted to Daoist, Buddhist, and/or local deity cults. Many early movie theaters were also renovated out of older ritual spaces. Ningxia's People's Cinema was built out of a money god temple, where the old idol was replaced with a movie screen and the old theater stage was turned into a projection booth.[78] A former communist activist in a northeastern county helped convert a local church into a movie theater in 1948 by building a projectionist's booth and digging a slope.[79] An early 1950s PLA manual provides detailed instructions on how to convert rural ancestral halls into army cultural clubs to cultivate the revolutionary spirit among soldiers (see figure 1.6). Mobile movie teams also conducted screenings within ancestral halls and temple during the day and in the case of rain.[80]

What did it mean to screen films in spaces originally designed to worship bodhisattvas, Christ, local deities, or ancestral spirits? Did showing films always secularize sacred spaces, or did those electric shadows bring new "gods and ghosts" that rubbed off a place's sacred aura and take on its time-honored reverberations? Did cinema help undo so-called superstitions, or did it introduce new deities and religiosities? Provincial film histories and projectionist memoirs report conflicts between cinema and indigenous religions. When a movie team came to a border town in Yunnan in 1953 to show movies, the locals did not allow those "Han men with horses . . . to bring gods and ghosts into our mountain hamlet." It took much persuasion to convince them that cinema was science rather than spirits.[81] Yet official discourse throughout the socialist era discussed public spaces as the spiritual battleground between revolutionary and reactionary forces. Where cinema failed to reach, "feudal superstitions" propagated by shadow puppets and traditional storytellers allegedly re-emerged, and "decadent tunes" reverberated through the soundscape.[82] In Hubei in the early 1970s,

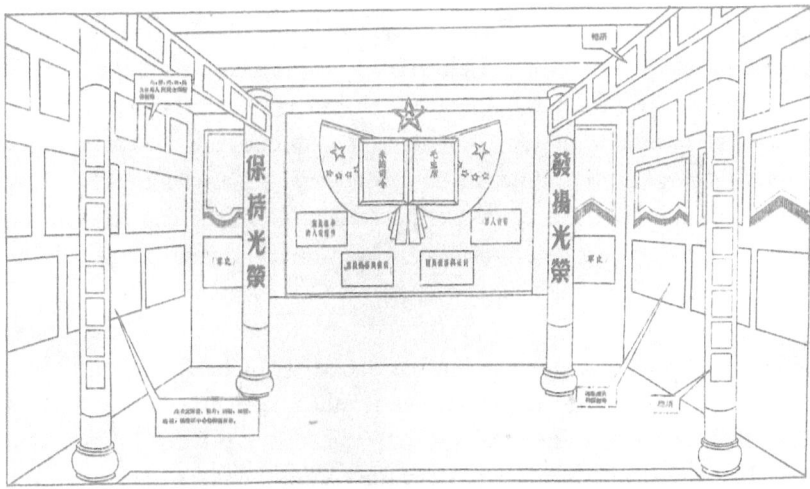

FIGURE 1.6 Illustration from an early 1950s People's Liberation Army manual on converting a rural ancestral hall into an army cultural club.

Cinematic Nation-Building 61

projectionists allegedly used revolutionary cinema to abolish "feudal practices" such as arranged marriages.[83] Noting the sparse attendance of their screenings, a Liaoning movie team detected villagers who read old novels and listened to old LP records in the house of a Rightist, so they alerted the local cadres to raid his home and confiscate his library. More than five thousand people attended the struggle session, which culminated with a slideshow of his crimes and the screening of the revolutionary model opera film *The Red Lantern* (红灯记) (1971).[84] Revolutionary cinema thus served as an exorcist medium to purge "feudal" or "bourgeois" spirits.

My fieldwork in a rural township in Zhejiang further suggested cinema's spiritual competition with local religiosities. After asking villagers of different generations where they watched films over the decades, I learned that most local screenings from the 1940s to the present day took place in spaces of worship: a Catholic church, an ancestral hall (祠堂), and a Buddhist temple.[85] Mr. Xu (1932–), a local Catholic who served as a caretaker of the church, recalled watching in his childhood silent films about the life and death of Christ over Christmas, shown with a hand-cranked projector by the priest.[86] In 1955, along with eight other Catholic villagers who joined the Legion of Mary, Mr. Xu was arrested as a counterrevolutionary and sent to Inner Mongolia to engage in "reform through labor."[87] Meanwhile, the township government confiscated all church property and converted it into administrative offices, held political meetings in the church auditorium, and used the bells to assemble villagers for mass rallies. The three characters above the church entrance, "*tianzhutang*" (天主堂) (literally "Catholic Hall"), were changed to "*dahuitang*" (大会堂) (literally "Big Meeting Hall"), with the character *tang* (堂) unaltered. Inside, Mao's portrait hung in the center with red flags flanking the sides, and the revolutionary masses replaced the Catholic congregation.[88]

While the Catholic church turned into a communist ritual space, villager memories of moviegoing "in the days of Chairman Mao" converged at the township's largest ancestral hall, burned down in the Second Sino-Japanese War and not rebuilt until the early 1980s. During the Mao era, the open ruins were used to dry the commune's rice harvest and to show films. Villagers born in the 1940s recalled watching *The White-Haired Girl* (白毛女) (1950), *Shangganling Ridge* (上甘岭) (1956), *The Fairy*

Couple (天仙配) (1955), and Mao's Tiananmen rally newsreels. Those in the back stood on benches or climbed up trees, as if they were the very masses Mao addressed. After Mao's death, a state-run movie team came to show his funeral documentary. Everyone was supposed to cry, but someone in the audience laughed. The projectionist demanded a denunciation, but the villagers did not comply and thus prevented an escalation.[89] After the Cultural Revolution, ticketed screenings required an enclosed rather than a porous space, so the commune movie team used the courtyard of a Buddhist temple wrecked in the campaign to "smash the four olds." Among the most popular films shown were opera films such as *The Monkey King Thrice Defeats the White-Boned Demon* (孙悟空三打白骨精) and *The Dream of the Red Chamber* (红楼梦)—both made in 1962, banned in the Cultural Revolution, and rehabilitated by 1978—reenchanting the ruins of the Buddhist temple with their otherworldly illusions.[90]

The late 1970s and early 1980s saw a construction boom of many "township movie theaters" (集镇电影院). Some were renovated from conference halls, canteens, ancestral shrines, or, in the case of this Wenzhou township, the Catholic church. Its guardian Mr. Xu recalled with scorching outrage how the renovation vandalized the architecture: the ground in front was dug up to raise the back to make a slope, two pillars were removed to clear the view of the screen, stained-glass windows were sealed to shut out the light, and two hundred more seats were added in the nave. A local militia member worked as the church cinema's security guard by catching and punishing ticket evaders. From 1986 onward, local Catholics petitioned the government to reclaim their church property and finally took the space back by 1992.

Screening films in communal religious and ritual spaces was part of modern Chinese nationalism's iconoclasm against local religiosities from the 1900s to the Cultural Revolution.[91] Yet as much as desecration, revolutionary cinema also brought new icons to old altars to convert local audiences with mixed success. While illuminating the darkness of the night, cinema brought the far near, prophesied utopian futures, and mobilized crowds that displaced and replaced local religious gatherings. Filmmaker Feng Xiaogang (冯小刚) spoke for many members of his generation when he likened the "ritual hall" (礼堂) where he watched movies as a child to a church (教堂).[92] Similarly, the overlap and contestation between local religious spaces and film-screening spaces highlight Maoist propaganda's "ritual competitions" not only for hearts and minds but also for material resources.[93]

As the party-state used mass media to conjure up, congregate, and mobilize the masses, the Chinese revolution was a media revolution. Human agents extended the existing media infrastructure to network the immense Chinese countryside not covered by any electrical grid. Film, radio, print, theater, exhibitions, and other visual and performing arts came together in a guerrilla media network that relied on the labor and creativity of local propagandists. At the heart of this network was a film-exhibition network that grew systematically in the Mao era. Party leaders saw cinema's power in its "mass character" and "socialist distant-horizon education," so their cinematic governance and nation-building aimed to extend the people's vision and to network a dispersed populace into the revolutionary masses. Projectionists fashioned themselves as Mao's emissaries and turned their screens into altars of worship, and local cadres reinvented ritual processions for local deities to receive celluloid Mao, while audiences of Mao newsreels learned to play their parts as a devout congregation. Cinema further industrialized and militarized the populace, which meant not only more film screenings for workers and soldiers but also labor mobilization and military discipline of civilians. As mobile projectionists vowed to "stick the red flag of communist thought in factories, mines, and the countryside," they brought cinema to the most remote areas and turned communal public spaces into spiritual battlegrounds between revolutionary and reactionary forces.

Official discourse tell us why the party was so invested in cinema and what the medium was supposed to do for the revolution. Yet retrospective accounts from projectionists and audiences suggest that revolutionary spirit mediumship did not always go according to prescription. Despite elaborate reports about bringing cinema into peripheral regions, guerrilla projectionists remained in more densely populated areas to meet economic targets, as will be discussed further in chapter 4. Union projectionists and activists sought to provide entertainment and relaxation to their constituents over education and propaganda. Even the cinematic apotheosis of Mao sometimes met with cynical comments and irreverent laughter.

Highlighting the question "who was cinema," the next three chapters shift perspectives from cinema's mission to its missionaries, from media networks to its human agents, from nation-building discourses to day-to-day practices, from media revolution to revolutionary mediums. The analytical lenses of generations, gender, and economics can historicize and provide nuances to our picture of the heterogeneous "army" of Chinese projectionists, as we unpack their material luggage, trace the making of a model movie team, and account for the costs of "spiritual food."

CHAPTER TWO

Mobile Projectionists and the Things They Carried

If the Communist revolution was a media revolution, then mobile projectionists were its rank-and-file guerrillas. Each movie team typically consisted of three or four members, sharing responsibilities to transport equipment, hang screens, generate electricity, project films and slideshows, make publicity, and manage finances. Even with a clear division of labor, projectionists were often multimedia performers and multitasking angels. Beyond operating machines and explaining the films they brought, projectionists also served as correspondents, editors, curators, commentators, storytellers, and singers. Some model projectionists even volunteered as medics, barbers, technicians, and social workers who carried water, chopped wood, washed laundry, and cooked for villagers in need. Thus movie teams were celebrated as "propaganda teams" (宣传队), "work teams" (工作队), and "cultural cavalries" (文化轻骑兵).[1]

From the 1950s to the 1970s, mobile projectionists grew a thousand-fold, from a cohort of fewer than 2,000 to an "army" of some 200,000.[2] Rather than identical bolts in the state's propaganda machine, these cinematic guerrillas came from heterogeneous backgrounds, cultivated diverse talents and skills, and embarked on distinct career trajectories. Drawing on both published (auto)biographies and oral history interviews of more than sixty projectionists across multiple provinces, this chapter tracks three "generations" of film exhibitors from the Republican era to the 1970s. It unpacks the material baggage they carried, starting from the cinematic assemblage of generators and projectors, screens, and film reels—heavy technological objects that were not hidden but rather spectacular and noisy, bulky and brittle, volatile and sacrosanct. It then examines bamboo clappers and lantern slides—two lightweight ritual paraphernalia projectionists used to localize propaganda with folk art and live performances. Finally, it considers the mobile projectionists' everyday necessities in terms of clothing, food, shelter, and transportation.

Through thick descriptions of mobile projectionists and the things they carried, this chapter examines the *physicality* of cinema at the grassroots, both the corporeality of bodily senses, needs, and performances and the materiality of media assemblages. Foregrounding the corporeality and materiality of cinema revises foundational "apparatus theory" that takes as its premise the invisibility, imperceptibility, and immateriality of film's *infra*structure, with classical Hollywood cinema magically unwinding in hermetically sealed spaces.[3] Whereas the *apparatus* connotes a "closed and binding structure," film scholar Francesco Casetti proposed the term *assemblage* to refer to an "open and flexible set of elements" that "recompose themselves in response to the circumstances."[4] With few purpose-built movie theaters in socialist China, mobile movie teams had to assemble cinema's infrastructure anew with every screening. Hence cinema's materiality was keenly seen, heard, touched, and even smelled and tasted by projectionists and audiences. The interaction between such materiality and bodies highlights cinema's physicality, foregrounded due to both technological wonders and technological failures.

Mobile movie teams and their practices demonstrate how people extended poor infrastructure, such that material shortages found compensation in bodily sacrifice and spiritual enrichment. We could thus reconceptualize propaganda not only as homogeneous indoctrination from above but also as heterogeneous ritual participation. Like religious clergy and ritual specialists, projectionists not only ventriloquized and transmitted messages from a central/divine authority but also addressed the particular needs of local communities. In this sense, as I will argue, their physical mediation of cinema was also a form of spirit mediumship.

PROJECTIONIST GENERATIONS: PIONEERS BEFORE 1949

Chinese film history has often been narrated in terms of filmmaker generations, with special attention given to the renowned fifth generation of directors who won global visibility at international film festivals in the 1980s and 1990s.[5] More broadly, cinema scholars have anchored their studies around auteurs, actors, and the films they produced, but what if we were to shift attention from elite makers to grassroots exhibitors as the primary human agents and subjects of film historiography? How might this transform our understandings of what, when, where, and who cinema was? I propose a rewriting of Chinese film history by tracking the generations of projectionists: designating pre-1949 pioneers as the first generation, state employees of the Seventeen Years (1949–1966) as the second generation, and commune projectionists of the 1970s as the third generation. The epilogue will follow up on private projectionists of the 1980s, the fourth generation, and the new millennium's digital projectionists, the fifth generation.

Cinema first came to China thanks to the entrepreneurial efforts of foreign itinerant exhibitors in treaty ports such as Shanghai and Hong Kong.[6] Provincial film gazetteers also note local film pioneers: adventurers, merchants, missionaries, or soldiers who screened films to curious crowds in temples, churches, schools, parks, or markets.[7] This section recounts the legendary careers of several pioneering projectionists from Ningxia, Shaanxi, and Heilongjiang provinces with connections to local royalty, Communist base areas, and Japanese colonizers. According to the *Ningxia Film Chronicles*, the Northwest region's first film projector was a dowry gift in 1906 from the empress dowager to the local Mongol prince, whose son married a Manchu princess. The prince's servant Zhang Wanbao (章万宝) learned to operate the machine, making him Ningxia's "first projectionist." After the royal bannermen grew weary of the same few films he screened, Zhang left the court in 1925 with the projector and reels to start his own movie show business. At first he collaborated with a Peking opera troupe so that audiences could watch both film and live performance in the same theatre. After accumulating some capital, he bought a courtyard house and furnished it as a photography studio that also doubled as a movie theatre. In 1935 an electrical engineer from the newly founded lightbulb company made technical improvements to brighten the projector, but the antiquated machine and worn film reels soon exited the historical stage, not to be seen again until the arrival of the PLA.[8]

In the 1930s and 1940s the Nationalist government and the Japanese occupation systematically sent roving projection units to show propaganda films in areas under their control. Most reports of such mobile screenings emphasize the delight and enthusiasm of their audiences, although a Chinese projectionist for the Manchurian Motion Picture Association recalled facing death threats in villages under strong communist influence.[9] In its Yan'an base area, the Communist Eighth Route Army founded its first film group in September 1938 with two film cameras, a 35mm portable projector, and some Soviet film prints. Without technical know-how, their first attempt at film projection resulted in a fire that killed one soldier and severely wounded another.[10] One year later the Yan'an Film Group established a specialized projection team. A new recruit, Xi Zhen (席珍), had just graduated from Yan'an's Anti-Japanese Military and Political University and was excited about his job assignment to "perform films" (演电影): "Although I had never seen a film, my classmate and I acted in spoken drama, so we thought we were chosen as actors. Only later did we realize that our jobs were to become *projectionists*."[11] After learning how to operate the machinery from comrades who had returned from Moscow, the projection team showed films for conferences and events sponsored by government organizations, schools, and the Eighth Route Army. With only a handful of Soviet films with Chinese subtitles or dubbing, they took the time between the changing of reels to summarize the story. "When showing films to soldiers, we first brought the greetings of central leaders, communicated party policies, propagated 'good people and good deeds,' or brought glad tidings from the battlefront. After every screening, we organized discussions to heighten consciousness and deepen impressions, and wrote reports for the authorities."[12]

The most celebrated "projectionist" in Yan'an, however, was CCP vice chairman Zhou Enlai. In March 1940, after medical treatment for his broken elbow in Moscow, Zhou brought back a hand-cranked 16mm projector and several reels of film. To demonstrate his recovery and the workings of this new machine, he personally projected a new Soviet film at a meeting to celebrate his return (figure 0.3).[13] In 1943 he brought an American-made RCA 16mm film projector from Chongqing and gave hands-on instruction to the Yan'an projection team, meanwhile telling them not only to master technical skills but also to study politics.[14] "Projectionist Zhou Enlai" became a legend taught to later projectionists so that they could consider their premier the guru of their profession.[15]

Whereas Yan'an's projectionists already proselytized the communist faith, most film exhibitors from the Republican era considered cinema entertainment business. The *Harbin Film Gazetteer* records the precipitous rise and fall of the film entrepreneur Zhu Andong (朱安东), a Shandong native who apprenticed as a projectionist at the Russian-owned Orient Cinema in Harbin before opening two movie theaters of his own. Local newspaper advertisements for his "New World Film Garden" (新世界电影园) from the 1920s and 1930s suggest a rich and varied program of action/war films, actualities, melodramas, and Chaplin comedies.[16] After the Japanese occupation of Manchuria in 1931, Zhu Andong changed his name to Tanaka Taro (田中太郎) and took two Japanese sisters as concubines. He allegedly collaborated with various Japanese military and spy networks, letting them use his New World hotel as a torture chamber for anti-Japanese guerrillas. Meanwhile, Zhu made a handsome profit from eight opium dens with Japanese colonial support and expanded his film distribution business to a chain of movie theatres all over Manchuria. After the war, however, the CCP took all of Zhu's property and sentenced him to death in 1950.[17]

In contrast to such legendary figures as Zhu Andong and Zhang Wanbao, most projectionists whose careers bridged the 1949 divide narrated their preliberation biographies as capitalist exploitation. At a Beijing conference for labor models in the film sector in 1957, a fifty-year-old senior projectionist recalled how his Chinese boss had abused him as a "coolie" to transport the machinery acquired from a "foreign capitalist." When there was a technical breakdown, the boss paid an exorbitant sum to a foreign engineer whose "repairs" damaged the projector even more. In the end, downtrodden Chinese projectionists fixed the machines with their own experimentation and passed on their hard-won technical expertise to the next generation.[18]

SECOND-GENERATION PROJECTIONISTS: PARTY MISSIONARIES AND STATE EMPLOYEES

Whereas pre-1949 projectionists never considered themselves a cohort, the state systematically recruited and employed what I am calling second-generation projectionists. In 1950, 1,800 young projectionists from all over the country attended a training program in Nanjing, later considered a "Cradle of the People's Cinema." As discussed in chapter 1, their class song prescribed their roles as enthusiastic soldiers and missionaries of Mao Zedong Thought who would inspire the workers, peasants, and soldiers to build the nation. According to former trainee Liu Zhenzhong (柳振忠), a fresh graduate from Fujian Provincial Industrial High School, he and his classmates were initially disappointed at the career prospect of merely showing rather than making films. To change their outlook, the teachers showed them new films every night—such as *The Birth of New China* (新中国的诞生), *The Sons and Daughters of China* (中华儿女), and *Radiant Light* (光芒万丈), all from 1949—and organized discussions afterward. Inspired by the heroes of these films, "many comrades made teary self-criticisms of their individualism and vowed to screen films to peasants for the rest of their lives." Liu also recalled the uneven educational background and babel of languages and dialects spoken by the trainees, such that translators were required for ethnic minorities. The trainees brought their own stools to a large auditorium temporarily constructed from straw mats. The teacher spoke through a loudspeaker, but the students in the back needed binoculars to see his diagrams on the blackboard, so they rotated seats and shared notes. In the absence of tables, chairs, and beds, students ate while sitting on the ground and laid their bedrolls on straw. They arose at five every morning for military drills before classes, and there was much choral singing throughout the day.[19] After returning from Nanjing, the 1800 plus graduates would go on not only to project films but also to replicate the training session in their respective provinces to cultivate more projectionists.

Second-generation projectionists were mostly born in the 1930s and 1940s and joined the film-exhibition sector in the 1950s and 1960s. Middle school graduates, young teachers, demobilized soldiers, and union activists were the most consistent pipeline for recruits. Many joined the Communist Youth League, but problematic class backgrounds hindered their paths to party membership.[20] Indeed, a 1958 report criticized the film-exhibition network for recruiting too few employees from worker and peasant families.[21] While the physical and itinerant aspects of the job discouraged female applicants, as will be discussed in chapter 3, there were targeted recruitments of women as well as of "ethnic minority" projectionists to reach historically marginalized audiences.[22]

After several months of training, the mobile projectionists hit the road. Their reports from the early 1950s highlight pioneering expeditions into inhospitable terrains—climbing mountains and traversing marshes, overcoming thin air at high altitudes and braving storms at sea, crossing perilous rivers and braving enemy fires, suffering tropical diseases and surviving bandit attacks.[23] After film screenings became more routine by the late 1950s, many projectionists still covered entire counties, so that each tour lasted several months.[24] Many had to delay their marriages, whereas married projectionists rarely returned home. As a popular doggerel put it: "Don't let your daughter marry a projectionist, otherwise she'd spend her days and nights all alone. On the rare occasion that he comes home, he'd throw you a pile of stinky clothes" (有女莫嫁放映郎，日日夜夜守空房，偶然一次回家转，丢下一堆臭衣裳).[25] *Film Projection* magazine also published common gripes about the job in the form of Spring Festival couplets: "Traveling fifteen kilometers a day to show films / Sleeping five hours a night in makeshift shelters" (日行三十里放映，夜眠五小时安身); "Hoping for a year of screenings without glitches, despairing at four seasons without respite" (但愿一年无故障，奈何四季不得闲); "Meeting a lowly third-rank official, getting a belly full of grievances. The horizontal inscription reads: Serve the People" (见官小三级，受气一肚皮，横批：为人民服务).[26] By the Great Leap Forward, however, projectionists' everyday hardships were sublimated through a rhetoric of sacrifice, and their (self-)representation was transformed from disgruntled state employees to labor models or superheroes who "ate one meal a day yet traveled one hundred *li*" and "climbed mountains at night instead of sleeping."[27]

Most second-generation projectionists I interviewed toured the countryside for only a few years before taking stationary jobs as propaganda officers, technicians, teachers, or managers at county movie stations.[28] They recruited local volunteers to help transport equipment, hang screens, check tickets, and maintain order. Some volunteers became the projectionists' apprentices, substitutes, and successors.²⁹ As projectionists rose in rank, however, they became more vulnerable to attack in the Cultural Revolution: many film managerial cadres and former model projectionists were paraded through the streets, demoted, incarcerated, exiled, injured, and even disabled or killed.³⁰ After the cadres were purged, the remaining employees became entangled in factional conflicts, whereas others conducted only the necessary screenings following political mandates.³¹ Survivors were rehabilitated after the Cultural Revolution, and by the time of my interviews, most were living off retirement pensions in work-unit housing built by their county movie company in the late 1970s and early 1980s.

THIRD GENERATION: COMMUNE-BASED BAREFOOT PROJECTIONISTS

After several years of paralysis and anarchy from 1966 to 1969, the release of the filmed versions of "revolutionary model works" (*yangbanxi* 样板戏), overseen by Mao's wife Jiang Qing, prompted a reorganization and expansion of the exhibition network, giving rise to a "third generation" of commune-based projectionists, also known as "barefoot projectionists" (赤脚放映员). Unlike earlier projectionists with long-term careers in the state cultural bureaucracy, barefoot projectionists remained commune members and were sometimes compensated with work points instead of salaries (see figure 2.1). Some held concurrent jobs as local broadcasters or barefoot doctors, so they called themselves a "light cavalry" serving the "poor and lower-middle peasants."³² Coming from the grassroots and remaining there, they constituted an unofficial army of cinematic guerrillas who feature most prominently in popular memories.

New technologies contributed to the creation of commune-run movie teams. Development of lightweight 8.75mm projectors and film prints, and pedal-powered generators allowed for easier transportation and greater mobility, thus enhancing the penetration of previously forbidding terrains.³³ Hubei's rural cadres came up with a ditty to describe the transformative impact of commune-run cinema:

天台山，天台山，山外还有山，...
看场电影难上难，吃了中饭就爬山，

FIGURE 2.1 "Commune member by day, projectionist by night." Drawing by Tao Yanling and Lu Zailiang, *Mass Cinema*, no. 10 (1964).

看完电影回到屋,鸡叫头遍莫安眠。
社办电影好的很,电影放到高山顶,
经常看到毛主席,革命生产添干劲。

Tiantai Mountain, Tiantai Mountain, mountains beyond mountains,
It's so hard to go to a movie: After lunch you climb a mountain,
Heading home after the movie, the rooster crows and it's time to rise.
Commune-run film is a great thing! The movie is shown on top of the mountain,
The frequent sight of Chairman Mao invigorates our revolutionary production.[34]

Thanks to commune-run movie teams, cinema became monthly or bimonthly events, and "barefoot projectionists" became familiar faces and bodies mediating cinema at the grassroots. Almost every older villager whom I asked during my fieldwork knew in which village their former projectionist had lived. Cinema for them was not so much a machine or a place, but rather a person.

The official selection criteria for commune projectionists included ideological rectitude, family class background, and educational level. "Poor and lower-middle peasants" were supposed to recommend suitable candidates, though cadres appointed most projectionists I interviewed.[35] Many had been schoolteachers, village broadcasters, telephone technicians, or tractor drivers. Several took part in amateur propaganda troupes as artists, writers, or performers. Most found film projection to be a more desirable job because of its respectability, mobility, and freedom.[36] Beyond class background, artistic talent, and technical skills, interviewees also mentioned *guanxi*, or private relationships, as an important selection criterion. For example, Mr. Xia (1947–) became a projectionist in 1965 because his uncle was the commune party secretary and lost the job ten years later with a change in the commune leadership—the new party secretary doled out the position to his own family member.[37]

Barefoot projectionists attended brief training sessions in county seats and participated in annual competitions in power generation, film projection, and slideshow performances. Winners became "advanced workers" honored at the "Congresses of Activists Studying Marxism-Leninism and Mao Zedong Thought," which could open up schooling and job opportunities to leave the countryside.[38] Celebrated feats included conducting special screenings for old grannies who had never before seen a film, transporting their equipment without local help, and working with severe injuries, so that the masses praised them for "not only projecting heroes in movies but also emulating them in practice."[39] Barefoot projectionists also showed films to mobilized laborers at construction sites, often full of chaos and scuffles because the workers did not belong to the same community. When projectionists encountered technical problems or when cadres gave long-winded speeches, the crowd might throw stones at them. "Even if your machine caught fire," one projectionist explained, "you had to keep calm, explain to your audience, troubleshoot, and not get into fights."[40]

Sent-down youths were a major subset of third-generation projectionists. These young people had grown up in the cities and attended many films with their schools. After they "went up to the mountains and down to the countryside," however, cinema became a rare and highly anticipated luxury. Chosen for their drawing, writing, singing, or acting skills, the four sent-down youth projectionists I interviewed did not have strong revolutionary family backgrounds or convictions, but propaganda work gave them welcome respite from agricultural labor and the opportunity to develop their artistic and intellectual ambitions. Some even carried a civilizing mission after seeing how "peasant homes had almost nothing made out of paper." They spoke of a broader sense of cultural deprivation: "The loudspeakers only relayed Central People's Radio or the provincial station. Even if you had your own radio set, listening to foreign stations was strictly forbidden. Most people just went to bed soon after sunset. Film was our only spiritual life."[41]

As their communes' "Mao Zedong Thought propaganda team," barefoot projectionists I interviewed in Hubei all performed multimedia propaganda. Beyond mobile film screenings, Mr. Xia would bring a red flag and portrait of Mao to the fields, lead villagers to recite Mao quotations, and project slideshows. First catching a cadre's attention for making an exquisite set of poker cards, Mr. Peng (1950–) was hired to paint historical panoramas for the county museum, make sets for

FIGURE 2.2 A sent-down youth projectionist. Courtesy of Pan Hengsheng.

FIGURE 2.3 A sent-down youth projectionist. Courtesy of Cheng Yuntao.

the local theater troupe, and produce lantern slides for the movie teams. A talented calligrapher and artist, Mr. Zhang (1955–) helped write slogans and paint propaganda on walls since his school days. He even spent a summer "broadcasting" Mao's little red book through a homemade megaphone on top of a hill to the tillers in the valleys. Although hardly anyone listened, he found the job of being a human loudspeaker easier than toiling under the sun. As a film projectionist, he first worked for the commune but later bought the equipment and hired help under the contract responsibility system. With the commune's dissolution and television's eclipse of film, he transferred his painting and calligraphy skills to advertising and sign-making. Indeed, many barefoot projectionists proved to be adaptable to the changing media ecology from socialist propaganda or capitalist advertising.

THE CINEMATIC ASSEMBLAGE: MACHINES AND HUMAN POWER

Having now delineated three generation of mobile projectionists in the Mao era, let us consider the things they carried, starting with the machinery. In the 1950s both power generators and projectors were foreign-made, either remnant American or Japanese machines or newer models imported from the Soviet Union or Eastern Europe.⁴² Weighing as much as two hundred kilograms, the power generator was the bulkiest, heaviest, loudest, and most volatile machine projectionists carried. Age, disrepair, bad roads, and difficult climates all led to frequent breakdowns. Since the generator burned flammable oil, the movie team also brought a long cable (some thirty meters) to keep it both connected and at a good distance from the projector and loudspeakers. To forestall fire and electrocution as children were running amok, the generator operator rarely watched the movie.⁴³

If technology was precarious and perilous, then projectionists' bodies played a compensatory role. Guidelines admonished them to shield their machines from shock, fall, rain, snow, sand, heat, and cold during transport and screenings. Refraining from drinking, smoking, and chatting, generator operators kept an eye on the transformer, listened carefully for noise, touched many buttons, and attended to burning smells.⁴⁴ Precautionary measures included regular cleaning of machine parts and sewing a cotton bag to keep the gasoline from freezing. Some projectionists risked their lives to save machines from a collapsing building or covered machines with their raincoats and blankets during thunderstorms.⁴⁵ Inventive bricolage helped resolve technical issues such as the wind blowing away the screen, failing generators, and brittle, overused film reels.⁴⁶ As the projectionists' embodied practices compensated for poor technology, their self-sacrifice emanated an electrifying spirit and pathos that reportedly moved the masses whom they served.

Indeed, the movie team not only *carried* a power generator—they *were* a power generator. The joining of projectionist bodies to their machines of image projection and sound amplification generated energy, passion, labor, and mass assembly needed for political campaigns and infrastructural construction. Especially during the Great Leap Forward and the Cultural Revolution, local cadres summoned movie teams to generate electricity for the lights and loudspeakers at mass rallies, and even for all-night shifts of agricultural or construction projects.⁴⁷ The films themselves became secondary, even dispensable. Cinema thus became sheer electrification that both inspired and conscripted the masses to "make revolution" day and night.

FILM REELS AS PRECIOUS SCROLLS

"Love machines as you would your life; protect reels as you would your eyes," *Film Projection* magazine admonished. "Damaging a film frame is equivalent to wasting a flatbread. Destroying a print is even more serious—you can account for the financial loss, but you cannot account for the political impact of millions of audiences not educated by the film."[48] Since each print had to be screened hundreds or even thousands of times, a ruined film reel could mean a ruined career. In work photos, projectionists often posed with their projector while checking a film print frame by frame for loose screws. Even sand blown in by the wind could cause reels to break, scratch, or burn.[49] Prints could also get wet from rain during screenings, or they could fall into a river during transportation, thus requiring fastidious care to prevent irredeemable damage. As central planning maximized usage of every print, it was also essential to return scarce copies on time.[50]

Despite all the care taken, overused celluloid inevitably snapped and became scratched, so an overused print unwound as a palimpsest scroll of human foibles. Scratched films and other technical issues contributed to fuzzy images, hissing sounds, and an overall sensorial experience of "disrepair and noise."[51] Snapped film reels provoked audiences to boo and hoot, while children jumped up and fought over the discarded "treasures" of celluloid fragments.[52] Scratches indicated a film's popularity and familiarity to audiences, who sometimes recited memorized dialogues or commented on the plot. Single copies of popular films with a brief rental period were sometimes shared among multiple movie teams on the same night, requiring "copy running" (跑片) to relay the film reels between two or more locations. Waiting for the copy-runner's arrival meant being held in suspense about what would happen next.[53] Skillful projectionists filled the gap by summarizing the plot of the last reel, sometimes in prosimetric form with a bamboo clapper, so that a feature-length film took on the quality of traditional serialized vernacular storytelling.

Film reels were thus like "precious scrolls" in two senses. The first refers to their treasured and fragile materiality, which demanded meticulous care. The second sense analogizes films to precious scrolls as *baojuan* (宝卷), a prosimetric vernacular narrative composed for performance in a ritual setting for a lay audience, popular from the fourteenth to the early twentieth centuries.[54] Like *baojuan*, film reels came to life through the incantation of projectionists and received reverent attention from audiences. If *baojuan* propagated Buddhist doctrines, Maoist films proselytized revolutionary messages. Whereas *baojuan* often began with an invitation to Buddha and bodhisattvas, socialist cinema began with revolutionary icons and mediated encounters between a revered Chairman Mao and his loyal masses. Yet just as *baojuan* evolved from tools of Buddhist proselytizing to folk ritualized storytelling, Maoist films served as both spiritual education and vernacular entertainment, ritual and leisure.[55]

BAMBOO CLAPPERS, LANTERN SLIDES, AND EXTRA-FILMIC PROPAGANDA

Projectionists were not merely machine operators but also talented performers using their voices, bamboo clappers, and lantern slides to enliven the cinematic event and enhance audience participation. They were as much entertainers as ritual specialists who disseminated, translated, and explicated propaganda for their grassroots congregations. Their *mediumship* transformed and diversified an industrialized, standardized mass cultural product to suit local needs (see figure 0.6).

The wooden clapper (often bamboo) is a pair of percussive instruments routinely used by opera troupes and traditional storytellers to punctuate their songs and narratives with a crisp, rhythmic, staccato sound. Popular in North China, clapper-talk (快板) developed from beggar ballads to stage performances in the Mao era.[56] A former projectionist from Hebei recalled her prescreening clapper-talk from the 1950s: "Audiences, settle down and be kind, a few rules to keep in mind. First rule, most crucial, onsite order is essential. No pushing, no fighting, no running, and no screaming. Tall chairs should be laid low, and a central path should be cleared out. Why clear out a middle road? So you don't block the projector's glow..." (观众们，请安静，说几件事情大家听。第一件，要记牢，场里的秩序很重要。别拥挤、别吵闹，不要乱跑和喊叫。坐高凳子的都放倒，中间要留路一条。哎，为啥要留路一条？挡住光线看不好...).[57] Since mobile film exhibition had no fixed infrastructure and could not count on sloped seating or fire safety, projectionists used clapper-talk to focus audience attention and discipline behavior.

The projectionists' oral performances also addressed the comprehension challenges faced by grassroots audiences at the cinematic, cultural, linguistic, and acoustic levels. When watching Soviet World War II films in the early 1950s, rank-and-file army audiences applauded at the wrong places, such as when the enemy (German) troops appeared.[58] Although imported films were dubbed in Mandarin, most rural folk only understood local dialects. The acoustic quality of the loudspeakers and film prints was often so poor, even the projectionists had trouble discerning the spoken dialogue, so they relied on print publications to follow the story.[59] Last, cinematic language such as flashbacks, intercutting, and dream sequences often baffled audiences, so projectionists provided introductions before, explanations during, and discussions after the screenings.[60] Absorption into the film's diegesis came to depend on extradiegetic live narrations (figure 2.4).

Such live lecturing harkens back to silent cinema's exhibition practices, especially Japanese *benshi* who drew on traditional storytelling arts to serve as narrator, voice actor, and audience representative at film

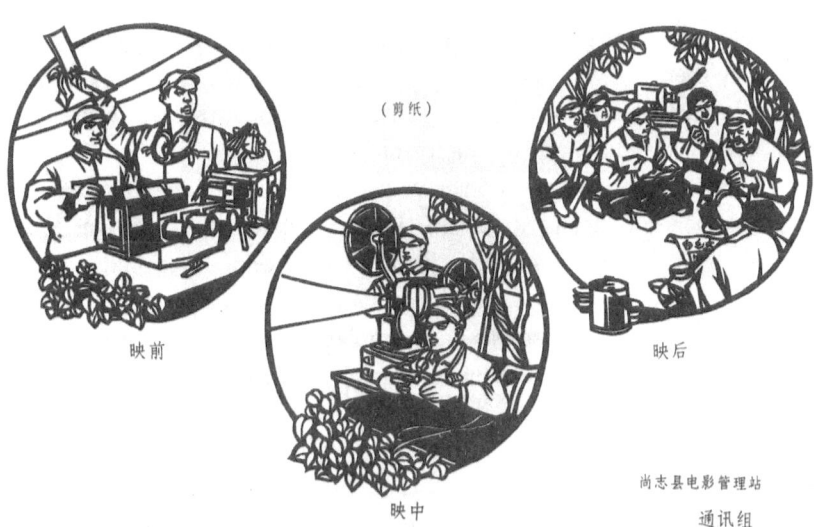

FIGURE 2.4 "Before, during, and after screenings." Papercut by Shangzhi County Movie Station, *Film Work Correspondence*, no. 1 (1972).

Mobile Projectionists and the Things They Carried 81

screenings.⁶¹ Whereas the introduction of talkies rendered film lecturers obsolete by the 1930s, oral performances continued to accompany sound cinema in rural China into the 1970s. Talent and experience in singing, storytelling, or improvisation became major criteria for the selection of projectionists. Some learned better intonation and Mandarin pronunciation from radio broadcasters; others apprenticed with folk storytellers, such that they became the heirs and disseminators of oral traditions.⁶² Their liveness, heterogeneity, and local color often made such performances even greater attractions than the films.

Apart from clapper-talk, mobile projectionists systematically produced, projected, and narrated lantern slides, which came to be known as "rustic cinema" (土电影). Light and portable, the magic lantern appeared in China as early as the seventeenth century and was widely used by the early twentieth century for performance, entertainment, preaching, and education.⁶³ Popularly known as *layangpian* (拉洋片, "pulling Western slides"), or *xiyangjing* (西洋镜, "Western mirror," or 西洋景, "Western scenery"), magic lanterns were fitted for public shows and peep shows at temple fairs, displaying foreign and domestic landscapes, fantastic depictions of heaven and hell, and photographs of nude women.⁶⁴ The imported technology became an important medium for local artists to exhibit and market their talent: merchants displayed slides and sold New Year prints of the same images; storytellers used slides to illustrate their ballads. At once both exotic and familiar, foreign (*yang* 洋), and folk/rustic/native (*tu* 土), the lantern slideshow thrived with other imported and indigenous media forms.⁶⁵

The CCP readily enlisted the versatile medium of the lantern slide in its propaganda network. All movie teams were asked to incorporate slideshows into their cinematic liturgy to introduce national policies and political campaigns, and to explicate the stories, characters, and morals of films. According to an exemplary agenda from 1954, when a movie team arrived at a township, projectionists asked local cadres about "good people and good deeds" (好人好事) and prepared relevant slides. Before the evening's screening, they played revolutionary songs over loudspeakers and used a slideshow to exhort their audience to attend the public tribunal of a "bad element." The team's "propagandist" sang a ballad about industrialization, which was followed by fifty slides depicting a new steel capital. Only then would she introduce the story and characters in the evening's film. While her colleagues changed reels, she summarized the previous reel. On the second evening, the team projected slides they had prepared the day before and sang newly composed songs to address local issues, such as the promulgation of thrift and savings, interspersed with speeches by local bank and irrigation officers. The following morning the team held a discussion about the films with cadres and militia members.⁶⁶

"If cinema is a cannon among propaganda weapons," *Film Projection* magazine proclaimed, "the slide projector is a machine gun."⁶⁷ In areas without electricity, the slides could be projected using gas lamps instead of bulky generators. The audiences would watch the slideshow as

FIGURE 2.5 Upon arrival in a village, mobile projectionists were supposed to interview the locals about "good people and good deeds" to make relevant slideshows. Papercut by Zhaodong County Movie Station, *Film Work Correspondence*, no. 1 (1972).

a concentrated collective in the darkness, except that the slideshow could be sped up, slowed down, or repeated on demand.⁶⁸ Sonically, the slideshow was usually accompanied by live performances of storytelling, poetry recitation, regional opera, or folk songs.⁶⁹ Standing amid the audience, the projectionist-performers often attracted as much attention as the projected slides. The local models who were being praised might interrupt the performance with flushed modesty, turning the show into a "crosstalk" (相声) as the audiences enlivened the scene with laughter.⁷⁰ Projectionists also facilitated the liturgical use of revolutionary music and quasi-congregational singing by projecting lyrics on lantern slides and teaching audiences to sing line by line (see figure 1.5).⁷¹

Apart from its economy, versatility, and interactivity, the slideshow format encouraged local media production that integrated and cultivated folk artists. Projectionists and lanternists applied various visual styles to enrich the medium's expressive means. Those interviewees recalled having to keep the colors transparent while ensuring accuracy in the miniature format, as all mistakes would be magnified through projection. The fastidious work was so strenuous for the eyes, hands, and shoulders that some lanternists were left with arthritis and other chronic illnesses. Yet hardly any interviewees considered those handmade slides to be works of art worthy of preservation, only an effective propaganda means that demanded craftsmanship.⁷²

Even projectionists with little artistic talent produced lantern slides in creative ways. When asked to advertise a new insecticide for a township government, a movie team tried to draw the rice planthopper but failed to capture its likeness, so they caught some with the help of the local cadre and trapped them inside the lantern slides to be projected live onto the screen. The heat of the light bulbs agitated the insects, so they became especially animated while agricultural technicians explained the workings of the insecticide. The magnification and illumination of living specimens turned out to be highly effective in convincing villagers to purchase insecticides to fight the pest. Thus the movie team was praised for turning the slide projector into a microscope and an "insect trap."⁷³

When projectionists researched, wrote, drew, and sang about local models, the honor of appearing onscreen gave incentives to work hard to "get into the movies."⁷⁴ Some teams invested in photographic technology to let rural villagers see "real local people, places, and events" on screen.⁷⁵ Some projectionists produced slideshow "screen newspapers" (银屏报) that not only honored models but also shamed "backward elements." One movie team contrasted the high and low yields of backyard steel furnaces in two production brigades by painting the former as a Sputnik and the latter as a turtle. An article even instructed projectionists to dab the faces of positive figures with warm flesh tones and to tint the faces of negative figures with blue and green.⁷⁶

In addition to clapper-talk and slideshows, movie teams made other extra-filmic propaganda to transform the broader visual and acoustic environment of villages. For example, the Hubei Sino-Soviet Movie Team decorated the projection site with posters depicting Soviet construction, used gramophones and loudspeakers to broadcast Sino-Soviet friendship songs, and mobilized elementary school children to form waist-drum marching bands to spread the word about upcoming screenings.⁷⁷ Other movie teams wrote poetry, painted murals, and made "propaganda lanterns" (宣传灯) in the form of Zoetropes (走马灯). Some composed new lyrics for popular melodies and taught them to villagers.⁷⁸ Others carried microphones, gramophones, and loudspeakers into the fields so that they could make "broadcasts" while participating in labor.⁷⁹ Indeed, one major incentive for local cadres to hire movie teams was to use their microphones and loudspeakers to address a crowd so that they could better assign agricultural production tasks and mobilize for mass campaigns.⁸⁰

During the Socialist Education Movement, movie teams projected films and slideshows that emphasized class struggle. They encouraged audience members to identify with the prerevolutionary suffering and to remember bitterness onstage, therefore providing a "vivid and concrete lesson on class struggle" for "young people unfamiliar with past bitterness."⁸¹ Human voices and gestures joined films, slides, microphones, and loudspeakers in a quasi-shamanistic performance that conjured up past grievances and transformed audience members into spirit mediums possessed by the ghosts of the feudal past, which had to be purged to ensure the purity of the revolutionary community.

Even though existing sources mostly testify to the efficacy of propaganda slideshows, Henrietta Harrison's microhistory of a Catholic village in Shanxi provides a more subversive account of their grassroots reception. During her fieldwork, Harrison heard many villagers recounting a "miracle of the flying bicycle" associated with four brave women who, in the 1960s, convinced many apostates to return to the church:

> On one occasion an old man responded to my obvious doubt by saying that he had a photograph of the flying bicycle. A short while later he came back with a pile of old glass slides. As we hunted through the slides looking without success for a flying bicycle, I realized that they had in fact been made as part of the Socialist Education Movement not to prove that miracles took place but, quite the opposite, to show the villagers how the miracles of that time had been faked and thus to persuade them not to believe in Christianity. For the old man, the original intention of the slides did not matter, instead he was preserving them as a record of what really happened.[82]

During the Cultural Revolution, as will be further discussed in chapter 8, extra-filmic propaganda was used to demonize and exorcize class enemies as "ox-demons and snake-spirits" at live denunciations. As many cultural cadres and models were attacked, projectionists became paranoid about making political mistakes with live performances and slideshows: "You can't pierce your hands by wiping your machines, but it's truly risky to wield a brush to write or paint." After 1971, however, extra-filmic propaganda become a criterion for selecting new projectionists, so that slideshows with live narration became *the* local media production of every commune.[83]

TRANSPORTATION, FOOD, CLOTHES, AND ACCOMMODATIONS: THE WEIGHT OF BODIES

Having discussed the material objects movie teams worked with, let us examine the materiality of their everyday lives, as captured by the idiom *yi shi zhu xing* (衣食住行)—clothing, food, shelter, and transportation. Depending on the local terrain and available infrastructure, mobile projectionists used transportation modes ranging from automobiles, horse-drawn carriages, donkeys, boats, bicycles, hand-pushed carts, and shoulder poles (see figure 0.4 on page 10). An all-female movie team from

Shaanxi rode on a horse cart with their machinery and personal belongings, but the team leader also had a bicycle for making logistical arrangements.[84] A Jiangsu movie team had a "movie boat" that served as its transportation and accommodations over three decades.[85] By the 1970s many commune movie teams could expect the next village on their itinerary to send a few men to pick up the machinery.[86] Former sent-down youth projectionists in the "Great Northern Wilderness" got lifts on jeeps, trucks, or, more commonly, tractors and horse carts. One interviewee, Mr. Lu (1950–), vividly recalled the roads his team traveled, and how they got soaked in the rain and froze in the winter even when wrapped up in thick blankets. To counter the cold, they drank liquor, but if a projectionist got drunk, he could mess up the screening, and the ruining of film was rumored to be punishable by heavy fines or prison sentences. In the summer heat, the horse sometimes galloped into the river with all the luggage and machinery. When the road was muddy and the horse was tired, they would sometimes be stranded in the grassland. The coachman would whip the horse, which would howl with pain but still refuse to budge, and the movie team would despair, thinking of the hundreds of people waiting for the movie.[87] The interviewee also showed me a drawing he had made while stranded on the road with his equipment after the truck giving them a ride tumbled into a ditch (figure 2.6).

Projection teams slept in schools, temples, shrines, silos, toolsheds, opera stages, and villagers' homes. When there were no beds, they slept on the ground, on desks and chairs pushed together, even inside empty coffins.[88] They brought bedrolls and mosquito nets yet still endured the bitter winter cold and the summer bug bites. A movie team working in Tibet described their accommodations in romantic terms: "The sky is our mosquito net, the earth our bed. Not enough blankets? We'll find cover under the snow. So long as the herders can watch movies, a thousand bitter hardships are swept aside" (天作蚊帐地当床，被盖不够雪帮忙，为了牧民看电影，千难万苦一扫光).[89]

Since there were few restaurants in the countryside, mobile movie teams often bought food from peddlers or ate in villager homes. One projectionist who was a rice eater from the South could not get used to eating steamed wheat buns in the Northern countryside, whereas her team member from an urban middle-class family had trouble swallowing the food prepared by villagers—often maize porridge mixed with

FIGURE 2.6 Sketch of a mobile projectionist and his equipment stranded on the road after the truck giving them a ride tumbled into a ditch. Courtesy of Hua Yilong.

vinegar and chili peppers.[90] Although movie-team members were supposed to pay for their meals, some local cadres drew on the collective budget to pay for feasts—in some instances killing a sheep and several chickens to feed two dozen minions, so Yunnan villagers composed the following doggerel: "When the movie is here, the cadres laugh. They drink like there's no tomorrow. Chicken and ducks fly in fright. Pigs and dogs fear for their plight" (电影来到，干部欢笑，一得喝酒，命都不要。鸡鸭吓飞，猪狗吓跳，如此下去，大为不妙).[91]

For grassroots audiences, film projectionists were a privileged class, as evidenced by what they wore and ate. A Ningxia villager recalled an all-female commune movie team whose members wore leather shoes and leather jackets: "You could tell at once that they received a state salary."[92] A villager from Gansu recalled how projectionists wore sheepskin coats or blue khaki Mao suit–like uniforms, with four pockets and buttoned up to the collar, whereas the clothing of those in the audiences was covered with patches. Along with the local cadres, movie-team members ate noodles or pancakes of fine flour instead of the villagers' daily fare of coarse grains.⁹³ Many of my parents' former sent-down youth friends spoke with retrospective envy of the projectionists as the ones who ate better than everyone else. The projectionists' material lives thus refracted the broader material conditions at the grassroots.

As we reconsider film history from the perspectives of projectionists rather than directors, we arrive at alternative understandings of what, when, where, and who cinema was. The various origin stories of cinema in different localities remind us that film did not arrive everywhere and for everyone at the same time or in the same way. This calls for writing histories of *cinematic accessibility* that take into account such differentials and mapping cinema's many global and local itineraries, its many centers and margins. Obscured by a film history of auteurs and masterpieces, the various career trajectories of film projectionists suggest alternative periodizations that take into account the uneven development of media infrastructure in fits and starts. More than a collection of audiovisual texts, mobile projectionists and their practices foreground cinema's physicality in terms of both corporeality and materiality. When machines had to be carried over mountains or across rivers because there were no mechanized modes of transportation, we pay more attention to their bulkiness and weight, as well as to the roads, geography, and weather. When films break down or when the electric voltage fluctuates, we notice the brittleness and flammability of celluloid, the human powering of the generator, and the makeshift shabbiness or absence of infrastructure.

Yet material scarcity demanded bodily sacrifice and contributed to a sense of the sacred. Carrying ungainly power generators, movie teams *became* power generators that contributed to the generation of revolutionary energy. Raising screens like flags, they enchanted audiences with luminous images in villages without electricity. Taking meticulous care of precious film reels, projectionists made celluloid "precious scrolls" serve liturgical, educational, and entertainment purposes with their retellings of revolutionary pious tales, just as Chinese popular religion relied on fiction, drama, and folk art for the dissemination of myths and images of the deities.⁹⁴ With lantern slideshows and bamboo clappers, projectionists localized, diversified, and enlivened propaganda for their grassroots audiences. Meanwhile, the official demand for slideshows and live performances helped certain folk arts and artists survive, even thrive, in a socialist media ecology. Projectionists also made extra-filmic propaganda using microphones, gramophones, radios, mimeographed pamphlets, and posters.[95] Indeed, cinema was only one component of their ritual paraphernalia for revolutionary liturgies. Even beyond the cinematic event, movie teams claimed to have been particularly efficacious at solving local problems, from labor mobilization to pest control, from technical repairs to transforming "feudal practices." One model team reportedly even solved a case of theft by projecting the documentary *Rent Collection Courtyard* (收租院) (1966) and animated film *Rooster Crows at Midnight* (半夜鸡叫) (1964) to inspire class struggle and mass denunciations.[96]

In both its constitution and function, Maoist cinema was a *physical and spirit medium.* By physical medium, I refer to the material and corporeal dimensions of film exhibition—a media assemblage of generators and projectors, screens and film reels, microphones and loudspeakers, lantern slides and bamboo clappers, as well as the voices, labor, and performance of mobile projectionists and their grassroots audiences. By spirit medium, I underscore the *human* mediation of cinema by mobile projectionists who wove together a mass media network and mobilized the masses with modern technologies, local traditions, and their own bodies and spirits. Like missionaries, priests, and shamans, mobile projectionists solicited and staged testimonies of revolutionary faith, be they bitter memories of a prerevolutionary past, denunciations of local landlords or other class enemies, or vows to contribute to a communist future. Thus Maoist cinema was also a form of spiritual enrichment that sought to compensate for material impoverishment, even if it sometimes highlighted the disjunctions between utopian images and material realities.

CHAPTER THREE

The Three Sisters Movie Team

Projecting Models, Model Projectionists, and Female Projectionists

In 1958 the authorities passed down a directive: "Every commune should form a film projection team, every village should hang a screen, and everyone should watch movies" (社社办电影,村村插银幕,人人看电影). Laishui County of Hebei Province recruited three female graduates from the local middle school to form a new movie team. "A projectionist is like a magician," the young women were quoted in a reportage, "with a sway of the fingers, mountains and rivers, people and horses, distant cities and villages can all appear before your eyes."[1] After overcoming technical failures, ideological wavering, and the rural folk's skepticism, the "Three Sisters Movie Team" (三姐妹电影队)—as they came to be known—crossed mountains and braved snowstorms to bring films to the county's most remote villages. Beyond screening films, they created and performed animated slideshows about local models with bamboo clapper-talk. Such "rustic cinema" won them nationwide renown until they became role models for projectionists around the country. Besides being featured in newspapers and magazines, the "Three Sisters" became the subjects of propaganda posters and appeared in a documentary newsreel in 1966.[2]

From projecting models to model projectionists, the Three Sisters Movie Team is a kaleidoscopic prism through which we can examine the production, circulation, and reception of models through mass media. Not only media representations in words and images, print, and

FIGURE 3.1 Propaganda poster from 1966 portraying Hebei's Three Sisters Movie Team, by Sun Yu, Liu Zhenye, and Yang Deshu.

celluloid, the Three Sisters were also media producers who disseminated propaganda techniques around the country. Furthermore, their gendered identities projected new socialist values of "women's liberation" and "what men can do, women can also do." Yet to what extent could a scholar "believe" the wealth of propaganda sources about the Three Sisters? Are those quotations and speeches in the first person these women's authentic voices, or were the Three Sisters ventriloquized mediums serving as the party's mouthpiece? Since media coverage of the Three Sisters Movie Team ceased by the summer of 1966, what happened to these women during the Cultural Revolution decade? Was their propaganda work as efficacious as trumpeted in the propaganda?

With these questions in mind, I took a fieldtrip to Laishui County with the generous help of historian Feng Xiaocai and two graduate students, Lyu Hongyun and Li Bingbing, to learn more about the Three Sisters Movie Team. We interviewed a dozen current and former employees of the county's film sector, visited the local "Three Sisters Memorial Hall," and perused new archival sources. We failed to interview any of the original "Three Sisters," however, for reasons that will become manifest. Nevertheless, we learned a great deal about Maoist media ecologies and gender politics that remain largely invisible from published sources. To supplement this chapter with women's perspectives, I conducted additional oral history interviews with female projectionists elsewhere to learn about their negotiations with and transformation of gender norms both traditional and revolutionary.

Shifting the analytical lens from generations to gender, from collective to individual biographies, from materialities to subjectivities, this chapter explores the relationship between propaganda and reality from several angles. The first section presents a media-centered retheorization of models as a utopian blueprint in socialist China by highlighting film and slide projection as the radiation of the revolutionary spirit. Since projectionists often became models because of their excellence in projecting models, the middle section reconstructs the making and unmaking of the Three Sisters Movie Team amid other female model projectionist stories. A juxtaposition of published propaganda against oral-history interviews reveals a complex media ecology behind the scenes and lays bare some contradictions in state-sponsored feminism. The last section analyzes oral-history interviews with "ordinary" female projectionists who received little press during their working lives between the 1950s and 1980s, highlighting what had been omitted from model narratives and how gender figured practically into a career in the film-exhibition sector.

PROJECTING MODELS: THE RADIATION OF REVOLUTIONARY SPIRIT

农村阵地要占牢，	To strengthen the hold of the rural front,
革命电影不可少，	We cannot do without revolutionary cinema,
银幕映出新气象，	The screen projects and radiates a new climate,
人变地变产量高。	Changing people and land and boosting our yield.

What did the Maoist projectionist project? Revolutionary films and slideshows would be the simple answer. But according to this jingle by a model movie team in Hubei in 1974, the projection did not stop at the two-dimensional screen but rather emanated farther into the atmosphere to create a "new climate" with a transformative impact on the people, land, and agricultural output.³ The verse is embedded in a report about the model movie team's projection of revolutionary model works to inspire emulation and raise productivity. If the films were only a means to an end, then what the Maoist projectionists projected were radiant models that emitted the revolutionary spirit into both the human psyche and the physical environment. If movie teams were the emissaries of Chairman Mao, their projections were also emissions of Mao's divine light and solar energy. Hailing Mao Zedong Thought as the source of inspiration and energy, models resembled solar panels that absorbed the sun's rays and converted them into labor power. Maoist cinema was thus not only a representational medium but also a climate-changing technology, tasked with not only "engineering the human soul" but also with agricultural engineering and geo-engineering. In this sense, the cult of Mao harkens back to time-honored cults of dragon kings and other weather-controlling deities, who also demanded sacrifices from their worshippers.

Maoist models went by various nomenclature—examples (模范), prototypes (样板), advanced [workers] (先进), activists (积极分子), paragons (榜样), typical cases (典型), pacesetters (标兵), and heroes (英雄)—but they can be broadly defined as people and places, individuals and collectives, that the officials considered worthy of emulation. Models included utopian blueprints for rural development from the Soviet communes to Dazhai; war heroes and martyrs from China's revolutionary past; and ordinary people making extraordinary contributions to socialism. A central mission of projectionists and other propagandists was to magnify, amplify, and multiply models. Serving as a "linchpin of the Communist Party's mass line," models were both mass mediated and technologies of mass mediation.⁴ Often undergoing a metamorphosis from receiver to transmitter of ideology, models were supposed to unleash a chain process of emulation whereby models begat models begat models. After all, they embodied, emanated, and transmitted the revolutionary spirit to their audiences.

What was the relationship between models and reality? Cultural historians of modern China conducted narrative and formal analyses of literary, visual, and media texts as idealized illustrations of ideology, often pointing out disjunctions between representation and reality.⁵

Cinema scholars often asked how documentaries "represent reality" and how films portray their subjects in terms of realism and verisimilitude.[6] But what if we shifted attention from *representations* vis-à-vis their referents to *projection* vis-à-vis their audiences? *Projection* links elite-produced moving images to the grassroots populations that receive them, so rather than asking "How real were the images?" the question becomes: "How did projections transform realities beyond the film?"

Has cinema ever changed the world?[7] Variations of this question have been asked of film texts rather than of the exhibition process, and studies of projection focus on the evolving technological apparatus and its psychological impact. Borrowing from Louis Althusser, film scholar Rey Chow discussed cinema as "projection with an invitation for introjection."[8] Whereas apparatus theory largely constructs audiences as passive spectators to preserve the status quo, Maoist projections of propaganda aimed to *activate* its audiences to make revolutionary changes. As Mao put it in 1958: "The outstanding thing about China's 600 million people is that they are 'poor and blank.' This may seem a bad thing, but in reality, it is a good thing. Poverty gives rise to the desire for changes, the desire for action and the desire for revolution. On a blank sheet of paper free from any mark, the freshest and most beautiful characters can be written; the freshest and most beautiful pictures can be painted."[9] The people, in other words, were not merely the subjects or objects of representation but the very *medium* of revolutionary politics and aesthetics.[10] They were the "poor and blank" canvases or screens onto which utopian models were to be inscribed and projected, and they were to *become* those utopian models through emulation. When projection teams entered the Qinling Mountains in Gansu Province, a commune member reportedly said: "Earning only 20 cents a day, I used to think, how can we build socialism in these poor mountains and deep forests? Now that I've watched the slideshow *Mountain Agricultural Cooperative Prospective Blueprint* (山区农业社远景规划) (1958) and the film *Great Leap Forward in the Countryside* (农村大跃进) (1958), my eyes have grown bright, and I will work all my life to turn these mountains into a paradise." After watching a slideshow entitled *Canal Prospective Blueprint* (运河远景规划) (1960), laborers at an irrigation project agreed that "three years of bitter battle will give happiness to ten thousand generations."[11]

As projected images authenticated revolutionary miracles, they also converted audiences to adopt the pictured methods. According to a projectionist report from Hubei, a villager skeptical of newspaper reports about high-yielding experimental wheat fields finally "believed his eyes" after watching the newsreel *The Aroma of a Wheat Harvest Travels a Thousand Miles* (麦香千里喜丰收) (1958).[12] Following the logic of "seeing is believing," communes built new hydroelectric power plants, dug irrigation ditches, and expanded backyard steel furnaces. Chosen for their local applicability to the tasks at hand, documentaries and science-education films modeled new agricultural and engineering techniques, which sometimes brought disastrous results. One example of this was a documentary newsreel entitled *Besieging Sparrows* (围剿麻雀) (1958) to support the campaign against the "Four Pests," to be further discussed in chapter 6.[13]

Despite cinema's role at mobilizing labor, only a few Mao-era film productions portrayed individual labor models, such as Xie Jin's "artistic documentary" *Huang Baomei* (黄宝妹) (1958). Most cinematic models tended to be agricultural and infrastructural projects in documentaries or revolutionary war heroes and martyrs emulated for their self-sacrificial spirit. Where labor models did get projected onscreen, however, was in the locally handmade slideshows, praised by many cadres for being even more efficacious than film at labor mobilization because they featured local faces.[14] As a slogan put it: "Everyone can get into the movies; each contends for honor and glory" (人人上电影，个个争光荣). As movie teams were dubbed "night luminescent pearls" (夜明珠), the radiance of the projected image could spread its luminosity onto all audiences, generating revolutionary energy until they were themselves absorbed into the utopian image.[15]

Film and slideshow projection as radiation of revolutionary energy had environmental, climatic, and atmospheric connotations for rural China. If we adopt not a linear model of mediation as a "direct transmission of a message," but instead "a spherical model that understands the medium as an immediate environment or field that encompasses a variety of media and constitutes a shared space of experience,"[16] Maoist projections literally sought to transform the rural landscape, as suggested by the following 1950s film titles: *Light Shines Onto a Mountain Village* (光明照到高地) (1956), *Under the Radiance of the General Line* (总路

线的光辉照耀下) (1958), *Moving Mountains and Filling Seas* (移山填海) (1955), *Chopping Mountains and Diverting Water* (劈山引水) (1958), *Reclaiming Virgin Land* (被开垦的处女地) (1960), *Waterlogged Land Turns Into Arable Field* (涝地变良田) (1958), and so forth. From the parable of the foolish old man who moved the mountains to the mythic Jingwei bird that filled up the ocean, from a Soviet collective farm to a new Chinese reservoir, the aim of such films was to reclaim wasteland and transform mountains and marshes into fertile fields that yielded bountiful harvests, a process aided by the radiant light of film projection and party leadership.

How did projected images alter the physical environment? Reports from projectionists and interviews suggest three ways of modeling: *illustration, illumination,* and *energy conversion*. First, the content of films and slideshows illustrated both the achievements and processes of land improvement through collective labor that their rural audiences could replicate. While resonating with ancient Chinese myths, cinema imparted cultural techniques in the original sense of *Kulturtechniken* as agricultural engineering, including irrigation, drainage, enclosure, and river regulation.[17] Beyond technical illustration, the illumination of cinema heightened the visibility and the "poetics of infrastructures" that existed as "forms of desire and fantasy."[18] Following such projected models, many infrastructural projects aimed to attract media attention, serving optical rather than practical purposes. Finally, apart from the projection image's technical and aesthetic dimensions, the collective ritual of attending such screenings generated revolutionary energy among the audience. Following Thomas Elsaesser's theorization of cinema as an "energy exchange system," Debashree Mukherjee studied the "cine-ecology" of Bombay cinema in the 1930s as "a web of energy relations," finding in films of this period a "pervasive aesthetics of vitality."[19] Similarly, Maoist cinematic models reportedly energized their off screen audiences to multiply their productivity and became a "power source for agricultural production" (农业生产的力量源泉).[20]

By the mid-1960s, as cultural studies scholar Laikwan Pang showed, a new word for model, *yangban* (样板), had gained widespread currency, referring at first to prototypes of industrial products with "a clear implication of design." In 1963 the National Agricultural Science Committee advanced "the idea of the *yangban* field [model field], a set of scientific agricultural strategies designed for high-yield output that could be adopted nationally."²¹ In her study of scientific farming in socialist China, historian Sigrid Schmalzer pointed out that "demonstration fields allowed the 'masses' to 'see' and 'touch' new technologies so that they would more quickly recognize their benefits and accept their use.... demonstration fields were expected to play a key role in increasing production 'from a single point to many points, and from many points to the whole plane.'"²² Mao's wife Jiang Qing appropriated this agricultural-industrial term for her influential revolutionary model works, created by the party and copied by the people. In contrast to earlier promotions of *mofan*, "the distinguished individuals or projects whose greatness merits imitation," *yangban* "are fictitiously constructed and represented as embodiments of perfection."²³

The agricultural point-to-plane system of proliferating the *yangban* field was also applied to the dissemination of *yangban* models. Especially after the model works were standardized on film, the film projection network grew rapidly through commune-run movie teams. As one county-level movie station put it in 1971: "We must erect models to lead the ordinary ... to go from a red point to a red line to a red plane."²⁴ Another movie station borrowed a conceit from the model opera *The Red Lantern*: the function of a model was to "light a single lantern" that "reddens a plane," so that "one model proliferates into many points, and a group of models advances the entire county."²⁵

The political imperative to popularize the revolutionary model works on film launched the fastest expansion of the rural projection network during the Cultural Revolution decade to ensure their ubiquitous radiation.²⁶ Admonishing audiences to "become revolutionaries through watching revolutionary films," projectionists solicited stories of transformation and turned them into slideshows: a mason reportedly increased his productivity threefold, and a seamstress threw away her gloves, a symbol of her bourgeois mentality. After watching *Sparks Amid the Reeds* (沙家浜) (1971) an older villager named Second Granny Lei formed her own "Granny Sha Combat Team" to plant peanuts as sideline production for her brigade, and a group of young women formed a "Li Tiemei Combat Team" after watching *The Red Lantern*.²⁷

Apart from the *yangbanxi*, Dazhai, a rural model of self-reliance, was a recurring subject of newsreel documentaries from 1964 to 1978

FIGURE 3.2 Stills from the documentary film *Path to Dazhai* (1964). *Mass Cinema*, no. 8–9 (1964).

(figure 3.2).²⁸ A Hubei projectionist reported that audiences likened viewing a film about Dazhai to a pilgrimage to seek Buddhist scriptures.²⁹ According to a village secretary in Chongqing: "If we were to visit Dazhai, it would cost us more than 100 yuan per person. By watching the film, our entire brigade was able to visit Dazhai and learn from its spirit."³⁰ A projection team from Heilongjiang collected similar audience testimonies in doggerel verse: "Iron arms cultivated Dazhai's land, sweat watered Dazhai flowers, Dazhai people's revolutionary labor created earth-shattering miracles—that is the great triumph of Mao Zedong Thought." A female labor model admired Dazhai's "Iron Girls" for carrying rocks while walking barefoot up the mountains to see distant horizons.³¹ Yet as far as I could gather from interviews conducted in Zhejiang, Hubei, and Ningxia provinces, remembrances of those Dazhai films were less inspired. As a Ningxia villager recalled: "Those documentaries about collective labor always showed how people elsewhere overcame hardships with a fighting spirit, carrying baskets of mud on their backs to build irrigation ditches. They didn't use anything with wheels, not even a single-wheeled cart. When we returned to the production brigade, the leaders told us to learn from the movies. We often had evening meetings for two hours to discuss what we had seen in the films, which we still enjoyed because there was nothing else to watch."[32]

Apart from labor mobilization, Dazhai films served as blueprints for rural infrastructural construction. They were shown specifically to mobilized workers who toiled on dams, reservoirs, and terraced fields so that they could better endure the hardships—"let us treat wind like a fan and rain like our sweat!"[33] The films were also screened at cadre conferences so that they might "look for disparities" between their own brigades and Dazhai, in order to intensify their "battle with heaven, earth, and class enemies."[34] As late as 1978 Dazhai films were supposed to serve as an antidote for the "capitalist tendencies" of villagers who had left their communes to do business.[35]

In Wenzhou I visited a mountainous village where Dazhai films had a major impact. It was not that those documentaries were widely or frequently shown there, since the location was remote even for the commune movie team. Instead, the village party secretary watched Dazhai films at cadre conferences and tried to transform his village into Dazhai. Whereas most nearby villages began dividing up their land, this party secretary insisted on keeping collectivization intact to build terraced fields and irrigation facilities. The county government and media wrote glowing reports about these heroic revolutionary efforts that eventually caught Madame Mao's attention, so she sent creative talent from a Shanghai film studio to "experience life" in this village.[36] The script was finished by 1976, but because Mao died and Jiang Qing was arrested, the film was never made. Meanwhile, efforts to re-create the terraced fields of Dazhai resulted in a mountain landslide that killed two villagers, finally terminating their model emulation.[37] In this and many other instances, the projection of utopian images onto the land and people had tangible consequences that strayed far from the original models.

MODEL FEMALE PROJECTIONISTS AND THE THREE SISTERS MOVIE TEAM

Having now considered the projection of models, let us consider model projectionists with a with a focus on Hebei's Three Sisters Movie Team, famous for their animated slideshows of local models and promoted as embodiments of gender equality. Indeed, those best at projecting models could themselves become labor models. As the career of the Three Sisters culminated in movie stardom in a documentary newsreel in 1966 before their comet-like downfall, however, they also offer a cautionary tale about the flammability of the Maoist media limelight.

The story of the Three Sisters must start with their mentor Wang Baoyi (王宝义), Laishui Movie Team's first projectionist and a pioneer of the animated slideshow with multiple lenses on the projector. A schoolteacher enlisted as propaganda worker, Wang organized village drama troupes and conducted rooftop broadcasting for the newly founded county cultural center, where he discovered an unused slide projector and a set of twenty slides about someone joining the army. The optical device reminded him of the *layangpian* (拉洋片) peepshows in temple fairs, except that the slide projector projected images outward to hundreds in the audience instead of a few paying customers. Wang began producing and narrating his own slideshows on market days to propagate the Marriage Law, the Three-Anti and Five-Anti campaigns, and the Korean War.[38]

In 1955, with the expansion of the film projection network, Wang Baoyi was assigned to the Laishui county movie team, responsible for itinerary planning and propaganda work.[39] Studying animated film prints frame by frame, he tinkered with the team's slide projector and experimented with slide formats to create special effects, such as blinking eyes, babbling mouths, radiating sunshine, and undulating waves. Those impressive slideshows inspired emulation from other teams and earned Wang the honor of attending the National Film Distribution and Projection Model Workers Conference in 1957 and meeting Chairman Mao in person.[40] From bringing luminous images of Mao to being summoned in his physical/divine presence, these 361 model projectionists reportedly saw their arduous labor as "glistening with light."[41] Nevertheless, Wang's application for party membership would be rejected time and again because his father had worked as a policeman under the Japanese occupation. With this chip on his shoulder, Wang eagerly answered the party's call with every campaign, such as expanding the film exhibition network during the Great Leap Forward. Having read about all-female movie teams in the press, he decided to recruit one for his county as well.[42]

Like iconic female tractor drivers and pilots, female projectionists took on a physically demanding job that also required mechanical and engineering skills.[43] According to an issue of *Mass Cinema* in 1952, members of Hubei's first all-female movie team did not want to rely on men, so they underwent physical training to carry their 150-kilogram generator. Conducting smooth screenings with clear explications, they won everyone's respect and set an example for rural young women: "Now women can drive trains, fly planes, and show films. Let's learn to read too because women can do everything!"[44] Even more than the films they showed, female projectionists who met with thousands of audiences at every screening countered patriarchal norms that kept women out of the labor force and public sphere. Their embodiment of new gender norms was celebrated as changing the rural sociocultural climate (风气, literally "wind and air").

Model profiles of female projectionists offer two variations of the socialist bildungsroman, highlighting either their humble origins or their overcoming of bourgeois privilege. In an example of the former, an illiterate female Tibetan shepherd became a model projectionist thanks to the benevolence of the party and Chairman Mao.[45] The intersection of her gender, ethnic, and geographic marginality brought revolutionary transformation into sharp relief. Such model narratives chronicled how the wretched became masters, how bitterness turned sweet, how the mute came to speak, and how the benighted became enlightened. By contrast, women projectionists from well-to-do urban family backgrounds learned to embrace physical labor and hardships in rural areas. With socialist education, their revolutionary spirit reportedly overcame their vulnerable bodies so that they no longer felt weakness, pain, or nausea while transporting heavy machinery, suffering injuries, or smelling gasoline.

Instead of addressing corporeal challenges, model narratives treated women's biological bodies as problems to be overcome. Rather than getting treatment for gynecological infections, a model projectionist and her teammate refused take a break and even volunteered to build a backyard furnace to temper steel and themselves.[46] Only one editorial of *Film Projection* in 1955 gave voice to complaints: when an eight-month-pregnant projectionist in Chongqing asked to work in the headquarters rather than conduct mobile screenings, her supervisor told her that "childbearing women are ideologically backward and lack political consciousness." The editorial called for special allowances for women projectionists, such as assigning them nearby itineraries and better machines, but most reports praised the triumph of the women's revolutionary spirit.[47]

Inspired by such media reports about female projectionists, Wang Baoyi recruited three young women into a new movie team responsible for screenings in villages close to the county seat. A year later, six young men were recruited to staff two other teams covering more remote and mountainous regions. At prefectural competitions to select labor models, all nine rookie projectionists honed their technical and performance skills while expanding and innovating their propaganda repertoire. Wang passed onto them various tricks he had developed on the slide projector, so that, in their propaganda slideshow to promote pig farming, the farmer's eyes and nose moved while the pigs flapped their ears and opened their mouths. At a nationwide conference on film exhibition in 1960, the Three Sister Movie Team performed a slideshow on the history of a local mountain village, with animated gimmicks such as "Leaping Horses Galloping," "East Is Red Sunshine," shooting guns and cannons, red flags fluttering, and various movements of people and animals.[48] A slideshow for the Socialist Education Movement began with a riddle: "Head like a crab, with joints at its waist, this animal has a long tail and eight legs." When the audience guessed the correct answer, a scorpion appeared and dissolved into a landlord.[49] Just as their production depended on handicraft, the performance of these animated slideshows depended on the hand that pulls the slides and on the commentary—"allowing for a variable temporality [of] gesture and speech" (see figure 3.3).[50] By the mid-1960s movie teams nationwide emulated the Three Sisters Movie Team to produce and perform animated slideshows featuring, for example, a lotus blooming with ever brighter colors, children waving flowers up and down, the character for "quiet" rising from a moonlit lake, and a Vietnamese anti-aircraft gun shooting into the sky, followed by an American plane tumbling down with a smoking tail.[51]

The Three Sisters won their renown not only through outstanding live performances at propaganda competitions and nationwide tours, but also through curated model narratives and images in print publications, photographic pictorials, and documentary newsreels.

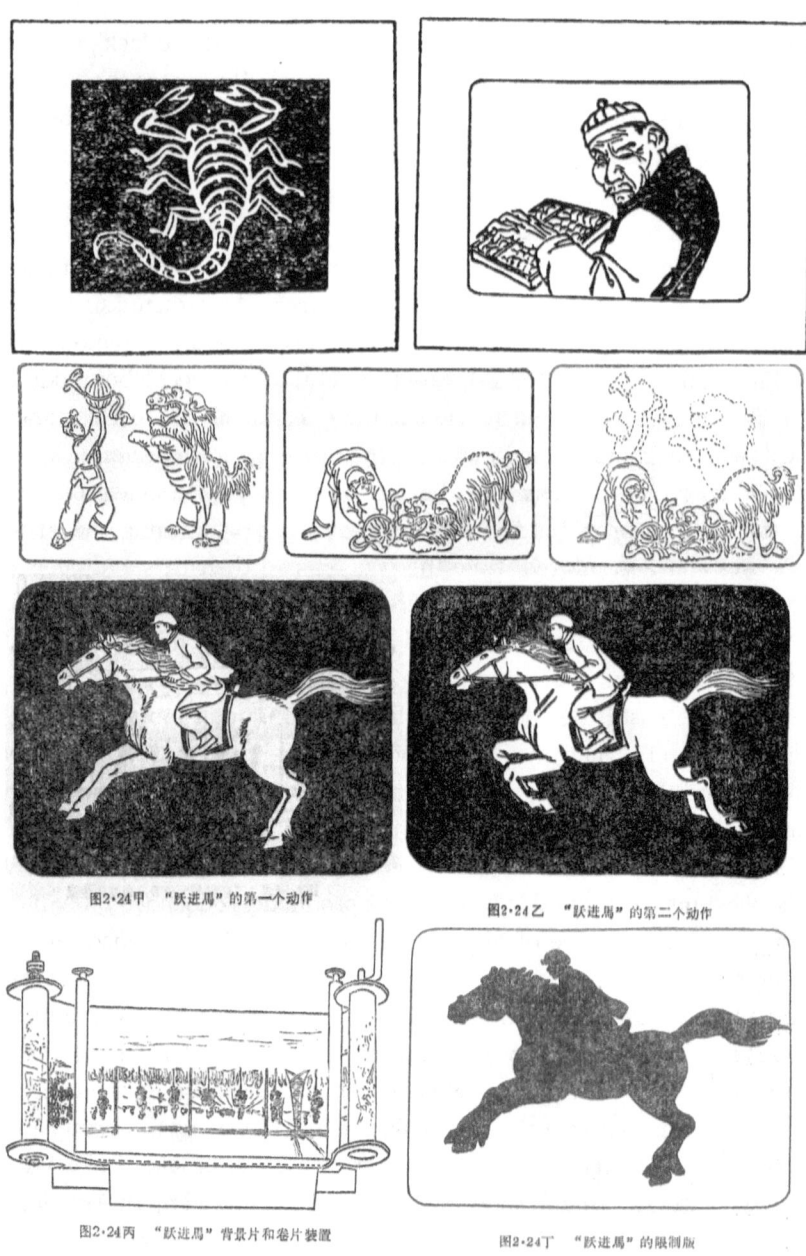

FIGURE 3.3 Animated slideshows attributed to the Three Sisters Movie Team, from *Making and Using Multilens Slide Projectors* (1965), manual by Hebei Film Distribution and Exhibition Company.

According to early reports penned by Wang Baoyi for the local press and for *Film Projection* magazine, the young women overcame the skeptical gossip of villagers and embarrassing failures as novices. As their propaganda and technical skills improved, they won and were won over by the masses. In the winter, their villager hosts treated them like daughters by reserving for them the warmest parts of their *kang* bed and boiling many eggs for them as snacks. The Three Sisters in turn braved snow and ice to bring cinema to mountain dwellers, to learn clapper-talk from local performers, and to research, produce, and perform slideshows.[52] Refining and updating this model narrative, the team leader Zheng Yizhen (郑义珍) delivered speeches at model conferences, such as one entitled "Chairman Mao's Works Gave Us Infinite Wisdom and Power," emphasizing how "we are not only a movie team but a propaganda team" that learned to write, to paint, to sing as well as to tinker with the slide projector to make "dead slides come to life."[53]

Was this really Zheng Yizhen's own voice speaking, or was she a medium through which the party-state ventriloquized its revolutionary agenda? How truthful or illusory are those photographic and filmic images of the Three Sisters in *China Pictorial* (人民画报) and *News Briefings* (新闻简报)? Since the women were assigned to screen films for the county seat and surrounding plains, why do the photos and newsreels show them lugging machinery on a donkey through mountain passes (figure 3.4)? What does it mean for a scholar to use these texts as historical sources, or to reproduce these images as illustrations for publication? Whereas there are many photographs of mobile projectionists taken in daylight, figure 3.5 is the only high-quality photograph I could find of open-air cinema under the moon, thanks to the professional camera and lighting of the *China Pictorial* photographer. But the light of official mass media obscures as much as it illuminates, as suggested by former colleagues of the Three Sisters with the colloquial phrase *deng xia hei* (灯下黑), literally "darkness under the lamp," meaning that the most invisible spot is right beneath the light.

Visiting Laishui in 2017, I hoped to supplement official narratives with retrospective testimonies. Yet Wang Baoyi and the clapper-talker Li Jingxian (李景贤) had just passed away, and no one had contact information for the generator operator Zhang Burong (张步荣). We found several acquaintances of Zheng Yizhen, but she declined to speak to us

让农民看到电影

何世尧 摄影

解放前，我国广大农民是与电影无缘的。象河北省的涉水县，即使在县城里也是解放后才有电影的。现在，这个太行山区的小县，已有四个农村电影放映队和一个电影院，全县百分之九十五以上的人都能从电影上看到激动人心的革命斗争生活和社会主义建设图景了。

这个县的农村电影放映队中有一个由三位农村姑娘——郑又珍、李景贤、陆晓春组成的电影放映队，很受农民欢迎，被称为"三姐妹电影放映队。"这个队成立于一九五八年，她们每年不辞劳苦地在农村流动放映，使一些处在高山峻岭上只有十多户人家的偏僻村庄，也能看到电影。

她们在为农民放映电影的同时，还采用当地农民喜闻乐见的鼓词、快板、讲故事、蓑鼓话等说唱形式，结合放映幻灯，让农民知道国内外大事和当前中心工作。她们经常在放映之余，一边参加劳动，一边搜集好人好事的生动材料，及时绘制成幻灯片给群众放映，鼓励社员的劳动热情。

目前，我国电影放映队已分布在广大农村，放映员们常年累月地跋山涉水，为让农民看到电影而辛勤劳动着。

FIGURES 3.4, 3.5, AND 3.6 Photo spread of the Three Sisters Movie Team. *China Pictorial*, no. 11 (1965).

FIGURES 3.4, 3.5, AND 3.6 (continued)

FIGURES 3.4, 3.5, AND 3.6 (continued)

despite phone calls on our behalf from her cousin and former teacher. Instead, we spoke to other former projectionists, propaganda officials, and villagers who had been their acquaintances and audiences. Those conversations not only paint a more complex picture of this model collective than published sources but also illuminate the very process and consequence of model-making.

As their fame grew in the early 1960s, the Three Sisters went on nationwide tours and had less time to spend in the countryside.[54] Live performance and showwomanship overtook the daily grind of routine screenings, and their audiences shifted from the grassroots to the political elite, from local cultural officials to national leaders. The honor and privilege given to the three women provoked resentment from their colleagues, whose retrospective testimonies contradicted and deconstructed media accounts. Although press photos showed the women painting lantern slides, it was Wang Baoyi and other male colleagues who made the slides they showed until the hiring of a local artist, Mr. Yan (1940–), as a professional lanternist for the Laishui movie station in 1962. For the Three Sisters' signature slideshow "Model Commune Member Xia Pu," Wang Baoyi was the producer, director, and scriptwriter, Mr. Yan was the artist, and the three women were the stars. Yan and others acknowledged their performance skills and challenges: without tape recorders, they had to change LP records dozens of times for musical accompaniment and manually execute the animation effects, all the while singing with bamboo clappers.[55] Rather than three individuals, the Three Sisters, as Mr. Yan suggested, was a larger model collective, even something of a corporate brand, with the women as the "red flowers above the green leaves."[56]

Other "green leaves" included two all-male movie teams recruited in 1959 and 1962. Mr. Zeng (1934–) made technical improvements to the multilens slide projector, and Mr. Han (1938–) wrote the texts and designed the animation effects for several famous slideshows later attributed to the Three Sisters. Mr. Guo (1937–) helped carry the heavy equipment for the women into the mountains when photojournalists came, but he had to step out of their cameras' viewfinders.[57] I also conducted a three-hour-long interview with a Mr. Liu (1935–), leader of a movie team responsible for Laishui County's hilliest terrain.[58] In the early 1950s, after a brief stint as a village teacher, Mr. Liu worked at the county cultural center to teach revolutionary songs, choreograph dances for amateur village theater troupes, and organize collective listening to radio. Traveling from village to village, he became acquainted with the county's physical and cultural geography even before becoming a mobile projectionist in 1962. As a multitalented cultural worker, Mr. Liu also researched, scripted, and produced slideshows accredited to the Three Sisters.

While other "green leaves" swallowed their pride, Mr. Liu vented his resentment when a *China Pictorial* photojournalist came to Laishui, and the cadres staged a screening by the Three Sisters at a mountain village they had never before visited. Knowing the magazine had an international distribution, Liu lashed out at the photojournalist and the Three Sisters: "You've deceived the entire nation, now you want to deceive the world?" Shortly after this incident, a Four Cleanups work team came to investigate corruption, and Liu's teammates accused him of having affairs with multiple female villagers. Liu denied those charges and attributed them to his colleagues' jealousy of his popularity, but when interrogated by the work team, he impetuously "admitted" all the allegations and told them to "shoot me here and now." He was henceforth sent to labor reform for three years.[59] Returning to Laishui in 1969, he led a quiet life as a farmer and electrician. Looking back, Liu considered himself fortunate to have dodged the struggle sessions of the Cultural Revolution, which traumatized, crippled, and even killed some of his colleagues. Because he was persecuted during the Four Cleanups, however, Mr. Liu was never rehabilitated, and he retained a peasant's sociopolitical status. Whereas other projectionist retirees lived in work-unit-allocated high-rise housing, he lived in a self-constructed and dilapidated brick house across from a new real estate development. He chain-smoked and drank a bitter tea during our interview, often becoming quite upset when recounting the injustices he had suffered.

Although my research assistants and I had explained my academic purpose to all interviewees, our presence and questions must still have reminded them of investigations by Maoist work teams or, alternatively, of the propaganda journalists who collected, embellished, and sometimes fabricated stories about the Three Sisters Movie Team. Perhaps it was the fear of another hijacking of her story and ventriloquism of her voice that prevented the original team leader of the Three Sisters from speaking to us. In fact, the more we learned, through interviews with other projectionists, about the gaps in the official history, the better we understood her silence. After all, the more they came into the limelight, the more their image became an illusion, and their meteoric rise to fame portended an equally spectacular downfall during the Cultural Revolution.

Since the Cultural Revolution began on the cultural front in 1966, Wang Baoyi, as the county's leader of "film workers" and coming from a "bad" class background, was among the first to be toppled. The rebels denounced him as a "capitalist-roader," gave him a "*yin-yang* haircut," and paraded him through the streets with a rope around his neck and a two-meter-long dunce cap painted with oxen and snakes.[60] According to several interviewees who attended a struggle session against Wang at a sports stadium, the clapper-talker of the Three Sisters led the crowd to shout slogans against her former mentor. Along with other cultural cadres, Wang Baoyi was imprisoned in an "ox-shed," forced to clean the public latrine, and escorted daily to read a special column of big-character posters and caricatures against him.[61]

While their mentor Wang Baoyi was denounced, the team leader of the Three Sisters became the vice county mayor, only to be toppled a month later with the fall of President Liu Shaoqi. This harkens back to an August 1965 slideshow performance by the Three Sisters for President Liu and First Lady Wang Guangmei, who invited the movie team to dinner, with fresh peaches for dessert. Instead of eating her peach, the team leader took it home, wrote "The Source of Power" (力量的源泉) on it, and enshrined it in a glass case in her office.[62] Wall posters depicted this incident in caricatures of her worshipping the disgraced First Lady's peach until it rotted. Now that the "fragrant flowers stank," the masses shouted "Down with the Putrid Three Sister Movie Team!" and paraded two of the three members through the streets with their hair in a tussle.[63] The third member responsible for the power generator joined a rebel faction to attack the other two.[64] While all projectionists were busy making revolution or being revolutionized, film screenings and slideshows came to a halt. Several years later some projectionists adapted their propaganda know-how to the latest political winds, but their jobs remained volatile. In 1969 a projectionist inadvertently superimposed a lantern slide of a "capitalist-roader" onto an image of Mao, an accident that made him an "active counterrevolutionary."[65] After the Cultural Revolution came to an end, projectionists who had been persecuted were rehabilitated and promoted to various leadership positions, but Wang Baoyi and the original Three Sisters never spoke to each other again, even when they shared the same office building.

By the time we visited Laishui in 2017, the county's rural film exhibition was managed by a Ms. Yu (1961–), a member of the "Little Three Sisters Movie Team," recruited in the late 1970s. Its headquarters was Laishui County Cinema, built in 1980 with a capacity to seat one thousand, but the cinema had long stopped showing films and only rarely hosted government conferences and stage performances. Manager Yu took us upstairs and unlocked two rooms that served as the Three Sisters Memorial Hall (三姐妹纪念馆), exhibiting film projectors and reels on a bicycle, the famous four-lens magic lantern, some slides, and press photos from the 1960s. Stylishly dressed in a Prada jacket and clutching a Michael Kors purse, Ms. Yu gave me a two-hour interview about her career in the film-exhibition sector. As a novice projectionist in the late 1970s, her physical training and everyday practice included bike- and horse-riding and throwing a rope, lasso-like, to hang the screen, and measuring the distance of the projector to the screen with a few strides. There was also voice training for narration and singing; manual training for bamboo clappers and slideshow projection; and coordination training like a chamber music trio. Their award-winning slideshow repertoire—handmade by Mr. Yan—kept up with new political priorities from the smashing of the Gang of Four to the commemoration of Premier Zhou Enlai to the one-child policy.[66] Watching Ms. Yu's gesticulations as she pantomimed the animated slideshow, I realized that, even while receiving the support of male authorship and craftsmanship, model female projectionists were neither puppets controlled by male cadres nor charlatans deceiving the public, but rather virtuoso performers who exercised their own voice and agency.

In 2017, Ms. Yu officially oversaw ten digital projectionists to "send movies to the countryside." With entrepreneurial savvy, she combined these government-sponsored screenings with advertising for local businesses and private event planning. Her white minivan bore the labels "public welfare cinema" (公益电影), "wedding services" (婚庆), and "film media" (电影传媒). When asked about "film media," Yu distinguished *chuanmei* (传媒, media, communications) from *xuanchuan* (宣传, propaganda), as she considered the latter to be governmental and the former to be commercial, though both required good communication skills. She saw little contradiction or irony in the adaptation of socialist propaganda infrastructure and technique into postsocialist guerrilla marketing of products and celebration of private rituals. When asked if I could attend a screening by one of her digital projectionists, she responded candidly: "If you need to take pictures of a screening, I can set one up for you, but the effect won't be so great because it's cold and windy today, and people would rather watch TV on their couches than come out and eat dust." Instead, she showed us some pictures on her phone of open-air screenings in the summer and spoke fondly of camping out under the stars.[67] Rather than mere images made by men, then, female projectionists were also entrepreneurial image-makers in their own right.

ORDINARY FEMALE PROJECTIONISTS

Despite their prominence in propaganda, women constituted a small fraction of mobile projectionists.[68] Besides grassroots prejudices against women doing "a man's job" in the public sphere, male and female projectionist interviewees cited concerns about safety on the road and difficulty of finding adequate accommodations.[69] Pregnancy and motherhood augmented the physical hardships of transporting bulky equipment, riding on bumpy roads, and eating unfamiliar foods. Without childcare, a Fujian projectionist reportedly locked up her older child at home and carried her younger child to screenings.[70] Most female projectionists stopped conducting mobile screenings after childbirth. If still employed in the film-exhibition sector, they might sell tickets at movie theaters, train new projectionists, or conduct technical maintenance.[71] As a result, my best efforts to find female projectionists yielded only six out of sixty plus interviews. Beside the aforementioned Manager Yu, who joined the Three Sisters Movie Team in the late 1970s, I also spoke with Ms. Dai (1934–), who projected films for the Suzhou Steel Factory from the 1950s to the 1980s; Ms. Gong (1944–), a propaganda activist and amateur projectionist for her township in Hubei from 1958 to 1965; Ms. Duan (1957–), who served as a commune projectionist in Hubei from the late 1970s to the early 1990s; and Ms. Chen (1969–), who showed films in her village ancestral hall in Zhejiang in the mid-1980s. My research assistant Peng Hai also interviewed Ms. Zhou (1960–), a rural projectionist in the Ningxia Hui Autonomous Region from the mid-1970s to the early 1990s. Their diverse experiences and subjectivities reveal gendered negotiations with political movements, cultural norms, material conditions, and, above all, family backgrounds and local relations.

Since none of my female interviewees conducted mobile screenings in the early 1950s, I first draw on a book-length oral history conducted in 2010 with former members of Shaanxi's first all-female projection team. Like many early recruits, Lu Shukun (1937–) and Yuan Xiuying (1936–) came from urban "bourgeois" families that could afford to send their daughters to secondary school. Yuan's father had studied engineering in Europe, whereas Lu's father worked for the KMT and was executed in the Campaign to Suppress Counterrevolutionaries in 1951, casting a long shadow of trauma and stigma on his daughter. Both Lu and Yuan grew up with modern values of gender equality but met with much more conservative gender norms in rural areas. Lu recalled, "The first day we left the city gate for the countryside, curious villagers lined the roads. We must have attracted a bigger crowd than a wedding parade. We sat on top of our luggage on an oxcart and felt very proud."[72] Yet, assuming that unmarried girls would not appear in public, villagers referred to them disparagingly as "film wives" (电影婆娘) and even laughed when one of them got bitten by a dog. Nevertheless, the female projectionists recalled little fear for their safety and gratitude toward their superiors for giving them nearby assignments and a lightweight generator. Unlike model projectionists in the press, they would have preferred a mixed-gender team, because male colleagues carried heavy machinery with ease, whereas women were more careful machine operators. The itinerant job presented challenges for motherhood: Lu miscarried her first pregnancy after extensive bike trips and climbing in the first trimester, and the second pregnancy made her so sick, she could not ingest the food offered by villagers. To continue their careers, she and her teammates all sent their children to be nursed by nannies and raised by grandparents. After several years as mobile projectionists, these women became teachers, technicians, and administrators in county seats or prefectural cities.[73]

Also belonging to a pioneering generation of female projectionists was Ms. Dai, who served as the trade union projectionist for Suzhou Steel Factory for three decades. Soft-spoken, petite, and athletic, she was one of the very few women to pass the projectionist's entrance exam that required applicants to climb up a pole to hang a loudspeaker. Since the factory built a movie theater for its ten thousand employees in 1958, however, she had a stationary workplace that was not physically strenuous. Instead of muscles, Dai pointed to her head as the secret of doing her job well. She surveyed factory employees on what films they liked—e.g., foreign films were popular among engineers but not among workers—so she procured film prints accordingly and often skipped documentary newsreels at the request of workers. As a Shanghai native, she forged connections to the Shanghai Film Studio so as to access the same films as Shanghai's first-run cinemas and cultivated good relationships with railway workers so that they delivered films to the factory. She always returned prints intact after tens of thousands of screenings, yet the only film story she could clearly remember was Zheng Junli's wartime epic *A Spring River Flows East* (一江春水向东流) (1947), which provoked a commotion of weeping among her audiences and resonated with her own memories of air raids. Ms. Dai was also temporarily in charge of factory broadcasting but outsourced the task to better Mandarin speakers. Coming from a family of small business owners, she never joined the party or rose through the ranks but was proud to share that her projectionist apprentices went as far as Xinjiang to screen films.[74]

For female projectionists who joined the film exhibition sector in the 1950s, the same class background that allowed for girls' schooling proved to be a stumbling block for their later career advancement. For the next four interviewees—all commune projectionists from peasant backgrounds—family mattered at a much more local level. From rural Hubei, Ms. Gong was recruited as an amateur projectionist in part because her father was the commune accountant and in part because she liked to sing and dance. During the Great Leap Forward in 1958, at age fourteen, she took part in the propaganda troupe to guide journalists, photographers, and cadres to the nationally famous "Sputnik" rice paddy of her village, with a harvest so bountiful, children could jump on it as if on a trampoline. When I spoke to her in 2015, Ms. Gong could still sing the old propaganda ditty about that rice paddy but also remembered how "at night they moved the crops over from other fields. . . . We knew but dared not talk. We were too young, just blindly following the cadres." Walking with me from the rice paddy back to the village, she spoke of the famine that followed, pointing to edible plants along the path that helped her family to survive. In 1964, during the Socialist Education Movement, Ms. Gong was recruited into a work team and received training in film and slide projection at the county government office. She recalled projecting slides with her fellow trainee and roommate onto their mosquito net for fun one night and receiving a sound scolding from the mayor. Showing films and slides for about two years, she could best recall "bitter films" (苦片), such as *The White-Haired Girl* and *Sow Thistle* (苦菜花) (1965). Gong spoke wistfully of the mid-1960s, when the authorities promoted women cadres, but because she never attended middle school and had to raise three children, she only became the leader of an all-women production team and later a birth planning propaganda officer in the 1980s.[75]

Ms. Gong's memory of "propaganda work" was framed by a childish innocence and playfulness, even as she was aware of propaganda's complicity in the famine, whose unspeakable bitterness was rechanneled through her memory of bitter films. Besides her own talent and hobby, her recruitment as a propagandist depended on patriarchal networks—her father and other cadres—but her career ambitions had to be curtailed with marriage and childbearing. Patriarchal networks also ushered Ms. Duan from a nearby village into a projectionist's career. The daughter of a party secretary, Ms. Duan began driving a tractor at the age of fifteen, thus acquiring the technical skills that equipped her to generate electricity for the commune movie team a few years later. Although the generator was powered by foot-pedaling, she found her new job less strenuous than operating the bulky tractor. Her first assignments were to screen documentary newsreels of Zhou Enlai's and Mao Zedong's funerals in early 1977. Villagers prepared a memorial arch of pine and cypress and sent marching bands and students with white paper flowers to greet the arrival of these two films. Her fellow projectionist led audiences to observe three minutes of silence, followed by speeches by the local cadres. After those ritual screenings, Ms. Duan most often showed guerrilla war films like *A Sparkling Red Star* (闪闪的红星) (1974), *Tunnel Warfare* (地道战) (1965), *Landmine Warfare* (地雷战) (1962), and *Red Guards at Honghu Lake* (洪湖赤卫队) (1961). With few prints to go around, her team and three others conducted simultaneous screenings in four neighboring villages with much shuttling of the film reels. Proud of her extensive travels, Ms. Duan also met her husband during mobile projection and continued showing films in his commune after marriage, even bringing their child on tours. After the rise of television reduced the demand for cinema, she only screened films for private celebrations and told me stories about fellow projectionists choosing films utterly inappropriate for the occasion, such as the bitter film *Serf* for a wedding ceremony.[76] Beginning her projectionist career with funerals and ending it with weddings, Ms. Duan was keenly attuned to the ritual function of cinema.

A Hui Muslim from rural Ningxia, Ms. Zhou was recruited as a commune projectionist in 1975. Betrothed to a young man from the same village, she had the approval of her future parents-in-law and other villagers: she was not just a daughter who would marry out but also a daughter-in-law who would remain within the community. Moreover, she had proven her capability and productivity two years earlier, when she dug out eight cubic meters of earth a day at a reservoir construction project. Zhou and a fellow Hui girl traveled to the county seat for training on a coal-transport truck, stayed overnight in a straw hut temple, and ate only one egg each because Halal food was not available on the road. Like half of the hundred students in her training class, Zhou had never learned to read or write, but she readily passed the "entrance exam" to tell a projector from a generator and learned by watching the teacher's hands instead of taking notes: "During practice, the teacher created malfunctions on the machines for us to troubleshoot. We illiterates were much better at this than the schooled ones." When the Hui girls began showing films, villagers would stare and gossip, which made them nervous and flustered. Their teacher told them not to mind the crowd, who got used to them and obeyed their instructions to sit down and be quiet during screenings. When the film reel snapped or when their generator broke down, villagers were nice and returned the next day. Zhou and her partner showed films for seven years until the commune was decollectivized, their township acquired electricity, and villagers bought TV sets.[77]

For female commune projectionists such as Duan and Zhou, showing films was less a step up on the career ladder than a livelihood that also served their grassroots communities. Even as Duan embodied the iconic Maoist female tractor driver and Zhou was effectively a socialist labor model, neither seemed invested in revolutionizing gender norms. Instead, they sought affirmation from their husbands' families and villages while transforming prejudices against women in public arenas. Zhou's pride in her technical competency despite (and because of) her illiteracy further resonates with another female projectionist interviewee from rural Zhejiang, Ms. Chen. With the introduction of the household responsibility system in 1979, Chen's father contracted the commune tractor—the ultimate technology and symbol of socialist collective farming—to transport people and products in and out of the mountains, thereby connecting former commune members to the market economy. A few years later, he expanded the tractor business to show business by purchasing a projector and generator, contracting the clan's ancestral hall as a movie theater, and sending his adolescent daughter for training as a film projectionist. To rent film prints, Chen used to set out at dawn with the tractor, cross a river with a rowboat, and catch the bus to the county seat. Returning by early afternoon, she held three free screenings per month for lineage members but sold tickets at varying prices on other nights, making an especially handsome profit with popular films like *Shaolin Temple* (少林寺) (1982) and around Chinese New Year. Since her village had no electricity until the 1990s, private families and the village chief often hired her to show films for various rituals so that they could also use her generator, microphone, loudspeakers, and slide projector. Ms. Chen recalled how "nobody wanted to listen to speeches or watch slideshows, even when they were free of charge." Instead, older people wanted opera films, whereas younger audiences preferred kungfu and romance. When asked to name specific films from a booklet of old movie posters, Ms. Chen was embarrassed to admit her illiteracy but explained that she never watched films but rather focused on the machines, thus causing fewer technical breakdowns than nearby male projectionists captivated by the films they showed. [78] With little interest in women's liberation or gender equality, Ms. Chen nevertheless took pride in her work ethic, technical focus, and entrepreneurial savvy. While working for profit and scornful of party propaganda, she still lent her machines and her labor to government events in a seamless blending of the socialist, market, and ritual economies.

Finally, as I learned through fieldwork, women not only constituted a small minority of projectionists but also watched far fewer films than men, especially soldiers, cadres, and adolescent boys who followed commune movie teams to different villages. If they went to movies at all, rural women described their cinematic memories as "watching hot noise" (see chapter 5). If they could remember any films, it was often traditional opera films or bitter melodramas (see chapters 6 and 7). My interview with an older couple in a Hubei mountain village best illustrates the gender disparity in film access. Having fought for both the Nationalists and the Communists, the husband had watched a film every month while in the army. After returning home in the mid-1950s, he was made village chief and often attended conferences with film screenings in the county seat, or he would stop by the worker's club to watch a film on his own. By contrast, his wife could not recall watching a single film, not even after her husband took up the business of mobile film projection in the 1980s. Apart from having to take care of the house and children, she had to cook for all the relatives who came to watch movies. Nevertheless, she partook in the heat and noise of the ritual event as a host: cinema for her, and for many other women, was as much about hospitality as it was about the film.

In Maoist China, cinema served not so much to reflect or represent, but rather to project and model reality as well as to *transform* people and places through the radiation of revolutionary energy. The efficacy of such projection relied on mobile projectionists, who not only showed the same films distributed nationwide but also made and performed slideshows featuring local models and addressing local audiences. Those best at projecting models themselves became model projectionists, with all-female movie teams receiving special attention in official propaganda.

Female projectionists performed revolutionary spirit mediumship as the producers and products, embodiments and disseminators of socialist gender ideals, thus connecting elite discourses and grassroots experiences in recent feminist scholarship.[79] As machine operators, female projectionists proved that women could also do "men's work" and embodied revolutionary transformation—either by virtue of being liberated from oppression or by steeling themselves against their "bourgeois" class backgrounds. Often hosted by elderly female villagers, female projectionists also had special access to rural women and convinced them to go to movies, enter the public domain, and become subjects of interpellation by the state.[80]

While female projectionists may have had some measure of success in promoting "women's liberation" and "gender equality," the rise and fall of the Three Sisters Movie Team takes us behind the scenes of a Maoist model media production and illuminates the male "green leaves" beneath the female "red flowers." From serving the people to posing for pictorials and newsreels, the Three Sisters followed and disseminated model-promotion techniques that incentivized labor models to get into slideshows. As oral history revealed, however, the growing media attention on the Three Sisters in the 1960s transformed their audiences from the grassroots to the authorities. The same attention economy persisted from the Great Leap Forward, when local cadres created Sputnik rice paddies to be photographed, to the later years of the Cultural Revolution, such that a Wenzhou village's emulation of the model village Dazhai attracted Madame Mao to send in a film crew.[81] This inversion of audiences was symptomatic of a broader media ecology, in which the creation and emulation of models meant attracting attention from upward rather than downward in the power hierarchy.

In contrast to model narratives, interviews with female projectionists with little claim to fame reveal diverse motivations and challenges, standards and strategies for success in their careers. Projectionists whose bourgeois class backgrounds afforded them a secondary education by the 1950s could not become models or advance through the ranks, whereas those who came from poor backgrounds could not be promoted further because of their semiliteracy. "Serving the people" meant less the propagation of revolutionary ideology than attentiveness to the needs and tastes of their local audiences. All of them prided themselves on technical competence to prevent breakdowns, and they took an entrepreneurial approach to procuring desirable film copies. Above all, these women projectionists gained acceptance and respect from their audiences due more to their embeddedness in local communities than to socialist gender ideals. Their pragmatism and resourcefulness point to another kind of cinematic guerrilla less concerned with ideological propaganda than economic sustainability, the focus of the next chapter.

CHAPTER FOUR

The Cost of Spiritual Food

A Ritual Economy of Rural Cinema

Whereas China's booming box office became a flashy news item in the new millennium, little attention has been paid to the "box office" in socialist China, when moviegoing was much more popular than it has been in the last three decades. The annual per capita cinema attendance rate underwent exponential growth, from 0.3 in 1949 to 6.5 in 1956 to 28 in 1978, only to dwindle to 0.2 in 2009 and 1.2 in 2019.[1] Despite growing audience numbers, socialist discourse disavowed the "market potential" of those moviegoing masses and highlighted cinema as education and propaganda. Following this logic, historians of Chinese film only mention the economics of socialist cinema as a foil to the era of market reforms, when "decentralization, privatization, conglomeration, and globalization" replaced "national subsidies, central planning, and tight management of output and exhibition."[2]

Even with politics in command, selling films and making ends meet remained a perennial obsession for grassroots projectionists. An article in the August 1957 issue of *Film Projection* collated "Ten Ways to Collect Rural Movie Fees" from around the country: a movie team from Henan's Luyi County deducted 40 yuan per screening from the township's public welfare fund; Guangxi's projectionists outsourced ticket sales and logistics to rural clubs and gave them bonuses from the surplus; projectionists of Shanxi's Yangcheng County collected funds for a year's worth of screenings from villagers during harvest season; and various movie teams in Jiangsu allowed villagers to barter for film admission with eggs, recyclable broken glass, torn fabric, even grass and manure from chicken, dogs, and other farm animals.[3] These charging practices suggest another kind of cinematic guerrilla at work than crusaders of communist ideology: economic guerrillas who adapted to local materials conditions with resourceful and pragmatic tactics.

This chapter analyzes the microeconomics of socialist rural film exhibition. What did cinema cost, how was it paid for, and who paid? Beyond ideological indoctrination, were there also economic incentives behind rural film screenings? Did they bring about "material" as well as "spiritual" benefits? While asking "What was cinema?" through an economic lens—commodity, welfare, or taxation?—we will also ask "What was it for?" and "At what price?"[4] Reprising the question "Who was cinema?" this chapter recasts film projectionists less as self-sacrificial model workers than as *homo economicus* looking after their own interests and livelihoods. And what if we were to rethink propaganda not only as ideological persuasion but also as publicity akin to advertising?

My findings derive from a number of sources: *Film Projection* magazine served as a forum for projectionists to share best practices; local film gazetteers chronicle the ups and downs in the economic sustainability of rural cinema; interviews with projectionists further yielded past and present concerns with wages, expenses, and livelihoods. Contrary to popular memories of socialist cinema as "free" or negligently cheap, rural film exhibition incurred various costs for the central government, local cadres, mobile projectionists, and grassroots audiences. Covering costs involved incentivization and coercion. When cinema appeared to be free, rural audiences had to pay out of collective funds during the harvest or by working harder. Thus, in addition to using cinema as an open means of political mobilization, cinema was also used as a veiled means of economic extraction: of money, labor, and grain from the rural masses.

Structured chronologically, this chapter tracks the shifting economic concerns and practices of mobile projectionists over the socialist decades. The first section analyzes how the growing film exhibition network sought to meet economic targets through ticket sales and flat fees. Having to sell unpopular films to impoverished villagers, movie teams came up with flexible, creative, and spurious charging practices, including bartering, child labor, deception, and price discrimination. The next section focuses on the Great Leap Forward in the film projection sector, which not only wrested movie fees from the communes' collective budget, but also helped the state extract labor and grain from the peasantry. The third section focuses on the mid-1960s, which saw the emergence of what I call "villagebusters"—the energizing and exhausting exhibition of films *with* and *as* mass campaigns—alongside the intensification of live, local performances to supplement propaganda films. The fourth section analyzes the growth of self-reliant commune-run movie teams launched to popularize revolutionary model operas, meanwhile cultivating a shadow economy of widespread corruption that became a "golden age" of film exhibition by the end of the decade. The conclusion reframes the Maoist cultural economy as a ritual economy, which paid for "spiritual food" outside of a capitalist commodity logic and exhorted sacrifices from audiences.

COLLECTIVIZATION AND COLLECTING MOVIE FEES, 1951–1957

While movie teams promoted rural collectivization through "socialist distant horizon education," cinema was considered not only a propaganda tool but also a commodity expected to yield "returns on the state's investment to develop the domestic film industry and to accumulate more capital for national construction."[5] Meeting both political and economic objectives was easier said than done, however, and charging admission in the countryside was a challenge from the start. In autumn 1951, for example, Jilin Province's five movie teams conducted 362 screenings for more than 1,000 audience members per showing and only charged about one-third of their total cost. Even then, village leaders found the fee much too expensive, as they could have used the money to buy more than 250 kilos of grain.[6] By 1954 the Film Bureau issued a directive for movie teams to set prices flexibly depending on local economic conditions.[7] Planners categorized screening locations by geography, climate, population density, transportation infrastructure, and local economies, so movie teams frequented densely populated, well-off, and easy-to-reach townships while subsidizing screenings to poor and peripheral regions.[8] However, even if "movie teams climbed mountains" and charged less per screening, the per capita economic burden for sparsely populated mountain folk still exceeded that for the townspeople and richer villagers in the plains.[9]

Although film screenings promoted collectivization, collectivization reduced film audiences. By 1956 the systematic growth of movie teams meant smaller crowds at every screening.[10] If earlier screenings were held in townships with over a thousand households, now they took place in villages with just a few hundred households, greatly driving up the overall per capita cost. In some smaller villages, every household was forced to pay ten cents per member over the age of ten regardless of attendance.[11] Besides having less cash in their pockets, villagers could no longer simply visit relatives to watch films because of food rationing and labor discipline. Even if they had the money, they would prefer to spend it on "oil and salt." Projectionists circulated sayings such as "The high tide of collectivization brought a low tide to movie teams" or "The era of villagers attracted to a curiosity is over."[12]

Movie teams charged either individual admissions through ticket sales or a flat fee per screening. Ticket sales were the norm for urban, prefectural and county cinemas, which worked with local schools, work units, and neighborhood committees to organize collective moviegoing that served political mobilization and promoted box office revenue. Cinemas outsourced ticket sales to their liaisons in the trade unions, youth leagues, and young pioneer organizations who set up mobile box offices.[13] For open-air screenings in the countryside, however, the precondition for ticket sales was the enclosure of the screening space, which could be improvised using ropes or fences, or rented from local schools, theaters, shrines, or temples.[14] When using existing infrastructure, movie teams tried not to interfere with local priorities such as harvests, conferences, and exams. They tried to preserve order and hygiene while preventing theft and vandalism. Nevertheless, most available village courtyards were too small or had walls too low to separate paying from nonpaying audiences. Even when the barriers were high, audiences would scale them in the dark, and local ushers would let their acquaintances in for free: "The movie team can tend to the east but not to the west; they can block the south, but people came in from the north."[15]

Apart from spatial challenges, ticket sales dampened the movie teams' relations with their rural audiences. Instead of helping them with food and lodging, villagers spoke of "peddling movie troupes" making handsome profits: "The three of you work one night and make 30 or 40 yuan!" Villagers were even less inclined to pay after joining collectives, making ticket sales unsustainable.[16] One movie team compared their income per screening from retail ticket sales—about 20 yuan for an average audience of about 300—and from charging a flat fee of 40 yuan per screening with an average audience of about 1,500. Another movie team reported having to meet their economic target by selling at least 800 tickets per screening, an impossible number given the "low quality of the films," so they had to resort to charging a flat fee per screening to increase revenues.[17]

Charging flat fees required less logistical hassle in terms of enclosed spaces, security, and accounting. Villages or townships paid the movie fee after every screening or signed up for a fixed number of annual screenings, with payment due at harvest from either the public welfare budget (公益金) or the production budget (生产资金).[18] Sharing the cost of cinema equally within a community disgruntled those who did not watch films, so some considered it an unjust "tax." To avoid trouble and save expenses, many grassroots cadres simply told movie teams not to come.[19] The easiest way for movie teams to meet economic targets was to sell tickets in densely populated and economically well-off county seats or townships, thereby abandoning "spiritual conquest" in mountain villages.[20]

As projectionists faced the problem of having to sell unpopular films, a common tactic was to show a double bill with the less-desirable film first. For example, a Zhejiang movie team showed a North Korean film, *Partisan Girl* (빨치산 처녀, 1954, the Chinese-dubbed version was released as 游击队的姑娘 in 1955), before the opera film *Hua Mulan* (花木兰) (1956) on a very cold evening. The audience muffled their ears and stomped their feet throughout the screening. Those who could not "withstand the test" just left. Villagers complained that movie teams "sold ham with claws—making moviegoing expensive and strenuous." A Hubei movie team was criticized for its conniving salesmanship: for fear of boring their audience, they showed only the first reel of a documentary and then screened the second reel of a film scheduled for the next evening as a preview of coming attractions, since that reel included a song, some fighting, and some romance.[21] A Jiangsu movie team showed the opera film *The Butterfly Lovers* (梁山伯与祝英台) (1954) and sold tickets for another opera film *Qin Xianglian* (秦香莲) (1955) even though they did not have a print on hand. Planning to borrow the print from another movie team five kilometers away, the projectionists bought time by sending the audience to another screening location, playing music, and showing highlights from a war film. When the opera film finally arrived at dawn, the audience was utterly exhausted and could hardly get up for work or school the next morning (figure 4.1).[22] Indeed, film exhibitors were keenly aware of villager preferences for opera films and war films over "rural-theme films" that bored them and foreign films that baffled them.[23] It took some guerrilla tactics on their part to address the stark disjunction between supply and demand, between what the party wanted to show and what the people wanted to see.

Projectionists had little say about *what* films were produced or imported, but they could maximize revenues with smart decisions

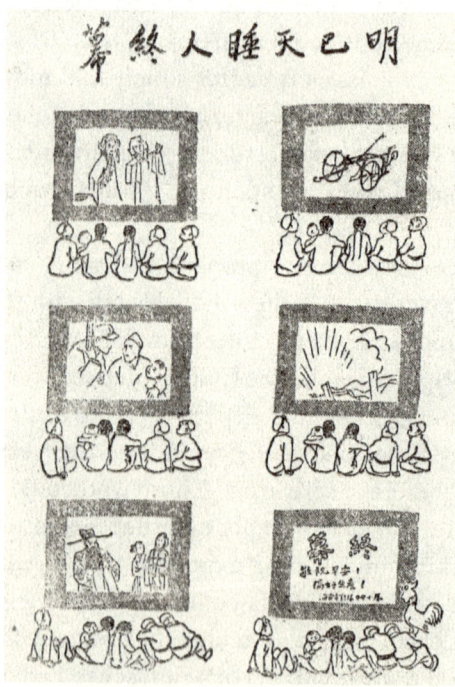

FIGURE 4.1 Screening ends amid audience slumber and sunrise. Caricature of a profit-seeking movie team. *Film Projection*, no. 6 (1956).

about *where* and *when* to conduct screenings. If you have an opera or war film, a *Film Projection* article advised, then show it in county seats; if you only have documentaries, then organize screenings in peripheral areas where cinema might still be a novelty. Go to sparsely populated areas on moonlit nights—when villagers would be more likely to trek to a film—and densely populated areas on cloudy, dark nights. Also consider the seasons: go to poor townships only after harvest, whereas richer places could afford movies year-round.[24] *Film Projection* hosted forums to discuss creative charging practices, such as outsourcing ticket sales and security to rural (cultural) clubs or "supply and marketing cooperatives" (供销社), while giving them a small share of the revenue. To address the villagers' lack of cash, a cadre could write down the names of all who attended a screening and then deduct from their work points afterward. Villagers could barter for admission with chicken eggs or recyclable material. Some movie teams organized voluntary labor to add income into a "cultural budget." If adults were too busy, an article recommended mobilizing the children to collect fertilizer in exchange for an animated film.[25] Instead of passive audiences, children were to actively contribute to socialist production and consumption, meanwhile serving as the movie teams' best advertisers. In the absence of modern communication infrastructures, projectionists recruited local youth as propagandist-cum-publicists and asked schoolteachers to relay information about the films to their pupils.[26]

As propaganda converged with advertising, the proselytizers of ideology were also self-interested employees. For much of the 1950s, projectionists received bonuses for saving costs and generating revenue.[27] *Film Projection* gave voice to their complaints about overwork, underpay, prolonged internships, nonexistent benefits, and disrespect from local cadres.[28] Projectionists considered themselves not only noble providers but also deserving recipients of socialist welfare. After the Anti-Rightist Campaign of 1957, however, the criteria for evaluating projectionists changed from technical expertise and revenue maximization to ideological rectitude, which meant sublimating the hardships of their itinerant work through the rhetoric of self-sacrifice.[29] Meanwhile, cinema transformed from a national cultural commodity to mass-mobilization rallies to extract ever greater sacrifices from the rural people for the nation's Great Leap Forward.

BOOM AND BUST, 1958–1962

From 1958 to 1959 there was a "great leap" in both the number of movie teams and the number of screenings per team.[30] Instead of discussing practical problems, *Film Projection* magazine published grandiose proposals and staged intensive competitions. Highlighting production over consumption, movie teams coordinated films with agricultural cycles and construction projects, promoted daytime screenings, and brought films to farm fields, steel furnaces, irrigation digs, and public canteens.[31] Some teams vowed to conduct three thousand screenings per year, and some conducted fifteen showings per day, mostly newsreel documentaries that supposedly accelerated peasant productivity, but they were also chosen for their brevity, with each fifteen- to thirty-minute documentary counting as one screening in the books.[32]

In 1958 cultural officials contrasted cinema's for-profit nature in capitalist countries against its educational mission in socialist countries, so "a film cannot be evaluated by the breadth or narrowness of its audience." Following this logic, documentaries cannot be faulted for having "no plot or beautiful actors" because they directly showcased "our national outlook."[33] Officials denounced "box office value" as capitalist managerial thinking: "If you attract an audience, you have to consider what kind of audience it is . . . screening pornographic or counterrevolutionary films is like discharging poisonous weeds to the people."[34] Despite such polemic, projectionists still had to cover their costs, but since commune kitchens were serving free food, it seemed unreasonable to make commune members pay for movie tickets. Tapping into the communes' collective budgets became the standard business model that both camouflaged costs and obviated the need to market entertaining films.[35] The creation of commune-run movie teams further facilitated local cadres' deployment of projectionist services and media equipment for labor mobilization.[36]

If the free food in canteens would run out in a matter of weeks, the free spiritual food of cinema was just as unsustainable. In Guangxi and Liaoning, many production brigades paid movie fees from a public welfare fund and deducted the amount from each brigade member's share of the collective income at harvest. By 1959, when public welfare funds were depleted, some production brigades owed as much as one thousand yuan of movie fees and had to pay off this cinema debt at the height of the famine.[37] In Hunan, conflicts arose when some communes prohibited screenings by other commune movie teams because they begrudged the flow of movie fees to their neighbors.[38]

While taxing movie fees from the communes' collective budget, movie teams helped the state extract labor and grain from the peasantry. Such *extractive* capacity is captured by the slogan "Emit What Little Light and Heat You Have" (有一分光，发一分热), sometimes shortened as "Emit Light and Heat" (发光发热). Paraphrased from an essay by writer Lu Xun,[39] this catechism admonished generations of Chinese to ignite their spirits and combust their bodies for the greater national cause, but such rhetoric of sacrifice was particularly consequential during the Great Leap Forward as bodies lost calories and lives were extinguished.

Examples of cinematic extraction abound even in official sources. Given the wild statistical claims of the Great Leap Forward, projectionist reports such as "After watching *Making Steel*, daily production increased by 20 percent" must be taken with a pinch of salt, yet even lies had real consequences and legitimized the government extraction of what little food the peasants actually had.[40] At a conference in 1960 for rural cadres to verify harvest yields, a movie team screened the guerrilla war film *Five Heroes on Langya Mountain* (狼牙山五壮士) (1958) to remind them that "today's liberation is sanctified by the blood of revolutionary martyrs, so we cannot think only about short-term gain and ignore long-term benefits." After the film, these cadres reported thirteen thousand kilograms of hidden grain and turned it over to the state.[41] The cinematic extraction of labor took place through "shock battalions," named after the heroes of war films who pledged to "do battle" or to work for days and nights without rest. Beyond showing films, movie teams used slideshows and microphones to stage labor competitions and lights and loudspeakers to illuminate and direct night work shifts.[42]

Electrified by the mobile movie teams, this cult of speed soon led to exhaustion, and the bubble of cinema burst as the Great Leap turned into the Great Famine. After publishing biweekly between mid-1958 and mid-1960, *Film Projection* stopped publication altogether between July 1960 and December 1962. Many commune projectionists returned to farming, whereas projectionists who remained state employees held only sporadic screenings in county seats. Amid financial insolvency, there was rampant corruption and waste as well as a black market for Hong Kong film tickets in major metropolises.[43]

After the famine, the film-exhibition network again tried to implement "whoever watches films should pay for them."[44] Some movie teams charged a flat fee and outsourced ticket sales to local cadres, who also organized screening locations and managed security logistics. When ticket sales exceeded the flat fee, the surplus could make up for occasional losses, compensate for damaged property, buy film publicity materials, and construct better screening locations to "consolidate the projection network."[45] Some local cadres asked better-off villagers to pay the movie fee for an entire production brigade. Yet when one Shanxi movie team contacted more than thirty production brigades, only four had the budget to pay for cinema, so their county-level managers teamed up with a local cooperative to collect agricultural sideline products instead of cash.[46]

Difficulties with ticket sales were not only financial but also logistical. The Hunan Film Distribution Company gave a vivid example of a screening in the township government auditorium that used to be an ancestral hall. Local cadres assisted the movie team with admission but managed to sell only two hundred tickets, while actual audience numbers went up to a thousand. Most entered by scaling the walls or rumbling in through the door, bruising and ripping the clothes of the party secretary who guarded the entrance and lost his fountain pen. The stampede wounded several children, destroyed the ancestral hall's roof tiles, and damaged the door and many tables and chairs. The township party secretary said: "Thank goodness, please don't show movies anymore. Never mind the property, what if lives are lost?" The same Hunan report also mentioned another screaming, stone-throwing, and nonpaying crowd that injured village children and the projectionist, who also lost his torch, wallet, and ration coupons. Local cadres became fearful of movies, and an area encompassing twenty-six communes that used to have fifteen-plus screening locations became a "blank spot."[47]

In 1963 a film exhibition conference across five provinces highlighted cinema's blank spots. Since the ban on dipping into collective funds, movie teams only sold tickets in more densely populated areas. With the revival of "feudal superstitions," representatives emphasized the spiritual conquest of the rural thought front and called for subsidizing screenings in poor and sparsely populated mountains.[48] In response, various movie stations differentiated movie fees and rationalized itinerary planning after surveying the region's natural, demographic, and economic conditions, as well as the local roads, distance between villages, moviegoing habits, schools, shops, markets, and the number of sent-down cadres and students. As investigations revealed, some mountain villagers paid ten times more per capita per film than villagers on the plains, so new policies prescribed keeping the average spending on cinema at 0.3–0.5 percent of the villagers' annual income while still ensuring every village to watch at least one film a year. *Film Projection* valorized such careful planning over the laissez-faire method of "grazing cows in the mountains—going where there is grass to eat."[49]

VILLAGEBUSTERS, 1963–1977

As film exhibition emerged from the boom and bust of the Great Leap, rural projectionists began showing what I call "villagebusters," films with wide release in the countryside because of either top-down policy or grassroots popularity. State-led villagebusters were the energizing and exhausting exhibition of films *with* and *as* mass campaigns, whereas popularity-driven villagebusters were the films that rural audiences actually wished to see. I derive "villagebuster" from "blockbuster," which originally referred to a heavy bomb deployed in World War II but in the 1950s came to mean large-scale Hollywood productions and box-office hits.[50] The Hollywood blockbuster came to China in the mid-1990s as the "American big film," whereas Chinese blockbusters emerged in the 2000s with popular "New Year films."[51] Yet as early as 1950, the CCP inaugurated blockbuster-style film distribution to conquer a film market previously dominated by Hollywood. The Film Bureau released patriotic films simultaneously in all major cities and advertised them on streets, buses, ferries, shops, newspapers, and matchboxes, radio commercials and loudspeakers, lantern slides and live speeches, hot air balloons and helicopters disseminating flyers, waist-drummers, lion dancers, and parades. Such publicity campaigns for "progressive films" (进步片) merged with political campaigns to resist America and aid Korea and to suppress counterrevolutionaries.[52]

The campaign-like releases of films in the 1950s were still urban blockbuster campaigns. For the Socialist Education Movement, however, the authorities selected a handful of "emphasis films" (重点片) to saturate rural distribution, starting in 1963 with *Li Shuangshuang* (李双双) (1962) and *Locust Tree Village* (槐树庄) (1961). Guangxi province's projection network received more than thirty prints of both films—an unprecedentedly high number—and required every team to prioritize their screening for half a year.[53] In 1964 five more emphasis films were added, among them a rerelease of *The White-Haired Girl* from 1950 and a North Korean import, *Red Propagandist* (붉은 선동원, 红色宣传员) (1962). Rural movie teams were required to devote at least 60 percent of their screenings to emphasis films and to supplement them with multimedia propaganda.[54]

In practice, many prints of socialist education films lay in storage. Some movie teams showed opera films, yet in the books attributed those screenings and audience numbers to emphasis films.[55] Such illicit guerrilla practices had to do with the unpopularity of didactic villagebusters. Guangxi's movie teams reported that, despite strenuous efforts to publicize *Red Propagandist*, many audiences left in the middle of the screening.[56] Even though *Li Shuangshuang* was meant to promote collectivism and gender equality, many rural audiences thought the protagonist was a vixen and busybody whose defiance and disobedience of her husband set a bad moral example, so that even the cadres clamored for the opera film *The Monkey King Thrice Defeats the White-Boned Demon* (孙悟空三打白骨精) (1962). Some movie teams even changed the film's title from *Li Shuangshuang* to *Xiwang's Wife* to refocus the film around patriarchal norms.[57] To persuade audiences to remain and the cadres to pay, projectionists performed extra-filmic propaganda: making and showing lantern slides, singing and explaining in local dialects, curating village history exhibitions, and staging "speaking bitterness" and struggle sessions—all to make such socialist villagebusters locally relevant and "come to life."[58]

In contrast to state-led villagebusters, the truly popular villagebusters were war films and opera films, most notably *The Monkey King Thrice Defeats the White-Boned Demon*.[59] A July 1964 editorial in *Film Projection* criticized movie teams in Inner Mongolia, Qinghai, Henan, and Shanghai for screening 16mm prints of this folktale opera film twice or thrice as often as available prints of socialist education films.[60] My interviews with projectionists and audiences in Hebei, Hubei, and Zhejiang provinces all mentioned the *Monkey King* as the first film to require copy-runners to shuttle reels between simultaneous screenings in different locations.[61]

The Cultural Revolution ushered in villagebusters of unprecedented scale, starting with the 1966 newsreels of Mao's meetings with the Red Guards, as discussed in chapter 1. Movie teams had to screen those "red treasure films" (红宝片) at every stop on their itineraries regardless of the locality's ability to pay, leading to extensive financial losses.[62] The Cultural Revolution Small Group lowered film ticket prices to "destroy Liu Shaoqi's counterrevolutionary revisionist profit-running 'box office value theory,' so that film could better serve workers, peasants, soldiers, proletarian politics, and socialism."[63] Total screenings and revenue in some provinces plummeted to 15–20 percent of 1965 numbers.[64] One county movie station described the early Cultural Revolution years as having "no limits or standards for spending, no efforts to save costs, and many violations of financial discipline."[65] Another county movie station recalled "anarchist tendencies and unhealthy winds that blended stench with fragrance," so that projectionists gained notoriety for "making money without showing films, using public funds to eat and drink, and taking wages for not going to work."[66]

Despite three chaotic years, the Cultural Revolution decade was hardly "ten years of catastrophe" for the film exhibition network. From 1965 to 1976 film projection units increased some fourfold, audience numbers nearly tripled, and the national film attendance rate more than doubled.[67] In 1971 the first filmed revolutionary model operas were released with fanfare. Audiences were already familiar with the story and the operatic numbers through radio broadcasts, but watching *Taking Tiger Mountain by Strategy* (智取威虎山) (1970) and *Shajiabang* (沙家浜) (1971) in vibrant colors was still something special.[68] Guangxi Province initially received only two prints of each film but maximized their screening by copy-running on the highway night and day. A Guangdong movie team had to screen a single copy of *Taking Tiger Mountain* in eighteen different locations over three days, so that children stayed up to wake up other villages upon the film's arrival with gongs and drums, firecrackers, and lion dances.[69]

The initial enthusiasm greeting the model opera films fizzled out after they were repeatedly screened in bundles between 1972 and 1976, despite the slogan to "watch them a hundred times and to see something new every time." To meet statistical targets, work units bought tickets for their employees and their families, schools received tickets for all teachers and pupils, and neighborhood committees delivered tickets to all residents, but those with tickets often did not attend or snuck out when the film began.[70] Southern audiences did not appreciate Peking opera. Even the new model opera *On the Docks* (海港) (1972) sold only 64 percent of all tickets in Guangxi. After the local culture bureau applied some pressure, 90.6 percent of all tickets were sold, but the cinemas were often empty. In rural Chongqing, a production brigade refused to pay for a model opera film, saying any other film would be preferable, especially a foreign film such as the Romanian *Waves of the Danube* (Valurile Dunarii, 1959, released in China as 多瑙河之波 in 1973).[71]

While the political priority to screen model opera films greatly expanded the exhibition network, the truly popular villagebusters before 1976 were a number of dubbed foreign imports from China's socialist allies, to be discussed further in chapter 7. Here I will just mention one incident that reveals the hierarchies of access to cinematic villagebusters in the Cultural Revolution. Shortly before Chinese New Year in 1973, an army unit stationed in the Chongqing suburbs obtained a print of the sensational North Korean film *The Flower Girl* (1972) and first screened it for the Revolutionary Committee and then for rank-and-file soldiers. By the second screening, civilians flooded the gates of the division headquarters and pestered the guards all night long without gaining entry. The army chief added an open-air screening for local civilians on the drilling grounds and distributed tickets via work units, but those without tickets still came to try their luck. Undeterred by the heavy security, the crowd climbed over walls and filled a screening site larger than four soccer fields. The film played amid growing pandemonium. The audience inside wanted to exit, but those on the outside refused to leave and began chanting Mao's poetry on the fish-and-water relationship between the army and people. A segment of the wall fell like dominos, and the screaming over injured bodies led to a stampede that resulted in fifteen dead and many more wounded.[72]

This tragic incident was one of many fatal accidents of walls crashing down on audiences or moviegoers falling into rivers and lakes.[73] Under the planned economy, film admission depended on, and showcased, the power and prestige of one's affiliation. The order of access to the film reflected the local power hierarchy from the revolutionary committee and army officers to rank-and-file soldiers and finally to townsfolks attached to work units. The unaffiliated who shouted Mao slogans of unity and harmony laid bare the reality of division and inequality. Their unquenched thirst for spiritual nourishment readily turned into an unplanned popular protest. Even at the height of Maoism, the "revolutionary masses" that the films and projectionists tried so hard to discipline readily transformed into unruly mobs.

The end of the Cultural Revolution ushered in a new era of village-busters, as films condemned as "poisonous weeds" were "liberated" from storage and rescreened to enthusiastic audiences. In this new "golden age" for cinema, it became common to raise ticket prices and conduct multiple showings to large crowds for nights on end.[74] Writer Ge Fei (格非) recalled how the rerelease of the opera film *The Dream of the Red Chamber* (红楼梦) (1962) attracted villagers from a ten-mile radius:

> By the end of the film, many people sitting at the back side of the screen were squeezed into ponds and cesspools. Clashing audiences from different villages paused the screening. To calm the riot, the local party secretary promised through the loudspeaker to show the film again the next evening, attracting an even bigger crowd. Before it got dark, audiences from afar passed through our villages, fields, and riverbanks like armies of ants—among them many elderly women with bound feet. Worried about another incident, the village cadres moved the screening to the rice paddies. It was late autumn right after the harvest, and the field stretched boundlessly into the horizon. My mother and I watched *The Dream of the Red Chamber* sitting on a ridge full of reaped rice. We were so far away, it was hard to see what was happening on screen, yet my mother and the women around her kept wiping away tears.... The movie was the talk of the village for weeks thereafter. Most men didn't like Lin Daiyu and had a soft spot for

the actress Jin Cai who played Xue Baochai. An unmarried carpenter already in his thirties kept sighing: "Does Jia Baoyu not want you? Don't pester him. Be my wife!"... A village cadre rebuked: "This film really deserves being banned. When it was rereleased, our landlords, rich peasants, counterrevolutionaries, bad elements, and Rightists—all those capitalist ox-demons and snake-spirits—came out and began wiggling, as if it were a damn festival!"[75]

THE RED, GRAY, AND GOLDEN ECONOMIES OF 1970S CINEMA

Did capitalism only return with the cathartic rerelease of "poisonous weed films" that unleashed a return of "bourgeois" sentiments? Or perhaps a gray economy of cinema had already grown in the shadows of revolutionary cinema's red economy? Studies of cinema's shadow economies—"the unmeasured, unregulated and extra-legal audiovisual commerce"—have focused on video piracy since the 1990s.[76] In the Chinese socialist context, I rehistoricize a gray economy of cinema against a red planned economy that prioritized revolutionary politics over market incentives. Indeed, illicit, unofficial, and corrupt economic networks emerged within and around the state-sponsored film exhibition network, consisting of a relationship-driven *guanxi* economy of film access, a parallel economy of peddlers, and unofficial circuits of audiovisual trade.

Collectivism and self-reliance, as opposed to profits, were supposed to guide the red economy of commune cinema. Yet the film exhibition network developed unevenly, and the inequitable access to cinema cultivated a *guanxi* economy, what anthropologist Mayfair Yang called "the political economy of gift relations."[77] Some communes established movie teams much earlier than others thanks to their special relationships to higher powers.[78] A commune in the Yunnan mountains organized a logging expedition to buy an 8.75mm projector and charged every commune member a kilo of grain to pay for a year of cinema, so they could invite their friends and relatives and friends as an "emotional linkage to the nearby masses."[79] Similar to temple festivals, film screenings often attracted much larger crowds than the local population, and poorer villagers often took long trips to movies hosted by richer villages, giving rise to pride and prejudice that fostered hospitality as well as hostility.

Following the self-reliant red economy of commune-run cinema, projectionists charged just enough to pay for the film rentals, machine repairs, and their own wages. Cinema's price was thus set according to cost, not demand.[80] Remaining members of their communes, barefoot projectionists were often compensated in work points plus a cash-and-ration-coupon stipend for meals on the move; some also received a monthly wage of 20–30 yuan to cover their expenses. If they ate in villagers' homes, they were supposed to pay a fixed amount of cash and ration coupons. In practice, however, many villages did not charge projectionists for their meals so that they would visit more often.[81] Some local cadres even took the occasion of a film screening to host a banquet using the commune budget. It became common to feast at the village's expense, so movie teams came to be called "lord teams" or "eat-and-drink teams."[82]

Despite the onscreen spiritual crusade against feudalism and capitalism, revolutionary cinema stimulated parallel economies of entertainment and enjoyment. A former projectionist in rural Hubei recalled competing with itinerant storytellers and shadow puppet troupes for the same audiences in the 1960s—also customers for hawkers of sugar cane, watermelon, and sunflower seeds.[83] An uncle of a projectionist interviewee in Zhejiang followed his movie team to sell corn cobs and roasted peanuts, earning twice as much as the projectionist every night.[84] As a former sent-down youth to rural Shanxi recalled, the film screen was encircled by the dim lamps of peddlers with baskets or carts selling roasted sunflower seeds, five-spice roasted peanuts, dried tofu, even lamb kebabs, liquor, and home-made cigars. While onscreen newsreels showed laboring or fist-raising masses shouting anticapitalist slogans, off-screen hawkers peddled their wares to eager consumers, sometimes beneath banners stating, "Learn from Dazhai," the model communist village of the 1960s and 1970s.[85]

In 1977 and 1978 *Film Projection* exposed rampant corruption and attributed it to the "Gang of Four." At county-seat cinemas, there was a scramble for tickets every time a new film arrived, and "folks went through the backdoor in a thousand and one ways." Instead of "serving the people," cinema employees were busy reserving and distributing tickets among their acquaintances. Movie tickets became a powerful gray currency to gain access to scarce commodities and services, including the attention of doctors in hospitals.[86] Those without paper tickets could enter through the "nodding tickets" (点头票) of ushers. Contentious crowds teemed at the box office and entrance. Inside the auditorium, smoking, whistling, littering, and spitting all contributed to a foul atmosphere; scuffles, theft, robbery, and sexual harassment were also commonplace.[87] Audiences in front sat on bricks and stones, and those in the back squatted on their seats. Blocked passages made it hard for anyone to go to the toilet. The damp summer heat drenched everyone in sweat, so the jeering audiences called moviegoing "taking a bath." One cinema calculated its annual lost revenue to be equivalent to the total salary of its employees, but reform efforts met with counterarguments: "The mountain dweller lives off the mountain, the shore dweller lives off the sea. All we have are a few tickets and the power to admit a few familiar faces." "You'd get nowhere if you totally block the backdoor: the energy bureau can cut off your electricity and the coach station can refuse to deliver your film prints."[88]

When supply fell far short of demand, movie tickets became social capital trophies and bootleg commodities. Wang Xinpeng (王昕朋), a sent-down youth in 1977, asked a friend nicknamed Cannon (local slang for boasting) to help him get tickets to the Yugoslav film *Walter Defends Sarajevo* (*Valter brani Sarajevo*, 1972, dubbed and released in China as 瓦尔特保卫萨拉热窝 in 1973): "I told him not to forfeit his promise because I had to borrow a friend's bicycle to get to town and would lose face if I couldn't get us tickets." Wang gave Cannon one yuan for five tickets at official prices. After waiting two days, Cannon brought three tickets and bragged about an uncle in the local culture bureau who sent a special note to the cinema manager—by contrast, another cadre who allocated thousands of bricks to the cinema only got one ticket in return. Wang was overjoyed and only later learned that Cannon had used his own money to buy three exorbitant tickets at the black market.[89]

Since cinema was most lucrative when catering to townsfolk, mobile movie teams became less inclined to tour the countryside. Instead of making distribution plans, film management stations increasingly functioned like retail shops that gave projectionists whatever they wanted, with little accounting or accountability. Many commune teams conducted free screenings without paying for the print rental. Whereas many documentaries languished in storage, more entertaining film prints were hijacked during transport for extra showings. Some projectionists even divided up and pocketed all the movie fees they collected, revealing anarchist "guerrilla activities" that corroded and sabotaged the socialist economy.[90]

Instead of proselytizers of communist ideology, these "anarchist" guerrilla projectionists were entrepreneurial *homo economicus* extracting private profits from public services. Their roles might be compared with Qing dynasty's "yamen runners" who helped the Qing state administer local affairs, collected rapacious fees, and increased the peasants' tax burden.[91] Similarly, as early as the 1950s many rural villagers regarded movie fees as a tax burden, especially if they had to pay for propaganda that failed to entertain. By the mid-1970s there was even wider economic resistance to unpopular films, such as the "Learn from Dazhai" documentaries, resulting in much foot-dragging in the payment of movie fees that turned into movie debts.[92] One "creative" solution was to turn movie fees into "fines" to be paid by commune members who had committed petty theft, illegal logging, or other infractions against the collective. Before such screenings, the offenders had to make public confessions, thereby paying not only an economic penalty but also the penance of shame so as to "educate" the entire village.[93] Similarly, rural cadres "saved" the cost of transporting cinema by extracting punitive free labor from villagers labeled landlords, rich peasants, counterrevolutionaries, "bad elements," or Rightists.[94]

An economic analytic sheds new light on projectionists as cinematic guerrillas and propagandists performing revolutionary spirit mediumship. Whereas chapter 1 analyzed Maoist media *networks* as infrastructure and as ideological nets, this chapter has explored cinema's *net value* to the state, to the projectionists, and to rural audiences. In projectionist lingo, the phrase "organizing audiences" (组织观众) meant various efforts to ensure that audiences came to (and somehow paid for) the movies. Similarly, their propaganda work was conflated with publicity and advertising. As much as missionaries who spread the communist gospel, projectionists were bureaucratic *intermediaries* between state and society. As much as rank-and-file soldiers seeking to "occupy the thought front," they were economic guerrillas who made ends meet by engaging in underground, illicit, even "capitalist" activities under a communist banner. In the Mao era, cinema's political economy underwent several booms and busts with socialist villagebusters—the exhibition of films *with* and *as* mass campaigns. These inspiring and energizing events contributed to the state extraction of grain and labor from the peasantry as well as to the combustion and exhaustion of their economies and bodies. The growth of commune movie teams gave rise to overlapping red, gray, and golden economies of socialist cinema in the 1970s.

Studying the changing economics of rural cinema can contribute to a broader understanding of the Maoist cultural economy. Laikwan Pang explored the economics of Maoist propaganda works "not in terms of the profits the works made but their production, circulation, and reception." She juxtaposed a revolutionary cultural economy that "emphasized integration instead of differentiation" against Pierre Bourdieu's conception of class distinctions through "cultural and political capital."[95] In practice, the Maoist cultural economy was full of unevenness and hierarchies, with enormous differentiations depending on geography, gender, age, professional affiliations, rank, and personal networks. Moreover, projectionist periodicals, gazetteers, and reminiscences evidence an underlying obsession with economics during the era of "politics in command," the salience of the market in the absence of a "market economy," and the roles of cultural and political capital in an era of "cutting all capitalist tails."

Nevertheless, paying for cinema as spiritual food operated outside a capitalist commodity logic, belonging rather to a *socialist ritual economy* defined by sacrifice for a collective cause. Mayfair Yang defined ritual economy in postsocialist Wenzhou as "expenditures of wealth on ritual, religious, ethical, and social bonding practices," whose internal logic of "giving out" contrasts against the "profit economy" of "taking in." While tracing contemporary ritual economy back to the imperial Chinese state's extravagant ritual expenditures to stimulate production, Yang considered it to have been "curtailed and almost abolished in the Maoist era."[96] Yet I have shown how cinema functioned as a (spi)ritual medium to sanctify the revolution and demand sacrifice at the grassroots.

Whereas the postsocialist ritual economy engaged in economic exchanges with the divine world, the Maoist ritual economy carved out a portion of its austere material economy for the spiritual food of cinema in order to congregate the masses in ritual spaces in communion with not only the divine Chairman Mao but also the spirits of revolutionary martyrs, the ghosts of the "Old Society," and millenarian visions of a communist paradise.

Serving a socialist ritual economy, the film exhibition network is reminiscent of the networks of village temples "providing services, raising funds, and mobilizing entire communities to participate in collective rituals" in pre- and postrevolutionary times.[97] As cinema replaced opera as entertainment and edification for the peasantry, movie teams attended to older cultural habits by scheduling more screenings around spring festivals and harvests. They also tried to generate a sense of revolutionary festivity by screening films and slideshows on "International Women's Day" or May Day. Instead of temple associations inviting opera troupes to celebrate the birthdays of the deities, cadres invited movie teams to screen films at political meetings. Just as "funds for a temple festival were collected from the community, generally on the basis of ability to pay,"[98] rural cinema relied mostly on communal funds instead of charging individual admission. As cinema facilitated cults of worship, mass mobilization, and shamanistic exorcism against class enemies, it gained currency in the Maoist ritual economy, which was also an economy of sacrifice and gratitude. Beyond paying movie fees out of tight collective budgets, the sacrifice of the revolutionary martyrs in the films exhorted the masses to be grateful to the party and to sacrifice their grain, labor, and bodies to collective endeavors. Perhaps it was also in this sense that a projectionist wrote that "brilliant flowers of political thought will bear bountiful economic fruits."[99]

PART TWO

Audiences as Creative Agents

CHAPTER FIVE

The Hot Noise of Open-Air Cinema

> For my generation, cinema is the gatekeeper of our childhood memory lane. When this gate opens, all the smells and flavors of that vanished era assault our senses: roasted sunflower seeds, the unique scorched flavor of pumpkin seeds, the aroma of dust and rain, the scent of women's vanishing cream, the odor of petroleum emanating from the generator, the smell of mysterious nights of distant moon and stars.
> —Ge Fei, "Xiangcun dianying" (Village cinema)

When I asked Chinese villagers, especially older women who spoke only local dialects, what films they had seen or liked, they often replied, "Film? We just went to 'watch hot noise'" (*kan renao* 看热闹). Sometimes they also said "approaching/gathering hot noise" (*cou renao* 凑热闹), suggesting that they were not passive audience members but active participants in the hustle and bustle. By calling cinema "hot noise," villagers usually meant two things. First, the movie team brought a festive ambience through an assembly of warm bodies, a polyphony of chatting voices, and a kaleidoscope of sense impressions. Second, they did not understand or care for the narratives, characters, aesthetics, or morals of the films. Instead, they were overwhelmed by the extra-filmic noises that constituted the milieu of open-air cinema.

"Hot noise" is a word-for-word yet altogether incommensurate translation of *renao*, more commonly rendered as "spectacle," "attraction," or "liveliness." A central feature of Chinese popular religion, theater, and markets, *renao* describes what Adam Chau called a "sociothermic affect," a lively, busy, and prosperous atmosphere sought after at New Year's celebrations, weddings, birthday parties, temple fairs, and

FIGURE 5.1 "Projection Team on the Lake." Papercut by Wang Mingqi, *Film Projection*, no. 3 (1965).

even funerals.[1] Robert Weller dubbed Chinese popular religion a "hot and noisy religion," whereby a successful large event "should be packed with people, chaotically boisterous, loud with different voices, and clashingly colorful."[2] Shuenn-Der Yu highlighted *renao*'s multisensory quality by describing how vendors of Taiwan's night markets attracted customers with bright lighting and decorations, music and sales pitches, smoke and steam, and overflowing wares and food ingredients.[3] Joshua Goldstein underscored the interactivity of *renao* through raucous Peking opera audience behavior at the turn of the twentieth century: while "loudly vocalizing their appreciation or discontent, [the teahouse] customers did not dole out their aesthetic currency—their attention—without a healthy haggle, nor was one expected to keep silent and still. . . . Disruption [*renao*] was part of the fun; indeed, it was an integral part of the communication between the audience and the actors."[4]

Renao belongs to what Svetlana Boym called a "Dictionary of Untranslatables," cultural common places that are "perceived as natural in a given culture but in fact were naturalized and their historical, political, or literary origins forgotten or disguised."[5] By rendering "untranslatable" *renao* into the literal yet jarring term "hot noise," I wish to defamiliarize the taken-for-granted everyday usage of *renao* to interrogate the sources, effects, and multiple valences of "heat" and "noise" as well as to rethink what we mean by *noise* in terms of both unwanted sound and disruption of signal. Whereas Jacques Attali claimed that noise "in all cultures [is] associated with the idea of the weapon, blasphemy, plague," *renao* as "hot noise" is the antonym of *lengqing*, "chilly and desolate," also associated with wandering ghosts and spirits.[6] Indeed, the amiable, noisy confusion of enthusiastic human interaction is nothing less than a celebration of life itself, the *yang* opposed to the *yin* in Chinese cosmology. Rather than unwanted disruption, hot noise is akin to the ambience of carnivals in medieval Europe, considered by Mikhail Bakhtin as emancipatory occasions when the grassroots populace could subvert the elite-made rules and hierarchies that govern their everyday lives.[7]

If the "hottest and noisiest" events in rural China tended to be temple festivals, operas, and markets, what happened when Chinese state socialism suppressed such communal events as feudal, superstitious, or capitalist? I argue that *socialist hot noise* took on politicized and technologically amplified new forms in radio broadcasts, open-air cinema, as well as mass rallies, parades, calisthenics, and struggle sessions. Whereas the "heat" in "hot noise" refers to the bodily heat of a gathered crowd, the "heat" of socialist hot noise derives from a *synergy between body and electricity* that soldered dispersed populations into the revolutionary masses. Rather than unofficial culture or commercial exchange, socialist hot noise was coordinated with political campaigns, and open-air cinema became its quintessential event. Gathering a crowd like a temple festival but disciplining them into a socialist congregation, open-air cinema occasioned the electrification of the countryside by literally bringing electricity to off-the-grid rural areas and by metaphorically electrifying the populace with the revolutionary spirit. As socialist hot noise, cinema was not only film as mass media but also the *masses as media*. The interaction of those warm bodies with both the film apparatus and the screening environment created a memorable ambience and vibe with visual, aural, olfactory, gustatory, and haptic dimensions. Although extra-filmic sensory noises interfered with absorption into the film texts, they could also be the very purpose of the spectacle, the object of attraction and consumption. Instead of drawing audiences centripetally into the film, open-air cinema radiated outward centrifugally like a disco ball and karaoke microphone-loudspeaker whose main functions are to emanate light and amplify sound.

How did cinema as socialist hot noise revolutionize the Chinese sensorium? Film scholars connected the beginnings of cinema to the invention of a new sensorium inseparable from urban industrial modernity.[8] Yet the vast majority of China's population lived in rural areas until the 1990s and would not have encountered cinema until mobile movie teams brought them in the 1950s and 1960s. Since the Chinese countryside had little infrastructure devoted to film exhibition, screenings took place mostly in open air, and the environment for cinema was more natural than built, more improvised than designed. From the 1950s to the 1970s, even urban Chinese encountered films primarily at open-air screenings in nontheatrical venues, such as schools, work units, and military courtyards. The open-air screenings intensified the audiences' *physical* memories of cinema due to their embodied interactions with the material spaces of film exhibition. This chapter will thus parse the senses—sight, hearing, smell, taste, and touch—with which grassroots audiences engaged with cinema *beyond* the film. While the multisensory environment of open-air cinema contributed to the making of socialist subjects, audiences' extra-filmic sensory experiences also went beyond state orchestration.

EYES: WATCHING HOT NOISE

Cinema is above all a *visual* medium, but moviegoing has always meant seeing more than just the films. As Zhiwei Xiao argued: "The site of film exhibition and the entire movie theater environment—from the ticket booth on the sidewalk to the posters in the hall, publicity materials in the display window, crowds in the lobby, and snack bars—all play a crucial role in shaping the audience's experience of a given film."[9] In the 1950s and 1960s, the CCP constructed cinemas, clubs, and cultural palaces for the "proletariat masses." These were often stand-alone monuments in industrial districts on urban peripheries and modeled after Soviet architecture.[10] According to a Chinese cinema architecture textbook from 1963, movie theaters should look "welcoming" and "vivacious" but not "sumptuous and palatial." Since socialist cinemas received priority in urban planning, they did not "have to compete with crammed and colorful storefronts," nor rely on "giant brassy signs." Under the socialist order, cinema audiences were no longer admitted on a rolling basis but rather filed into the auditorium at the beginning and cleared out at the end of every showing. The audience lounge became an important space decorated with movie posters, star photos, and film reviews, whereas the box office became less prominent with advance group ticket sales and shorter queues.[11] In county seats and large townships, movie theaters were often the highest and grandest architectural monuments, so they loomed large in the visual experiences and memories of audiences.

Whereas movie theater façades and decorations remained fixtures in the everyday lives of urban citizens, the arrival of cinema marked a festive event for rural villagers. Although the projector, projectionist, and electricity that produced audiovisual images were usually camouflaged *infrastructure* in purpose-built cinemas, the itinerant movie team—their embodied presence and the machines they brought—were spectacular attractions in the countryside. According to projectionist reports, first-time audiences often marveled at the electrical miracle of film technology, giving rise to many comic anecdotes: old peasants tried lighting their pipes at an electric light bulb; audiences of a war film returned the next morning to look for leftover artillery. In tales reminiscent of the myth of the spectators' terrified reactions to Lumière brothers' *Arrival of a Train* (1895), older villagers reportedly cleared out a path between them when a character in *The White-Haired Girl* shouted, "Get out of the way" as his entourage drove toward the camera.[12] After their initial curiosity about the new technology subsided, however, some of these "primitive" audiences became bored with films. In rural Guangxi, audiences initially hiked through the mountains with food and blankets to attend a screening for the first time. Since they could not understand the film's Mandarin dialogue, however, they didn't come the next time and said they had "already seen film." Only after the movie team introduced live narration in the local language did the audience return, understanding cinema to be like the itinerant storyteller who brought new stories every time.[13]

Even after cinema was no longer a novelty in the 1970s, the arrival of a movie team to a village remained a special yet unpredictable event, augured by the sight of the cart transporting equipment or a villager shoveling holes to erect bamboo poles to hang a screen. Such sights unleashed a swift wind of rumors that would travel to neighboring villages, followed by scores or even hundreds of individual decisions about whether to hike to the screening, decisions that would take account of distance, road and weather conditions, the company, and the availability of torches and moonlight. The rumors might not be true, so the sight of fellow travelers from other villages congregating along the way, some holding flashlights, was reassuring.[14] Sometimes rural audiences traveled a long way only to see a "white cloth film" (白布电影) when the projector or generator broke down. Even when screenings went smoothly, audiences often watched a blank screen during the reel changes or when waiting for copy-runners to bring the next reel.[15]

Various reminiscences of open-air cinema liken the screen to a flag, a sail, or a lighthouse—all belonging to what John Durham Peters called

FIGURE 5.2 "Happy at Cinema's Return." Woodcut by Zhang Zhentao, *Film Projection*, no. 11 (1964).

"sky media," which also include towers, bells, weather, and clouds.[16] As argued in chapter 1, with the extension of the film-exhibition network to ever more grassroots levels, hanging up movie screens became akin to raising flags in territorial conquests. Yet in the countryside, as an article in *Film Projection* in 1954 put it: "The screen could encounter many enemies, such as inappropriate locations, moonlight, wind and sand, and mosquitos." To "triumph over these enemies," the author urged projectionists not to hang the screen too high (leading to audience fatigue) or too low (leading to overcrowding), while taking the weather into consideration.[17] The fixing of the screen was itself an attraction and a spectacular display of the projectionists' acrobatic virtuosity, whether it was scaling up the pillars of the temple theater or using a rope like a cowboy's lasso. Audiences were also eager to help tamp down the earth to stabilize the bamboo poles, to tighten the rope that secured the screen, and to cast shadows with their hands when the lights were turned on.[18]

Lighting up a dark firmament in open air, the screen had an enchanted quality, "enveloping thousands of troops," magnifying tiny insects, drawing the far near, conjuring the past, and divining the future. Some compared the screen to a sailboat that navigated audiences across an ocean of dreams.[19] And if, in the words of a hosanna to Chairman Mao, "Sailing the Sea Depends on the Great Helmsman" (大海航行靠舵手), then Mao's illuminated image on the screen both provided the illusion of live presence and summoned otherwise dispersed villagers into a congregation at his beck and call. In this sense, the screen was a lighthouse that provided orientation and anchor in the midst of Mao's "revolutionary wind and waves."

Real wind blowing the screen twisted the metaphor of the sail, as the screen itself became distorted and the film characters took on grotesque grimaces and warped bodies.[20] Bending the very surface of the screen, the wind created out of didactic film texts unpredictable comedy, farce, and a sense of the uncanny. Shanghai writer Wang Anyi (王安忆) described in a novella how students sent to a collective farm in Anhui in the 1970s assembled at the sound of a bugle for the screening of the revolutionary ballet film *The White-Haired Girl* (白毛女) (1972):

> The wind blew the screen like a sail on the sea, twisting the bodies of the characters onscreen so they all looked miserable. Zhao

> Zhiguo walked from behind the screen toward the audience. In the wind, the students sat on their backpacks in phalanx formation. The light and shadow of the screen reflected off their tanned, solemn, and indistinguishable faces.... The exaggerated gestures of the characters seemed absurd in this kind of night. The sound of music was engulfed by the wilderness, but the sound of the wind was omnipresent, filling the space between sky and earth.[21]

The film's visual and auditory signals were not only distorted by the wind but swallowed up, overpowered, and rendered infinitesimal by the sky, the earth, and the air in between. Besides the wind-blown screen-as-sail and thunderstorms, sunlight also affected a film's visibility. Since most of rural China did not have the infrastructural conditions to engineer "artificial darkness,"[22] the start-time of open-air cinema depended on nightfall. When films on a short rental period had to be screened in multiple villages, the last screening of the night might end with sunrise, leaving at first faint shadows and eventually nothing but a blank screen, though audience members could still hear the film's heroic music and dialogue alongside the snoring and laughter of their fellow viewers.[23]

Even under optimal conditions, open-air screens, often two by three meters or the size of a "two-person blanket," were tiny compared to the vast audience. Those in the back could see sometimes little more than "heads and butts."[24] Yet reminiscences also mention the beautiful spectacle of audiences arriving or departing with flashlights, lanterns, and torches, like twinkling stars scattered across the mountain paths and embankments of the paddies.[25] Moviegoers looked at one another and compared whose clothes were smarter and whose clothes were full of holes with cotton falling out. Villagers often dressed up in their best clothes, but even those were shabby in many instances. With a heightened consciousness of the self as spectacle, many moviegoers recollected their pride or shame under the scrutiny of many eyes much better than any film.[26]

EARS AND MOUTHS: SOUNDING HOT NOISE

Besides spectacles for the eyes, cinema's hot noise also attracted and assailed the ears. If Tom Gunning's "cinema of attraction" originally referred to early *silent* cinema, Chinese grassroots cinema featured a "noise of attraction."[27] Since one can better project sound than images across wide distances, the sound of the loudspeaker has helped attract audiences to open-air screenings to this day. Besides the apparatus, the audience and environment also contributed extra-filmic sounds to the rural cinematic experience.

Due to haphazard, makeshift spaces without fixed seating or clear boundaries, much hullabaloo at open-air cinema had to do with friction over desirable spots to sit or stand, over blockages of the projector or of the audience vision, over the hurling of insults and food waste, or over unauthorized audiences forcing their way in or being forced out. From livestock cries to children's tantrums, from gossiping to catcalling, from smoking to spitting, much hot noise at the cinema might be considered "uncivilized" and tamed in urban cinemas, but they would enliven rural open-air screenings well into the 1990s.[28]

In the Mao era, mobile projectionists did not so much suppress as summon audience noise, often inviting them to shout political slogans, sing revolutionary songs, or speak up after the screening on how the film affected them personally. Channeling audience pandemonium as the sound and fury of the "revolutionary masses," projectionists solicited, even staged, postscreening testimonies of revolutionary faith, be they bitter memories of a prerevolutionary past, denunciations of local landlords or other class enemies, or vows to contribute to a communist future.[29] During the Great Leap Forward, for example, a Jiangsu movie team found an independent farmer who was ready to join the commune, so the projectionists invited him onstage with a microphone to publicly declare his desire, which supposedly helped convert others. Another projection team staged a "martial contest" for young commune members, giving them microphones so that they could pledge to finish the harvest at unprecedented speed.[30]

While waiting for the movie teams to arrive, schoolchildren and soldiers often sang revolutionary songs to pass the time.[31] Many Maoist films introduced theme songs within the film narrative and then repeated them in the ending credits, so moviegoers would already be singing or humming the tunes on their way home. Indeed, every new film ushered in the learning of new songs. Audiences clipped and copied the sheet music printed in newspapers and magazines as well as transcribed songs from radio and loudspeaker broadcasts. Rural youths often followed the local movie team to various villages. Because radios, gramophones, cassette players, and even song-books were unaffordable luxuries, many villagers learned film songs by writing down the lyrics at screenings.[32] Thus films became the wings of songs that took further flight as they reverberated through the voices of audience members.

Audience noise could thus enhance and prolong the efficacy of film propaganda, but it could also disrupt and mock political communication. Take applause: projectionists recalled loud clapping at the sight of Mao or at the triumphant climax of war films (see figures 1.2 and 1.3).[33] Audiences also applauded when the projectionist fixed a technical problem or when the copy-runner arrived with the next reel.[34] Yet applause could become booing when impatient children clapped to cut short speeches by party secretaries carried away with the amplification of their own voices.[35] Bored by repetitive and predictable films, audiences sometimes shouted lines before they were uttered onscreen.[36] Even disruptive mechanical noise could give rise to humor and parody that subverted the propaganda messages. Writer Ah Cheng (阿城) described open-air screenings in Yunnan's mountains in the 1970s:

> You needed several men to take turns powering the generator by pedaling. Sometimes the man pedaling tired and the electricity would fluctuate, causing the sound from the loudspeakers to become slurred, distorting the well-known arias. Meanwhile on the screen, an uplifting scene of "heroic deeds" might have started boldly but would suddenly lapse into hesitation. In the mountains, though, everyone enjoyed watching anyway. Other times the man on the pedals changed the tempo on purpose, creatively improvising, and the old films would send the audience into fits of laughter.[37]

If noise could become more meaningful than the film proper, different audiences picked out different signals from the polyphonous sonic environment of an open-air film screening. Whereas village children treated cadre speeches as boring noise to battle with their own noise-making, local cadres paid for cinema precisely for the opportunity to address an assembly of villagers. Thus the hot noise of rural cinema served political communication regardless of the films' content. Many adult villagers did listen patiently and carefully when the cadres laid out production plans, when newsreels showed them the latest political winds, or when "science education films" introduced new agricultural techniques more pertinent to their livelihoods than fictional features.[38]

The sonic environment of open-air cinema complicates theories of film sound. Consider, for example Michel Chion's three listening modes.[39] Audiences attracted to open-air screenings practiced *causal listening* to identify the sound source; those absorbed in the films' diegesis were *semantic listeners* who decoded the film's content; projectionists practiced a *reduced listening* to their machines to forestall breakdown and accidents. Some audience members practiced another form of "reduced listening" when they eavesdropped outside cinemas or listened to a neighbor's radio for programs featuring sound clips from feature films.[40] Rural women too busy with domestic chores could listen to film sound only over the loudspeakers.

Yet to Chion's trio of causal, semantic, and reduced listening can be added another mode: the *emplaced listening* to the soundscape of the film screening location. Situated, live, and highly variable from person to person, emplaced listening tied audiences to their local environments so they could be as attentive to extra-filmic noises as to the film's diegetic sounds. Outdoor moviegoers listened for distant thunder that signaled imminent rain, while elderly villagers listened for barking dogs warning against thieves.[41] Other atmospheric noises—such as howling wind, singing cicadas, or croaking frogs—could fall into the background as ambient sound, but they were still "noises of the real" that grounded audiences in the here and now.[42] The natural environment further generated reactive audience noise: buzzing mosquitos provoked smacking, heat prompted fanning, and cold compelled the stomping of feet.

NOSE AND TONGUE: CINEMA AND COMMENSALITY

What did cinema smell and taste like? Apart from audiovisual representations and evocations of smell and taste, film scholars also discussed movie theaters as "an instrument for public hygiene and a technology for the creation of controlled olfactory environments."[43] In contrast to the deodorization of urban movie theaters, open-air cinemas in rural China were heightened olfactory and gustatory experiences, as the writer Ge Fei suggested in the Proust-inspired text quoted in the epigraph to this chapter. Grassroots moviegoing was often accompanied by homemade or peddler-sold snacks consumed only on Chinese New Year. Moreover, the coming of the movies occasioned gatherings of bodies that emanated scents, sweat, smoke, and other odors in open-air environments, also perfumed by fragrant plants and fetid manure.[44]

Smoke, not only a nuisance to the nose, could also blur the vision.[45] Yet in open-air cinema, fire and smoke could provide light, warmth, sustenance, and protection: a lantern or a torch could illuminate the way home; portable bamboo hand warmers burning charcoal helped many withstand the winter cold; some learned to smoke to drive away insects attracted to the cinema's light; some made bonfires to roast corn or sweet potatoes.[46] Smoking was also part of local leisure and consumption. A former sent-down youth to rural Shanxi recalled cigarette vendors who bought cigarettes at fourteen cents a pack and retailed single cigarettes at three cents each. Teased for her "snowballing usury," the vendor "radiated a smile and said: 'Not expensive at all. For three cents you get to enjoy the life of a city person.'"[47] The smell and taste of smoke thus added to the alchemy of fantasy created by the audiovisual images.

The synesthetic delights of open-air cinema are praised in one projectionist's poem from 1959:

人群汇集广场，灯光亮，歌声扬，男女老少喜洋洋。
银幕上，拖拉机嚓嚓响，谷子低头尺来长，
苹果红梨子黄，葡萄一串又一串，
惹得小伢直流涎...
队长：只因为看了电影，鼓足了干劲，才捕得这样鱼满舱

People gather at the square, lights shine, songs ripple,
Men and women are merry, old and young are jubilant
On the screen, tractors roll, bountiful ears of grain curl
Red apples, yellow pears, bunches of grapes make children salivate . . .
The brigade leader says: watching movies made us work harder,
That's how we filled up our boats with fish.[48]

In both contemporary and retrospective writings, cinema during the Mao era was dubbed "spiritual food" (精神食粮) that motivated food production and/or compensated for food scarcity.[49] Projected images of plenty were intended to inspire audiences to work hard and turn utopian visions into reality. Yet even this propaganda poem suggests a tension between abundance and scarcity, aspiration and reality, production and consumption, as the food onscreen pinpoints its lack off screen. If we read this poem with retrospective knowledge of the Great Leap famine, we can see the delectable fruits as a mirage and taste the saliva as the gastric acid of hunger. What we have here, then, is phantom commensality.

In classical sociological theories of commensality, "sharing food is a way of establishing closeness, while, conversely, the refusal to share is one of the clearest marks of distance and enmity."[50] The public canteens of China's Great Leap Forward, however, instituted what James Watson called "coercive commensality" to mobilize women's labor from domestic chores as well as "imagined commensality" that fed on utopian fantasies.[51] The collective canteens collapsed a few months after their introduction, but cinema as a form of phantom, illusory, or spiritual commensality continued in the absence of food.

In Chinese socialist cinema, the bounty and scarcity of food onscreen projected future utopias and recalled past sacrifices to contextualize the present in gustatory metaphors: past bitterness gave rise to present sweetness, and present bitterness would give rise to future sweetness. Meanwhile, lavish feasts and gluttony were negatively coded as the rapacious sin of Japanese invaders, KMT officials, landlords, capitalists, and bandits. And yet many audiences living amid socialist austerity could not help but vicariously "consume" the onscreen food meant to inspire productive labor, even secretly identifying with the "bad guys." Even in the 1970s, audiences salivated after the appearance of foods in newsreels featuring diplomatic feasts or North Korean films showcasing harvest surpluses.[52]

Beyond "feasting" their eyes, audiences also literally ate at the cinema. To arrive at the screening early, many would hurry through schoolwork, farmwork, or domestic chores and eat early or skip supper altogether, instead bringing or buying food, which often meant not staples but snacks such as roasted peanuts, soybeans, sunflower seeds, sweet potato chips, tea eggs, sugar cane, candied hawthorns, and red bean popsicles.[53] Homemade snacks required ingredients, time, and labor, so anticipation of the film was folded into food preparation. Made in haste, some snacks might still taste raw, but that, too, was savored as cinema's delight. From the 1970s onward, as mentioned in chapter 4, a growing peddler economy added steaming aromas and hawking cries to screenings. Snacks could be shared as tokens of sentiment, friendship, and infatuation—or rouse envy and aggression.[54]

Beyond onscreen food or eating at the screening, village cadres often invited the movie team to meals before or after the film. Projectionists recalled the touching hospitality of the rural folk alongside comical anecdotes about naïve villagers mistaking onscreen characters for live actors or cooking enough food to feed a large theater troupe.[55] Other stories highlight the villagers' abject poverty. A former projectionist recalled staying with "the richest man of a village," also its party secretary, who treated the movie team to cured meat that his family had parsimoniously hoarded for two weeks after Chinese New Year, not realizing that it had already gone rancid.[56] Although movie teams were supposed to pay for their meals with cash and ration coupons, some cadres drew on the collective budget to pay for feasts that gave the whole village leadership an excuse to eat and drink, also leading to inebriated, long-winded speeches.[57] Beyond the movie team, local villagers had to feed relatives and friends who came for the screenings, so the spiritual food of cinema came to be associated with literal feasting.[58]

HANDS AND FEET: TOUCHING HOT NOISE

In *The Skin of Film*, Laura Marks wrote about how grainy, densely textured, and sensuous images taken by cameras close to the body evoke "haptic visuality" so that "the eyes themselves function like organs of touch."[59] In her phenomenology of film, Vivian Sobchack traced theoretical antecedents for the "carnal sensuality of the film experience": "Our fingers, our skin and nose and lips and tongue and stomach and all the other parts of us understand what we see."[60] As much as filmic images evoked the sense of touch through synesthesia, cinema was enabled by and gave rise to literal acts of touching, from the projectionists' magic touch that made images come to life, the feet that carried audience members to and from the screening, to the touching of bodies as audience members stood or sat during the film.

Like onscreen guerrillas and mobile projectionists who spent extensive time on the road, rural audiences often had to travel long distances to get to screenings, climbing hills and fording streams, so that memories of filmgoing often focused more on the *going* than on the film, their feet bearing the corporeal brunt of the adventure. Some villagers without adequate shoes walked barefoot along kilometers of mountainous paths, making this an era not only of "barefoot projectionists" but "barefoot audiences." A sent-down youth to the "Great Northern Wilderness" recalled walking fifteen kilometers with friends through the snowy wilderness at night, with frost on their eyelashes and wolves on their heels.[61] Some Ningxia villagers recalled having to wade through streams in a mountain valley, making it necessary to take off their shoes and roll up their pants. In the winter, the streams would be frozen on top, but it was still easy to break the ice and splash water on pants and shoes, made of worn cotton or straw because most villagers could not afford rubber boots. The wet pants and shoes in turn froze as temperatures dropped during the screening, "but our hearts were hot, and we might just take off our wet shoes and jump up and down to get warm."[62] This added a special sound effect to the hot noise of cinema: the thunderous sound of stomping feet. Meanwhile, since technical problems often interrupted screenings or prevented them from starting at all, some audiences playfully dubbed those filmgoing journeys without a film "Guerrillas Running in Vain" (白跑游击队), with playful reference to the many guerrilla films they watched.[63]

In contrast to the soft sofas of today's multiplex cinemas where we might forget our bodies, open-air cinema often stimulated an intense awareness of one's body between the sky and earth, vulnerable to wind, rain, snow, heat, and cold. Bug bites and frostbite, scratches and rashes all became cinema's corporeal souvenirs.[64] A former sent-down youth recalled an open-air screening on a school drilling ground in Inner Mongolia in 1974:

> Each of us sat on a brick or stone found on the spot. After the first reel, we waited for the copy-runner to bring the second reel. The cold air seeped into my military coat and cotton shoes. My face, hands, and feet became numb. We rubbed our hands and faces and hopped up and down. Even though no one forced us to stay,

hardly anybody left. We could no longer distinguish between enjoyment and torment, or judge whether the film was even worth such endurance. The loudspeaker kept reporting how close the copy-runner was, but the second reel still hadn't arrived. When it finally came and was screened, we had to wait for the third reel, and so on and so forth. I've forgotten if we eventually finished the movie. I can only remember the growing pain, fatigue, and the numb stupidity of not leaving. I returned to the dorm at dawn and worked in the fields the next morning, but by the end of the day I began to urinate blood and was diagnosed with severe nephritis.[65]

Open-air screening locations not only had no roofs but no seats. Every shred of bodily comfort depended on makeshift bricolage and personal resourcefulness. Local villagers brought benches from schools, stools from home, and stones from the rivers. Audiences who arrived late from farther away climbed on trees, walls, roofs, haystacks, bicycles, and shoulders.[66] Most simply stood, some on their tiptoes. As one recalled: "You needed a strong body to go to the cinema in the countryside because the crowd sometimes left you with nowhere to stand. The elderly who got tired and took a break often lost their spot when they came back."[67]

Where one sat or stood at a screening could also indicate the social and political mapping of a community, its hierarchies and networks, centers and margins, inclusions and exclusions. The village leader often sat next to the projectionist and could decide when the film was to begin. Young people came early to occupy the best spots for their friends and relatives. While waiting for the film to start, audiences would chat, snack, knit, play cards, or get into scuffles.[68] Some attended open-air cinema as a family, with children sitting on their grandparents' laps or riding on their fathers' shoulders, but most socialized with members of the same generation.[69] As the only nightlife available to Chinese villagers without electricity, open-air cinema broke down everyday taboos. Adolescents fraternized and flirted. The shadows of lovers could be spotted farther from the screen, while some pairs disappeared from view altogether.[70] Cinema thus provided a camouflage for couples who otherwise might find no occasion to touch, talk, or even look at each other under the moral surveillance of other villagers. Many later cited open-air cinema as their matchmaker.[71]

This chapter studied the extra-filmic senses associated with cinemagoing in socialist China. Besides the ideological content of the film texts, the arrival of a movie team constituted festive occasions for mass congregation, spectacle, commensality, intimacy, and nightlife against a backdrop of poverty and hardship. Often serving as both labor mobilization and respite from labor, film screenings stimulated and amplified the senses while modeling austerity measures through an economy of gratitude. Even though the state's aim was to attract, discipline, and collectivize a scattered population into the "revolutionary masses," cinema audiences remained an unruly crowd whose hot noise eluded, even subverted, state control.

In the postsocialist era, the hot noise of open-air cinema has cooled, abated, and drifted to the margins of the Chinese sensorium, featuring ever-flashier sights and ever-louder sounds. During fieldwork from 2015 to 2019, I followed various mobile projectionists as they conducted state-sponsored, free open-air cinema in rural counties, townships, and villages, but attendance was sparse except for screenings conducted by a "model projectionist" in rural Wenzhou in the courtyards of various ancestral shrines, where mahjong and other forms of gambling generated greater interest than the films. In rural Hebei, not too far from Beijing, I waited around for days for an open-air screening that never took place because "the wind is too great," or "there will be a sandstorm," or "the air quality is bad." I never saw the moon or the stars during the open-air screenings, which took place not in fresh air but in air rendered toxic by the smog of the nearby factories banished from the big cities. Air pollution, light pollution, noise pollution, as well as mass deracination through demolition and migration assail the sensorium of today's grassroots China. Sensory overstimulation can lead to shock and numbness, so open-air cinema has become dull and muffled, invisible and inaudible, against audiovisual saturation, just as satiated bellies blunted the flavors of traditional snacks. Sensory overload can go some way to explain the paradoxical nostalgia for the sensory austerity under socialism.

What, then, was cinema in socialist China? The villager elders I interviewed were probably right: cinema was not so much the films shown as the hot noise of extra-filmic sights, sounds, smells, taste, and touch. Emanating from the apparatus, the audience, or the atmosphere, hot noise included heat and cold, wind and rain, moon and mosquitos, snacks and feasts, shoes and roads, hand shadows and stomping feet, screens and seating, power generators and loudspeakers. Cinema as hot noise was a participatory and heightened sensory experience for grassroots audiences. As special occasions for mass congregation, carnival, and consumption against a backdrop of sensory deprivation, open-air cinema brought together bodies that moved and acted, sensed, and reacted; bodies that emanated and absorbed sights, sounds, and smells; bodies that touched and were touched. Those extra-filmic visual, aural, olfactory, gustatory, and haptic noises at open-air screenings often drowned out the films' propaganda messages. If socialist cinema's open-air screen was intended as a flag, a sail, and a lighthouse, its utopian visions arrived at the grassroots as mirages and phantoms that paled against the noises of a lived reality.

By discussing cinema as "hot noise," however, I do not wish to conclude that the films themselves had minimal impact on their audiences. The next two chapters will show how certain domestic and foreign films became canonical classics because of their wide release, repeated screenings, and coordination with mass campaigns. More than textual analyses, I will draw on memoirs, oral histories, and projectionist reports to explore a broad range of intellectual and emotional, public and private, performed and repressed responses to films over time.

CHAPTER SIX

Guerrilla Cinema and Guerrilla Reception

What influence do propaganda films have on their audiences? Was cinema a technology of mind control, as might be suggested by the Cold War imaginary of communist "brainwashing"? Or was cinema part of the CCP's social engineering to create new socialist persons, "emancipated people who not only mastered their own fates but also decided the country's destiny"?[1] This chapter proposes a more elastic and nuanced approach to audience reception of propaganda cinema than the polarizing binaries of passivity and agency, submission and resistance. I argue that guerrilla films projected by guerrilla projectionists trained guerrilla audiences in guerrilla techniques that could both support and undermine propaganda goals.

By *guerrilla cinema*, I refer to PRC films depicting Communist-led revolutionary warfare before 1949 as well as struggles against internal or external enemies after 1949. Red Army, Eighth Route Army, and People's Liberation Army soldiers engage in open or furtive battles against the Japanese, the KMT, local tyrants and bandits, as well as against spies, traitors, and saboteurs who infiltrated revolutionary time and space.[2] Adapting characters and stories from real life, folktales, fiction and theatre to the screen, guerrilla cinema had transmedia afterlives in comic books, live performances, slideshows, audio broadcasts, and audience emulation. Produced and distributed from the 1940s to the present, Chinese guerrilla cinema was mostly a state-sponsored meta genre aimed at mass mobilization.³ Furthermore, the PLA sponsorship of the August First Film Studio, the vast military film exhibition network, and cinema as military training made guerrilla films an "industrial-military genre."⁴

Although imposed from above, guerrilla films enjoyed tremendous grassroots popularity, such that any film title with the word *battle* (战) was sure to attract a large crowd.⁵ This had to thank their kinesthetic action, intriguing plots, idiosyncratic characters, musical interludes, emotional catharsis, and occasional slapstick comedy. As ordinary villagers, including women and children, are recruited into battles of strength and wit against their better-equipped enemies, guerrilla cinema blurred the line between soldiers and civilians to invite identification from large swathes of the Chinese population and instilled a sense of wartime emergency even in times of peace.⁶

By militarizing its audiences' way of seeing and thinking, Maoist guerrilla cinema became logistical media that assembled and trained its audiences for warlike campaigns, at once resonating with and going beyond media theories connecting war and cinema through their shared technologies.⁷ To mobilize audiences, projectionists amplified and even staged ideal audience responses to "prove" cinema's propaganda efficacy. Film magazines published selective testimonies of the films' ideal reception, whereas school broadcasting stations and blackboard bulletins amplified the correct takeaways—mediating processes that transformed a film's intended reception into a performative, even prescriptive reception. Beyond echoing a film's ideological messages, audiences were supposed to show their emotions through their sighs and vows, their fists and tears, and then respond through action. As projectionists and local cadres deployed multimedia propaganda for mass mobilization in successive campaigns, onscreen guerrillas mythologized war memories and transmitted the revolutionary spirit to their audiences.

This chapter begins by analyzing how revolutionary war films inspired childhood mimicry of guerrilla war heroes and prepared audiences for ever-greater sacrifices. As guerrilla war films often highlighted human-woven defense and communication infrastructure, embodied mediation became a key message, yet the same films also taught guerrilla tactics of subterfuge and encryption. In fact, a synonym for guerrilla warfare was "sparrow tactic" (麻雀战术), the main weapon for which was noise in both the acoustic sense of sound and the informational sense of interference. Mediated by cinema, sparrow warfare as noise warfare had off-screen resonances in mass movements from the Great Leap Forward to the Cultural Revolution. The next section focuses on revolutionary spy thrillers that fostered participatory surveillance while also allowing guerrilla audiences to indulge in bourgeois temptations and carnal desires. Featuring communist soldiers as saviors in deus ex machina endings, the final section discusses how bitter films such as *The White-Haired Girl* and *Serf* moved audiences to shed tears of catharsis, to "speak bitterness" about the "hell" of Old Society, and to express gratitude to the party. All three subgenres of guerrilla cinema networked audience sentiments into revolutionary solidarity, even as prescriptive public responses camouflaged heterodox interpretations, identifications, and pleasures by guerrilla audiences.

REVOLUTIONARY WAR FILMS AND MILITANT PEDAGOGY

War films were often screened as the first contact with cinema for many rural Chinese audiences in the 1950s, but not everyone appreciated them at first. For those who had experienced its horrors firsthand, war was frightening rather than entertaining. The combat and explosions onscreen may well have triggered traumatic memories and survival instincts.[8] A Hunan movie team reported initial peasant responses to the film *Fighting South and North* (南征北战) (1952): "This film really chills the heart—so many people were killed!" To overcome their humanist sentiments, the projectionists explained "why we fight" and "what kind of people we kill." Afterward, the movie team quoted an eight-year-old boy speaking to his mother: "Mama, our PLA is great at fighting—they killed so many iron-capped bandits in Chiang Kai-shek's army!" A sixty-year-old peasant provided another model response: "The PLA fought so hard for our liberation. When I go home, I will sell my surplus grain to the state to support the liberation of Taiwan."[9]

Thanks to the projectionists' intervention, public reactions to war films shifted from horror to pride and gratitude, articulated in testimonials such as "Our forefathers fought fierce battles against Japanese imperialism and paid a heavy price. Our happy lives today are inseparable from their bloodshed and sacrifice."[10] A villager provided a model response to *The Storm on South Island* (南岛风云) (1955): "Guerrillas [in the film] had to share a single bowl of porridge, so what if we have to mix rice with some coarse cereals?" After screening *Shanggan Ridge* at a dam construction site, a movie team interviewed a female labor model who responded: "I am only toiling to harness a river—it's nothing compared to the People's Volunteer Army!"[11] War films thus trained audiences to endure physical hardships and material austerity as profoundly meaningful, as well as to engage in virtual revolutionary competitions with the soldiers onscreen.

Beyond such prescriptive responses, war films inspired many role-playing games, such that children of the same village or neighborhood would form guerrilla squads under whistle-blowing sergeants and throw clods of mud as if they were hand grenades.[12] In a self-reflexive mode, the child protagonists of many guerrilla war films, such as the beloved *Little Soldier Zhang Ga* (小兵张嘎) (1963), play at war before participating in real warfare, suggesting how mimicry should serve as rehearsal for revolutionary action. Children growing up in military compounds identified even more with soldiers in war films and borrowed their parents' uniforms, insignia, even headphones and walkie-talkies as costumes and props for their war games. Army brats also boasted their privileged access to more and better films by brandishing their movie tickets or recounting movie stories to their nonmilitary classmates. Children of high officers even sat on film reel containers next to the projectionist and decided when a movie was to start. Some strategically placed their folding stools in open-air courtyards, less for a good view of the screen than to attract attention to their army caps. While civilian children in the same schools and neighborhoods envied military kids, they nevertheless benefited from physical proximity to army headquarters, if only by sneaking into screenings like guerrillas.[13]

While encouraging playful fantasies, guerrilla war films also cultivated patriotic sentiment, militant discipline, and a self-sacrificial spirit. A Ningxia villager recalled *Guerrilla on the Plains* (平原游击队) (1955; remade in color, 1974) most vividly for an infectious gesture of the clenched fist: a village child finds an unused bullet after a skirmish and tells the guerrilla hero that he plans to use it to kill "Japanese devils." Later, when pressed by a Japanese officer to reveal the whereabouts of the guerrilla hero, the child bites the officer's hand and gets shot. The guerrilla hero finds the bullet in the dead child's clenched fist and later uses it to kill the Japanese officer. Visualizing hatred of the enemy, the clenched fist of the sacrificed child is emulated by both the intradiegetic spectators in the film and the extradiegetic audiences watching the film in anger and solidarity.[14] Insofar as guerrilla war films networked militant sentiments and inspired many audience members to join the army, it was also a *cinema of conscription*.[15]

Amid the geopolitical tensions of the Cold War, the PLA's August First Film Studio produced two "military pedagogical films" (军事教育片) that were shown repeatedly throughout the Cultural Revolution decade. In *Landmine Warfare*, villagers-turned-guerrillas bury homemade landmines in strategic locations to vanquish the Japanese invaders. According to projectionist reports, this film "greatly enhanced the war-readiness of the local militia, who built rustic weapons with class hatred and swept the whole commune in a vigorous mass campaign of indigenous weapon production."[16] In *Tunnel Warfare*, villagers-turned-guerrillas build a network of tunnels as a hideaway from enemy troops, who eventually invade the village but become trapped inside the underground maze. Highlighting Mao's pamphlet *On Protracted Warfare* (论持久战) (1938) as a sacred text enlightening its readers, the film itself became an audiovisual manual on guerrilla warfare, demonstrating how to use low-tech methods and local knowledge to build an effective defense infrastructure (figure 6.1).

With an estimated 1.8 billion viewings,[17] *Tunnel Warfare* taught the entire populace how to dig nuclear bunkers at the height of Sino-Soviet tensions in 1969, resulting in immense labyrinths dubbed the "Underground Great Wall."[18] A viewer from Fujian recalled how all the primary- and secondary-school students in his township dug tunnels beneath their schools following the techniques introduced in the film. Two teams would start digging two-meter deep holes one hundred meters apart and burrow horizontally toward each other until the tunnels connected. Only one person could crawl forward at a time, yet the underground labyrinth grew so sprawling as to trap some adventurous explorers. Before any war broke out, a few torrential downpours waterlogged

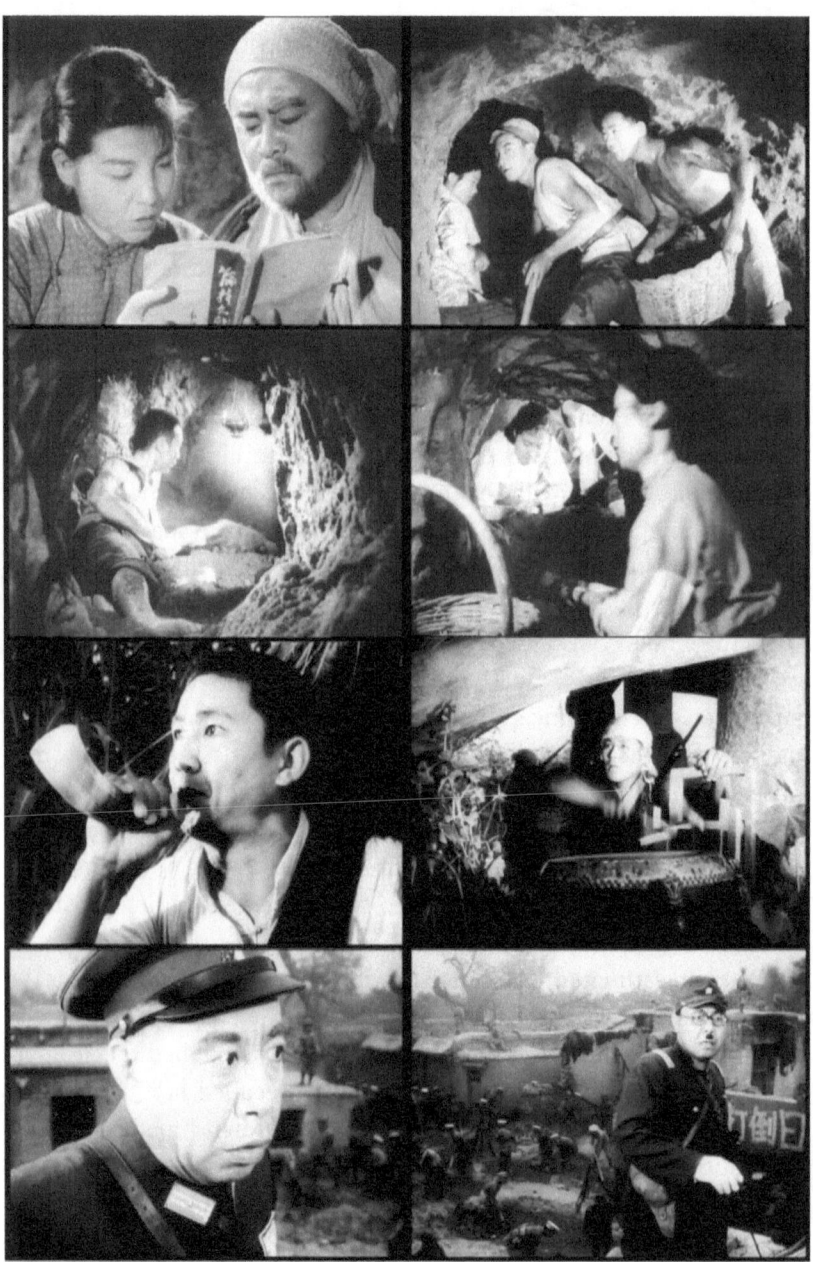

FIGURE 6.1 Guerrilla tactics from tunnel digging to "sparrow warfare" from the military pedagogical film *Tunnel Warfare* (1965).

the tunnels, which fell into oblivion and became a hideout for young lovers—another kind of "guerrilla" seeking subterfuge for private sentiments.[19]

Besides defense infrastructure, Maoist guerrilla films often highlight human-woven communication networks. The opening of *Letter with Feather* (鸡毛信) (1954) shows its twelve-year-old protagonist standing sentinel with his flock of sheep atop a hill at an "information tree" (信息树), a small fake tree that can be erected or knocked down to indicate safety or danger, a binary code inspired by ancient smoke towers (figure 6.2). We see this alarm system in action a bit later, when the boy knocks over his information tree after seeing that other trees closer to the Japanese fortress have tumbled, signaling that "the devils are coming." He shouts out to his friends in the valley to sound their gongs and cymbals to warn villagers to hide their food from the plundering enemy. Meanwhile, the child hero's father composes an urgent letter marked by chicken feathers for him to deliver to the nearby Communist guerrillas so that they might attack the unmanned Japanese fortress. In the absence of such modern technologies as cameras, telephones, wireless radios, loudspeakers, and wheeled vehicles, a carefully constructed network of eyes, ears, voices, and youthful legs constituted a surveillance, alarm, and telecommunication and transportation network.

FIGURE 6.2 Child sentinel at an "information tree," from the film *Letter with Feather* (1954).

In guerrilla war films, embodied mediation was the message. In *The Red Lantern*, the act of passing on the encoded message is more significant than the encoded content.[20] In *The Everlasting Radio Signals*, when the Communist guerrilla risks his life to tap out telegraphic signals that are never deciphered for the audience, he is transmitting not so much ideology or intelligence, but rather the revolutionary spirit of martyrdom (see figure 0.2). As receivers of such revolutionary spirit, audiences were supposed to further transmit it through performative sacrifice. At the same time, audiences learned from guerrilla war films to turn everyday realms into battlegrounds of signals and noises. According to memoirist Cui Jizhe (崔济哲), he and his childhood pals were inspired by *Letter with Feather* to install sentinels to protect themselves from discovery as they tried tuning into enemy radio on his parents' "Red Lantern" receiver, as concentrated "as underground party agents noting down secret codes" in *The Everlasting Radio Signals*, but all they heard were "noises resembling wind, rain, thunder, gongs, and firecrackers," and they could just barely make out the faint tone of foreigners speaking Chinese but not much rhyme and reason.[21]

SPARROW WARFARE

Among the most interesting and impactful guerrilla tactics imparted by military pedagogical films was the "sparrow tactic" (麻雀战术). Invented during the Second Sino-Japanese War, communist guerrillas imitating nimble sparrows dispersed forces in the mountains and "pecked" at the Japanese troops through scattershot attacks.[22] Sparrow warfare's primary weapon was noise, both in the acoustic sense of sound and in the informational sense of interference. As illustrated by military pedagogical films of the 1960s, guerrillas made noises with firecrackers, drums, whistles, and one or two gunshots in order to perplex, unsettle, and sow chaos among the enemy (see figure 6.1). The short-term goal was to divert their attention or mislead them onto landmines and other traps, whereas the long-term goal was to consume their energy and weaken their spirit, so that that they "couldn't eat or sleep in peace."

Mao's own talk of sparrows shed light not only on his guerrilla tactics but also on his biopolitical vision that would affect myriad lives, human and animal. At the Seventh Party Congress in 1945, Mao spoke of sparrow warfare as synonymous with guerrilla warfare:

> In the early phase of the War of Resistance against Japanese Aggression, our [military] force was like that of a little finger. How did we grow our prowess? With sparrow warfare, guerrilla warfare. Sparrows fly wherever they can find food.... The sparrows in the sky were our seeds that grew many sprouts. With those seeds, we grew the party, the base areas, the people, the food, and training for cadres. Back then we flew everywhere, sandwiched between the Japanese enemies and the Nationalist reactionaries.... Even though sparrows are opportunists that follow food, even though they are little, when you add them up, they amount to 910,000 strong. Will we be sparrows forever? Long Live the Sparrow? History has proven that our sparrow is no ordinary sparrow; it can grow into an eagle. In ancient Chinese mythology, there is an eagle that can fly from the North Sea to the South Sea with one swoop of its wings. We will be like that too and grow to three million, five million. Our little sparrow will grow into an eagle swooping up all of China with its wings.[23]

Mao's use of the sparrow as a parable for his guerrilla army can be put into productive conversation with the biblical allegory of the shepherd and his flock. Michel Foucault devoted his lecture series "Security, Territory, Population" in 1977–1978 to a lengthy analysis of pastoral power "not exercised over a territory but by definition over a flock in its movement from one place to another." The shepherd was to "ensure the salvation of his flock," leading them to "fertile grasslands ... the best routes to take, and the places suitable for resting."[24] While Mao's sparrows were also "a multiplicity on the move" that looked up to their leader as a savior, they were not merely passive followers but active, swift, and militant creatures. Likened to seeds, they were small but proliferated swiftly. They were "opportunists" because they forage for food, but once mobilized, they added up to a formidable force that could take over a whole country.

Even though Mao likened peasants-turned-into-guerrillas to sparrows and praised their collective vitality, he clearly placed little value

Guerrilla Cinema and Guerrilla Reception

on their individual lives. In 1956, speaking with representatives of some Latin American Communist parties, Mao again likened the peasantry to sparrows when calling for investigations in rural areas: "The method is to ... spend a few weeks [in one village] to get a clear idea of the class forces, the economic situation, living conditions, and so on in the countryside.... Though there are plenty of sparrows, it is not necessary to dissect every one of them; to dissect one or two is enough.... This is called 'anatomy.'"[25] Around the same time Mao spoke of "dissecting a sparrow" in metaphorical terms, he began calling for the literal extermination of all sparrows, which had catastrophic ecological ramifications. After hearing from peasant representatives about sparrows eating their crops, Mao wrote a decree to wipe out mice, sparrows, flies, and mosquitoes in the coming years.[26] Following his proposal, the years 1956 and 1957 saw local efforts to kill sparrows and the publication of various manuals for catching, trapping, and poisoning the birds. In the spring of 1958, the Four Pests Campaign ushered in a nationwide total war against sparrows as the masses deployed a new weapon of mass destruction: noise.[27]

In March 1958, after attending the Four Pests Great Leap Forward Conference in Beijing, leaders of Sichuan's Eliminate the Four Pest Headquarters learned from local peasants an annual practice of shooing sparrows from the fields before harvest. The headquarters mobilized the populations of entire counties to "exhaust and bombard" (疲劳轰炸) the sparrows.[28] Sichuan's Emei Film Studio made a documentary about Xinfan county's war against sparrows between March 11 and 18, *Besieging Sparrows* (围剿麻雀) (1958) (figure 6.3), which was then screened around the country ahead of similar campaigns. After a brief credit sequence accompanied by chirpy Chinese orchestral music, the film opens with a middle-aged cadre pointing a stick at a "besieging map" and then at flocks of sparrows overhead. Following his command, his youthful audience march off in single file and join other columns of villagers holding long bamboo sticks or rifles. The voiceover states: "A mass battle to eliminate sparrows with sound and fury is about to begin. Men, women, children, and the elderly—carrying all sorts of weapons—are coming to the battleground from all directions. Since this is war, strategy matters. The first task is to occupy the enemy front." The next sequence intercuts between the sparrows in the sky—the orchestral

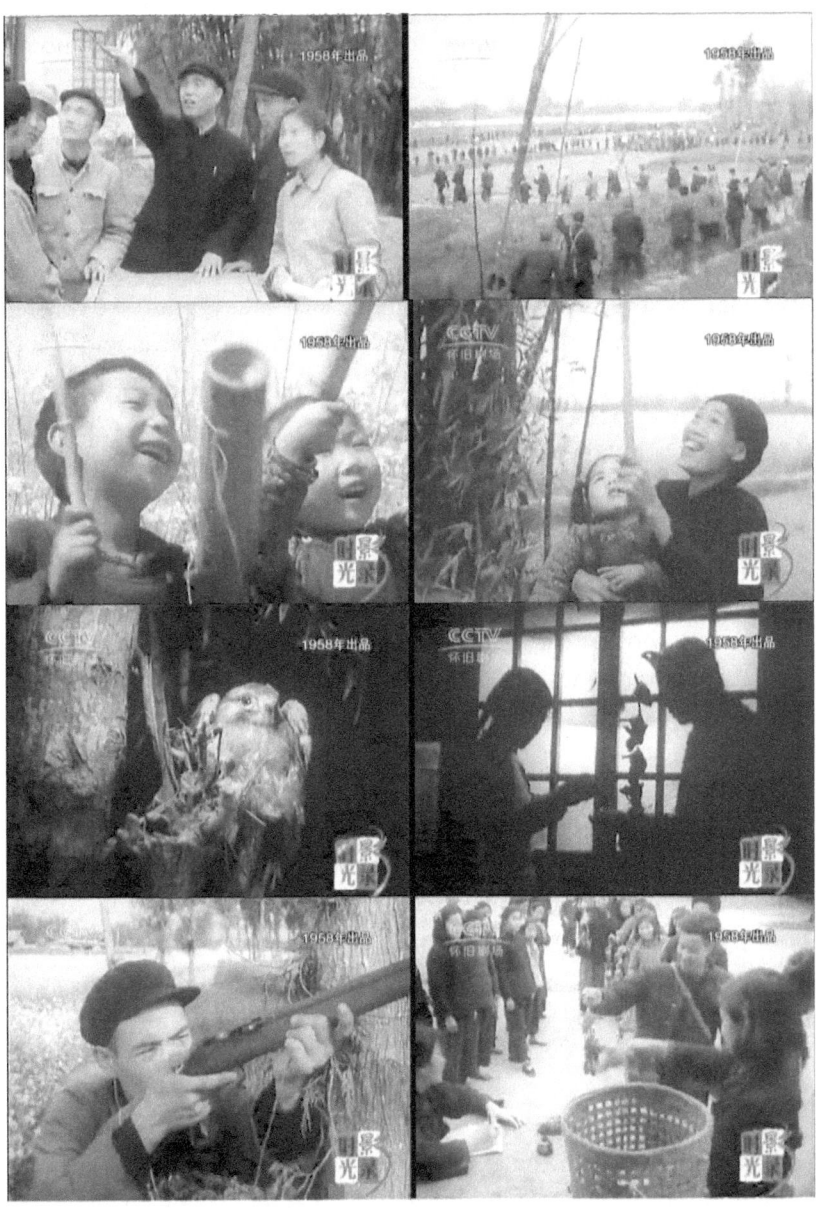

FIGURE 6.3 Stills from the Sichuan Emei Film Studio documentary *Besieging Sparrows* (1958).

score sinks in pitch as if enemy airplanes are poised to drop bombs—and a squad of women on the ground, including a granny with a toddler in her arms—their clicking bamboo sticks and loud hollering drown out the music. We then see men shooting at sparrows with rifles and scattering poisoned grain on a roof. As the camera pans over the dying birds, the voiceover quips: "Please look—this is what happens to those who are too fond of eating and too lazy to work." At night, villagers prepare bonfires, and flocks of panicked birds swoop down into the conflagration. Scouts with flashlights catch the remaining birds with their bare hands. The battle continues into the next day with a cacophony of gongs, cymbals, pans, basins, bamboo utensils, and human voices. As children pick up the cadavers, string them up, and dump them into barrels, the voiceover states cheerfully: "Days of hunger and fatigue have totally exhausted these sparrows. All you have to do now is lift a finger to pick up the dead or half-dead birds. This is indeed an earth-shattering battle. The peasants achieved glorious victory and vanquished more than twenty thousand sparrows in just six days." Closing with a panoramic shot over countless bird cadavers, the voiceover concludes: "As long as we set up nets above and snares below, sparrows cannot escape even with wings."

Although *Besieging Sparrows* is formally a documentary newsreel, its exhibition and reception turned it effectively into a military pedagogical film that taught the rest of the country how to massacre sparrows. For example, Beijing's "Suppress Sparrows Headquarters" organized residents in various neighborhoods to watch the Sichuan newsreel. Loudspeaker vans decked with dead sparrows toured the streets ahead of a three-day citywide campaign from April 19 and 22 in 1958.[29] Writer Ye Shengtao (叶圣陶) described the first day of the Beijing battle in his diary:

> The campaign to encircle the sparrows began after four o'clock in the morning. In the high-rise building opposite of the air force office, someone gave orders from a loudspeaker. Each family banged on pots and pans, set off firecrackers, or shouted loudly, so that the sparrows could not stop flying until they dropped from exhaustion. On top of all the roofs, people stood waving long poles with a red or otherwise colorful cloth. Behind a tall tree outside the back

of my room lived Lao Tian, who regularly beat a bucket made of galvanized sheet iron. [My grandchildren] all joined their school organizations to fight on campus or outside the city.[30]

Ye speculated that the purpose of such mass participation was not merely to annihilate the sparrows but also to "immerse the people in a collective fighting spirit."[31] On April 21 *Beijing Evening Paper* published Guo Moruo's (郭沫若) doggerel "To Curse Sparrows" (咒麻雀):

麻雀麻雀气太官，天垮下来你不管。
麻雀麻雀气太阔，吃起米来如风刮。
麻雀麻雀气太暮，光是偷懒没事做。
麻雀麻雀气太傲，既怕红来又怕闹。
麻雀麻雀气太骄，虽有翅膀飞不高。
你真是个混蛋鸟，五气俱全到处跳。
犯下罪恶几千年，今天和你总清算。
毒打轰掏齐进攻，最后方使烈火烘。
连同武器齐烧空，四害俱无天下同。

Sparrow, Sparrow, you are so arrogant, little do you care if the sky falls.
Sparrow, Sparrow, you are so extravagant, you eat rice like a whirlwind.
Sparrow, Sparrow, you are so lethargic, you loaf about with nothing
   to do.
Sparrow, Sparrow, you are so proud, yet fear red and noise.
Sparrow, Sparrow, you are so pampered, even with wings you cannot
   soar.
You are truly a bastard bird, with these five airs you've hopped around
And sinned for thousands of years. Today we shall settle accounts
   with you.
Poisoning, banging, bombarding, and dredging in a coordinated
   assault, finally throwing you into a raging fire.
Ablaze with weapons till you are gone! Without the Four Pests, great
   harmony will prevail.[32]

Other participants in the Great Sparrow Massacre recalled local loudspeakers mobilizing them in a coordinated assault against the birds with various homemade "weapons": firecrackers and hammers, metal pails, gong-and-drum parades, or human voices.[33] After three days, Beijing eliminated some 400,000 sparrows; a few days later, Shanghai eliminated about 500,000. The nationwide toll was estimated to be around 2.1 billion sparrows, some four times China's population at the time.[34] The following year, as poet Sally Wen Mao put it, "locusts surged and a plague laying to waste the grain supply. The trees webbed with caterpillars. The children who tortured the birds with pots and slingshots starved to death. The ghosts of rats, flies, and mosquitoes buzzed in the air. The ghosts of children and sparrows. Ghost formations, migrating across the sky."[35]

Modeled by cinema and directed by loudspeakers, the Great Sparrow Massacre and its associated Four Pests Campaign became a nationwide rite of passage through the crucible of collective violence. In *Confessions of a Red Guard*, Liang Xiaosheng (梁晓声) recounted how his entire primary school marched to the beat of gongs and drums to besiege all local public toilets with the battle cry: "Digging out a pupa is the same as unearthing a class enemy hiding deep inside society." A few years later, on the eve of the Cultural Revolution, Liang and his classmates set out to help a local village fight an insect infestation by pinching the green caterpillars with their fingers: "The size of those green, meaty caterpillars sent shock waves through us; we screamed, we jumped back, we ran off, many of us still quaking even when were safe." Their teachers told them to think of revolutionary martyrs who did not even flinch before the swords of reactionaries. As omnipresent loudspeakers warned against hidden internal enemies, Liang often had nightmares of green caterpillars crawling all over his body and gnawing on his flesh.[36] If finding and squashing a pupa or caterpillar was equated with ferreting out a hidden enemy, the equation also worked vice versa, and the barefisted "war" against various pests served as an embodied pedagogy of violence and compliance. The children who tortured the sparrows with noise would grow up into Red Guards who applied the noisy "sparrow warfare" tactics they learned from *Landmine Warfare* and *Tunnel Warfare* to torture class enemies with loudspeakers.[37] Meanwhile, their ability and method to "detect" class enemies had to thank their spectatorship of revolutionary spy thrillers.

REVOLUTIONARY SPY THRILLERS

Contemporaneous with Western film noir and James Bond movies, Chinese revolutionary spy thrillers, known as counterespionage films (反特片), featured either Communist agents infiltrating enemy territory or enemy agents conspiring to sabotage the Communist order. Cultural studies scholars Dai Jinhua and Haiyan Lee associate this genre with "Cold War boundaries and antagonisms" as well as with the "Maoist ideology of permanent revolution."[38] Beyond critical readings of these films as cultural symptoms, how did historical audiences engage with them? Distinguishing Maoist "participatory surveillance" from Foucauldian "panoptic surveillance," film scholar Xiaoning Lu argued that counterespionage films mobilized "the masses to become surveillance agents rather than defining them as surveillance subjects."[39] Indeed, rather than dulling their viewers' critical acumen, revolutionary spy thrillers trained the vigilance of the masses as omnipresent guerrilla agents against hidden enemies.

Many members of the Red Guard generation remembered looking for spies in their everyday lives based on the typecasting of villains in counterespionage films with "triangular eyes and skinny cheeks."[40] The open-air screening environment and moviegoing paths through the wilderness created the perfect mise-en-scène for fear and adventure. Writer Shi Tiesheng (史铁生) recalled how, after watching *The Case of Xu Qiuying* (徐秋影案件) (1958), he and his friends thought an old man smoking in the dark was sending smoke signals to class enemies, so they surrounded him only to realize he was one of their grandpas.[41] After watching *Secret Post in Canton* (羊城暗哨) (1956) and *Secret Drawings* (秘密图纸) (1965), composer Zhang Zhuoya (张卓亚) recalled how her middle school class began keeping watch over their local convenience shopkeeper—a woman in her thirties who smoked, permed her hair, and wore floral-patterned clothes. Each scout on duty kept a detailed log of all those who entered and exited her shop and home in a notebook to be submitted to the local police.[42]

Spy thrillers cultivated a hermeneutics of suspicion that guided participatory surveillance, as film audiences learned to overread their everyday environments as crime scenes and to detect potential enemies in their midst. For detective fiction author Wei Binhai (魏滨海),

counterespionage films enshrouded his hometown with a mysterious air: its winding streams, secluded corners, and bunker ruins all seemed to harbor secret clues. Fantasizing about cracking a spy ring like those clever investigators in films, he tried to decipher the graffiti on walls and scratches on trees for intelligence. During the Cultural Revolution, Wei's townsfolk caught an astonishing number of "hidden KMT agents" who seemed like amiable neighbors, familiar salespeople, and respected cadres. Denunciations via big-character posters suggested that these agents could readily strip off their humane masks and reveal their hideous true colors by killing, poisoning, and setting off explosions. The young Wei found all this exciting until a few Red Guards summoned his mother as a spy suspect after her colleague "confessed" under torture to have shared intelligence with her. Afterward, Wei became terrified of the film-inspired imaginations of his townsfolk, who allegedly ferreted out a former warden for the revolutionary martyr Sister Jiang from the film *Red Crag* (红岩) (1965) and uncovered a nationwide secret agent conference convened by Chiang Kai-shek himself.[43]

In the Cultural Revolution, spy-catching games evolved into ever more far-fetched denunciations of imagined enemies, justifying home searches, arrests, incarceration, and torture. A former KMT officer found his home ransacked by Red Guards who had watched *The Everlasting Radio Signals* and imagined that he must have a radio transmitter to communicate with the KMT in Taiwan.[44] When threatened with torture to "admit" his espionage activities, a nuclear scientist wrote a satisfactory "confession" by combining the "clues" from his interrogators with the genre conventions of counterespionage films.[45] Even after the Red Guard movement, spy thrillers continued to train the children in participatory surveillance. A first-grader in rural Anhui in the mid-1970s, recalled watching the North Korean spy thriller *The Disclosed Identity* (숨길 수 없는 정체, 1970, the Chinese dubbed version was released as 原形毕露 in 1973) in the commune auditorium—the walls of which were imprinted with the slogan "Never Forget Class Struggle." Afterward, she and a few friends spotted a woman in her fifties "with tangled hair, fair skin, and small, fierce eyes. She wore ragged urban clothes [and] red leather shoes we had only seen on female spies in movies." When accosted, she spoke in an incomprehensible dialect, so the children reported her to the commune revolutionary committee. The local militia fetched her for interrogations, searched her baggage for radio transmitters, and detained her in a straw hut for several days.⁴⁶

While instilling vigilance and violence, spy thrillers also aroused secret admiration for the villains and their extravagant milieu, sometimes leading to schizophrenic interior struggles against the self as enemy.⁴⁷ Indulgence in those concealed desires belonged to an ever-widening guerrilla reception of propaganda films. In particular, sensuous female spy characters mesmerized both diegetic male heroes and extra-diegetic audiences.⁴⁸ A former Red Guard recalled his own obsession with the female agent Ah Lan in *Adventures in the Bandit's Den* (英雄虎胆) (1958): "My favorite scene [in the film] was of Ah Lan dancing the rumba. I thought the way she moved was very beautiful, but the message of the film was that she was shameless and depraved . . . yet the actress was pretty; she had a great figure. For a bunch of boys at an all-boys' school, her appeal was obvious. At the time, I would criticize myself. I believed I was some sort of pervert. Now with scientific knowledge I see that I was sexually repressed" (see figure 6.4).⁴⁹

Others recalled watching Ah Lan with contradictory feelings of enchantment and shame, such that they secretly agonized over her final

FIGURE 6.4 Memorable scene with a female spy from the film *Adventures in the Bandit's Den* (1958).

execution. "Miss Ah Lan" became a compliment and a jeer to stylish young women with a captivating gait. With their tight-fitting dresses, leather pants, high-heel shoes, and permed hair, female agents on film were scorned, revered, and desired not only as erotic objects by men but also as fashion icons by women and girls.[50] One viewer recalled a neighbor's little daughter imitating Ah Lan by puffing on a "cigarette" she had made with paper over a ballpoint pen. Another viewer recalled how a girl in her village often volunteered to play the female agent with a flower in her hair.[51]

Feminist film scholars conducted psychoanalytical readings of femme fatales as projections of male desire and anxiety, but some also argued that film noir "offers a space for the playing out of *various* gender fantasies."[52] Even before Laura Mulvey published her seminal "Visual Pleasure and Narrative Cinema" in 1975, however, Mao's wife Jiang Qing had readily detected the subliminal pleasures of counterespionage films like *Adventures in the Bandit's Den*: "It prettifies the agent Ah Lan. That dance scene is an egregious display of the bourgeois lifestyle. It distorts the image of the underground [party] agent. Made up, Commander Lei looks more like the enemy than the enemy."[53] When supervising the production of revolutionary cinema, Jiang Qing always ensured correct viewer identification with the heroes rather than the villains. Sensitive to cinematic suturing in continuity editing that privileged certain points of view over others, she became outraged at a rough cut of a scene from *Taking Tiger Mountain by Strategy*, in which a high-angle extreme long shot of the guerrilla hero followed a medium close-up of the bandits: "You are letting the enemies hold dictatorship over the hero rather than vice versa—are your butts sitting on the side of the enemy?"[54] Applying Jiang Qing's theory of the "three prominences" (三突出)—foregrounding the main hero over other heroic figures, positive characters over everyone else—the model revolutionary works often shone a bright, reddish spotlight on the front-facing hero, meanwhile casting a dim and bluish light on diminutive enemies, seen sideways on the margins of the frame. As the model revolutionary works modeled behavior, they eliminated the ambiguity of characters and fluidity of identification in the spy thrillers of the Seventeen Years.

Another popular counterespionage film denounced by Jiang Qing was *Visitors on Ice Mountain* (冰山上的来客) (1963). The film's multiethnic cast and crew included a Nanai scriptwriter, a Han director and composer, a Tajik consultant, as well as Mongol, Manchu, Hui, Uyghur and Kazak actors.⁵⁵ Set in Xinjiang in 1951, the film's protagonist Amir, a young Tajik soldier in the PLA, believes to have found his long-lost childhood sweetheart Gulandam, but when she fails to respond to their shared favorite song, he realizes that this young woman is actually an enemy agent. Since *Visitors on Ice Mountain* featured the PLA defending the nation's borders, many schools organized viewings for their students. When asked to share their "thoughts and feelings after viewing" (观后感) with their classes, students usually cited the martyrdom of a sentinel who froze to death while guarding his post during a snowstorm, vowing to emulate his revolutionary spirit (figure 6.5 left).⁵⁶ Yet beyond prescriptive reception in public, what more likely resonated with the audience was the film's theme song, "Why Are the Flowers So Red," repeated three times in the diegesis and masterfully tying together its intricate plot:

花儿为什么这样红？为什么这样红？
哎 红得好像，红得好像燃烧的火
它象征著纯洁的友谊和爱情
花儿为什么这样鲜？为什么这样鲜？
哎 鲜得使人，鲜得使人不忍离去
它是用青春的血液染红

Why are the flowers so red? Why so red?
Hey so red just like, just like a burning flame

FIGURE 6.5 Stills from the film *Visitors on Ice Mountain* (1963).

It symbolizes the purity of friendship and love.
Why are the flowers so fresh? Why so fresh?
So fresh that, people could not bear to leave.
It is irrigated with the blood of youth.

While the musical composition was inspired by Tajik folk songs, the lyrics tie together revolution and love, as youthful blood can refer to both martyrdom and romance. The song went viral via the radio, the loudspeakers, and the lips of even those who had never seen the film.[57] A viewer recalled it as the first love song he had ever heard in public: "Its lyricism and melancholy presented an astonishing contrast with the militaristic marches of struggle and triumph. Appearing with the song was a beautiful, mysterious Eurasian woman named Gulandam, who lifted her veil to cast a penetrating gaze to the soldier protagonist and audience" (figure 6.5 right).[58] For many Han audiences, the film's ethnic minority characters and landscapes blended with its minor notes, chords, and themes, which went against the main melody of the time. Condemning the song for making its listeners "droop their heads" instead of "clenching their fists," articles in *People's Music* noted how young people humming the song with intoxication on trams or in public parks was "incongruous with the nation's vigorous fighting spirit."[59] A discussion in *China Youth Daily* considered the song's "unstable ornamentation" to have a "weeping effect," for its "melodic turns and twists complicate the sparse lyrics so as to sound lingering and arduous."[60] A critic for *Film Art* faulted *Visitors on Ice Mountain* for its "excessive pursuit of a bizarre and twisted storyline"—the surprising revelation of the villain who pretends to be the heroine's benefactor is no more than a "fun enigma," thereby failing to make the audience shudder with hatred.[61] Jiang Qing criticized the film for "lacking the leadership of the party, exaggerating the role of the individual, and neglecting political work. The platoon leader directs the battle with his flute and uses the songs to detect the agent. The score is soft and obscene throughout, and its love songs cover Manchukuo's songs." Jiang Qing further indicted the film's scriptwriter Wu Baixin (乌白辛) (1920–1966) for having worked under the "puppet state of Manchukuo," an accusation that led to his suicide.[62]

With this onslaught of denunciation, *Visitors on Ice Mountain* disappeared from the exhibition circuit in the Cultural Revolution, but its musical memories persisted with audiences. A young woman whose father was persecuted as a "traitor" and "capitalist roader" would sing a musical interlude from the film, "Snow Lotus on Ice Mountain," with other "five black element" children as they were banished to toil in a tilery:

眼泪会使玉石更白，痛苦使人意志更坚 ...
我是戈壁滩上的流沙，任凭风暴啊把我带到地角天边

Tears will further bleach the jade
Suffering will harden the human will . . .
I am the quicksand on the Gobi Desert
Let the storm bring me to the end of the earth.[63]

Guerrilla audiences appropriated lyrical moments from counterespionage films to express their own pain and suffering under the revolutionaries. This might account for the collective catharsis that greeted the rerelease of *Visitors on Ice Mountain* and other Seventeen Year productions after the Cultural Revolution.

REVOLUTIONARY HORROR AND REDEMPTION

A final category of Maoist guerrilla cinema features bitter redemptive melodramas that depict the horrors and sufferings in the "hell" of the Old Society and end with deus ex machina deliverance by Communist soldier-saviors. Two seminal films in this subgenre—*The White-Haired Girl* and *Serf*—were meant to move their audiences to shed tears of catharsis, to "speak bitterness," and to express gratitude to the party. While addressing and politicizing women and ethnic minorities, both films sought to expose religious worship and hypocritical sham and resorted to horror and ghost film aesthetics to appall their audiences. They thus built political religiosity on the ruins of indigenous beliefs, even while performative public responses camouflage hidden transcripts and subversive interpretations by guerrilla audiences.

When I asked projectionists and audiences, especially older women, for their most memorable films, they often mentioned *The White-Haired Girl*, which had multiple stage and screen versions from the 1940s to the 1970s. Feminist scholar Meng Yue tracked the changing image and sexuality of the eponymous protagonist from the original folktale to opera to film to ballet, finding its story of gender oppression to have been displaced by class oppression.[64] Others examined the film's demonization and caricature of the evil landlord as well as the actor's villain stardom.[65] Religion scholar Xiaofei Kang argued that the story owes its original popularity to folk-religious elements, yet propaganda workers adapted it into an antisuperstition narrative only "to build a new faith" in the CCP as a new embodiment of heavenly justice.[66] In the 1950 film's most powerful indictment of traditional religion and morality, the evil landlord sneaks up on Xi'er while she is lighting a candle at the altar of the family's Buddhist worship hall. As he proceeds to rape her, the camera pans up to the crossboards overhead reading "Mercy and Compassion" as well as "House of Accumulating Goodness."

Whereas the opera version of *The White-Haired Girl* in 1946 helped establish and consolidate the ritual of "speaking bitterness" in areas "liberated" by the CCP, the release of the 1950 film coincided with nationwide land reform.[67] When the film first screened at its filming location, the villagers were reportedly excited to see themselves and the land that then belonged to them. In scenes portraying peasant suffering, some "cursed angrily and others cried inconsolably—they forgot that they were watching a film and instead recalled the landlords' exploitation."[68] In this exemplary account, the screen became a mirror that invited complete identification, and mistaking the film for reality was not mocked as bumpkin naiveté but valorized as proof of the film's authenticity. Along those lines, there are reports of militia members firing shots at the screen or of villagers who poked knives into the screen upon the appearance of the villain Huang Shiren.[69] According to former work-team members, the very invocation of Huang "heated up" the hatred of the masses and intensified their struggle against local landlords, such that activists who came forth later became cadres. Local cadres thus praised cinema as more efficacious than guns for grassroots mobilization.[70]

Beyond the power of the film text, projectionists prescribed reception by mobilizing audience emotions into class exorcism. After interviewing local villagers, a Guangdong movie team integrated their grievances into slideshows and folk songs before the screening and solicited audiences to speak bitterness afterward.[71] An all-female movie team in

Sichuan "collected facts about the local tyrant's crimes and the bitterest instances of peasant suffering" to integrate into their film introduction and plot summaries between reels. Clarifying the class represented by each character during the screening so the audience would "know whom to love and hate," the projectionist-narrator would lower the pitch of her voice when introducing the poor peasant Yang Bailao—the protagonist's father—and speak with loathing when introducing the landlord's mother.[72]

The projectionists' ventriloquism reached a new height by the mid-1960s, when *The White-Haired Girl* was rereleased alongside other new "emphasis films" to support the Socialist Education Movement.[73] "Although the landlord class has been overthrown," a projectionist lecture script states, "its ghostly spirit has not yet dissipated."[74] Projectionists thus served as shamans who conjured up those haunting ghosts of class enemies with "bitter films" to involve their audiences in collective exorcist rituals. According to a Qinghai projectionist, an old Muslim woman pointed to the landlord onscreen and said: "It was he who ruined my husband and daughter!" After the screening, she told her story and provided a "vivid and concrete lesson on class struggle for young people unfamiliar with past bitterness."[75] In a Zhejiang village, however, the bitterness testimonies collected and staged by a Four Cleanups work team often derailed into nostalgia for the landlords who worked alongside and shared meals with their tenants. Even the party secretary could not muster up a compelling account of class struggle. Nevertheless, as the movie team continued showing and the local propaganda troupe continued performing *The White-Haired Girl*, the children also enacted their revolutionary exorcism by throwing stones at the few former "landlords" and "rich peasants" in their village.[76]

Cinematic shamanism persisted into the 1970s with the growth of commune-run movie teams and villagebuster distribution of the model revolutionary films. A Hubei projectionist wrote a poem detailing a choreographed collective response to the ballet version of *The White-Haired Girl* in 1971:

大爹看见黄世仁的"文明"棍，摸着被地主打的旧鞭伤。
大婶看见喜儿的"卖身契"，想起雪夜卖儿走他乡。

炮声隆，军号响，八路军来到杨各庄，
斗地主，分田地，千年苦水全倒光！
多少人心随喜儿跳，银幕上下掌声响，
忆苦思甜激情涌呵！泪水滴湿新衣裳。
电影放完人不散，批林批孔摆战场 . . .
批判会越开越热火，愤怒吼声震山岗。

When Old Uncle saw Huang Shiren's "civilized walking stick,"
He caressed his scars from the landlord's whip.
When Auntie saw Xi'er's "body-selling contract"
She remembered selling her child on a snowy night.
A cannon fires, a bugle sounds,
The Eighth Route Army is here!
Struggle against landlords, divide up the land!
Pour out the bitter water accruing over a thousand years,
How many hearts jump and dance with Xi'er
How many hands clap on and off screen.
Recall past bitterness and think of today's sweetness
Tears drop and soak new clothes
After the movie, the crowd doesn't dissipate
Get ready to criticize Lin Biao and Confucius . . .
The criticism meeting heats up like a flame,
Raging roar thunders through the hills.[77]

In such prescriptive reception, the film's sights and sounds evoked visceral memories of pain and catharsis through synesthesia and guided the hearts, hands, tears, and voices off-screen. Its revolutionary spirit mediumship thus crossed diegetic and extra-diegetic spaces and conflated past, present, and future. With such on- and off-screen resonances, *The White-Haired Girl* in its many versions served as a script for exorcist rituals of class struggle in successive campaigns for nearly three decades.

Notably, official accounts of *The White-Haired Girl*'s reception emphasized its special resonance with rural women. During land reform, a Guangdong movie team reported that "backward and fainthearted women became bold and active" as they vowed to "avenge Xi'er."[78] After a screening in rural Guangxi, a former maid spoke up: "I used to think some landlords are good, but after seeing *The White-Haired Girl*, I realized that all crows are equally black, and a dog cannot help eating shit. Landlords everywhere have black hearts."[79] Similarly moved by the film, a woman in rural Chongqing denounced her uncle in a literacy class, exposed his whereabouts, and testified to his former bandit activities.[80]

These official accounts made me wonder how such gendered reception mapped onto women's cinematic memories. During my fieldwork in rural Hubei and Zhejiang in the 2010s, *The White-Haired Girl* was indeed the one film that always elicited a response from the older women I accosted. Otherwise reticent and impervious when questioned about their cinematic memories, those grannies, whose hands were always busy peeling corn or some other domestic chore, would pause, furrow their brows, and click their tongues as if to savor the film's bitterness; or to whisper to a daughter-in-law or neighbor: "She was raped." In these reminiscences, however, there was never any mention of a landlord or any other class enemy in those reminiscences. The film, instead, became a medium to channel whatever suffering they had known but had no means of expression.

Another classic bitter film to cultivate sympathy and hatred onward was the film *Serf* (1963). Set in Tibet in the 1950s, this film depicts the trials and tribulations of a boy named Jampa. After his parents were killed by the serf owner, Jampa grew up with his devout grandmother and had to act as a human horse for his master's child until his emancipation by the People's Liberation Army (fig. 6.6). This film served as a sensational and shocking illustration of official Chinese historiography on conditions in Tibet before 1959 as "theocratic feudal serfdom," a verdict discredited by Tibetan and Western scholars.[81] As late as 2019, however, the party's white paper on "Democratic Reform in Tibet" continued to rehash appalling stories of torture and violence in "Old Tibet," described as a "living hell" where "serfs were tortured and slaughtered at will to supply the upper class of the Kashag (cabinet) regime and high-ranking monks with such horrible offerings as human head, skin, flesh, heart, and intestines, which were considered 'necessary' when chanting certain scriptures."[82]

The very production of *Serf* was intended as a scathing attack on Tibetan Buddhism. Xia Chuan (夏川)—vice president of August First

FIGURE 6.6 Stills from the film *Serf* (1963).

Film Studio and former propaganda chief of the PLA troops that occupied Tibet in 1951—outlined three cultural approaches to religion: the first "conducts atheist propaganda and education to weaken religion's influence on the masses"; the second "consciously promotes religious superstition." A third approach presents "objective and naturalistic depiction" that risked "exhibiting with undue fascination" sacred art or exotic customs that would become "de facto propaganda for religion and superstition." For example, the film script for *Serf* described Jampa's hallucinations of a bodhisattva offering him food and of demons holding broken limbs based on temple murals that depict torture in hell: "Such 'hallucinations' can be difficult to distinguish from superstitions.... We must seriously consider their impact among ethnic minority audiences." Yet Xia Chuan was gratified to see the "paling of religious color" in the final film and praised its sharp yet subtle jabs at religion, showing how the devotion of Jampa's grandmother brought no blessing to her grandson and how the lama hid rifles inside the golden statue of a bodhisattva.[83] This last plot device likely borrowed from the film *The Bell Rings at the Old Temple* (古刹钟声) (1958), in which an old monk hides a radiotelegraphic transmitter behind a bodhisattva.

For many Han audiences, *Serf* was their first introduction to Tibet as an exotic, beautiful, and "barbaric" land.[84] Watching it with their schools, many recoiled from horror and shed tears of pity at the cruel treatment of its protagonist.[85] Some forgot the film's plot and characters and could recall only a haunting atmosphere: "Two heavy gates squeaked open, and the camera slowly tracked into the gloomy temple. Rows of candle flames fluttered on the altar. The wretched and hair-raising sound of a sonorous horn echoed in the dark movie theater."[86] A viewer from Kunming recalled watching *Serf* as a preliterate child, drifting in and out of sleep: "A horn's repressive dull sound kept waking me up, and I would open my eyes to tattered clothes and appalled countenances." This viewer further misremembered tongue-cutting and eye-gouging—threatened punishments never carried out in the diegesis—and concluded that *Serf* was a veritable "horror film" whose "exotic appeal far outweighed its ideological propaganda." Thereafter, many used the phrase "miserable as Jampa" to mean someone down on his luck.[87] My interviewees in Shanghai shared such horrific impressions and similarly misremembered scenes of flaying and mutilations.[88]

If the film *Serf* convinced Han audiences that Tibet before the PLA "liberation" in 1959 was a "living hell on earth," the film's reception by Tibetan audiences is much harder to assess.[89] A book companion to the film from 1965 reprinted twenty first-person testimonies from various newspapers and periodicals by "emancipated serfs." With titles such as "I was Jampa," "From Hell to Heaven," and "Where There is Oppression There is Resistance," these testimonies mirror Jampa's story with personal anecdotes of hunger, abuse, and torture by Tibetan landlords as well as salvation by the party.[90] Yet Tibetan historian Tsering Shakya recalled a very different reception of this film in Lhasa:

> Many of the local audience had watched [Director] Li Jun and his crew shooting the film; they also knew the actors and had heard stories that they were just following instructions and were not allowed to correct many of the inaccuracies in the film.... In one famous scene, Jampa is shown being beaten by monks after hunger had forced him to steal food left as an offering on a temple shrine. Lhasa people at the time saw this not so much as a moment of class oppression but as the karmic reward due to a sacrilegious thief. The film became known locally as *Jampa Torma Kuma* (*Jampa, the Offering Thief*): even today hardly any Tibetan uses the official title when referring to the film.[91]

Despite their contempt for the film's hero, Shakya recalled that "everyone in Tibet was supposed to watch the film and cry; in those days, if you did not cry, you risked being accused of harboring sympathy for the feudal landlords. So my mother and her friends would put tiger-balm under their eyes to make them water."[92] What film scholar Linda Williams dubbed the "body genre" of melodrama took on intense political implications and performative qualities during the Mao era when film audiences had to abide by what literary scholar Haiyan Lee called a "socialist grammar of feelings," a "monstrous marriage of the regime of theatricality with the regime of authenticity."[93]

Perhaps even more influential than the film *Serf* was its music and singer Tseten Drolma, a model "emancipated serf" whose renditions of revolutionary songs became, as one reminiscence put it, "the blood of the era, flowing with the pulse of the time."[94] Her voice reverberated into the new millennium by official fiat. When writer Woeser in 2012 revisited the Tibetan sites her father had photographed during the Cultural Revolution, she heard Tseten Drolma's voice singing over the loudspeakers:

喜马拉雅山再高也有顶
雅鲁藏布江再长也有源
藏族人民再苦啊再苦也有边啊

共产党来了苦变甜哟
共产党来了苦变甜哟

No matter how tall the Himalayas are, we will reach their summit,
No matter how long the Yarlung Tsangbo River is, we will find its source;
No matter how hard Tibetans' life has been,
The Communist Party came, bitterness is now sweet,
The Communist Party came, bitterness is now sweet.

According to Woeser, "it was the same 'red song' that had been adapted from Tibetan folk music and popularized during the Cultural Revolution: the words and music had not changed. It did not belong only to the past; it was still with us. The sense of temporal dislocation that I felt was absurd. It was deeply painful to realize, through such a small sign, that the Cultural Revolution had not finished."[95]

Over the socialist and postsocialist decades, revolutionary films centering on how communist soldiers liberated the people and vanquished class enemies achieved canonical status as "red classics" for several generations through widespread distribution, repeated screenings, as well as televisual broadcasts and remakes. As the most celebrated heroes of Maoist cinema, onscreen guerrilla fighters blurred the lines between soldiers and civilians and recruited grassroots Chinese audiences for various mass campaigns with war-like readiness. As a *cinema of conscription*, guerrilla war films instilled patriotic sentiment, militant discipline, a spirit of self-sacrifice, and a willingness to participate in state-sponsored violence. In an era of technological underdevelopment, guerrilla cinema also trained Chinese audiences to give the labor of their bodies to infrastructural construction and to use their eyes, ears, voices to constitute human-woven media networks, effectively demonstrating how to "build our new Great Wall"—as the Chinese national anthem puts it—"with our blood and flesh."

With the guidance of projectionists, guerrilla cinema activated guerrilla audience members to perform revolutionary (re)actions. The interplay of onscreen and off screen dynamics was crucial for Maoist cinema's revolutionary spirit mediumship and ritual efficacy. Yet far from powerless victims of ideological interpellation, guerrilla audiences both performed public transcripts and harbored hidden transcripts. With frequent disjunctions between intended and received meanings, guerrilla cinema's genre elasticity had to thank not only the savviness of the filmmakers to make propaganda popular but also the creative agency of the projectionists and audiences, who adopted guerrilla tactics in their cinematic reception. Ranging between the playful and the subversive, the guerrilla reception of cinema did not always mean conscious resistance to hegemonic messages; it also arose out of boredom, fatigue, attraction to a film's extra-ideological content or formal elements (such as its music or décor), or out of cinema's exhibition context. Guerrilla audiences used Maoist guerrilla tactics to evade, even subvert, the Communist Party's ideological control. They identified not only with the revolutionary heroes but also with their bourgeois enemies. Alternatively, audiences appropriated lyrical moments from bitter films to express their own pain and suffering under the revolutionaries. The next chapter will continue the discussion of the guerrilla reception of foreign films screened in socialist China.

CHAPTER SEVEN

Transcultural Guerrillas

The Reception of Foreign Films in Socialist China

Hollywood cinema was expelled from Chinese screens from the 1950s to the 1970s, yet thanks to cultural diplomacy with the Socialist bloc and nonaligned nations, Chinese audiences still had access to an impressive array of international cinema.[1] Apart from hundreds of Soviet films dubbed into Chinese, "film weeks" held in major cities showcased films from countries as diverse as Bulgaria, Czechoslovakia, Egypt, England, Hungary, India, Iraq, Italy, Japan, Mexico, and Poland.[2] Even during the Cultural Revolution decade, a popular saying captures the cosmopolitanism of the masses' cinematic diet: "Chinese films: documentary newsreels; Vietnamese films: planes and cannons; North Korean films: weep, weep, smile, smile; Romanian films: hugs and embraces; Albanian films: baffling and bizarre" (中国电影新闻简报，越南电影飞机大炮，朝鲜电影哭哭笑笑，罗马尼亚电影搂搂抱抱，阿尔巴尼亚电影莫名其妙).[3] The cultural Cold War thus both delimited and expanded the gamut of films on Chinese screens. Much as cinema was an important weapon in the ideological warfare, there was also considerable grassroots diversity and creativity in the reception of cinema intended as propaganda.

Whether we speak of subtitles or dubbing, we usually assume that something of the original film is lost in translation, but we can also follow writer Salman Rushdie's suggestion to look for what might also be "gained in translation."[4] What is gained, I suggest, lies with film reception, inseparable from specific exhibition conditions. Here "translation" refers not only to the linguistic translation of film dialogue, but also to the transcultural interpretation of ordinary audience members who bring their personal sentiments, cultural repertoires, and historical circumstances to bear on cinematic meanings. Whereas studies of transcultural cinema focused largely on the *filmmakers*' strategic borrowings from other cultures,[5] scholars have rarely delved into the creative agency of audiences in the work of transculturation—"the many different processes of [the texts'] assimilation, adaptation, rejection, parody, resistance, loss, and ultimately transformation."[6] I consider such audiences *transcultural guerrillas* who adapt foreign films to their national, local, or personal contexts, thereby enriching even the most formulaic texts with a multiplicity of *extra-filmic meanings*: audience-generated meanings that go beyond the intentions and repressions of a film's creators.

In his textbook guidelines for film interpretation, David Bordwell argued that we can construct four levels of meanings in any film: *referential* meaning draws on a spectator's prior knowledge of the real world; *explicit* meaning is often stated by a character to drive home a film's message; *implicit* meaning is usually thematic, symbolic, or allegorical, whereas *symptomatic* meaning is divulged "involuntarily" either as "the consequence of the artist's obsessions" or "traced to economic, political, or ideological processes."[7] These four layers of meaning are complicated in transcultural reception, since a film's referential meaning can get lost; its explicit message can be ignored or mocked; and audiences may construct implicit or symptomatic meanings based on their lived experiences. Rather than teasing out hidden meanings intrinsic to a film text, transcultural guerrillas make extra-filmic meanings through everyday appropriation and transmedial re-creation, thus giving multiple, even subversive intellectual, affective, and aesthetic afterlives to foreign cinema.

This chapter delves into the Chinese reception of four sets of foreign films chosen for their wide release and enduring influence, thereby lending themselves to diachronic analysis. I begin with two Soviet films—Mikhail Romm's biopics *Lenin in October* (Ленин в Октябре, 列宁在十月) (1937) and *Lenin in 1918* (Ленин в 1918 году, 列宁在一九一八) (1939)—because their reception in China lasted nearly four decades from the 1940s to the 1970s. The next two sections examine the Chinese reception of North Korean and Albanian films—with special focus on Ch'oe Ik-kyu's *The Flower Girl* (꽃파는 처녀, 卖花姑娘) (1972) and Gëzim

Erebara and Piro Milkani's *Victory Over Death (Ngadhënjim mbi vdekjen,* 宁死不屈) (1967)—which enchanted audiences with emotional and aesthetic elements unavailable in domestic productions. My last case study will be the evolving resonances of Raj Kapoor's *Awaara* (1951), as Chinese audiences reinterpreted the film through their experiences of mass campaigns from the mid-1950s to the late 1970s. Over the decades and in a variety of exhibition contexts, these foreign films turned into unexpected canonical classics for audiences in socialist China.

SOVIET FILMS FROM UTOPIAN MODEL TO PARODIC FOLKLORE

Prior to the Communist revolution, Chinese urban audiences watched foreign films with explanatory booklets, subtitles on lantern slides, or live interpretations through earphones in the best cinemas.[8] Linguistic barriers, literacy requirements, and expensive ticket prices limited audiences to those with economic means and cultural capital. Even elite audiences did not necessarily find foreign talkies intelligible but went in part to show off their social status.[9] While Hollywood occupied the lion's share of film imports, film scholar Xuelei Huang found that some Russian and Soviet films were also screened in Harbin, Shanghai, Hankou, Chongqing, Guangxi, and Xinjiang, often relying on the eroticism of female bodies to attract moviegoers even as intellectuals considered Soviet films "to counter the 'decadent' capitalist culture."[10]

In the Communist base area of Yan'an, Soviet cinema did not have to compete with Hollywood but provided the only film prints available to Mao's guerrilla army. Among the first films shown in Yan'an were two Lenin biopics that also screened in the United States and received a lukewarm review in the *New York Times*: "The Soviet film biography of Lenin begun so well last season with *Lenin in October* is threatening, in its second chapter, to degenerate (dramatically) into a minutiae-swamped personal and party history of almost exclusively partisan interest.... Except for a few sequences of vivid action—the downhill route of the White Army, the mob scene after Lenin's shooting—the film is uncommonly static, a sign that Director Mikhail Romm was more concerned with party duty than camera duty."[11] Although sneered at as humdrum propaganda in North America, these two Soviet films reportedly caused quite a stir in Yan'an when CCP Vice Chairman Zhou Enlai himself projected them, with live interpretation. According to the semifictional account by popular historian Ye Yonglie, a soldier asked after the screening: "When will we have our own films?" Mao, who was also in the audience, supposedly quoted from the movie, "'There will be bread.' We will have our own films" (figure 0.3).[12]

A decade after the screening of Soviet films in Yan'an, the CCP took over the nation's film industry, and Soviet cinema replaced Hollywood's dominance of Chinese screens.[13] From 1949 to 1957 more than four hundred Soviet films were dubbed in Chinese, a number exceeding the total Chinese domestic feature-film production of the 1950s decade. Paired with the expansion of film exhibition, this massive film-translation project launched an unprecedented encounter between Chinese grassroots audiences and foreign films. While Soviet films "provided socialist heroes and heroines through whom the Chinese could envision their future," many rural audiences had trouble with basic comprehension of the plot and characters. Many could not even tell which character was Lenin in the Lenin biopics—so projectionists had to provide explanations before, during, and after the screenings.[14] Since Northeast Film Studio dubbed many Soviet films in the 1950s, the northeastern accents of voice actors posed linguistic barriers for southern audiences, causing considerable pushback from private cinemas.[15] Sino-Soviet tensions reduced Soviet film imports, so that Stalinist classics were the only Soviet films still screened in China in the 1960s. Ironically, as Tina Mai Chen observed, "many of the same films shown in the 1950s under the byline 'The Soviet Union Is China's Tomorrow' now functioned to inspire . . . struggle against [Soviet] revisionism."[16]

In the Cultural Revolution decade, *Lenin in 1918* and *Lenin in October* became the only Soviet feature films openly and repeatedly screened to the Chinese public.[17] Writer Shi Tiesheng recalled how the rerelease of these biopics in 1969 coincided with the reopening of cinemas after a few years of closure:

> The shot from Aurora [that began the October Revolution] would sound again! People would watch them again and again (what else would they watch?), rehearse their lines again and again (humor after a long gap), appreciate the ballet sequence again and again

(beautiful short skirts and legs . . .), and hold our breaths to watch Vasily and his wife kiss again and again (this couple is really daring). This moment shook up the aesthetic position of Chinese nationals, scavenging for tenderness amidst fire and smoke, longing for romance amid stalwart hatred.[18]

Translator Lu Gusun (陆谷孙) recalled how Red Guards, inspired by the films' revolutionary heroism, would put their thumbs inside their vests during orations as they imitated the Bolshevik leader's speech to the proletariat masses in the closing scenes of *Lenin in October*.[19]

With repetition, however, the heroic could become the banal, and emulation could turn into parody. Instead of relaying the films' explicit messages, guerrilla audiences playfully quoted the film dialogues to imbue them with new meanings. For example, the line "there will be bread" refers to prerevolutionary hardship and postrevolutionary bounty in the film, but repeating the phrase in 1970s China became a wry commentary on the eternal postponement of socialist promises. Repeated screenings of the same films also facilitated the memorization of dialogue, as demonstrated in Jiang Wen's film *In the Heat of the Sun* (阳光灿烂的日子) (1994). During an open-air screening of *Lenin in 1918* in a military courtyard, audiences shout in unison, "Careful, it's poison," before the camera tilts up to the screen where a villain utters the same line, provoking roaring laughter from the crowd. The exhibition and reception context here radically transforms the meaning of the film text: from idealism into cynicism, from mystery into mockery (see figure 7.1 top).

Instead of Lenin's revolutionary heroism, however, the most frequently invoked scenes of *Lenin in 1918* in Chinese memories are a ballet performance of *Swan Lake* and an intimate exchange between Vasily and his wife. Both scenes conveyed essential plot information and were thus never cut out of the film, but following orders from their superiors, some projectionists placed their hands in front of projector lenses to shield off the dancers' bare legs and the close-up of a kiss. As a military projectionist recalled: "Every time I did this, audience members turned around and stared at me resentfully. As they imagined what was being blocked, sometimes I would open my fingers just a crack to grant them a few glimpses of the forbidden images."[20] Obstructing the images thus

FIGURE 7.1 Metacinematic references to *Lenin in 1918* and other foreign films in the film *In the Heat of the Sun* (1994).

had the opposite effect of enhancing their tantalizing eroticism. Moreover, even when audiences were denied the sight of the ballet, some rewatched *Lenin in 1918* again and again just to listen to Tchaikovsky.[21] With repeated screenings of this film in county seats and military headquarters, audiences often left the auditorium in droves after the *Swan Lake* scene and made a racket with their flapping seats.[22]

While deriving aesthetic and sensual pleasure from the Soviet biopics, Chinese audiences also assimilated them into local folk culture. After writer Mo Yan (莫言) saw *Lenin in 1918* at age sixteen, he wrote a plot summary to Shandong's Maoqiang opera tune: "Mr. Lenin faces an emergency. He dispatches people to find Vasily. There's a food shortage in the city. Go get some food from the country" (列宁同志很着急，城里粮食有问题。马上去找瓦西里，赶快下乡搞粮食).[23] What is gained through Mo Yan's "translation" is both irreverent humor and sardonic commentary on the urban extraction of rural resources under Chinese socialism. In 2011 performing artist Guo Degang (郭德纲) created a *xiangsheng* (comedic crosstalk) entitled *Lenin in 1918* about the plight during the Cultural Revolution of Ping opera performers who could no longer perform their traditional repertoire, so they remixed highlights from both Lenin biopics into a Ping aria by setting long Russian names to familiar Chinese operatic cadences to achieve farcical effect. As transcultural guerrillas who adapted the foreign to the native, the Ping opera troupe managed to sustain their livelihoods and their art form by giving it a revolutionary makeover. Thus screened in China from the 1940s to the 1970s, these Lenin biopics took on different connotations for their Chinese audiences over time: from a model for China's revolution to a target of playful parody, from a glimpse of Western culture to a subject of local folklore.

NORTH KOREAN MELODRAMA AND CHINESE CATHARSIS

Even though Soviet films constituted 49 percent of all translated cinema during the Seventeen Years, North Korean films came to dominate Chinese screens in the first half of the 1970s. Film historian Tan Hui categorized North Korean film imports into three genres: films about revolutionary struggle or guerrilla warfare, films about constructing a new society, and counterespionage thrillers.[24] However, we can also think about film genres beyond thematic content to focus on audience reactions. Taking a cue from the popular saying, "North Korean films, weep, weep, laugh, laugh," I argue that their vivid and expressive palette of emotions filled an affective and aesthetic gap in the Chinese media landscape.[25]

Let us begin with two North Korean comedies released in 1970 and 1971: *The Flourishing Village* (꽃피는 마을, 鲜花盛开的村庄) and *When We Pick Apples* (사과 딸 때, 摘苹果的时候). Both films showcased modernized agriculture with tractors and mechanized irrigation systems, much in contrast to the self-reliance of manual labor in the Dazhai documentaries discussed in chapter 3. Insofar as they worked with machines rather than toiled with their bodies, the North Korean farmers resembled factory workers for many Chinese viewers. The vibrant colors of nature and the harmonious human relationships within the communes also contrasted starkly with Cultural Revolution slogans to "struggle against heaven, against earth, and against people."[26] As the heroine of *When We Pick Apples* and her friends make applesauce out of a harvest surplus, one viewer commented, "The girls are beautiful and well-dressed; folks are catching and eating fish at the riverside; you even see a lazy bum napping under a tree ... that's real communism."[27] A subplot of *The Flourishing Village* features a stout and hardworking girl who earns six hundred work points a day. An elderly villager tries to persuade his son to marry her by saying: "You cannot grow rice out of a beautiful face." After the movie, "six hundred work points" became a new epithet for chubby and robust young women and politically sanctioned matchmaking.[28] With gentle humor and choral music coursing throughout, both North Korean comedies had a pastoral quality that touched Chinese audiences with "utopian sensibilities" attributed to the film musical by Richard Dyer: "an image of 'something better' to escape into, or something we want deeply that our day-to-day lives do not provide."[29]

The best-known North Korean film and the most sensational film release in 1970s China, however, was the musical melodrama *The Flower Girl*. As stated in the opening credits, the film is an adaptation of an opera script written by Kim Il-sung in the 1930s, and its production was overseen by Kim Jong-il.[30] Living under Japanese colonization, the eponymous "flower girl," Kkot-bun, sells flowers on the streets to help her sick mother and her little sister who was blinded by the landlord's wife. Since the landlord killed her father, Kkot-bun's only hope is the return of her imprisoned brother, a guerrilla fighter. Pictured on North Korean currency, the film's heroine served as a model of emulation for

North Korean farmers and factory workers,[31] but the film's appeal in China went far beyond its propaganda messages.

The Flower Girl was made in widescreen format, which, according to Kim Jong-il, allows fewer transitions between shots and a longer duration of shots to depict the psychological and emotional development of the characters.[32] To accommodate this new aspect ratio, cinemas and projection units throughout China broadened their screens and installed widescreen lenses, further enhancing the films' aesthetic appeal and technological hype.[33] A former projectionist in northern Manchuria recalled how his entire division had only one widescreen lens for a 35mm projector. Since the film copy of *Flower Girl* was in such high demand and had such a short rental period, the division headquarters dispatched a special jeep so that the movie team could screen the film at every regiment headquarters, with audiences packing auditoriums to twice or three times their usual capacity.[34] As discussed in chapter 4, overcrowding incidents because of *The Flower Girl* were reported throughout the country, often with fatalities.[35]

What made *The Flower Girl* such a sensation in China in the 1970s? "Sensation" here refers to both the passionate crowds that flocked to this film and to the feeling of "overwhelming pathos in the weepie."[36] As Ben Singer explicates, "Melodramatic excess is a question of the body, of physical responses. The term tearjerker underscores the idea that powerful sentiment is in fact a physical sensation."[37] There are many exaggerated stories about weeping for *The Flower Girl*, such as women's tears turning into icicles in the Northeast.[38] Some recalled fellow audience members who jumped up from their seats in tearful rage and waved their fists at the landlord's wife onscreen as she pushed over a cooking pot at Kkot-bun's sister and scorched her eyes, a scene made with all the aesthetic conventions of a horror film.[39] Another scene of the blind sister knocking over their mother's boiling medicine made a viewer collapse on the ground, such that the next morning her swollen eyes convinced all her friends that she had watched a great, bitter movie.[40] In each of these cases, tear-oozing eyes mimicked overboiling pots under a lid of repression.

Why did Chinese audiences cry? Following official prescription, schoolchildren wrote that the film reinforced a sense of international class solidarity: "The Korean people, like the Chinese people, are full of class revenge and national rancor. Crows everywhere are equally black"; "All over the world, the poor help the poor."[41] Similar to the account of tears by Tsering Shakya in the previous chapter, weeping for *The Flower Girl* was sometimes performative. A viewer from Beijing recalled that whoever did *not* cry at the movie might be considered lacking in political consciousness—her neighbor had watched it nine times and shed theatrical tears of class sympathy every time.[42] Yet Mo Yan offers another explanation: growing up in rural Shandong, he first heard about the weepie through the village loudspeakers and from a woman who had seen it in a nearby city. To earn a half-day vacation to see this movie in town, Mo Yan and two friends arose at dawn to collect dung. After lunch, they walked twenty-five kilometers to the county seat, only to learn that the movie tickets were sold out. They pleaded with a relative to pull some strings to get them three tickets. Walking happily into the cinema, they met exiting audiences who looked like "paper lanterns that had just weathered a storm." During the movie, the tears of young Mo Yan gushed out "when the sister was blinded.... Some people in the audience fainted, and when the villains are punished at the end, those in the cinema broke out in a round of applause."[43]

In hindsight, Mo Yan wondered why such a "formulaic, simplistic, and hackneyed" film could move so many Chinese to tears in the 1970s: "The Cultural Revolution had already been ongoing for seven years. For a very long time, people had not only lost their bodily freedom but also their emotional freedom. Moreover, the Lin Biao incident sank the Chinese into disappointment, despair, and revulsion. The only Chinese films screened were the model revolutionary works that were empty, didactic, otherworldly, and emotionless." By contrast, *The Flower Girl*'s lyrical and melancholic music, vibrant colors, the beautiful girl's desolate plight, and the "grand reunion" ending helped to "fill an emotional void of the Chinese people" and became an "outlet of their catharsis." Thus Mo Yan concluded: "We were not crying for the Flower Girl. We were crying for ourselves."

The memories of many Chinese audiences support Mo Yan's views. A blogger put it bluntly: "The flower girl had a bitter fate? But my mother's fate is even bitterer."[44] Another recalled her "shared plight" with the heroine: she lost her mother as a child, whereas her father was arrested as a counterrevolutionary, leaving her and her siblings to look after themselves.[45] A former sent-down youth speculated that if the film camera had turned to Chinese families that at the time were poor, sick, or oppressed, it would have found many tales that were even more tragic. Moreover, it was forbidden to sell flowers—at once a bourgeois good and a capitalist venture—in the Cultural Revolution.[46] Transculturating *The Flower Girl* into 1970s China, these audience members found as much pathos in the differences as in the similarities.

Besides emotional catharsis, *The Flower Girl* appealed to Chinese audiences also for aesthetic reasons. Many interviewees reminisced about its melodious songs that had circulated beyond the film via radio and printed song-books, whereas some others, such as my mother Wang Yaqing, appreciated its vivid colors and widescreen format; she even tried painting various shots from the film while attending an art college for "workers, peasants, and soldiers" (figure 7.2). Finding *The Flower Girl* less than impressive upon rewatching it in 2018, she reflected on the dearth of art books and other reproductions of masterpieces in the 1970s. As a result, cinema became a significant resource for art students

FIGURE 7.2 Painting frames from *The Flower Girl* by Wang Yaqing.

to experiment with composition and color and to hone their sketching skills and visual memories with impressionable scenes and beautiful vistas.[47]

Another kind of creative reproduction of *The Flower Girl* was fictionalized in Dai Sijie's novel and film *Balzac and the Little Chinese Seamstress* (小裁缝) (2002), in which a mountain village leader dispatches two sent-down youths to watch *The Flower Girl* in town and then recount its plot to the villagers. Their ingenious storytelling, embellished with alternative details from forbidden European novels they read, mesmerizes their listeners. Later, a girl from the village goes to see the movie, but finds the "oral cinema show" of *The Flower Girl* to be much better. Her disappointment with the actual film speaks to the disjunction between Mao-era film texts, which may seem dull to today's audiences, and the enchanted cinematic memories of the period, indebted to the imaginations of the films' historical audiences. It was the Chinese audience's "translation" of the North Korean films into the diversity and austerity of their own lives that turned them into influential classics.

ALBANIAN CINEMA AND WESTERN BOURGEOIS AESTHETICS

Dubbed a "socialist bright lamp in Europe," Albania became one of China's closest allies after the Sino-Soviet split. From 1956 to 1977, a total of twenty-eight Albanian films were translated and released in China.[48] Most of these featured antifascist guerrilla fighters during World War II and thus were akin to Chinese revolutionary cinema about guerrilla resistance. Yet their attraction to Chinese audiences in the 1970s often lay more with their "bourgeois" sentiments and aesthetics.

The earliest foreign film to be released during the Cultural Revolution was the Albanian film *Echo on the Seaside* (*Oshëtime në bregdet*, 1966, dubbed and released in China in 1967 as 海岸风雷). Set in a fishing village during World War II, the film featured a family with four sons: three who worked for the resistance and one who collaborated with the fascists. "The basic revolutionary message," as one viewer recalled, "was similar to Chinese revolutionary cinema, but we enjoyed its exotic backdrop and complicated plot."[49] Audiences liked to repeat the traitor's line—"As a fisher, I can't even afford to buy a rope to hang myself in my old age"—as well as lines used to condemn the traitor: "How could you be so degenerate?" The latter took on ironic overtones in an age of material scarcity. "On behalf of the People, I sentence you to death!" became a favorite line for guerrilla role-playing games.[50]

Other Chinese guerrilla audiences, however, derived a sentimental education from the film *Victory Over Death* (dubbed and released in China in 1969), featuring two young women resistance fighters imprisoned and tortured by the Gestapo; rather than betray their comrades, the heroines walk unflinchingly to their deaths. Interspersed between their arrest and execution are nine flashbacks, mostly depicting one of the female fighters' memories of her middle-school days and a chaste romance with a guerrilla leader. In the film's most beloved scene, the young couple sing a melancholic song accompanied by his guitar: "Let's go up the mountain, warriors. Let's join the guerrillas this spring." The revolutionary message in the lyrics dissolves in the young man's grainy baritone voice, while the heroine leans her head on his shoulder. The guitar, once considered a "bourgeois" and "hooligan" instrument at the start of the Cultural Revolution, regained legitimacy and popularity through this film.[51] This film's release in China also coincided with the sent-down youth movement to "go up to the mountains and down to the countryside," so the song lyrics also found special resonance with this cohort.[52]

Long after the Cultural Revolution was over, *Victory Over Death* remained so popular that Chinatown video-store owners in California recalled renting out the film on VHS and DVD well into the 2000s.[53] In Xiao Jiang's film *Electric Shadows* (梦影童年) (2005), the female protagonist is a cinephile who gets pregnant out of wedlock and goes into labor during an open-air screening of *Victory Over Death*. The film roused her to stand up for herself and stay in town even after the disappearance of her lover. Despite the contrived plotting, the sentiments in *Electric Shadows* align with other memoirs that recalled the courageous heroine as an inspiring idol for overcoming the adversities in their own lives (see figure 7.3).[54]

The reputation of Albanian films as "strange and bizarre," "without rhyme and reason," and "going back and forth" (莫名其妙，没头没脑，颠颠倒倒) refers to their nonlinear narrative structure and subtle visual storytelling. While the flashbacks in *Victory Over Death* were still anchored

FIGURE 7.3 Watching the Albanian film *Victory Over Death* in the film *Electric Shadows* (2005).

in one character, the film that confused a generation of Chinese was *The Eighth Is Bronze* (*I teti në bronx*, 1970, dubbed and released in China as 第八个是铜像 in 1973). Set in Nazi-occupied Albania between 1943 and 1944, the film shows flashbacks of seven guerrillas carrying a statue of their deceased comrade. The *Rashomon*-like structure perplexed many Chinese viewers used to classical, clear, and didactic revolutionary narratives. Poet Yi Sha recalled it as a "war film from my childhood, but . . . had no idea who was fighting against whom."[55] Other audiences speculated that the censors had cut out so many parts that the film no longer made sense. Whereas Chinese revolutionary model films imposed singular interpretations, *The Eighth Is Bronze* and other Albanian films were polysemic and ambiguous, introducing many audience members to avant-garde and modernist aesthetics such as stream-of-consciousness storytelling.[56]

Even if viewers failed to comprehend a film's plot or characters, they could still have aesthetic takeaways. After the screening of *The Eighth Is Bronze*, according to writer Chen Naishan (程乃珊), Shanghai women began knitting a black-and-white striped collar that decorated the film protagonist's wool coat, adding warmth and variation to their own winter outfits.[57] Since the Chinese often made their own clothes in the 1970s, they could easily add individuated fashionable touches.[58] The heroine's curly braids also inspired urban women to quietly reintroduce the perm, whereas another Albanian film, *Old Wounds* (*Plagë të vjetra*, 1968, dubbed and released in China in 1970 as 创伤) created a vogue for "Vera's Hairdo"—coiling long braids into a little hill on one's head.[59] A former audience of *Victory Over Death* recalled being most impressed by a pan across the interior of the protagonist's room with its elegant furniture, lamps, and decorations, as her family lived in a factory dormitory with little furnishing inside its bare walls.[60]

In 2017 the director of Albania's state-funded Institute for Communist Crimes planned to initiate legislation outlawing television broadcasts of Communist-era films, calling them "a massive brainwashing tool" and "an ethical and aesthetic catastrophe" for the younger generation.[61] He was clearly unaware that for millions in Chinese audiences during the Cultural Revolution, those films he wished to ban were the very antithesis of political propaganda, instead serving as a major outlet for romantic sentiments and an exclusive window to Western aesthetics, fashion, and style.

INDIAN FILM *AWAARA* AND EVOLVING CHINESE RESONANCES

In contrast to the many Soviet, North Korean, and Albanian film imports, only eight Indian films were dubbed and released in socialist

China. Translated as 流浪者 or *Vagabond*, *Awaara* stirred up immense emotional, intellectual, and aesthetic reverberations that lasted from the 1950s to the 1980s. Much has been written of the global reach of Indian films, which featured sympathetic protagonists, socially conscious melodrama, and light-hearted fantasy. For Soviet viewers, these films presented a welcome diversion from didactic domestic films about factory workers and war heroes.[62] For Nigeria's Hausa audiences, Indian films offered images of a "parallel modernity to the West, one intimately concerned with the changing basis of social life, but rooted in conservative cultural values."[63] *Awaara*'s masala mixture of comedy and pathos combined with its spectacular mise-en-scène and musical sequences, such that its catchy title song was "popular like a national anthem" in Turkey.[64] In no other country, however, did the reception of *Awaara* have such a longue durée as it did in the PRC, where the film's socialist critique over time became a critique of socialism.

Part of a broader cultural diplomacy between China and India, *Awaara* was screened alongside two other features in twenty Chinese cities during Indian Film Week in 1955. Around the same time, a delegation of Indian filmmakers visited China, among them the actor Prithviraj Kapoor, who played the father and judge in *Awaara* and whose real-life son Raj Kapoor directed the film and starred as the son-protagonist. Prithviraj Kapoor's photos with Mao and Zhou Enlai (figure 7.4) are prominently featured in the magazine *Mass Cinema*, which also commissioned an article by Raj Kapoor, who wrote: "*Awaara* is our small contribution to the creation of a good society that does not produce 'vagabonds'; I hope that the audience in China, rapidly advancing to a perfect socialist society, even though you do not need the revelations presented in the film, will nevertheless appreciate the main content and the moving conflict in the film."[65] In 1955 both the Indian filmmaker and Chinese audiences assumed that a "liberated China" had already solved the social inequalities represented in the film. Along these lines, Krista Van Fleit's compared *Awaara* to 1930s and 1940s left-wing Shanghai cinema that featured urban poverty and vagabonds, as both "engaged in constructing an alternative to the Western experience of modernity."[66] Yet *Awaara* also took on an unintended and unexpected afterlife through its Chinese reception in the next few decades.

FIGURE 7.4 A delegation of Indian filmmakers visits China in 1955 and meets with Chinese leaders. *Mass Cinema*, no. 21 (1955).

Awaara's first Chinese audiences were cultural bureaucrats who watched the film in censorship screenings and wrote articles to guide its reception in terms of "socialist brotherhood."[67] After its release in cinemas in two dozen Chinese cities, *Awaara* became a huge hit among students and intellectuals. Its theme song, known in Chinese as "The Vagabond's Ballad" (流浪者之歌), circulated via radio, gramophone records, and collective singing.[68] The film had fans among CCP leaders such as Hu Yaobang, whose daughter and her middle school classmates used to sing *Awaara*'s songs to accordion accompaniment.[69] Even then, official critics raised some alarm concerning the film's popularity. One cited confessions from juvenile delinquents who imitated the film's hero. Another argued that the Chinese cover of "The Vagabond's Ballad" turned "a song of remorseful indictment into a frivolous and flirtatious tune."[70] "The Vagabond's Ballad" also took on new extra-filmic

Transcultural Guerrillas 209

meanings with the changing Maoist political ecology. Poet Ai Qing (艾青), who first met his wife Gao Ying (高瑛) at a screening of *Awaara* in 1955, was condemned as a "Rightist" in 1957 and banished to Xinjiang in 1959. The couple heard "The Vagabond's Ballad" on the westward-bound train and reinterpreted it as a song of exile for the wrongly accused like themselves.[71]

Although *Awaara* was no longer playing in cinemas by the 1960s, memories of its tragic plot resonated anew with audiences who had suffered due to their "bad class backgrounds." In the film, what ruins the protagonist's life is his birth father's conviction that "the son of a judge will be a judge; the son of a thief will be a thief." This motto uncannily resembles the later "bloodline theory" distilled into a notorious Red Guard couplet of 1966: "If the father's a hero, the son's a great fellow; if the father's a reactionary, the son's a rotten egg" (老子英雄儿好汉，老子反动儿混蛋). The revolutionary model opera *The Red Lantern* put it more elegantly: "What sapling you plant determines what fruit it yields, what seed you sow determines what flower blooms" (栽什么树苗结什么果，撒什么种子开什么花). Yu Luoke (遇罗克), a Beijing worker who critiqued the bloodline theory in a series of essays in 1967, once recounted *Awaara*'s plot to his younger siblings and commented: "Who could have thought that such an absurd viewpoint, long criticized in foreign countries, is gaining ground in China today?"[72] The Indian film contributed to Yu's reflections on China's actually existing socialism that crystallized into an essay, "On Family Background" (出身论) (1967), a trenchant and widely circulating critique of the bloodline theory that a year later resulted in his arrest and execution.

After the Cultural Revolution, *Awaara* received a much wider rerelease in China. A sent-down youth who watched the film upon his return to Shanghai in 1979 recalled: "Even three-year-olds were singing its theme song on the streets. This film moved many of us to tears, especially those of us who had been denied educational or employment opportunities because of our less than 'red' class backgrounds."[73] A comedic crosstalk piece entitled "The Fate of the Vagabond" (1978) touched on various registers of the Indian film's appeal: Performer A starts singing "The Vagabond's Ballad" and encourages Performer B to dance along, telling him that "you have to move all your joints to Indian music so that it stimulates blood circulation, helps the muscles to relax, clears the mind, and helps digestion." Performer A, however, recounts how the song made him think of his mother, a "victim of fascist dictatorship" like the mother of the film protagonist. In the Cultural Revolution, she was denounced as a spy because of a distant relative in Taiwan: her second aunt's mother-in-law's niece's husband's brother-in-law. If the Gang of Four had not fallen, he would have been labeled "Little Spy" and sentenced to twenty years in prison. No beautiful Rita would have waited for him, since the bloodline theory would doom their children's future.[74] This hypothetical transplantation of the Indian film's plot thus served as a salient commentary on various injustices during the Cultural Revolution.

By the early 1980s *Awaara* had become popular among a younger generation who grew their hair long or got it permed, wore bell bottom pants, and blasted the "Vagabond's Ballad" from their cassette players. As many sent-down youths returned from the countryside and tried to find a place for themselves in urban society, what struck the greatest chord was the protagonist's futile attempts to find employment.[75] The theme of vagabond youth also echoed through the works of celebrated filmmaker Jia Zhangke (贾樟柯). His first feature film, *Pickpocket* (小武) (1997), centers on a thief who finds innocence and redemption through romantic love, whereas his second film, *Platform* (站台) (2000), an epic chronicle of a small-town performance troupe, paid explicit tribute to *Awaara* by showing the young protagonists going on a date to see the film. As the musical sequence "Vagabond's Ballad" plays onscreen, the loudspeaker calls out the young woman from the audience. It turns out that her father, a policeman, does not want his daughter to go to the movies with a young man who is so much like the vagabond in the movie. Jia Zhangke emphasized the influence this Hindi film had on him at the Mumbai Film Festival in 2016: "I loved the Hindi film *Awaara* as a child. Now I am also an 'awaara' in the film world and shall continue to wander into the future"[76]

Jia Zhangke was not the only contemporary Chinese filmmaker to pay homage to the foreign films he had watched in his youth. As noted, memories of many films discussed in this chapter are staged as metacinema in works such as Jiang Wen's *In the Heat of the Sun*, Dai Sijie's *Balzac and the Little Chinese Seamstress*, and Xiao Jiang's *Electric*

Shadows. The frequent appearance of cinema itself in Chinese domestic features of the 1990s and 2000s serves as a kind of elegy for cinema "imbued with nostalgia for a lost golden age."[77] In postsocialist China, foreign films took on aesthetic afterlives in the creative responses of their audiences and exerted more diverse and enduring impact than in their countries of origin.

In his conceptualization of national cinema, Andrew Higson called for "an exhibition-led, or consumption-based, approach" that would include foreign films screened in a domestic context.[78] Studies of transnational cinemas have also paid increasing attention to films that cross national borders with an overwhelming focus on diasporic and intercultural filmmakers, coproductions, and international film festivals.[79] Yet cinematic border-crossing and transcultural meaning-making happened not only at the elite level of directors and producers, curators and critics, but also at the grassroots level of exhibitors and audiences. The transnational exhibition and reception can add rich ambiguities and poignant afterlives to popular and propagandistic film texts. Such an audience-centered methodology also broadens the field of "Chinese cinema" to include "cinema in China" with all its cosmopolitan connections.[80]

Analyzing literary exchanges and influences between the PRC and other socialist countries from 1945 to 1965, Nicolai Volland defined "socialist cosmopolitanism" as "a set of attitudes and practices that appreciates a shared yet diverse socialist culture and promotes transnational circulation across the socialist world."[81] In the cinematic universe, the transnational circulation of films from China's "socialist brothers" also shared utopian models and represented class struggle, but Chinese audiences often appreciated foreign films precisely for their differences from the domestic fare. More than film texts, the reception contexts helped generate humor, irony, and pathos. These guerrilla audiences share the memory of a Spartan cultural life: either having no films to watch for months on end or watching the same films again and again, which drew their attention to formal elements unrelated to the films' ideological messages. Audiences actively, creatively, and sometimes subversively poached everyday witticisms, political lessons, emotional catharsis, fashion tips, and hidden pleasures from even the most didactic texts. These films thus constituted the unintended cultural canon anchoring the structure of feelings and collective memories of several generations.

Finally, the rejection of Hollywood and the import of foreign films, complemented by the state-sponsored expansion of the exhibition network, made it possible for national cinemas as "unknown" and "minor" as North Korean and Albanian cinema to find a mainstream, even mass audience in China. Digging out an old notebook that logged all the films he watched in his adolescence, Shanghai cinephile Ye Zhiguang (叶智广) compared the media ecology of the 1960s to that of the new millennium:

> My family should be considered ordinary working class, with all six of us living on my father's 80-yuan monthly salary.... In 1962, I watched 125 films, about one film every three days, [of which] 91 films (or 72 percent) were foreign movies from the Soviet Union, Czechoslovakia, Hungary, Poland, Romania, Bulgaria, East Germany, England, France, West Germany, Spain, Norway, Finland, Argentina, Colombia, Mexico, Korea, Cambodia, Thailand, and Egypt.... [Let us compare all those choices to] today's ever more luxurious environment, ever bigger screens, ever more advanced technology, ever louder and flashier publicity, and ever more astronomical figures in the remuneration of stars. Yet audiences eating popcorn and sipping Coke face these pale, anemic films. Is this progress or retrogression? Are we living in the best of times or the worst of times?[82]

Ye Zhiguang's experiences, however, cannot speak for all grassroots audiences, as his Shanghai citizenship gave him privileged access to various international "film weeks" never held beyond the metropolises.[83] Although also screened in the countryside, the Soviet, North Korean, Albanian, and Indian films discussed in this chapter were popular mainly with sent-down youths and left little impression on rural villagers interviewed for this book. For example, when I chatted with about a dozen older people before a county movie theater in Zhejiang, none of them had heard of *Lenin in 1918*—one former village teacher thought I meant the refrain "9–18" from the song "On the Songhua River," lamenting Japan's invasion of Manchuria on September 18, 1931. Villagers from

Ningxia named *Shanggan Ridge*, a Chinese film about the Korean War, and *Doctor Bethune* (白求恩大夫) (1964), a Chinese biopic of the Canadian doctor who supported Chinese Communist troops, as the only "foreign films" they had seen.[84] A former projectionist in rural Hubei recalled that villagers only went to foreign films to "watch hot noise," suggesting that they neither understood nor cared much about the content.[85] Such apathy, even antipathy, toward foreign films persisted into the present day, as a digital projectionist in rural Zhejiang said his mostly older audiences would protest at the sight of any foreigners onscreen, so he showed only Chinese films. Transcultural guerrillas were thus more urban than rural, a distinction that also holds true for the next chapter, on the exhibition and reception of "poisonous weed cinema."

CHAPTER EIGHT

Poisonous Weeds and Censorship as Exorcism

In his adolescent years, literary scholar Chen Sihe (陈思和) often walked several miles with his middle school classmates from their industrial neighborhood to the Shanghai city center, where the major movie theaters were located, using their bus fare to buy plum juice or popsicles. Chen's mother worked as a telephone operator for a work unit that distributed tickets to "poisonous weed films" (毒草影片)—those films that Mao's wife Jiang Qing and her radical allies had condemned as reactionary and revisionist.[1] Part of a nationwide cinematic vaccination campaign that began in 1964 and climaxed in 1968, the "criticism screenings" Chen attended were meant to expose and expel the "ox-demons and snake-spirits" (牛鬼蛇神) that had been haunting the socialist screen before the Cultural Revolution. Public exposure was also a form of inoculation, as poisonous weed films were labeled "living specimens of revisionist thought" whose sugar-coated toxins replaced class struggle with humanist feelings. (Re)screening them was meant to "open the eyes" of the masses, sharpen their "political sense of smell," and increase their "intellectual immunity."[2] For Chen's generation, however, those poisonous weed films were eye-opening in a different way, creating a channel for "receiving culture in an environment of cultural destruction."[3]

This final chapter on Maoist cinema's spirit mediumship discusses the exhibition and reception of poisonous weed films before and during the Cultural Revolution. Shifting attention from propaganda to criticism,

I propose to reconceptualize Maoist censorship as exorcism, in which cinema served as poison and medicine, cause and symptom, illness and prescription, epidemic and vaccination. First appearing in Mao's speeches in the spring of 1957, "poisonous weeds" and "ox-demons and snake-spirits" went on to become the most potent curses for designating problematic cultural expressions and enemies of the people in the Cultural Revolution. With agricultural, pharmacological, and religious roots and resonances, these keywords, along with "spiritual opium" (精神鸦片), were at the center of a hygienic and demonological discourse undergirding Chinese mass movements, whereby the stage and the screen became the most symptomatic sites of ills and cures, haunting and exorcism, pollution and cleanliness. Indeed, those collective and participatory rituals of mass criticism against poisonous weed films helped the masses discern the counterrevolutionary in their everyday lives and functioned as incantatory exorcism to clean the revolutionary air of demonic pestilences.

Poisonous weeds, ox-demons and snake-spirits, and spiritual opium also find felicitous synthesis in the ancient Greek term *pharmakon*, which brings together the meanings of poison, remedy, and scapegoat—"that which pertains to an attack of demonic possession or is used as a curative against such an attack."[4] With the source term denoting "drug," pharmakon might be an herb, a drink, a lotion, a perfume, a pigment, a spell, or a charm that had the "perception-altering powers of *intoxication*."[5] Pharmakon took on philosophical analogues as speech, writing, and painting that mesmerized their audiences.[6] In "Plato's Pharmacy," philosopher Jacques Derrida unpacks the multivalence and ambivalence of writing as pharmakon, whereas Bernard Stiegler discusses all technology and technicity as pharmakon, an inescapable poison with curative potential.[7] While informed by this European intellectual genealogy, I am interested not so much in applying existing theories of pharmakon to media history in China but rather in excavating some parallel Maoist *prescriptive theories*—theory as top-down cultural policy and as pharmacological prescriptions to address the people's spiritual health. Inspired by Derrida's examination of "Plato's Pharmacy," I shall parse some of the ingredients and concoctions of "(Madame) Mao's Pharmacy" in which poisonous weed films helped disseminate Maoist cultural logic and practice to the masses.

This chapter begins by tracing the etymologies and usages of *poisonous weeds* and *ox-demons and snake-spirits* to develop a new theory of Maoist censorship that is more exposure than disappearance, more sound than silence. The next section brings weeds and demons together in an evolving understanding of cinema as "spiritual opium" from the 1930s to the 1970s, with a focus on Jiang Qing, who used cinema as a sedative for her nerves and banned films as an opiate for the people. I zero in on Jiang Qing's critical exorcism of poisonous weed films from 1964 to 1968 as well as on exhibition practices associated with the exposure and criticism of dozens of films, such as denunciatory voiceovers, pamphlets, and other forms of disinfection and incantation. Yet this mass campaign of cinematic vaccination often had the unintended effect of (re)infecting audiences.

POISONOUS WEEDS

While the word *du* (毒) is the modern Chinese equivalent for poison, it was defined in the first-century canonical dictionary, *Shuowen jiezi* (说文解字), as "thickness" (厚) associated with a harmful grass that grows luxuriantly. In medieval Chinese medicine, as medical historian Yan Liu showed, *du* had the core meaning of potency—"the power not just to harm as a poison but also to cure as a medicine." With dosage control and drug combination, Chinese doctors deployed toxic substances strategically for therapeutic purposes so that the saying "use poison to attack poison" (以毒攻毒) has persisted to this day.[8] The term *ducao* came into currency in the sixteenth century to designate a category of potent herbs in the celebrated pharmacopoeia *Systematic Materia Medica* (本草纲目) (1596), compiled by the doctor Li Shizhen (李时珍) (1518–1593). Following the legendary Divine Farmer (Shennong 神农), who "tasted hundreds of herbs," Li traveled extensively to gain firsthand experience with various local medicines. His pharmacopoeia characterized each drug as having or lacking *du*, which "indicated that a substance must be treated with caution, that it was potent, and that it ought to be used in moderation."[9] In his later speeches, Mao commended Li Shizhen for "going up to the mountains to pick medicine," thus learning from the literal grassroots.[10] In 1956 Shanghai Film Studio produced the biopic *Li Shizhen* to celebrate the doctor's odyssey to compile a medical encyclopedia that truly "served the people." The film dramatizes distinctions between healing and toxic herbs, "useful" practical knowledge and "useless" Confucian classics, scientific methods and Daoist alchemy.[11] *Li Shizhen* played in cinemas in spring 1957, when Mao first elaborated on the difficulties of distinguishing "poisonous weeds" from "fragrant flowers": "Often, correct and good things were first regarded not as fragrant flowers but as poisonous weeds," so that "a period of trial is often needed to determine whether something is right or wrong." Mao grafted onto this dialectic of flowers and weeds a more modern medical logic: "Fighting against wrong ideas is like being vaccinated—a person develops greater immunity from disease as a result of vaccination."[12]

Besides traditional Chinese medicine and modern Western vaccination, Mao's distinction between fragrant flowers and poisonous weeds drew on what Geremie Barmé called a "gardening impulse," obsessed with "setting apart useful elements destined to live and thrive from harmful and morbid ones, which ought to be exterminated."[13] In 1938 Mao likened China to "Prospect Garden" (大观园), the setting of the classic novel *The Dream of the Red Chamber*, and asked writers and journalists "to get off the horse and look at the flowers [up close]" to understand China's complex sociopolitical topography.[14] In 1951 he calligraphed "Weed Out the Old So That the New May Flourish, Let a Hundred Flowers Bloom" (推陈出新, 百花齐放) as an inscription for the National Academy of Chinese Theatre Arts. The children's film *Flowers of the Motherland* (祖国的花朵) (1955), set in Beijing's garden parks, was formative for what later became the Red Guard generation.[15] In sum, flowers refer to the literature, arts, theater, culture, and education as well as the children, youth, actors, and intellectuals—everyone was cultivated and cultivating in a socialist garden.

As the Hundred Flowers Movement garnered growing criticism of the CCP in the spring of 1957, Mao launched the Anti-Rightist Campaign by circulating an article among party cadres entitled "Things Are Beginning to Change": "As we expected and hoped, poisonous weeds have been growing side by side with fragrant flowers and ghosts and monsters appearing together with the unicorn and phoenix.... Why is such a torrent of reactionary, vicious statements being allowed to appear in the press? To let the people have some idea of these poisonous weeds and toxic fumes so as to have them uprooted or dispelled."[16] In a July 1 editorial in *People's Daily*, Mao further explained his shifting strategy with an agricultural metaphor: "Only when poisonous weeds are allowed to sprout from the soil can they be uprooted. Don't the peasants weed several times a year? Besides, uprooted weeds can be used as manure."[17]

Mao's dialectic of fragrant flowers and poisonous weeds advanced a horticultural and pharmacological conception of literature, art, and thought. The idea was not only to interdict particular authors and works but to teach the masses to become censors and self-censors. Rather than withdrawing poisonous weeds from circulation altogether, he suggested exposing small doses to the masses as quasi-vaccination against wrong ideas. Mao's call for the detection and extermination of poisonous weeds had immediate ramifications on the mass denunciations of half a million "Rightists" in 1957.[18] First used to refer to spoken or written dissent, the notion of poisonous weeds and their mass criticism would expand to all cultural realms by the mid-1960s. As a mass medium, cinema was meant to sharpen the masses' senses against "bourgeois" or "revisionist" thoughts and feelings stirred by poisonous weeds. Their immunological defenses would grow even stronger with the introduction of an exorcist logic of censorship that appropriates time-honored folk demonology.

THE DEMON-EXPOSING MIRROR: CENSORSHIP AND EXORCISM

Together with poisonous weeds, Mao's speeches in the spring of 1957 introduced the concept, or curse, of "ox-demons and snake-spirits" (*niugui sheshen* 牛鬼蛇神, with the character *gui* 鬼 translatable into "ghosts" or "demons").[19] Rooted in Buddhist demonology, the compound word first appeared in a preface written by the Tang dynasty poet Du Mu (杜牧) (803–852) to praise the fantastic supernatural world of Li He's (李贺) poetry.[20] Mao first used the term in a March 1957 speech to refer to popular "ghost plays" in traditional operas: "I don't approve of ox-demons and snake-spirits. Let them be performed so we can criticize them.... There are plenty of ox-demons and snake-spirits in society! Not all Chinese people believe in ghosts, and there is nothing to fear about such performances. Many young people do not know what ox-demons and snake spirits are, so they should watch some of these for educational purposes."²¹ As Mao's conceptual slippage between ghosts onstage and ghosts in society suggests, ghost operas help audiences see—indeed, see *through*—the ghosts and demons in their lives.²² Thus art could enhance the critical faculty of the masses, a view reminiscent of the cultural theorist Siegfried Kracauer's valorization of cinema as "the mirror of the prevailing society," capable of "expos[ing] disintegration instead of masking it."²³ Meanwhile, Chinese critics used the classical expression "using history as a mirror for the present" (以史为鉴) to defend onstage ghosts and spirits as possible reflections of class struggle. Protected by such reasoning, ghost plays and other "feudal remnants" of traditional opera remained popular and would not be banned until 1963.²⁴

Beyond the arts as a mirror of society and the past as a mirror of the present, CCP leaders likened class analysis to the folkloric demon-deflecting mirror (照妖镜), which was "to reflect the real appearance of a noxious spirit, ghost, or wraith. The true mien of the spirit thus revealed would also scare the specter away."²⁵ Although the revolutionaries dismantled the custom of placing a mirror in front of one's home as superstition, party leaders appropriated the metaphor to refer to Marxism-Leninism: "In the hands of the fighting Chinese people, [Marxism-Leninism] is like a demon-deflecting mirror that shines through all smokescreens and disguises to strip the enemies naked and expose their ferocious true shapes, so that they can become the targets of ten-thousand crossbows from the Chinese people."²⁶ The demons exposed by this magical mirror first referred to the KMT and the Americans, but starting in the mid-1950s, they applied increasingly to domestic campaign targets including "Hu Feng elements" in 1955 and "Rightists" in 1957.²⁷ Critics of the party were exposed, denounced, and exiled to purify the ranks of the revolutionary masses—practices reminiscent of the ancient Greek *pharmakos* rite of sacrificing scapegoats and expelling them from the city.²⁸

Maoist censorship treated the arts as symptoms of social ills and resorted to exorcist healing techniques that exposed the demons to the masses to exterminate them. In a discussion of the press, theater, and cinema in April 1957, Mao called for letting "ox-demons and snake-spirits come out to make some noise," because "the masses want to see them."²⁹ In the next few months, Mao condemned Rightists as ox-demons and snake-spirits; by letting them "air their views freely ... the people, now shocked to find these ugly things still existing in the world, would take action to wipe them out."[30] A *People's Daily* article in 1958 elucidated "ox-demons and snake-spirits" with classical novels such as *Journey to the West* (西游记) (1592) and reminded the readers of the power of the demon-deflecting mirror: "As a folk saying has it: an evil deity cannot meet an upright deity . . . if you ask who has seen real ox-demons and snake-spirits, then recall the wind from last spring that blew them into the open. Later people exposed their original forms on stage as *One Hundred Portraits of Ugly Rightists*."[31] In conversations with foreign diplomats in 1959, Mao compared imperialists worldwide to ghosts and demons and called for the compilation of *Stories About Not Being Afraid of Ghosts* (不怕鬼的故事) (1959).[32] Instead of taking the rational, secular, and "scientific" position on the nonexistence of ghosts, he insinuated the omnipresence of demons for the masses to combat.

Mao's talk of ghosts in 1959 could not be disassociated from the tens of millions of hungry ghosts who died during the Great Leap Famine (1959–1961), which also inspired widely circulating ghost stories.[33] Seeking to reestablish faith in socialism after the famine, the Socialist Education Movement launched a campaign against "superstitions" from ghost stories to religious practices. While formally banning ghosts and spirits from the stage and screen, state-sponsored rituals to "recall bitterness" conjured up countless ghosts from the "Old Society" through multisensory mass media and collective rituals.[34] My informants who came of age in the 1950s and 1960s recalled school trips to see socialist education films and exhibitions with vivid images and sculptures depicting a horrific past before their births. Also memorable were nauseating "remembering bitterness meals" (忆苦饭) accompanied by dolorous songs on the loudspeakers or stirring testimonies by older peasants and workers to their trials and tribulations under evil landlords and capitalists. As these "spirit mediums" became possessed by the ghosts of the prerevolutionary past, their young audiences also wept tears of sympathy and gratitude to the party. Along these lines, Mao spoke of the Socialist Education Campaign as being particularly efficacious (灵) at "lifting the lid on class struggle in the countryside" and "exposing the ox-demons and snake-spirits that sabotage socialism."[35]

Maoist antisuperstition films often exposed rumored ghosts as victims forced to go underground or spies hiding to avoid arrest. Yet, as

Laikwan Pang pointed out, such films "tread a thin line between the ghost story and the anti-ghost story: in their condemnation of spiritualism they chimed with the ideology of the CCP, but what usually attracted the audience was not the lessons learned by the film's end but the depictions of the supernatural at the beginning."[36] I further argue that Maoist cinema often depicted the "hell of the Old Society" with ghost film aesthetics to enhance an exorcist fervor. Even the documentary *Rent Collection Courtyard* (1966) turned a landlord's house into a haunted house with horror cinema's chiaroscuro lighting and ominous sound effects as well as a mise-en-scène of a water dungeon and clay statues inspired by City God Temple arhats.[37]

Such exorcist fervor reached a feverish pitch during the Cultural Revolution with the omnipresent slogan "Sweep Away All Ox-Demons and Snake-Spirits," often illustrated in Red Guard art with a broom that also served as a prop or weapon of spirit mediums. Literary scholar Wang Yi likened various Cultural Revolution practices to witchcraft (巫术) when words are deployed like magic spells.[38] Similarly, Barend J. Ter Haar argued for an understanding of the Cultural Revolution's violence through a "demonological paradigm" by comparing Red Guards to "divine soldiers charged with an exorcist task" and struggle sessions and parades of political targets to festival processions in popular religion.[39]

Censorship and exorcism converged under the banner of "Great Criticism" (大批判), which was more exposure than disappearance, more sound than silence. Great Criticism reinvented medieval Daoist and Buddhist associations of incantation (咒) with interdiction (禁), which together referred to exorcist healing rituals that relied on the power of words to eliminate malevolent demons that caused pestilence. The eighth-century Tang court even had a Department of Incantation to combat epidemics.[40] In the Cultural Revolution, vehement incantations against enemies of the people were chanted at struggle sessions, printed in newspapers, and calligraphed onto big-character posters, which the *People's Daily* praised as "devil-deflecting mirrors that reveal all monsters and demons."[41] The divine light of Mao as the "red sun" supposedly gave his words and images talismanic power to shine through all "poisonous mist and delusional dust" and penetrate all disguises so that "ox-demons and snake-spirits would reveal their ugly true shapes."[42]

Maoist censorship was further enhanced through the spirit mediumship of modern audiovisual technologies. Loudspeakers contributed to the soundscape of pandemonium, and film screenings became sites of phantasmagoria. Rather than association with science and rationality, audiovisual media rendered socialist China's "demons" visible and audible so as to dispel them with the light and spell of sacred images and texts. In mid-1960s China, the master censor-exorcist of the stage and screen was none other than Mao's wife, Jiang Qing (figures 8.1 and 8.2). In the campaigns she helped to launch, opera and cinema were at once targets and weapons of attack, at once the demons and the "demon-exposing mirror." Not only censoring individual films, Jiang Qing's exorcist crusade was also a hygiene campaign against what she believed to be a polluted mediasphere, whereby cinema's poison was particularly pervasive and analogous to opium.

FIGURE 8.1 Propaganda poster of Jiang Qing around 1967: "Let Socialist New Culture Occupy All Stages!" Bridgeman Images.

FIGURE 8.2 Jiang Qing addressing the Red Guards on March 19, 1969. Bridgeman Images.

CINEMA AS OPIUM IN MADAME MAO'S PHARMACY

In 1843, a year after the first Opium War, Karl Marx declared religion "the opium of the people." Since opium addiction was rampant in China, many intellectuals also saw their countrymen as sick not only in body but also in spirit. Writer Lu Xun best articulated such a view in his "Preface to *A Call to Arms*" (1923), recounting an anecdote from 1906 about seeing apathetic Chinese spectators of a compatriot's beheading in a lantern slide projection in his Japanese medical school classroom: "After this film I felt that medical science was not so important after all. The people of a weak and backward country, however strong and healthy they may be, can only serve to be made examples of, or to witness such futile spectacles.... The most important thing, therefore, was to change their spirit, and since at that time I felt that literature was the best means to this end, I determined to promote a literary movement." Lu Xun's "Preface" then used the famous parable of the iron house to explain how literature was to change the national spirit—by sensitizing the numb and awakening the lethargic: "Imagine an iron house without windows, absolutely indestructible, with many people fast asleep inside who will soon die of suffocation. But you know since they will die in their sleep, they will not feel the pain of death. Now if you cry aloud to wake a few of the lighter sleepers, making those unfortunate few suffer the agony of irrevocable death, do you think you are doing them a good turn?"[43]

Lu Xun's epiphany to take up literature instead of medicine to heal spirits rather than bodies is reminiscent of Plato's understanding of the philosopher as the moral physician who diagnoses and treats not only somatic ill health but also the "disease of the soul."[44] Although Lu Xun never used the term "spiritual opium," his call to arms against apathy and complacency reverberated through later Maoist discourses against the narcotic influences of poisonous weeds.

Also in the 1920s, Siegfried Kracauer described the modern cinemagoer as someone whose spirit "squats as a fake Chinaman in a fake opium den."[45] Soviet filmmaker Dziga Vertov condemned the "toxic sweetness of artistic drama and its kisses, sighs and murders" as the "opium of the people": "Under the electric narcotic of the movie theaters, the more or less starving proletariat, the jobless, unclenched its iron fist and unwittingly submitted to the corrupting influence of the master's cinema." Vertov interjected his treatise with slogans: "Against film-sorcery. Against film-mystification!" "Down with the immortal kings and queens of the screen! Long live the ordinary mortal, filmed in life at his daily tasks."[46]

Although Jiang Qing probably had not read Vertov, she would later also denounce poisonous weed cinema as opium and sorcery, haunted by "emperors, generals, ministers, gifted scholars, and beautiful ladies."[47] These ideas may be indebted to Shanghai's left-wing critics from the 1930s, including her former husband Tang Na (唐纳), who accused American cinema of "narcosis, deception, sermon, and seduction."[48] A decade before Bertolt Brecht dubbed Hollywood as "the very center of world drug-trafficking," Shanghai critic Wang Chenwu (王尘无) published an article in 1932 entitled "Down with All Hallucinogens and Poison, Cinema Should Become Nourishment for the Masses," criticizing American cinema for "using wine and women, song and dance to numb and intoxicate the people's consciousness," so that they "forget the times, the society, the classes."[49]

After 1949 CCP cultural bureaucrats began a systematic attack against American "screen-opium" alongside antidrug campaigns, and a ban on American films became part of the "Resist U.S., Aid Korea" war effort. While calculating the profits Hollywood studios "cheated out of China," critics attacked their "immersive and corrosive poisoning of our people's spirit."[50] If American cinema was "a cocktail of poison," the most toxic substance was the "stimulation of the senses—its dexterous use of color, sound, gestures, and music so that art degenerates into nicotine and alcohol."[51] Peking University professor Miao Langshan (缪朗山) wrote an "ode" to American culture as "a poisonous flower growing on a rotten garbage hill," whose "narcotic venom drizzles everywhere." The poem accused American warmongers of exporting lethal cultural commodities alongside poison gas and biological weapons to spread fascist germs.[52] Meanwhile, just as Vertov considered newsreels an antidote to sober audiences, China's cultural censors replaced Hollywood's "spiritual opium" with "healthy" Soviet imports and new domestic productions to "awaken" the people to devote themselves to socialist construction.[53]

Once American films were expelled from China, film censorship turned to domestic productions, beginning with the campaign against *The Life of Wu Xun* (武训传) (1950), a biopic of a philanthropist who begged to raise funds for free schools in the final days of the Qing dynasty. The film was well received at first and praised by General Zhu De and Premier Zhou Enlai, but after Jiang Qing brought it to Mao's attention, his criticism appeared as an anonymous editorial in *People's Daily*. Referring to the Opium Wars as "an era of great struggle against foreign aggressors and domestic reactionary rulers," Mao condemned the film's protagonist for "not lift[ing] a finger against the feudal economic base or its superstructure; on the contrary, he strove fanatically to spread feudal culture."[54] His editorial further criticized the film's positive reception as the "loss of critical faculties" and "capitulation to reactionary ideas." Not only analyzing the film per se, Mao saw its popularity as a *symptom* of the broader social psychology, an interpretive strategy remarkably similar to later Western ideological film criticism.[55] Yet *People's Daily* was not a forum for academic debates, but rather a platform to launch a mass campaign. As deputy director of the Film Guidance Committee that evaluated all movie projects from 1949 to 1951, Jiang Qing led an investigation team to Wu Xun's home county to collect oral "testimonies" from local peasants on the man's "greed and evil doings."[56]

Due to illness for the remainder of the 1950s, Jiang Qing retreated from her official position at the Film Bureau, but—according to Mao's physician Li Zhisui (李志绥)—"watched movies incessantly—morning, afternoon, and evening... as a treatment for her neurasthenia." She asked her personal physician to screen films as a treatment against insomnia and "accused him of mental torture" when she disliked his selections. Jiang Qing often watched *Gone with the Wind*, "all the while deriding it as propaganda for the Southern slave system and accusing those of us who openly enjoyed the movie of being 'stinking counter-revolutionaries.'"[57] After recovering from cervical cancer in 1957, Jiang Qing continued to believe she was ill, even though her doctors believed her to be in good physical health, so they recommended movies, music, photography, theatre, and concerts as therapy. Li Zhisui also recalled her acute reactions to all kinds of sensory stimuli:

> She was afraid of bright lights and ordered her nurses to pull down the shades to keep out the sun. But she wanted fresh air, so she ordered the windows open. When the windows were open, she hated the draft. When they were closed it was too stuffy. The slightest noise, even the rustle of her attendants' clothes, drove her to distraction, and she was constantly yelling at them about the noise they made when they moved. She was bothered by color. Pinks and browns were especially troublesome. They hurt her eyes. She had everything in her residence—walls and furniture alike—painted a pale light green.[58]

Although not entirely reliable, Li Zhisui's account suggests conflicting paradigms for understanding illness and healing between the doctors and Jiang Qing. Whereas the physicians held onto an ontological view of illness "as a concrete agent located at a specific site of the body," Jiang Qing was far more concerned with her sensory functions and sensory environment, effectively subscribing to a functional conception of illness as "discordance between the body and the cosmos."[59] Her secretary Yang Yinlu (杨银禄) provided collaborating testimony to Jiang Qing's cinephilia and cinephobia, her hypersensitivities and fastidiousness. According to Yang, well into the 1960s and 1970s, Jiang Qing often watched films into the wee hours of the morning before she would retreat to bed with sleeping pills.[60]

While these memoirs portray cinema as Jiang Qing's addiction, therapy, and placebo, Jiang Qing herself connected her illness with the performing arts and the spiritual health of the nation in a November 1966 speech to "comrades in the field of literature and arts." Following her doctors' advice to "spend more time on my cultural life" to "improve hearing and vision weakened by illness," she claimed to have gained "a relatively systematic perception of the state of our literature and arts" and wondered why there were "ghost plays on the stage of socialist China." All those "emperors, generals, ministers, gifted scholars, and beautiful ladies" onstage produced a "foul air" and "repugnant atmosphere" that favored the past over the present, the foreign over the native, the dead over the living. She then condemned imperialism as "capitalism in its death throes, parasitic and rotten," incapable of producing new works beyond stagnant classics. She summarized modern Western arts—"hooligan dance, jazz, striptease, impressionism, symbolism, abstract expressionism, animalism, modernism"—as "decadent and obscene, poisoning, and paralyzing the people."[61]

This speech moved from Jiang Qing's private illness to a broader diagnosis of a toxic atmosphere haunted by the ghostly, the dead, the rotten, the foreign, and the parasitic. Her narrative proceeded from vision and hearing to smell and taste, from a numbing of the senses to a sharpening of the senses, and then again from stimulants to paralysis. Adopting a militant mode of cinephobia,[62] Jiang Qing concluded with a call to arms: "Amidst the Great Proletarian Cultural Revolution, we have to fight with culture rather than with violence. Don't beat people up. Militant struggle can only touch the skin and flesh, whereas literature and arts can touch the soul."[63] Offering a succinct answer to the question "What is cultural about the Cultural Revolution?" this speech highlights the connections between Jiang Qing's own medical history and her pharmacological understandings of the arts as poisonous weed or opium.

With the Cultural Revolution, Jiang Qing transformed from a patient to a doctor who—emulating Shennong's and Li Shizhen's pharmacology—used her own sense perceptions to diagnose nationwide (feudal/bourgeois) pestilences and to prescribe (revolutionary) remedies. "Madame Mao's

Pharmacy" parses the ingredients of poisonous weed films and later remixes them into revolutionary model opera films. Noting how Plato used *pharmakon* to refer to artificial colors, dye, and perfume, Derrida extrapolated that "the magic of writing and painting is like a cosmetic concealing the dead under the appearance of the living."[64] Jiang Qing's sensitivity to color, sound, and smell similarly highlighted her vigilance against death and its masking in decadent, feudal, and imperialist arts and culture, whose remnants concentrated in the "big dyeing vat of Shanghai."[65]

CRITICISM SCREENINGS OF POISONOUS WEED FILMS

Dubbed a "flagbearer" (旗手) of the Cultural Revolution, Jiang Qing waved a flag that was at once the flag of the military avant-garde, a major prop of revolutionary model opera, and above all the movie screen, a major site of *exposure* in two senses: exposure to the toxins of poisonous weeds aiming at inoculation and exposure of "demons" aiming at exorcism. Led by Jiang Qing, the condemnation of poisonous weed films starting in 1964 already marked, as Paul Clark put it, "the opening salvoes of the Cultural Revolution" because "the film audience ... became a political audience for the radicals' messages."[66]

At her first public speech at a Peking Opera convention in June 1964, Jiang Qing condemned China's 2,800 regional opera troupes for their glorification of "emperors, kings, generals and ministers, scholars and beauties, ox-demons and snake-demons."[67] At the convention's closing ceremony, her political ally Kang Sheng criticized a number of films for their bourgeois humanism, sentimentalism and "middle characters" who were neither heroes nor villains. The Propaganda Department selected two criticized films, *Jiangnan in the North* (北国江南) (1963) and *Early Spring in February* (早春二月) (1964), for screening in major cities to stimulate criticism in newspapers to raise the audiences' "ideological consciousness and discerning abilities." In August Mao added that criticism screenings of these films should be expanded to "expose these revisionist materials to the public."[68]

For the remainder of 1964, Jiang Qing often headed to the Film Bureau to watch films, some still in production, and called the Propaganda Department to voice her condemnation of this or that film.

A director recalled those days: "Every morning, you had to watch the weather and identify the wind direction. Often a sneeze from high up could mean a force 8 wind down here."[69] By the end of the year, Jiang Qing labeled ten more films as poisonous weeds, but the Cultural Ministry winnowed the list down to two: *The Lin Family Shop* (林家铺子) (1959) and *City Without Night* (不夜城) (1957). "Criticism screenings" were followed by hundreds of newspaper criticisms.[70] In January 1965 Jiang Qing instructed the Shanghai Municipal Party Committee not to revise the criticized films before screening: "Don't obscure their ugliness, let them be exposed to broad daylight so as to receive thorough criticism."[71] Criticism screenings were supposed to recycle poisonous weeds as manure to achieve an "ideological and economic double harvest."[72] Meanwhile, she proposed revolutionary changes to film production: replace "capitalist director-centrism" (资产阶级的导演中心制) with "party-led democratic centralism" (党的民主集中制): gather the creative team in discussion and collect their best proposals for the director to execute.[73]

How should audiences receive poisonous weed films? An advice book for youth in 1965 had a chapter entitled "Take a Sniff," which warned readers against "beautiful characters, bizarre storylines, and honeyed words" that seek to "lead you by the nose." The author quoted Lu Xun: "Does reading them numb you, or make things clearer? Do they leave you feeling dazed, or do they accentuate what you feel?" Similarly for literature and film: "Does the work clarify your brain so you know who is the enemy and rouse your spirit so you join the struggle? Or does it make you apathetic and lethargic?" The chapter concluded that poisonous weeds can be excellent pedagogical tools by providing negative examples.[74] Citing a conversation with a young friend who decided to read fewer books to avoid encountering poisonous weeds, another article in *People's Daily* urged readers not to "stop eating for fear of choking" and concluded: "If you don't go watch *Early Spring in February*, how can you spot its toxicity and improve your critical faculties?"[75]

In February 1966 Jiang Qing hosted a "forum on artistic work in the armed forces" with army officers, thanks to Lin Biao's sponsorship. Over two weeks, they read and discussed Mao's writings, watched dozens of films and a few plays, and met with the cast and crew of an ongoing film production, finally concluding that a "black line" of bourgeois thought had reigned over the arts since the PRC's founding. The officers synthesized Jiang Qing's comments into a summary that would be widely disseminated to guide the Cultural Revolution.[76] Between April 8 and June 11, Jiang Qing presided over an All-Army Artistic Creation Conference in Beijing with more than two hundred representatives to watch sixty-eight domestic and twelve foreign films. Approving of only seven as conforming to Mao Zedong Thought, Jiang Qing categorized the remaining films as (1) "antiparty, antisocialist poisonous weeds," (2) propagating the wrong line and rehabilitating counterrevolutionaries, (3) uglifying army cadres and depicting heterosexual romance, and (4) focusing on middle characters.[77]

Despite these crude categories, Jiang Qing's snappy comments on individual films were often trenchant, as discussed in chapter 6 regarding counterespionage thrillers. Not only keenly observant of moving images, she was sharply attuned to the soundtrack, often calling the film music "unhealthy," "soft," "smacking of human feeling," or "full of petit bourgeois sentiment." She considered the film music in *Five Heroes on Langya Mountain* (狼牙山五壮士) (1958) "funeral dirges" to lament the cruelties of war and accused *The Cuckoo Sings Again* (布谷鸟又叫了) (1958) and *Visitors on Ice Mountain* (冰山上的来客) (1963) of "cloning yellow music" from the Republican era. She peppered her film criticism with musical keywords, using song (*ge* 歌) in conjunction with *gesong* (歌颂) (praise or extol), *qu* (曲) (music or melody, also meaning bend) in the compound *waiqu* (歪曲) (distort), and *diao* (调) (tune), as in *qingdiao* (情调) (sentiments), to refer to some films' petit bourgeois overtones.

While using her eyes and ears, Jiang Qing further took an olfactory and gustatory approach to cinema, catching a "whiff of *Butterfly Lovers* (梁山伯与祝英台)" in *Adolescence in the Flames of War* (战火中的青春) (1959), condemning *Revolutionary Family* (革命家庭) (1961) and *The Story of Liubao* (柳堡的故事) (1957) for "reeking of personal sentiments" (人情味) and having aesthetics that leave an "aftertaste" (后味). She found films depicting PLA struggles against bandits, such as *Snow in the Forest* (林海雪原) (1960) and *Independent Brigade* (独立大队) (1964), to "reek of banditry."[78] Sensitivity to the smell (气) and taste (味) of films harkens back to Li Shizhen's pharmacology. The purpose of criticism was to bring out the "stench" (臭) so people wouldn't mistake poisonous weeds for fragrant flowers.

On April 23, 1966, *PLA Daily* published an extensive film criticism under the pen name Gao Ju (高炬) (literally, "high torch" and a homonym with "uphold"), rumored to be Jiang Qing's writing group. Accusing the film *Besieged City* (兵临城下) (1963) of "taking the enemy's standpoint to promote bourgeois humanism," the article called this film "a dose of toxin that paralyzes the revolutionary will"; hence it was "necessary to cut through its deception and engage in thorough criticism."[79] Similar articles accused the "feudal loyalty" (气节) in *Peach Blossom Fan* (桃花扇) (1963) and the begging for charity in *The Life of Wu Xun* as "spiritual opium that eroded the revolutionary will and reinforced the reactionary regime."[80] Rather than an "accidental phenomenon," Jiang Qing and her entourage of critics considered every poisonous weed film symptomatic of the Zeitgeist. For example, *Besieged City*'s "adaptation from the stage to the screen took place against acute international and domestic class struggle," whereby "ox-demons and snake-spirits took advantage of our nation's temporary economic hardships to rouse an antiparty, antisocialist demonic wind. In this political climate, a large number of poisonous and bad works on the literary and artistic fronts emerged."[81]

CRITICISM SCREENINGS AND CINEMATIC INOCULATION

Not only censoring individual films, Madame Mao modeled a critical methodology for the rest of the country. From mid-1966 to the end of 1968, the film distribution and exhibition network "publicly exposed" about a dozen poisonous weed films to hundreds of millions of audiences.[82] These "living specimens of revisionist thought" were meant to "open the eyes" of the masses, sharpen their "political sense of smell," and increase their "intellectual immunity."[83] This cinematic vaccination campaign took place in movie theaters as well as in the courtyards and auditoriums of schools, factories, and work units that distributed tickets to their members. Meanwhile, crowds teemed before such criticism-screening venues, seeking to buy, sell, or exchange tickets.[84] Prior to every "criticism screening," the Shanghai Film Bureau collected and reprinted the screenplays, their literary sources, and all relevant film criticism as internal publications for writing groups.[85] Red Guard groups created special criticism bulletins as "preventive disinfection"

(预防消毒), drew caricatures, and prepared lantern slides to highlight the films' "most lethal and reactionary essence."[86] Each dose of a poisonous weed film was accompanied by a piercing voiceover that criticized the film before, during, and after the screening. Many received assignments to write criticism essays and disseminated them through big-character posters, local loudspeaker broadcasts, and Red Guard tabloids.[87]

Serving as the pharmacopoeia for this cinematic vaccination campaign were newspapers, periodicals, pamphlets, and books with titles such as *400 Poisonous Weed Films with Major Mistakes* and *Criticism of Poisonous Weed Films: Wherein Lies the Poison of Forty Films?* The latter book's preamble refers to the "cultural battlefront" of the seventeen years as "a *danse macabre* of demons" and "an overgrowth of poisonous weeds," whereby "cinema became a propaganda tool of counterrevolutionary restoration." The book called for using Mao Zedong Thought as a weapon to "cleanse the leaking poison from the depths of our souls" and to "thoroughly criticize the reactionary ideas in poisonous-weed films until they fall and stink."[88] Its table of contents resembled a series of slogans introducing struggle sessions: "Ferret out XXX reactionary films for criticism," followed by a list of five to nine titles. The films are thus grouped as culprits of similar crimes for exhibition and exposure to the public.

The exhibition of poisonous weed films was sometimes spectacularly combined with struggle sessions. Live targets, amplified voices, and audience participation enhanced the theatricality of screenings, while film images and sounds made the "ox-demons and snake-spirits" on stage even more spectral. Prior to a Shanghai screening of the film *City Without Night* (1957), for example, there was first a struggle session of its starring actor Sun Daolin (孙道临).[89] More commonly, viewers recall a live acousmatic commentary over the loudspeakers. An extant script for criticizing the film *Indignant Tide* (怒潮) (1962) includes slurs, curses, and rude language, such as "Pooh-pooh!" (呸) and "Shut up!" (住口).[90] At a screening of *Liu Shaoqi Visits Indonesia* (刘少奇访问印度尼西亚) (1963) organized by her middle school, my mother recalled a male voice speaking Mandarin with a heavy Shanghainese accent, cursing every time Liu Shaoqi's wife Wang Guangmei appeared: "Look, that stinky bitch" (看，这个臭婆娘).[91] Another viewer from Beijing remembered watching the same documentary with not only a denunciatory voiceover but also

FIGURE 8.3 Graphic of a booklet to criticize poisonous weed films, depicting Liu Shaoqi as a snake with a film reel as its body.

Liu's and Wang's faces manually crossed out on the celluloid.[92] When watching the film *Sorrows of the Forbidden City* (清宫秘史) (1948), a viewer recalled how the voiceover sneered at the death of the Manchu princess to undo a moment of pathos. Sometimes planted members of the audience stood up and shouted slogans, and the projectionist would pause the film for audiences to take center stage in the exorcist ritual.[93]

GUERRILLA AUDIENCES OF INFECTIOUS CINEMA

Despite attempts to patrol the meanings of poisonous weed films, huge gaps opened between intention and reception. After all, what moved audiences was often precisely the films' censured "humanistic sentiment." In Beijing, Xie Jin's *Two Stage Sisters* (舞台姐妹) (1964) was screened 2,674 times to 2.75 million viewers. Many shed tears and wanted to watch it again. Indeed, a female worker from No. 3 Wool Factory was particularly sympathetic to the "middle character."⁹⁴ In Shanghai, female cotton workers organized to watch *Two Stage Sisters* were told to fold their arms in front of them to maintain a critical posture, but audiences still couldn't help weeping out loud.⁹⁵

Nearly all retrospective accounts of poisonous weed screenings suggest that they had the opposite effects than the authorities' intentions, instead inspiring "guerrilla reception." For some young people, such films ironically made the Cultural Revolution an age of enlightenment. As Chen Sihe recalled, many of the poisonous weed films were literary adaptations, so he would afterward search out the novels on which they were based: "I became a lover of literature through cinema, which concentrated China's most talented writers, directors, and actors."⁹⁶ For this generation, school closures provided unprecedented time and freedom to read banned books and to watch poisonous weed films that provided them with an alternative sentimental education. Films featuring stars from the Republican era gave rise to intergenerational conversations. Despite Chen Sihe's dislike of the protagonist in *The Life of Wu Xun*, his elders were fans of the actor Zhao Dan (赵丹) and gossiped about his quick wit at his own struggle session. After watching *Sorrows of the Forbidden City*, his mother, uncle, and grandfather reminisced nostalgically about the "golden voice" of actress Zhou Xuan (周璇). Yet what Chen found most memorable in this film was a scene from the Boxer riots, with a bare-chested "big brother" leading a crowd shouting mumbo-jumbo and fighting its way through a civilian alley. For him, the scene evoked the street brawls of various Red Guard factions and planted a distaste for such mob violence.⁹⁷

Multiple memoirs and interviewees mentioned the poisonous weed film *Indignant Tide*, criticized in 1967 as a veiled celebration of the disgraced general Peng Dehuai, especially its musical interlude, a song of farewell condemned as "a tune to summon back Peng Dehuai's spirit" (彭德怀的招魂曲).⁹⁸ One former Red Guard responsible for producing revolutionary big-character posters for her school could pick up free movie tickets at the cinema, so she sneaked into several criticism screenings of *Indignant Tide*. The song's instrumental prelude served as a cue for the rebel to begin his husky and crude voiceover over the loudspeakers, yet she remained mesmerized by the singer's baritone voice.⁹⁹ Two interviewees in Shanghai recalled how, in the darkness of the auditorium, some began to sing along. The sing-along became louder and bolder as more in the audience joined in. The loudspeaker barked to stop the singing but could not find the instigator camouflaged by the crowd.[100]

To counter such infectious film songs, Xinhua News Agency reported an exemplary incident at the Mudanjiang train station in March 1968. One day, the railway workers heard a blind man playing on his flute the theme song "Sunny Sky in Autumn" (九九艳阳天) from the film *The Story of Liubao*. The tune transported the workers back to the era before the Cultural Revolution, when the waiting room was painted a pastel turquoise and decorated with large landscape paintings. The kiosk rented out comic books depicting scholars and beauties. The broadcasting station played "soft, venom-seeping songs" so as to turn this public space into a "bourgeois dyeing vat." During a shift-changing meeting, these revolutionary railway workers lined up before a Mao portrait, studied Jiang Qing's speeches, and mobilized the passengers and passersby into a criticism parade. Thereafter the loudspeakers always broadcast Mao quotation songs to greet all trains entering the station.[101]

In other peripheral parts of the country, poisonous weed films met with unintended and carnivalesque reception. In the winter of 1968 a sent-down youth walked into a county cinema in Inner Mongolia. The film being screened turned out to be *Liu Shaoqi Visits Indonesia*, which he had seen in Beijing a year earlier when the original soundtrack had been drowned out by a live denunciation over the loudspeaker, leading the audience to shout denunciations. In the grasslands, by contrast, the audience seemed altogether oblivious of Liu's downfall and clapped every time he appeared in a close-up, while the exotic tropical landscape onscreen contrasted with the cold snowy fields outside.[102] The same film met with an altogether different reception in Henan's mountains. After seeing First Lady Wang Guangmei changing her dress several times in the film, villagers began fantasizing about her other "bourgeois extravagances," such as frying pancakes next to her bed. Caricatures of Liu with a big nose and of Wang with necklaces the size of ping-pong balls filled big-character posters, and the brigade revolutionary committee ordered every local "ox-demon and ghost-spirit" to make a life-size Liu Shaoqi effigy to take to struggle sessions.[103]

In the 1970s mass-criticism screenings gave way to what came to be called "internal reference films" (內参片)—closed screenings of banned or archived films for limited audiences. According to various viewer accounts, internal reference films included denounced poisonous weeds as well as "science education films" about birth planning that explained sex with anatomical drawings, newsreels about domestic disasters such as a reservoir flood not reported in the official press, and a documentary about the Apollo moon landing.[104] Above all, internal reference films were foreign films never approved for public release in China, so their screening had a secretive aura, as if smuggling intelligence from the enemy. Among the earliest and most systematic internal reference screenings were those of three Japanese films set in World War II—*Admiral Yamamoto* (三本五十六) (1968), *Gateway to Glory* (あゝ海軍) (1969), and *Battle of the Japan Sea* (日本海大海战) (1969). These titles caught Premier Zhou Enlai's attention as symptomatic of the "revival of Japanese militarism," so he ordered their dubbing, distribution, and exhibition among government cadres, revolutionary committee members, factory managerial staff, educators at all schools, medical personnel in hospitals, and military officers above the platoon rank.[105]

Internal screenings began in the upper echelons of power, with an increasingly number of foreign films dubbed specifically for Jiang Qing and her entourage. The same film prints would ripple outward from the former imperial city and trickle down the ranks. By 1973 the State Council issued a notice warning against the widespread phenomenon of holding unauthorized screenings of banned films without holding any "disinfection criticisms" before or after.[106] Internal screenings became especially prevalent in military complexes, as dramatized in Jiang Wen's feature film *In the Heat of the Sun* (1994).[107] In one scene, army brats leave an open-air screening for rank-and-file soldiers to steal into an auditorium where high-ranking cadres were watching a European "internal reference film" that featured scenes of female nudity. After discovering the teenagers hiding in the aisles, the projectionist stops the film and turns on the light. In the front row, an elderly general stands up to scold the gatekeeper. Next to him, a much younger woman, resembling a thirty-year-old Jiang Qing, gives a speech mimicking Jiang Qing's voice: "This film is under criticism and is extremely poisonous. If children watch it, they could commit crimes. They could commit major crimes." She then commands all the parents in the audience to pick up their children so that the screening can resume (see figure 7.1).

The film within the film was the West German–Italian historical drama *The Last Roman* (*Kampf um Rom*, 罗马之战), made in 1968 and dubbed into Chinese in 1971. A voice actor at Shanghai Dubbing Studio recalled how her small team had only nine days to finish dubbing this three-hour multilingual film with many characters and a complicated plot, because "top leaders were waiting to watch it." With a single film print and no original script, everyone worked in shifts around the clock. Amid a hot and humid summer, the studio had no air conditioning, the electric fan had to be turned off during the recording, and several actors had to simultaneously speak into the same microphone. By the time this voice actor finally watched the dubbed movie, the print was extremely worn and scratched, suggesting just how often it had been screened.[108]

Internal reference film screenings persisted into the late 1970s and early 1980s. Living next to a Beijing theater, writer Shi Tiesheng remembered seeing mysterious cars arriving at night and important-looking people hurrying up the steps, as if to attend some secret meeting. He then speculated on the circumscription and expansion of "insiders" for internal screenings:

> "Insiders" were those with a high enough rank, a stable enough ideological stance, and a strong enough critical ability—the types who couldn't be poisoned by whatever colors that assailed them. Then there were the insiders of insiders, such as wives and good friends. The films came from the East (Japan) and the West. Rumor had it that lucky audiences could run into half naked or fully naked women, depending on the insiders' rank. But there was no impermeable wall—the ticket inspector came from the outside and the projectionist came from the outside. These outsiders inevitably had their insiders, such as wives and good friends.... When such screenings were held, there would be a boiling, fiery atmosphere in front of the theater—we had no idea from where so many insiders and outsiders mushroomed.

I close this section with one last anecdote on the reception of a Japanese internal reference film, *Admiral Yamamoto*. At its climactic end, the protagonist is shot in the back so that his blood seeps through his yellow uniform. Amid elegiac orchestral music, his plane crashes, with a large tail of smoke in slow motion. Infected by such an aesthetic rendering, a comrade involuntarily utters: "Hei!" (something to the effect of a muted "Bravo"). Another comrade pokes him in the arm, and he immediately adds: "So poisonous!" (真毒啊)![109]

A MAOIST PHARMACOLOGY OF THE SPIRIT

In the Mao era, film censorship took on a shamanistic logic of exorcist healing, as encapsulated through viral keywords like *poisonous weeds, ox-demons and snake-spirits,* and *spiritual opium*. Introduced by CCP leaders, these terms proliferated in official and popular discourse, with an ominous impact on the nation's art, culture, and politics. The traditional roots and revolutionary usages of these concepts suggest intriguing parallels between Maoist prescriptive theories and European theories of pharmakon. Inspired by Derrida's "Plato's Pharmacy," I have shown how poisonous weed films were important drugs in (Madame) Mao's Pharmacy, and that cinema as a mass medium helped to disseminate ideological rectitude as prescriptions to the masses.

Drawing on traditional herbal medicine and agricultural commonsense, this Maoist pharmacology taught the people to tell poisonous weeds from fragrant flowers so as to "uproot them" and "turn them into manure." Drawing also on the modern principle of vaccination, Mao suggested exposing small dosages of poisonous weeds to the masses to sharpen their senses, activate their cognitive defenses, and thus achieve herd immunity against spiritual pollution. Meanwhile, the masses were also called on to detect, unmask, and exorcise counterrevolutionaries as ox-demons and snake-spirits, deploying the "demon-deflecting mirror" of class analysis.

This immunological and exorcist logic of censorship trickled down to the grassroots masses through cinema, thanks largely to Madame Mao's interventions. While turning to cinema as her personal therapy, Jiang Qing conducted a symptomatic reading of films as a diagnosis of the nation's spiritual pestilence. To exorcise the "demonic wind" of feudal and bourgeois remnants, she prescribed criticism screenings that exposed some dozen poisonous weed films to hundreds of millions of audiences—at once a cultural vaccination campaign and a mass exorcist ritual. The militant rhetoric to fight against poisons and demons to protect the spiritual health of the nation contributed to the mass violence of the Cultural Revolution.

What, then, was cultural about the Cultural Revolution? Dubbed a "revolution to touch people's souls," the Cultural Revolution was meant to transform the people's spirits, to sensitize them against complacency, and to heighten their vigilance against internal enemies. As a form of exposure, cinema was to help audiences recognize the threats, ills, and demons in their everyday milieus. The criticism screening of poisonous weed films expanded revolutionary participation in the "Great Criticism," often spectacularly combined with or modeled after struggle sessions. A mass medium that congregated the masses, cinema also became a shamanistic medium that amplified and reproduced collective rituals. As proliferating "demon-exposing mirrors," audiovisual media made socialist China's "demons" visible and audible, so that those demonic reflections and echoes could be dispelled with the sacred images and words of the Mao cult. Yet instead of sharpening their class-analysis skills and hardening their revolutionary resolve, this cinematic vaccination/exorcism ended up reinfecting and reenchanting their guerrilla audiences with their humanistic sentiments, sensual seductions, and mesmerizing aesthetics. As "criticism screenings" gave way to "internal screenings" of mostly foreign films in the 1970s, the pharmakon of cinema also underwent a profanation that returned to common usage what had been placed in a separate sphere through consecration.[110] The epilogue will turn to the post-Mao legacies of cinematic guerrillas and revolutionary spirit mediumship.

Epilogue

During fieldwork in Zhejiang in 2015, I learned from a local county historian that Madame Mao once sent a film crew to a nearby mountain village to create a cinematic model of rural collectivization, but the production came to an abrupt end with Mao's death in 1976.[1] Intrigued by this story, my research team took a drive up the winding mountain paths to the said village. Stepping out of the van, we saw before us a courtyard house with an outer wall that bore a prominent but faded slogan: "People's Commune is the Bridge, Communism is the Paradise" (see figure 9.1). Was this the People's Commune headquarters from the Great Leap Forward in 1958? Or was this Jiang Qing's film set from 1976? Yet wasn't the house and the red paint, though somewhat faded, still too fresh to be half a century old? Excited and skeptical, we walked about the courtyard house but found its gates locked and nobody inside. After conversations with villagers, we finally learned that this used to be a *nongjiale* (农家乐) (literally, a "rural family delight") guesthouse renovated from an ancestral hall for rural ecotourism in the 1990s that had gone bankrupt in the 2000s. What we chanced upon, then, was the veritable ruins of a failed rural capitalist enterprise cross-dressed in the garbs of socialist nostalgia.

In "What Is Film History? Or the Riddle of the Sphinxes," Vivian Sobchack used the excavated film set of Cecil DeMille's *The Ten Commandments* (1923) near Santa Barbara, California, as "a symbol of the

FIGURE 9.1 Faded slogan from the Great Leap Forward on the wall of a mountain village that Jiang Qing wanted to turn into a cinematic model. Photo by the author.

destabilized grounds of contemporary historical theory and practice," calling attention to "our pervasively 'mediated' relation not only to the past, but also to our supposedly 'immediate' present."[2] Although this book has focused on cinema exhibition and memories between the 1950s and the 1970s, my research, fieldwork, and interviews took place between 2010 and 2020. The intervening decades are beyond the scope of this study, yet my excavation through the palimpsestic layers of film history kept stumbling on more recent rubble, nerves, and concerns. With similar "historiographic consciousness," this epilogue considers the legacies of cinematic guerrillas and revolutionary spirit mediumship in contemporary China while pointing to some future research pathways.

What were the plights of cinematic guerrillas in the postsocialist decades? After Mao's death in 1976, cinematic "poisonous weeds" were rereleased from storage to meet ardent audiences, who soon could also consume an influx of imported films alongside new domestic (co-)productions. As cinema attendance grew to nearly thirty films per capita nationwide by the early 1980s, projectionist numbers per county increased from double to triple digits.[3] Under the contract responsibility system, many third-generation "barefoot projectionists" purchased their equipment from the commune, rented screening spaces, hired labor, and pocketed profits. Meanwhile, tens of thousands of "private projection teams" (私人放映队) joined this flourishing business. No longer bound by propaganda imperatives, planned itineraries, or fixed prices, this fourth generation of projectionist-entrepreneurs procured copies of the most popular films available and showed them to the largest paying audiences they could find.[4] With the liberalization of the media market, the smuggling of film copies and piracy of VHS tapes grew rampant, such that guerrilla projectionists who sought to "occupy the thought front" with revolutionary films transformed into VHS guerrillas who peddled kungfu and pornography while dodging official crackdowns on "spiritual pollution."

Yet the golden age of rural cinema was also the beginning of its demise as television ownership grew. This boom and bust happened so swiftly that some projectionists barely recovered their investment.[5] Those who contracted the communes' film equipment instead of land could not even return to farming for their livelihood. One projectionist interviewee was so busy showing films in the late 1970s that he missed preparing for university entrance exams.[6] With decollectivization, most county-level film companies became financially sustainable and underwent privatization.[7] State-employed projectionists received retirement pensions, whereas most commune projectionists took up other jobs as technicians, vendors, or migrant workers.[8]

Since the 2000s, tens of thousands of former commune projectionists formed informal grassroots networks to petition their provincial governments for retirement pensions. In this context, their socialist memories, along with their old ID cards, certificates, and notebooks, became precious proof of their contributions.[9] My interviewees compared their roles to village cadres or other "rural officers/technicians" (八大员) administering agricultural machinery, animal husbandry, or broadcasting stations. Depending on the specific policies of each province, former projectionists received uneven amounts of retirement benefits. A projectionist who showed film for more than thirty-five years in rural Zhejiang spoke indignantly of how even farm vets received better treatment, and how pensions for old projectionists were hijacked by local broadcasters who bribed the authorities. Another petitioner speculated that the Zhejiang provincial government worried that paying pensions to some 5,600 barefoot projectionists might oblige them to take care of 300,000 plus former village teachers. According to a petitioner in Hubei, the provincial government dragged its feet on these settlements year after year, as if waiting for the petitioners to die out. In 2013 and 2017 thousands of former commune projectionists surrounded the Hunan provincial government, holding up banners that read, "The pioneers of cinema have no support in their old age; while the government procrastinates, we can only sit still and wait for death" (电影的开拓者老无所养，久拖不决，只能静坐等死), before being dispersed by the local police and other "stability maintenance" forces (see figure 9.2).¹⁰

The cinematic guerrillas recruited to help the Communist Party "occupy the thought front" thus grew into an aging guerrilla army of petitioners who struggled for their own livelihoods. In the socialist era, the young bodies of these "red propagandists" physically brought cinema to the countryside to project the party's image and amplify its voice to network and forge a scattered population into the revolutionary masses. In the new millennium, when former propagandists gathered to seek compensation and care for their twilight years, the government wanted them to disappear and shut up. Indeed, when these embodied mouthpieces of the state's media network tried to speak up for themselves, their uprisings were reported only in foreign media outlets.¹¹ Apart from the poignant irony of the CCP's failure to provide for its rank-and-file propagandists and give voice to its former speakers, the aging bodies and precarious plight of some hundred thousand former projectionists also foreground the question of "Who is cinema?" Whereas Debashree Mukherjee used "cine-worker" to refer to "any person involved

FIGURE 9.2 Thousands of former projectionists petition the Hunan provincial government in 2017 for a retirement pension. New Tang Dynasty Television.

in the production of films, irrespective of pay scale,"[12] this book expands our critical attention to the embodied practices and creative agencies of projectionists and audiences. All contributed to the multiplicity of cinematic experiences interwoven into broader political, economic, social, cultural, and media tapestries. Future researchers in different historical and geographic contexts can further rewrite media histories from grassroots perspectives by incorporating local archives, memories and memorabilia, oral histories, and ethnographic fieldwork. As much as asking "how cinema and media changed *the* world?" we can ask "how cinema and media changed *your* world(view)s?" These sources, methods, and questions can tease out the diverse and inventive ways ordinary people accessed, made sense of, and interacted with media texts and technologies.

If Chinese cinematic guerrillas turned into petitioning guerillas, what are the legacies of their revolutionary spirit mediumship? In the socialist era, tens of thousands of mobile movie teams wove together an expansive media propaganda network that sought to capture and occupy not only the landscape but also the mindscape of the vast country and dispersed populace. Using films and lantern slides, gramophones, and loudspeakers together with their bodies, cinematic guerrillas were akin to missionaries and priests who made the party's propaganda local as well as to shamanistic spirit mediums who enchanted their audiences with utopian visions of "socialist horizons" and conjured up the "hell of the Old Society" to exorcise its demons. As much as the films themselves, it was the collective ritual of organized moviegoing that revolutionized, industrialized, and militarized their audiences. Initially attracted by cinema's temple-festival-like "hot noise," socialist film audiences were disciplined into the congregational worship of Chairman Mao, communist futures, and revolutionary martyrs. Even when grassroots audiences could barely pay the movie fees extracted out of their collective budgets, the "spiritual food" of cinema compelled them to perform a Maoist ritual economy of sacrifice with their labor and grain.

After the Cultural Revolution, cinema as a "spirit medium" underwent a "profanation" that returned to common usage what had been placed in a separate sphere through consecration.[13] Kungfu action in *Shaolin Temple* replaced guerrilla warfare in *Landmine Warfare*; the evil mother-in-law in Taiwanese tearjerker *Mom Love Me Once Again*

(媽媽再愛我一次) (1988) replaced the evil landlords in *The White-Haired Girl* and *The Flower Girl*. With popular melodic shifts from red songs to yellow music, from revolutionary righteousness to irreverent laughter, even official discourse acknowledged cinema's entertainment and commercial value over propaganda and education.[14] Yet state-sponsored film exhibitors still used cinema to counter proliferating "superstitious activities" and rising "religious fever" in their respective territories, for example, by showing films next to Christian churches or Buddhist pilgrimage sites during times of worship."[15]

In the 1990s, as the army of cinematic guerrillas dwindled, remaining projectionists made ends meet by showing "patriotic education movies" in schools and "hot and noisy" films at private ceremonies such as weddings, elderly birthdays and sometimes funerals. In 1993 the central government issued the "Circular on Carrying Out Education in Patriotism in Primary and Secondary Schools Throughout the Country by Films and Television." Most required and recommended films on the list were guerrilla war movies made during the Mao era.[16] By May 1994, more than 95 percent of Beijing's primary and middle school students attended such organized screenings and wrote more than 1.5 million essays about the films, often vowing to emulate the resilient and self-sacrificial spirit of the guerrilla protagonists.[17] In the ensuing decades, the state invested in various "red" films and television dramas that remade or reinvented guerrilla cinema into so-called anti-Japanese mythic drama (抗日神劇) in the 2010s. Film scholar Julian Ward attributed the new genre's popularity to "kungfu style fighting, the casting of attractive, youthful stars on the Chinese side, and the contrasting portrayal of Japanese soldiers as ugly, their clothes awry, with little moustaches on their evil faces."[18] During fieldwork I watched a few such "anti-Japanese mythic dramas" that attracted the young and the elderly alike with their shifting registers between the sacred and the absurd, between tribute and parody.

In 1998 the Chinese Ministry of Culture revived mobile rural cinema with the "2131 project"—aimed at 100 percent coverage of "one movie per month per village" in rural China in the twenty-first century. By 2010 all their analogue equipment was upgraded to digital projectors. Instead of bulky 16mm celluloid prints, they downloaded a handful of HD film files at a time from a central server. With the mass urban migration of the rural work force, however, the 2131 project became a cinema in search of an audience, eventually shedding its initial name and ambition. Now known as "sending films to the countryside" (电影下乡), "public good cinema" (公益电影), or "rural digital cinema" (农村数字电影), film projection in the countryside since the 2010s operated under the informal slogan of "screening where there are people." Each county-level "digital film company" that we visited employed between ten and thirty personnel. Some were former "barefoot projectionists," and others were younger men with different day jobs, constituting a "fifth generation" of digital projectionists.

During fieldwork between 2015 and 2019, I attended some dozen open-air screenings in various counties of Zhejiang and Hubei provinces, often by following a mobile projectionist with a high-definition digital projector on a minivan or pickup truck. Most such screenings attracted only a handful of villagers, who stayed for about half an hour before heading home to their TV sets, while the projectionist looked at his cell phone. Sometimes a projectionist lost his audience completely to drizzle or a nearby "square dance" (广场舞) with booming loudspeakers. Still, he would finish showing the film—to the GPS surveillance chip built into the projector so that he would be paid later. All digital projectionists I encountered were men with except Manager Yu, a member of the Little Three Sisters Movie Team discussed in chapter 3.

Although most rural film screenings I witnessed were sparsely attended, one "model projectionist" in Zhejiang consistently garnered crowds of over a hundred at every screening (figure 9.3). The secret to Mr. Xu's success had much to do with the infrastructure of the screening spaces inside the courtyards of ancestral hall, where many of the village's older people had already gathered to chat, play mahjong, or watch their grandchildren play. Arriving at dusk, Mr. Xu would first connect the loudspeakers and play some music at top volume—often revolutionary songs such as the theme from *The Red Detachment of Women* set to a rock beat. While this "noise of attraction" brought in a trickle of villagers, he would unfurl the screen, often over an opera stage that faced the ancestral spirit tablets. Burning candles and incense occasionally animated those spirit tablets, but before a prefectural cadre's visit Mr. Xu took care to cover the tablets and hang red banners promoting

FIGURE 9.3 Screening in the courtyard of an ancestral shrine converted into a "cultural ritual hall" in Wenzhou, 2015. Photos by the author.

the "China Dream" over the traditional calligraphy on the pillars. When darkness descended, Mr. Xu would play one or two trailers—often an opera film, martial arts action, or guerrilla war film—and invite his audiences. The feature screening would be preceded by a slideshow of advertisements for local businesses as well as "legal propaganda" (法制宣传) and "propaganda against evil cults" (反邪教宣传). In fact, many of these ancestral halls had been renovated into "cultural ritual halls" (文化礼堂) with government subsidy.[19] One guardian of a cultural ritual hall told me that film screenings and other congregational activities were crucial for the government's spiritual competition with local Christian churches.

In western China's "autonomous regions" inhabited by "ethnic minorities," the government's spiritual crusade against local religiosities became increasingly militant. In 2003 the central government dispatched some four hundred film projection vans to Tibet and Xinjiang to oppose "separatism, Westernization, and ideological permeation," even recruiting young monks to form "monastic projection teams" (寺庙放映队).[20] In Xinjiang, a model Uyghur projectionist in 2010 spoke of occupying the rural thought front and competing for converts with mosques, whereas local party organs organized cultural activities during Friday prayers.[21] From 2012 onward, the party sent "patriotic education films" like *Serf* into Tibet's monasteries with prescriptive responses such as "Seeing the tragic fate of farmers and herdsmen in old Tibet, we will cherish today's hard-won happy life even more."[22] By 2019, of the 1,024 designated film-screening locations in Lhasa municipality, 76 were inside monasteries, with at least twenty monks who watched a "patriotic education film" once a month.[23] Meanwhile, classic revolutionary war films have been remediated through online databases for screenings at local party events, where audiences are exhorted to recite dialogues, reenact scenes, and review their vows.[24]

Even as the party-state has continued to use audiovisual propaganda to transmit the "great spirits" of the Chinese revolution, a digital revolution has empowered new cinematic guerrillas in China's media ecology. Like their Third Cinema counterparts of the 1970s, Chinese cinematic guerrillas since the 1990s have been those using digital media to document counterhegemonic histories and to engage in guerrilla warfare against the censors. Among these filmmakers, Hu Jie (胡杰) excavated the violence of the Mao era through poignant oral histories with victims and survivors, whereas audiences circulated his films via pirated VCDs and online streaming. Wu Wenguang (吴文光) dispatched young filmmakers to their family villages to interview older people about experiences of the Great Leap famine and to organize screenings of these memories within the same communities.[25] Zhan Juying (詹菊英), a semiliterate villager in Yunnan, made her own feature film about her family's traumatic experiences during the Cultural Revolution and screened it for her fellow villagers.[26] From underground to independent to underground,

Epilogue 249

China's DV filmmakers no longer tried to win a revolutionary struggle but rather sought to give voice to untold stories.

I conclude this book amid the November 2022 protests against China's zero-COVID policies, when every Chinese citizen equipped with a cell phone became a cinematic guerrilla insofar as they filmed, circulated, and consumed video footage of China's three-year-long "war on COVID." The nationwide emergency mobilizations militarized language and action with echoes of Maoist propaganda, whereas citizens cracking under the pressures of technologized biopolitical dictatorship often evoked comparisons to Maoist mass campaigns—from the viral voice recording of a Shanghainese old man's April rant that began by referring to the zero-sparrow movement of 1958 to Beijing's "bridge man," who in October unfurled a banner against the return of the Cultural Revolution.[27] Inspired by the latter's courageous act—staged and mediated through online video—November's protestors not only chanted the bridge man's slogans but also performed semiotic guerrilla warfare by repeating and repurposing official propaganda songs such as the "Internationale" and the Chinese national anthem. Viral videos of guerrilla protesters circulated via various technical guerrilla tactics, from flipping videos on their side to the sheer flooding of audiovisual media, to evade algorithmic censors. Meanwhile, savvy media guerrillas practiced digital tunnel warfare to circulate videos beneath the Great Firewall via foreign social media platforms like Twitter and Instagram as well as organized via encrypted messaging platforms like Telegram.[28] Like the "heroic little guerrillas" at the start of this book, today's digital guerrillas reconstitute networks after human censors aided by AI "bomb" their WeChat or weibo accounts (炸号), deleting all their digital archives and contacts. Above all, even amid high-tech totalitarianism, we are witnessing the centrality of the human in media networks, whether in terms of propaganda, surveillance, or resistance. With a blurring line between putting bodies online and putting bodies on the line, cinematic guerrillas and mediation as mediumship are not just socialist legacies but also part of our ongoing media revolution.

APPENDIX

Interviews

The interviewees are listed alphabetically by surname (and by age for those with the same surname) within the province or cities in which the interviews took place.

ZHEJIANG PROVINCE

Surname	Birth Year	Interview Date(s)	Notes
Anonymous villagers	1930s–1960s	July 2015, March 2017, June 2019	Brief interviews with some thirty villagers encountered before or during open-air screenings
Mr. Chen	1964	2015.7.28; 2017.3.17	Manager of a county film company, first hired as a mobile projectionist in the early 1980s
Ms. Chen	1969	2017.3.20	Private projectionist who showed films in her village ancestral hall, 1985–1990
Mr. Dai	1934	2015.7.28–29	County-level mobile projectionist, 1958–1990s

Surname	Birth Year	Interview Date(s)	Notes
Mr. Jin	1930s	2019.6.17	County-level mobile projectionist, 1950s–1980s
Mr. Jin	1934	2015.7.30	Former party secretary of a model village to which Jiang Qing sent a film crew in the 1970s
Mr. Jin	1937	2015.7.24	County-level mobile projectionist, 1965–2000s; interview by Li Bingbing, Lin Ruyi
Mr. Jin	1950s	2015.7.30	Former village teacher who lived next door to the film crew sent by Jiang Qing
Mr. Jin	1954	2015.7.30	Villager who traveled around the country as a cotton fluffer in the 1970s and watched many films
Mr. Qian	1960s	2019.6.15, 17	Manager of a county film company, first hired as a projectionist in the early 1980s
Mr. Xing	1940s	2019.6.17	County-level mobile projectionist, 1960–1990s
Mr. Xu	1932	2017.3.18–20	Guardian of a Catholic church
Mr. Xu	1947	2017.3.18	Head of an elderly association
Mr. Xu	1947	2017.3.18	Former security guard for a township cinema within a Catholic church in the 1970s and early 1980s
Mr. Xu	1965	2015.7.28–31; 2017.3.17–20	County-level projectionist, 1982–present
Mr. Xu	1970	2017.3.17	County historian

Surname	Birth Year	Interview Date(s)	Notes
Mr. Yang	1955	2012.7.7	Commune projectionist, 1976–late 1990s; interview by Li Shizhong, Wang Sisi
Mr. Yao	1935	2019.6.16	Former village party secretary who first watched a film when mobilized for reservoir construction in the mid-1950s
Mr. Zhan	1950	2015.8.2	Commune projectionist, 1970–1998; hired again as digital projectionist from 2010
Mr. Zheng	1941	2015.7.28	County-level mobile projectionist, 1966–2000s
Mr. Zheng	1930s	2019.6.17	County-level mobile projectionist, 1950s–1980s
Mr. Zhu	1967	2017.3.21	Vice manager of a county film company

HUBEI PROVINCE

Surname	Birth Year	Interview Date(s)	Notes
Anonymous villagers	1930s–1960s	August 2015	Brief interviews with some twenty villagers encountered before or during open-air screenings
Mr. Dong	1943	2015.8.9	Commune projectionist, 1972–1990s
Ms. Duan	1957	2015.8.12	Commune projectionist, 1976–1990s

Surname	Birth Year	Interview Date(s)	Notes
Mr. Duan	1956	2015.8.12	Commune projectionist, 1975–1990s
Ms. Gong	1944	2015.8.10	Amateur projectionist for the Four Clean-ups Movement, 1964–1966
Mr. He	1956	2015.8.9	Worked on and off as a private projectionist, 1982–2010s
Ms. He	1960	2015.8.9	Sold tickets in the township cinema and occasionally showed films in local schools 1980s–2010s
Mr. Hu	1956	2015.8.9	Commune projectionist, 1975–2003
Mr. Lei	1931	2015.8.15	County-level mobile projectionist, 1955–1988
Ms. Li	1951	2015.8.8	County historian
Mr. Li	1950	2015.8.11	Commune projectionist, 1976–1984, interviewed by Feng Xiaocai
Mr. Liang	1952	2015.8.9	Commune projectionist, 1975–1992
Mr. Liu	1961	2015.8.10	Commune projectionist, 1978–1995
Mr. Peng	1932	2015.8.11	PLA soldier in the early 1950s; village chief, 1950s–1970s; private projectionist, 1985–1988
Mr. Peng	1950	2015.8.14	Commune projectionist, 1979–1990s

Surname	Birth Year	Interview Date(s)	Notes
Mr. Qin	1952	2015.8.16	County-level mobile projectionist from 1971 and county movie theater manager
Mr. Tan	1934	2015.8.12	Commune projectionist, 1975–1990s
Mr. Tan	1942	2015.8.12	Private projectionist, 1982–1990s
Mr. Wang	1946	2015.8.12	Commune projectionist, 1976–1990s
Mr. Xia	1947	2015.8.10	County-level projectionist, 1965–1975
Mr. Xu	1954	2015.8.14	Commune projectionist, 1970–1974, 1979–1990s
Mr. Ye	1945	2015.8.10	County-level projectionist, 1961–1978
Mr. Ye	1946	2015.8.12	Private projectionist, 1981–1990s
Mr. Zhang	1950s	2015.8.15 & 8.16	Manager of a county film company, first hired as a projectionist in the early 1980s
Mr. Zhang	1955	2015.8.13	Commune projectionist, 1977–1988
Mr. Zeng	1934	2015.8.15	County-level mobile projectionist, 1956–1995
Mr. Zheng	1947	2015.8.8	County-level projectionist from 1965, manager of a county film company in the 1990s
Mr. Zheng	1956	2015.8.11	Mobile projectionist, 1998–2015

Surname	Birth Year	Interview Date(s)	Notes
Mr. Zhou	1956	2015.8.13	Commune projectionist, 1975–2015
Mr. Zhu	1952	2015.8.9	Commune projectionist, 1974–2004

HEBEI PROVINCE

Surname	Birth Year	Interview Date(s)	Notes
Anonymous villagers	1930s–1960s	February 2017	Brief interviews with about a dozen villagers encountered during our search for former projectionists
Mr. Guo	1937	2017.2.10	County-level projectionist, 1959–1990s
Mr. Han	1938	2017.2.10	County-level projectionist, 1962–1990s
Mr. Liu	1931	2017.2.10	County-level projectionist, 1955–1990s
Mr. Liu	1935	2017.2.11	County-level projectionist, 1961–1965
Mr. Wang	1955	2017.2.8	Local historian and propaganda officer; author of book-length oral history with Wang Baoyi
Mr. Yan	1940	2017.1.11; 2017.2.7	Lanternist for the "Three Sisters Movie Team," 1962–1980s; first interview by Lyu Hongyun

Surname	Birth Year	Interview Date(s)	Notes
Ms. Yu	1961	2017.2.9	Member of the "Little Three Sisters Movie Team" from 1978; current manager of the county film company
Mr. Zeng	1962	2017.2.9	Son of former projectionist who managed the county movie theater, 1978–1990s

SHANGHAI

Surname	Birth Year	Interview Date(s)	Notes
Ms. Chen	1952	2016.11.09	Shanghai urban youth sent down to rural Henan
Mr. Chen	1953	2016.11.15	Shanghai youth sent down to rural Inner Mongolia
Ms. Chen	1958	2016.11.16	Daughter of a cinephile Shanghai union cultural activist who helped local cinemas sell tickets in his silk factory
Ms. Fang	1947	2016.11.11	Watched many Hong Kong movies in Shanghai in the 1950s and 1960s; collected photos of Hong Kong movie stars.
Ms. Ge	1952	2016.11.15	Shanghai youth sent down to rural Jiangxi; KMT and landlord family background led to different interpretations of revolutionary cinema

Surname	Birth Year	Interview Date(s)	Notes
Mr. Gong	1949	2016.11.15	Shanghai youth sent down to the "Great Northern Wilderness"; cited *Awaara* as one of his favorite films
Mr. Gu	1942	2016.11.14	Former projectionist and later manager of Shanghai movie theater
Ms. He	1949	2016.11.15	Shanghai youth sent down to rural Jilin
Mr. Hu	1947	2016.11.15	Grew up in Shanghai; recalled going to watch many war films with his school
Mr. Jiang	1941	2016.11.09; 2016.11.14	Publicity officer for Shanghai Film Distribution and Exhibition Company, 1970s–1990
Ms. Li Rong	1960	2016.11.10	Childhood in Beijing; followed her parents to the Third Front in Sichuan in the early 1970s
Mr. Lin	1950	2016.11.15	Shanghai sent-down youth; volunteered to go to the "Great Northern Wilderness" after seeing documentaries about pioneers on China's frontiers
Ms. Lin	1951	2016.11.15	Shanghai youth sent down to rural Jilin, cited *The Flower Girl* as her most memorable film
Mr. Lou	1953	2016.11.07	Sent-down youth projectionist in the "Great Northern Wilderness," 1971–1979

Surname	Birth Year	Interview Date(s)	Notes
Mr. Lu	1948	2016.11.13	Cinephile who did not always have the money to go to the cinema, but watched *Visitors on Ice Mountain* four times to learn the film songs.
Mr. Lu	1950	2012.8.16	Sent-down youth projectionist in the "Great Northern Wilderness," 1974–1978
Mr. Ma	1947	2016.11.15	Shanghai youth sent down to the "Great Northern Wilderness"; recalled many socialist movie stars as well as cinema's influence on class and patriotic feelings
Mr. Pan	1948	2012.8.16; 2015.7.24	Sent-down youth projectionist in the "Great Northern Wilderness," 1972–1978
Mr. Qin	1952	2013.7.21	Sent-down youth projectionist in the "Great Northern Wilderness," 1971–1979
Mr. Shang	1951	2016.11	Grew up in Qiqiha'er; managed a worker union cinema in early 1980s; interview via written questionnaire
Mr. Sun	1930s	2016.11.14	Former mobile projectionist trained in Nanjing in 1950, later manager of a Shanghai movie theater
Mr. Sun	1954	2016.11.13	Recalled watching many poisonous weed films in Shanghai in the late 1960s

Surname	Birth Year	Interview Date(s)	Notes
Mr. Wang	1947	2016.11.15	Shanghai youth sent down to the "Great Northern Wilderness"; enjoyed watching documentaries
Ms. Wu	1949	2016.11.15	Shanghai youth sent down to the "Great Northern Wilderness"; associated cinema with "recall bitterness" rituals
Ms. Xu Xiaoli	1953	2016.11.09	Beijing urban youth sent down to Inner Mongolia; interview via written questionnaire
Ms. Yan	1962	2016.11.13	Grew up between rural Anhui and Shanghai; recalled listening to edited film clips on a neighbor's radio
Ms. Yuan	1957	2016.11.13	Grew up in the Shanghai suburbs and took long trips to open-air cinemas run by commune movie teams; cited *Tunnel Warfare* as her most memorable film
Mr. Zhang	1953	2016.11.13	Fan of old Shanghai's movie stars; recalled watching many poisonous weed films in the late 1960s
Mr. Zhou	1930s	2016.11.14	Trade union projectionist in the 1950s, later manager of three Shanghai movie theaters
Mr. Zhu	1954	2016.11.09	Shanghai urban youth sent down to rural Henan
Mr. Zhu	1954	2016.11.15	Shanghai youth sent down to the "Great Northern Wilderness"

CHANGCHUN, HANGZHOU, HARBIN, SUZHOU

Surname	Birth Year	Interview Date(s)	Notes
Ms. Dai	1934	2017.1.27 Suzhou	Suzhou Steel Factory union projectionist, 1956–1990s
Mr. Fan	1946	2016.11.11 Hangzhou	Artist and film critic; ran a cinephile club in Hangzhou in the 2000s
Ms. Han	1950s	2016.11.11 Hangzhou	Worked for Zhejiang Film Distribution and Exhibition Company, 1970s–1990s
Mr. Jia	1940s	2016.11.11 Hangzhou	Worked for Zhejiang Film Distribution and Exhibition Company, 1960s–1990s; specialized in propaganda and music
Mr. Li	1921	2017.4.15 Changchun	Recalled watching Shanghai films in Harbin in the 1930s; wrote film reviews in the 1940s for the Manchurian Motion Picture Association
Mr. Liu	1930	2016.11.11 Hangzhou	Worked for Zhejiang Film Distribution and Exhibition Company, 1950s–1990s; propaganda officer, 1950s; worked on *Zhejiang Film Gazetteer*, 1990s
Mr. Liu	1922	2017.4.17 Changchun	Grew up in Harbin and worked as an art designer for the Manchurian Motion Picture Association and for Changchun Film Studio
Mr. Sun	1976	2017.4.9 Harbin	Private collector of memorabilia related to Harbin's film history

Appendix

Surname	Birth Year	Interview Date(s)	Notes
Ms. Wang	1940	2016.11.11 Hangzhou	Cinephile who fondly recalled watching Hollywood films as a child in Shanghai during the 1940s
Mr. Yang	1924	2017.4.7 Harbin	Cinema poster painter in Harbin, 1941–1945; helped convert a church in a nearby county into a cinema in 1948

NINGXIA, INTERVIEWS BY PENG HAI, APRIL 2017

Surname	Birth Year	Notes
Ms. Guo	1950	Villager who watched films screened for petroleum drillers near her village, 1950s–1960s
Mr. Hai	1962	Bricklayer who recalled mainly guerrilla war films
Mr. Hai	1969	Village teacher who had to cross two half-frozen rivers to get to open-air screenings in his childhood
Mr. Li	1959	Village teacher who recalled taking long trips to open-air screenings
Ms. Li	1961	Grew up in rural Gansu; cited *Sparkling Red Star* and *The Flower Girl* as her most memorable films
Ms. Li	1962	Villager who vividly recalled the first film she saw, *The Red Lantern*, and the female projectionists who showed it
Mr. Luo	1960	Village teacher who best recalled action films and fighting between young men during open-air screenings

Surname	Birth Year	Notes
Mr. Ma	1949	Villager activist who helped organize moviegoing trips and film screenings in his production brigade in the 1960s and 1970s
Ms. Ma	1955	Villager whose childhood memories of rare moviegoing trips are dominated by the shame of her dirty and tattered clothes from carrying dung all day
Ms. Ma	1957	Daughter of an Iman who rarely allowed her to watch films; could recall three revolutionary model opera films
Mr. Ma	1960	Vendor who helped to transport equipment for the commune movie team in the 1970s
Mr. Ma	1962	Bricklayer who frequented the county cinema behind his father's back in the 1960s and 1970s
Mr. Mu	1949	Mosque manager who recalled many films from the 1960s and 1970s
Mr. Yuan	1953	Carpenter who cited *Guerrillas on the Plains* as his most memorable film
Ms. Zhou	1960	Commune projectionist, mid-1970s–1990s

Notes

INTRODUCTION

1. *Yunnansheng dianying faxing fangying gongzuo jinian tekan* (Commemorative publication on film distribution and exhibition work in Yunnan province) (internal publication, 1984).
2. "Yingxiong xiaobalu ruhe zouxiang pingmu" (How the "Heroic Little Guerrillas" became a film), *Dongnan zaobao* (Southeast morning post), May 26, 2005, http://news.sina.com.cn/o/2005-05-26/04185989652s.shtml.
3. Marshall McLuhan, *Understanding Media: The Extensions of Man* (Cambridge, Mass.: MIT Press, 1994). My notion of human extensions of media also builds on more recent discussions of people as (media) infrastructure. For example, drawing on anthropologist AbdouMaliq Simone's notion of "people as infrastructure" to describe economic collaboration among urban residents in South Africa, media scholar Joshua Neves used "people as media infrastructure" to describe pirated video vendors in Beijing. See AbdouMaliq Simone, "People as Infrastructure: Intersecting Fragments in Johannesburg," *Public Culture* 16, no. 3 (2004): 407-29; Joshua Neves, *Underglobalization: Beijing's Media Urbanism and the Chimera of Legitimacy* (Durham, N.C.: Duke University Press, 2020), chap. 6.
4. For more on "masses as media," see the introduction and first chapter of my book *Utopian Ruins: A Memorial Museum of the Mao Era* (Durham, N.C.: Duke University Press, 2020).

5. Jeffrey Sconce, *Haunted Media: Electronic Presence from Telegraphy to Television* (Durham, N.C.: Duke University Press, 2000), 24–25.
6. Weihong Bao, *Fiery Cinema: The Emergence of an Affective Medium in China, 1915–1945* (Minneapolis: University of Minnesota Press, 2015); Shaoling Ma, *The Stone and the Wireless: Mediating China, 1861–1906* (Durham, N.C.: Duke University Press, 2021).
7. Sebastian Heilmann and Elizabeth J. Perry, "Embracing Uncertainty: Guerrilla Policy Style and Adaptive Governance in China," in *Mao's Invisible Hand: The Political Foundations of Adaptive Governance in China* (Cambridge, Mass.: Asia Center, Harvard University, 2011), 1–29.
8. Mao Tse-tung, *On Guerrilla Warfare*, trans. Samuel B. Griffith (New York: Praeger, 1961), 46. This translation is based primarily on Mao's treatise *KangRi youji zhanzheng de yiban wenti* (Common problems in the anti-Japanese guerrilla war) (Yan'an: Jiefangshe, 1938).
9. Mao, *On Guerrilla Warfare*, 101.
10. Mao, 116; Bao, *Fiery Cinema*, 300.
11. Mao, *On Guerrilla Warfare*, appendix, table 1.
12. Mao Zedong, "Beat Back at the Attacks of the Bourgeois Rightists," speech at a conference of cadres in Shanghai, July 9, 1957, https://www.marxists.org/reference/archive/mao/selected-works/volume-5/mswv5_65.htm.
13. Samuel B. Griffith, "Introduction," in Mao, *On Guerrilla Warfare*, 7.
14. Mao Zedong, "Report on an Investigation of the Peasant Movement in Hunan," March 1927, https://www.marxists.org/reference/archive/mao/selected-works/volume-1/mswv1_2.htm.
15. Peter Kenez, *The Birth of the Propaganda State: Soviet Methods of Mass Mobilization, 1917–1929* (Cambridge: Cambridge University Press, 1985), 106; Walter Benjamin, *The Work of Art in the Age of Its Technological Reproducibility, and Other Writings on Media* (Cambridge, Mass.: Harvard University Press, 2008).
16. Bao, *Fiery Cinema*, chap. 5; Hongwei Thorn Chen, "Cinemas, Highways, and the Making of Provincial Space: Mobile Screenings in Jiangsu, China, 1933–1937," *Wide Screen* 7, no. 1 (2018); Jie Li, "A National Cinema for a Puppet State: The Manchurian Motion Picture Association," in *Oxford Handbook of Chinese Cinemas*, ed. Eileen Cheng-yin Chow and Carlos Rojas (Oxford: Oxford University Press, 2013), 82.
17. Wu Zhuqing and Zhang Dai, eds., *Zhongguo dianying de fengbei: Yan'an dianying tuan gushi* (Monument of Chinese cinema: The story of the Yan'an Film Group) (Beijing: Renmin daxue chubanshe, 2008), 119.
18. Zhao Junyi, "*Sheying Wang* de shi yu mo" (The beginning and end of *Photography Web*), https://news.artron.net/20130108/n298304.html.

19. Charles A. Laughlin, *Chinese Reportage: The Aesthetics of Historical Experience* (Durham, N.C.: Duke University Press, 2002), chap. 5; Chang-tai Hung, *Going to the People: Chinese Intellectuals and Folk Literature, 1918–1937* (Cambridge, Mass.: Council on East Asian Studies, Harvard University, 1985).
20. Brian DeMare, *Mao's Cultural Army: Drama Troupes in China's Rural Revolution* (Cambridge: Cambridge University Press, 2015), 5.
21. *Dianying fangying* (Film projection) (hereafter DYFY), no. 4 (1957): 16–19.
22. DYFY, no. 10 (1960): 17.
23. DYFY, no. 9 (1960): 1–7.
24. Ji Pu, "Ba dianying song dao nongcun li qu" (Send movies into the countryside), *Dazhong dianying* (Mass cinema) (hereafter DZDY), no. 4 (1952): 28.
25. DYFY, no. 10 (1960): 10; no. 10 (1959): 20–21.
26. Among early film reception studies that treat audience as historical, corporeal, and heterogeneous subjects rather than textually implied spectators are Miriam Hansen, *Babel and Babylon: Spectatorship in American Silent Film* (Cambridge, Mass.: Harvard University Press, 1994); and Yuri Tsivian, *Early Cinema in Russia and Its Cultural Reception* (New York: Routledge, 1994). Among major studies of nontheatrical film exhibition infrastructures are Brian Larkin, *Signal and Noise: Media, Infrastructure, and Urban Culture in Nigeria* (Durham, N.C.: Duke University Press, 2008); and Sudhir Mahadevan, *A Very Old Machine: The Many Origins of the Cinema in India* (Albany: State University of New York Press, 2015).
27. Jean-Louis Baudry and Alan Williams, "Ideological Effects of the Basic Cinematographic Apparatus," *Film Quarterly* 28, no. 2 (1974): 39–47.
28. These two positions are best represented by the legacies of the Frankfurt School and British cultural studies.
29. Michel de Certeau, *The Practice of Everyday Life*, trans. Steven F. Rendall (Berkeley: University of California Press, 1984), part 3; John Fiske, *Television Culture* (London: Methuen, 1987), 316.
30. Interview with various members of the Red Guard generation, Shanghai, 2016.
31. DYFY, no. 1 (1963): 20–22; no. 8 (1963): 15–16; no. 10 (1964): 4; no. 10 (1965): 15.
32. James C. Scott, *Domination and the Arts of Resistance: Hidden Transcripts* (New Haven, Conn.: Yale University Press, 1990).
33. Tsering Shakya, "Tibet and China: The Past in the Present," blogpost, *Open Democracy*, March 28, 2009, https://www.opendemocracy.net/en/tibet-and-china-the-past-in-the-present/.
34. *Guangxi dianying faxing fangying shi* (History of film distribution and exhibition in Guangxi) (Guilin: Guangxi dianying faxing fangying gongsi, 1995), 189–205.
35. Paul Clark, *The Chinese Cultural Revolution: A History* (Cambridge: Cambridge University Press, 2008), 259.

36. Xiaoning Lu, *Moulding the Socialist Subject: Cinema and Chinese Modernity (1949–1966)* (Leiden: Brill, 2020).
37. Fernando Solanas and Octavio Getino, "Toward a Third Cinema," *Cineaste* 4, no. 3 (1970): 1–10.
38. Anthony Guneratne and Wimal Dissanayake, eds., *Rethinking Third Cinema* (New York: Routledge, 2003), 8.
39. Solanas, and Getino, "Toward a Third Cinema," 2.
40. Haidee Wasson and Lee Grieveson, eds., *Cinema's Military Industrial Complex* (Berkeley: University of California Press, 2018).
41. Paul Virilio, *War and Cinema: The Logistics of Perception* (London: Verso, 1989).
42. Friedrich Kittler, *Operation Valhalla: Writings on War, Weapons, and Media* (Durham, N.C.: Duke University Press, 2021), 3–35.
43. John Durham Peters, "Foreword: Some Assembly Required," in *Assembly Codes: The Logistics of Media*, ed. Matthew Hockenberry, Nicole Starosielski, and Susan Zieger (Durham, N.C.: Duke University Press, 2021), viii.
44. Screened in coordination with land reform and the Socialist Education Movement, *The White-Haired Girl* tells the story of how "Old Society turns people into ghosts, and New Society turns ghosts back into humans." This and similar films became haunting reminders of the prerevolutionary past as hell and prompted local audiences to "remember bitterness." After Mao's call in 1963 to learn from Dazhai, a rural model of self-reliance, Dazhai became a recurring subject of newsreel documentaries, with at least one documentary made every year from 1964 to 1978. For a comprehensive list, see Liu Guangyu, *Xin Zhongguo chengli yilai nongcun dianying fangying yanjiu* (Study of rural film exhibitions since the founding of New China) (Beijing: Wenhua yishu chubanshe, 2015), 161.
45. Liu Xiaobo, "That Holy Word, 'Revolution,'" in *Popular Protest and Political Culture in Modern China*, ed. Jeffrey N. Wasserstrom, 2nd ed. (New York: Routledge, 1992), 309–24.
46. Rebecca Nedostup, *Superstitious Regimes: Religion and the Politics of Chinese Modernity* (Cambridge, Mass.: Asia Center, Harvard University, 2010); Henrietta Harrison, *The Missionary's Curse and Other Tales from a Chinese Catholic Village* (Berkeley: University of California Press, 2013).
47. Chiang Kai-shek, *Geming de jingshen jiaoyu* (Revolutionary spiritual education) (Shanghai: Taipingyang shudian, 1929). See also Jianhua Chen, "Chinese 'Revolution' in the Syntax of World Revolution," in *Tokens of Exchange*, ed. Lydia H. Liu (Durham, N.C.: Duke University Press, 1990), 355–74.
48. Nedostup, *Superstitious Regimes*, 14, 228; Mayfair Mei-hui Yang, ed., *Chinese Religiosities: Afflictions of Modernity and State Formation* (Berkeley: University of California Press, 2008), 1–8.

49. Brian Tsui, *China's Conservative Revolution: The Quest for a New Order, 1927–1949* (Cambridge: Cambridge University Press, 2018), chap. 4; Mao Zedong, "Report to the 2nd National Congress of Worker's and Peasant's Representatives," January 23, 1934, https://www.marxists.org/reference/archive/mao/selected-works/volume-6/mswv6_18.htm.
50. Maurice J. Meisner, *Marxism, Maoism, and Utopianism: Eight Essays* (Madison: University of Wisconsin Press, 1982), 112–20.
51. Wendy Larson, *From Ah Q to Lei Feng: Freud and Revolutionary Spirit in 20th Century China* (Stanford, Calif.: Stanford University Press, 2009), 77–97.
52. Nedostup, *Superstitious Regimes*; Xiaoxuan Wang, *Maoism and Grassroots Religion: The Communist Revolution and the Reinvention of Religious Life in China* (Oxford: Oxford University Press, 2020).
53. "CPC's Spiritual Legacy Has Been Carried Forward Through a Journey of 100 Years," *Global Times*, November 8, 2021, https://www.globaltimes.cn/page/202111/1238439.shtml.
54. Garth S. Jowett, and Victoria O'Donnell, *Propaganda and Persuasion*, 7th ed. (Newbury Park, Calif.: Sage, 2018), 72–73.
55. Timothy Cheek, *Propaganda and Culture in Mao's China: Deng Tuo and the Intelligentsia* (Oxford: Clarendon, 1997), 2; Bao, *Fiery Cinema*, chap. 5.
56. Cheek, *Propaganda and Culture in Mao's China*, 14–15.
57. Nedostup, *Superstitious Regimes*, 13, 48; Elizabeth J. Perry, "Missionaries of the Party: Work-team Participation and Intellectual Incorporation," *China Quarterly*, no. 248 (2021): 78, 82.
58. More than the term "religion," Mayfair Yang called for the study of Chinese "religiosities" in order to "avoid two damaging distinctions . . . between religion and superstition [and] between inner (individual) faith and collective religious institution." Yang, *Chinese Religiosities*, 18.
59. Vincent Goossaert and David A. Palmer, *The Religious Question in Modern China* (Chicago: University of Chicago Press, 2011), 168.
60. Robert Jay Lifton, *Revolutionary Immortality: Mao Tse-tung and the Chinese Cultural Revolution* (New York: Random House, 1968), 8; Meisner, *Marxism, Maoism, and Utopianism*, 70, 168–69.
61. Richard Madsen, *Morality and Power in a Chinese Village* (Berkeley: University of California Press, 1984), esp. chap. 5; Elizabeth J. Perry, *Anyuan: Mining China's Revolutionary Tradition* (Berkeley: University of California Press, 2012), 206, 242–46.
62. Stefan R. Landsberger, "Mao as the Kitchen God: Religious Aspects of the Mao Cult During the Cultural Revolution," *China Information* 11, nos. 2–3 (1996): 196–214; Perry, *Anyuan*, 216–20.

63. Rudolf G. Wagner, "Reading the Chairman Mao Memorial Hall in Peking: The Tribulations of the Implied Pilgrim," in *Pilgrims and Sacred Sites in China*, ed. Susan Naquin and Chun-Fang Yu (Berkeley: University of California Press, 1992), 378–423; Adam Yuet Chau, "Mao's Travelling Mangoes: Food as Relic in Revolutionary China," *Past and Present* 206 (2010): 256–75; Barend J. Ter Haar, "China's Inner Demons: The Political Impact of the Demonological Paradigm," *China Information* 11, no. 2–3 (1996): 54–85.
64. John Durham Peters, *The Marvelous Clouds: Toward a Philosophy of Elemental Media* (Chicago: University of Chicago Press, 2015), 333–34; Jeremy Stolow, "Religion and/as Media," *Theory, Culture & Society* 22, no. 4 (2005): 125.
65. Birgit Meyer, ed., *Aesthetic Formations: Media, Religion, and the Senses* (New York: Palgrave Macmillan, 2009), 11.
66. John Durham Peters, *Speaking Into the Air: A History of the Idea of Communication* (Chicago: University of Chicago Press, 2012), 100; Sconce, *Haunted Media*; Stefan Andriopoulos, *Possessed: Hypnotic Crimes, Corporate Fiction, and the Invention of Cinema* (Chicago: University of Chicago Press, 2008), 91–127.
67. Bao, *Fiery Cinema*, 116–17.
68. Xiao Liu, *Information Fantasies: Precarious Mediation in Postsocialist China* (Minneapolis: University of Minnesota Press, 2019).
69. Benjamin, *The Work of Art*, 23–26.
70. See, for example, *Yunnansheng*, 16, 24, 92; *Fujiansheng*, 4–5, 31, 53; *Qinghai dianying zhi* (Qinghai film gazetteer) (Xining: Qinghaisheng wenhuating, 1989), 42. For accounts of early film exhibition in treaty ports, see Zhen Zhang, *An Amorous History of the Silver Screen: Shanghai Cinema, 1896–1937* (Chicago: University of Chicago Press, 2005); Laikwan Pang, "Walking Into and Out of the Spectacle: China's Earliest Film Scene," *Screen* 47, no. 1 (2006): 66–80.
71. Chen Mo, *Huaji fangying: Shaanxi nüzi fangyingren* (Blooming projection: Shaanxi's female projectionists) (Beijing: Zhongguo dianying chubanshe, 2014), 57.
72. Donald S. Sutton, "From Credulity to Scorn: Confucians Confront the Spirit Mediums in Late Imperial China," *Late Imperial China* 21, no. 2 (2000): 2.
73. Steve A. Smith, "Supernatural Politics: Popular Religion in Maoist China," ms., chapter on spirit mediumship; Steve A. Smith, "Local Cadres Confront the Supernatural: The Politics of Holy Water (*Shenshui*) in the PRC, 1949–1966, *China Quarterly*, no. 188 (2006): 999–1022.
74. On the notion of *lingying*, see Adam Chau, *Miraculous Response: Doing Popular Religion in Contemporary China* (Stanford, Calif.: Stanford University Press, 2005). Two additional "antisuperstition films" from the CCP are *A Reactionary Secret Society* (一贯害人道) (1952) and *Farewell to the Plague Spirit* (送瘟神) (1959).

75. *Qinghai dianying zhi* (Qinghai film gazetteer) (Xining: Qinghaisheng wenhuating, 1989), 194–95.
76. Michael Taussig, *Mimesis and Alterity: A Particular History of the Senses* (New York: Routledge, 1993), 207–8.
77. Larkin, *Signal and Noise*, 39.
78. DZDY, no. 5 (1952): 28.
79. Richard Taylor, "A Medium for the Masses: Agitation in the Soviet Civil War," *Soviet Studies* 22, no. 4 (April 1971): 569.
80. Interview with Mr. Zheng (1941–), Zhejiang, 2015; and Mr. Zeng (1934–), Hubei, 2015.
81. *Dianying fangying ziliao* (Film projection materials) (hereafter DYFYZL) 2, no. 2–3 (1954).
82. DYFY 1959.18.1; 1959.2.19.
83. David Johnson, *Spectacle and Sacrifice: The Ritual Foundations of Village Life in North China* (Cambridge, Mass.: Asia Center, Harvard University, 2010).
84. DYFY, no. 8 (1957): 17; "Xuexi nongcun fangying dui de geming jingshen" (Learn the revolutionary spirit of the rural screening team), *Dianying yishu* (Film art), no. 5 (1965): 2–3. On "shadow opera," see Chris Berry and Mary Farquhar, *China on Screen: Cinema and Nation* (New York: Columbia University Press, 2006), 47–48.
85. Johnson, *Spectacle and Sacrifice*, 1–3.
86. Adam B. Seligman, Robert P. Weller, Michael J. Puett, and Bennett Simon, *Ritual and Its Consequences: An Essay on the Limits of Sincerity* (New York: Oxford University Press, 2008), 22, 179–82.
87. Chau, *Miraculous Response*, 51; Xudong Zhao and Duran Bell, "Miaohui, the Temples Meeting Festival in North China," *China Information* 21, no. 3 (2007): 457–79.
88. Emily Ng, *A Time of Lost Gods: Mediumship, Madness, and the Ghost After Mao* (Berkeley: University of California Press, 2020).
89. Erik Mueggler, *The Age of Wild Ghosts: Memory, Violence, and Place in Southwest China* (Berkeley: University of California Press, 2001).
90. Thomas Elsaesser, *Film History as Media Archaeology: Tracking Digital Cinema* (Amsterdam: Amsterdam University Press, 2016), 94–100. Also see an interview with Elsaesser at Amsterdam University Press, https://www.aup.nl/en/articles/film-history-as-media-archaeology-an-interview-with-thomas-elsaesser-and.
91. André Bazin, *What Is Cinema?* (Berkeley: University of California Press, 2005); D. N. Rodowick, *The Virtual Life of Film* (Cambridge, Mass.: Harvard University Press, 2007), 8; Robert C. Allen, "Getting to Going to the Show," *New Review of Film and Television Studies* 8, no. 3 (2010): 265.

92. Zhang, *An Amorous History*, 89–117; Pang, "Walking Into and Out"; Emilie Yueh-yu Yeh, "Translating *Yingxi*: Chinese Film Genealogy and Early Cinema in Hong Kong," *Journal of Chinese Cinemas* 9, no. 1 (2015): 76–109.
93. Richard Maltby, Daniël Biltereyst, and Philippe Meers, eds., *Explorations in New Cinema History: Approaches and Case Studies* (Malden, Mass.: Wiley and Blackwell, 2011), xii.
94. I borrow this phrase from Larkin, *Signal and Noise*, 81.
95. Zhang, *An Amorous History*, xv–xvi.
96. Yomi Braester, and Tina Mai Chen, "Film in the People's Republic of China, 1949–1979: The Missing Years?," *Journal of Chinese Cinemas* 5, no. 1 (2011): 5–12; Yingjin Zhang, "Chinese Film History and Historiography," *Journal of Chinese Cinemas* 10, no. 1 (2016): 38–47.
97. Chenshu Zhou, *Cinema Off Screen: Moviegoing in Socialist China* (Berkeley: University of California Press, 2021).
98. Elsaesser, *Film History as Media Archeology*, 97. Many essays in Ina Rae Hark, ed., *Exhibition, the Film Reader* (New York: Routledge, 2002), are also grouped under a section called "Where the Movies Were."
99. Zhang, *An Amorous History*; Pang, "Walking Into and Out"; Yeh, "Translating *Yingxi*." On Harbin, see Zhang Jingwu, "Bei zhebi de Ha'erbin: Zhongguo zhuanye yingyuan zhi dansheng yu zaoqi dianying wenhua geju" (Concealed Harbin: the birth of movie theaters in China and the cultural scene of early cinema), *Zhongguo yingshi* (Chinese film history) 127, no. 1 (2016), 80–89.
100. Nicolai Volland, *Socialist Cosmopolitanism: The Chinese Literary Universe, 1945–1965* (New York: Columbia University Press, 2017); Poshek Fu and Man-Fung Yip, eds., *The Cold War and Asian Cinemas* (New York: Routledge, 2019).
101. Friedrich A. Kittler, *Austreibung des Geistes aus den Geisteswissenschaften* (The expulsion of spirit from the humanities) (Zurich: Schöningh, 1980). Rather than human interests and intentions, Kittler favors analysis of how medial, technical, and institutional arrangements shaped cultural forms. See Bernard Dionysius Geoghegan, "After Kittler: On the Cultural Techniques of Recent German Media Theory," *Theory, Culture & Society* 30, no. 6 (November 2013): 68.
102. Bernhard Siegert, *Cultural Techniques: Grids, Filters, Doors, and Other Articulations of the Real* (New York: Fordham University Press, 2015), 3; Erikki Huhtamo and Jussi Parikka, eds., *Media Archaeology: Approaches, Applications, and Implications* (Berkeley: University of California Press, 2011).
103. Larkin, *Signal and Noise*; Bao, *Fiery Cinema*.
104. Haidee Wasson, *Everyday Movies: Portable Film Projectors and the Transformation of American Culture* (Berkeley: University of California Press, 2020).

105. Charles Musser, *The Emergence of Cinema: The American Screen to 1907* (Berkeley: University of California Press, 1994), 15–45; Zhou, *Cinema Off Screen*, chap. 3.
106. Craig Buckley, Rüdiger Campe, and Francesco Casetti, *Screen Genealogies: From Optical Device to Environmental Medium* (Amsterdam: Amsterdam University Press, 2019).
107. Debashree Mukherjee, *Bombay Hustle: Making Movies in a Colonial City* (New York: Columbia University Press, 2020), chaps. 4 and 5; Elsaesser, *Film History as Media Archeology*, chap. 5.
108. Vivian Carol Sobchack, *Carnal Thoughts: Embodiment and Moving Image Culture* (Berkeley: University of California Press, 2004); Laura W. Marks, *The Skin of the Film: Intercultural Cinema, Embodiment, and the Senses* (Durham, N.C.: Duke University Press, 2000).
109. This is inspired by and paraphrases Barbara Mittler's reframing of the question from "What does propaganda do to the people?" to "What do people do to propaganda?" See Barbara Mittler, *A Continuous Revolution: Making Sense of Cultural Revolution Culture* (Cambridge, Mass.: Asia Center, Harvard University, 2012), 12–14.
110. On participatory propaganda, see Denise Y. Ho, *Curating Revolution: Politics on Display in Mao's China* (Cambridge: Cambridge University Press, 2018).
111. First launched at the end of 1953, *Dianying fangying ziliao* (Film projection materials) was published roughly monthly between 1954 and 1956. The title was shortened to *Dianying fangying* and was published monthly or bimonthly between 1957 and mid-1960 and again between 1963 and mid-1966. The magazine ceased publication during the Cultural Revolution decade, but I was able to find similar projectionist publications from 1971 to 1976 under various titles such as *Dianying gongzuo qingkuang jianbao* (Film work briefings).
112. Tina Mai Chen, "Propagating the Propaganda Film: The Meaning of Film in Chinese Communist Party Writings, 1949–1965," *Modern Chinese Literature and Culture* 15, no. 2 (2003): 154–93.
113. Kuhn, *An Everyday Magic*, 6–11; Annette Kuhn, Daniel Biltereyst, and Philippe Meers, "Memories of Cinemagoing and Film Experience: An Introduction," *Memory Studies* 10, no. 1 (2017): 11.
114. Jacqueline Najima Stewart, *Migrating to the Movies: Cinema and Black Urban Modernity* (Berkeley: University of California Press, 2005), 95–97.
115. Tsivian, *Early Cinema in Russia*, 1.
116. Jie Li, *Shanghai Homes: Palimpsests of Private Life* (New York: Columbia University Press, 2015), 11–17.
117. Gail Hershatter, *The Gender of Memory: Rural Women and China's Collective Past* (Berkeley: University of California Press, 2011), 23.

1. CINEMATIC NATION-BUILDING

1. Mao Zedong, "Report on an Investigation of the Peasant Movement in Hunan," March 1927, https://www.marxists.org/reference/archive/mao/selected-works/volume-1/mswv1_2.htm.
2. Dangdai Zhongguo de guangbo dianshi bianji bu (Contemporary Chinese Radio and Television Editorial Board), ed., *Zhongguo de youxian guangbo* (China's wired broadcasting) (Beijing: Beijing guangbo xueyuan, 1988), 201.
3. John Durham Peters, "Calendar, Clock, Towers," in *Deus in Machina: Religion, Technology, and the Things in Between*, ed. Jeremy Stolow (New York: Fordham University Press, 2013), 41–42.
4. Sebastian Heilmann and Elizabeth J. Perry, "Embracing Uncertainty: Guerrilla Policy Style and Adaptive Governance in China," in *Mao's Invisible Hand: The Political Foundations of Adaptive Governance in China* (Cambridge, Mass.: Asia Center, Harvard University, 2011), 1–29.
5. Xu Jilin and Luo Gang, *Chengshi de jiyi: Shanghai wenhua de duoyuan lishi chuantong* (Metropolitan memories: The plural historical legacy of Shanghai culture) (Shanghai: Shanghai shudian chubanshe, 2011), 159–66.
6. Jie Li, "Revolutionary Echoes: Radios and Loudspeakers in the Mao Era," *Twentieth-Century China* 45, no. 1 (2020): 32–33.
7. *Dianying fangying* (Film projection) (hereafter DYFY), no. 5 (1957): 14.
8. Following the 1917 revolution, the Bolsheviks dispatched agit-prop trains and steamers equipped with cinemas to the nation's peripheries to show newsreels of national leaders. See Adelheid Heftberger, "Propaganda in Motion: Dziga Vertovs and Aleksandr Medvedkin's Film Trains and Agit Steamers of the 1920s and 1930s," *Apparatus. Film, Media and Digital Cultures of Central and Eastern Europe*, no. 1 (2015): 7–22; Jamie Miller, "Soviet Cinema, 1929–41: The Development of Industry and Infrastructure," *Europe-Asia Studies* 58, no. 1 (January 2006): 103–24.
9. DYFY, no. 9 (1960): 19.
10. Hongwei Thorn Chen, "Cinemas, Highways, and the Making of Provincial Space: Mobile Screenings in Jiangsu, China, 1933–1937," *Wide Screen* 7, no. 1 (2018); Weihong Bao, *Fiery Cinema: The Emergence of an Affective Medium in China, 1915–1945* (Minneapolis: University of Minnesota Press, 2015), chap. 5.
11. Jie Li, "Phantasmagoric Manchukuo: Documentaries Produced by the South Manchurian Railway Company, 1932–1940," *positions: east asia cultures critique* 22, no. 2 (2014): 334–36; Jie Li, "A National Cinema for a Puppet State: The Manchurian Motion Picture Association," in *Oxford Handbook of Chinese Cinemas*, ed. Eileen Cheng-yin Chow and Carlos Rojas (Oxford: Oxford University Press, 2013), 82.

12. Wu Zhuqing and Zhang Dai, eds., *Zhongguo dianying de fengbei: Yan'an dianying tuan gushi* (Monument of Chinese cinema: The story of the Yan'an Film Group) (Beijing: Renmin University Press, 2008), 58–115; Luo Guangda, "Yuan Muzhi yu xin Zhongguo chuqi de dianying faxing fangying gongzuo" (Yuan Muzhi and film distribution and projection work in the early days of New China), *Dianying puji* (Popularizing cinema), no. 2 (1986): 7; Chen Bo, ed., *Zhongguo dianying biannian jishi—Faxing fangyingjuan* (Chronicle of Chinese cinema—on distribution and exhibition) (Beijing: Zhongguo wenxian chubanshe, 2005) 1, no. 1: 343.
13. DYFY, no. 18 (1959): 1–8; *Yunnansheng dianying faxing fangying gongzuo jinian tekan* (Commemorative publication on film distribution and exhibition work in Yunnan province) (Internal publication, 1984), 2. The numbers of projection units included movie theaters and clubs, but the majority were mobile projection teams.
14. *Jilinsheng wenhua gongzuo wenjian xuanbian: Dianying faxing fangying 1951–1966* (Jilin cultural work documents: Film distribution and exhibition, 1951–1966) (Changchun: Jilin wenhuaju, 1988), appendix; *Qinghai dianying zhi* (Qinghai film gazetteer) (Xining: Qinghai Culture Bureau, 1989), 46–47; *Shaanxi dianying zhi* (Shaanxi film gazetteer) (Xi'an: Shaanxi Culture Bureau, 1999), 162, 228, 383–84; *Liaoning dianying faxing fangying jishi (1906–1994)* (Liaoning film distribution and exhibition chronicles [1906–1994]) (Shenyang: Liaoning Film Distribution and Exhibition Company, 1994), 215–16; *Hunan dianying shiye (1949–1990)* (Hunan film enterprise [1949–1990]) (Beijing: Wenhua yishu, 1992), 19–33; *Anhuisheng dianying zhi* (Anhui film gazetteer) (Hefei: Anhui Culture Bureau, 2000), 62, 132–33.
15. Zhengwu yuan (State Council), "Guanyu jianli dianying fangying wang yu dianying gongye de jueding" (Decision on establishing a film projection network and the film industry), Beijing fayuan fagui jiansuo (Beijing court regulations), January 12, 1954, http://fgcx.bjcourt.gov.cn:4601/law?fn=chl521s663.txt&truetag=2686&titles=&contents=&dbt=chl.
16. *Dianying fangying ziliao* (Film projection materials) (hereafter DYFYZL), no. 7 (1954): 12–19; *Guangxi dianying faxing fangying shi* (History of film distribution and exhibition in Guangxi) (Guilin: Guangxi dianying faxing fangying gongsi, 1995), 44–45.
17. DYFYZL, no. 9 (1955): 10–17; DYFY, no. 1 (1963): 9–10; *Guangxi*, 79.
18. *Guangdongsheng dianying faxing fangying gongzuo shiliao* (Historical materials concerning film distribution and exhibition in Guangdong), 3 vols. (Guangzhou: Guangdong wenhuaju, 1991), 2:151.
19. Zhu Zhigang, "Shixi jianguo chuqi xuanchuan wang de jianli he chexiao" (A trial analysis of the establishment and revocation of propaganda networks in

1. Cinematic Nation-Building 275

the early stages of the People's Republic), *Xiandai chuanbo* (Modern communication), no. 11 (2011).
20. Brian DeMare, *Mao's Cultural Army: Drama Troupes in China's Rural Revolution* (Cambridge: Cambridge University Press, 2015), 23.
21. "Dali fazhan wenyi chuangzuo he nongcun qunzhong wenhua shiye" (Vigorously develop artistic creations and rural mass cultural enterprises), *Wenyi bao* (Literature and art newspaper), no. 24 (1955): 10; Cultural Ministry of the People's Republic of China, "Guanyu peihe nongcun hezuohua yundong gaochao kaizhan nongcun wenhua gongzuo de zhishi" (Directive to develop rural cultural work in coordination with rural collectivization), *Renmin ribao* (People's daily), February 22, 1956, 3; Wang Baoyi and Wang Xuying, *Wangshi ruyan: Yesanpo de tuohuangzhe—Wang Baoyi koushu shilu* (The past is like smoke: Yesanpo's pioneer—Wang Baoyi's oral history) (Beijing: Xinhua, 2011), 28–30.
22. Cao Hua, "Zai wenhua gongzuo de juese lai tantan" (Talking about the role of cultural work), *Zhongguo qingnian*, no. 3 (1956).
23. DYFY, no. 2 (1960): 9–12.
24. Wu Xinjun, "'Renmin wenyi' de chuanbo wangluo yu chuanbo jizhi" (The dissemination network of "People's Literature and Art"), *Wenyi yanjiu* (Studies of literature and art), no. 8 (2011): 72–80.
25. Henry Jenkins, *Convergence Culture: Where Old and New Media* Collide (New York: New York University Press, 2006); Wu Xinjun, "'Renmin wenyi,'" 74, 77–79.
26. Prasenjit Duara, *Culture, Power, and the State: Rural North China, 1900–1942* (Stanford, Calif.: Stanford University Press, 1991), 15–41, 73–77.
27. Li Daoxin, "Xin Zhongguo dianying faxing fangying wang: Yige lishi de kaocha" (Film distribution and exhibition network in New China: A historical perspective), *Zhejiang chuanmei xueyuan xuebao* (Zhejiang University journal of communications), no. 3 (2017): 2–19; *Guangdongsheng* 3: 159–71; *Fujiansheng dianying fangying dadui chengli wushi zhounian jinian ce* (Commemorative volume for the fiftieth anniversary of the founding of the Fujian Film Projection Brigade) (Fuzhou, 2001), 12–14.
28. Benedict Anderson, *Imagined Communities: Reflections on the Origin and Spread of Nationalism* (London: Verso. 2006); Noel Carroll, and Sally Banes, "Cinematic Nation-Building: Eisenstein's *The Old and the New*," in *Cinema and Nation*, ed. Mette Hjort and Scott MacKenzie (New York: Routledge, 2000), 121.
29. DYFYZL, no. 2 (1953): 2–3.
30. *Dazhong dianying* (Mass cinema) (hereafter DZDY), no. 1 (1953): 18–20.
31. DYFYZL, no. 4 (1954): 44–46.
32. DYFYZL, no. 5 (1954): 42–50; no. 7 (1954): 62–63; no 11 (1955): 39–40; no. 1 (1956): 7–8, 14–15.

33. André Bazin, *What Is Cinema?* (Berkeley: University of California Press, 2005); DYFYZL, no. 1 (1956): 26–28.
34. Chen Huangmei, "Dianying faxing fangying gongzuo ruhe geng hao de wei guangda qunzhong fuwu" (How to better serve the general public through film distribution and projection), DYFY, no. 9 (1960): 1–7.
35. Walter Benjamin, *The Work of Art in the Age of Its Technological Reproducibility and Other Writings on Media* (Cambridge, Mass.: Harvard University Press, 2008), 40–42.
36. DYFYZL, no. 7 (1954): 32–35; no. 6 (1954): 75–76; DYFY, no. 1 (1960): 8–10.
37. *Guangdongsheng* 3:149–51.
38. Rey Chow, *Primitive Passions: Visuality, Sexuality, Ethnography, and Contemporary Chinese Cinema* (New York: Columbia University Press, 1995), 29–33; Andrew F. Jones, *Circuit Listening: Chinese Popular Music in the Global 1960s* (Minneapolis: University of Minnesota Press, 2020), 56; Haiyan Lee, "The Charisma of Power and the Military Sublime in Tiananmen Square," *Journal of Asian Studies* 70, no. 2 (2011): 399.
39. Daniel Leese, *Mao Cult: Rhetoric and Ritual in the Cultural Revolution* (Cambridge: Cambridge University Press, 2011), 253–61.
40. DYFYZL, no. 1 (1956): 7–8.
41. Benjamin, *The Work of Art*, 23–26; DYFY, no. 11 (1958): 12; no. 1 (1960): 8–10.
42. DYFY, no. 15 (1958): 40; no. 16 (1958): 23.
43. DYFY, no. 11 (1959): 2–21; no. 24 (1959): 4–5.
44. DYFY, no. 2 (1958): 24; no. 1 (1959): 8–10.
45. DYFY, no. 8 (1964): 2.
46. Marshall McLuhan, and Quentin Fiore, *The Medium Is the Message* (New York: Random House, 1967).
47. Paul Clark, "The Triumph of Cinema: Chinese Film Culture from the 1960s to the 1980s," in *Art, Politics, and Commerce in Chinese Cinema*, ed. Ying Zhu and Stanley Rosen (Hong Kong: Hong Kong University Press, 2010); Bai Andan, ed., *Beijingshi dianying faxing fangying danwei shi* (History of film distribution and exhibition in Beijing municipality) (Beijing: Beijing wenhuaju, 1995), 158; *Jilinsheng*, 149–50; *Liaoning*, 210; *Hunan dianying shiye*, 660.
48. Interview with Mr. Zheng (1941–), Zhejiang, 2015; Mr. Zeng (1934–), Hubei, 2015.
49. *Guangxi*, 174.
50. Interview by Peng Hai with Mr. Ma (1949–), Ningxia, 2017.
51. Guoxin Xing, "Urban Workers' Leisure Culture and the 'Public Sphere': A Study of the Transformation of the Workers' Cultural Palace in Reform-Era China," *Critical Sociology* 37, no. 6 (2011): 817–18.
52. Chenshu Zhou, *Cinema Off Screen: Moviegoing in Socialist China* (Berkeley: University of California Press, 2021), 43–45.

53. "Zhonghua quanguo zong gonghui guanyu gonghui dianying fangying gongzuo de guiding" (Provisions of the All-China Federation of Trade Unions on the work of trade union film projection), DYFYZL, no. 9 (1955): 18–19.
54. Interview with Ms. Dai (1934–), Suzhou, 2017.
55. Interview with Ms. Chen (1958–), Shanghai, 2016.
56. DYFYZL, no. 6 (1954): 1–5; no. 11 (1955): 4–5; DYFY, no. 1 (1958): 22–26; no. 13 (1958): 7.
57. Interview with Mr. Yao (1935–), Zhejiang, 2019.
58. Ying Qian, "When Taylorism Met Revolutionary Romanticism: Documentary Cinema in China's Great Leap Forward," *Critical Inquiry* 46, no. 3 (2020): 578–604.
59. Wang Baoyi and Wang Xuying, *Wangshi ruyan*, 28–29.
60. DYFY, no. 9 (1960): 19, 22; no. 1 (1959): 15; no. 9 (1960): 26.
61. DYFY, no. 9 (1960): 19; no. 12 (1958): 12; no. 16 (1958): 4–5, 16–17; no. 18 (1959): 1–8; no. 4 (1960): 19; no. 12 (1960): 8–10.
62. Susan Buck-Morss, *Dreamworld and Catastrophe: The Passing of Mass Utopia in East and West* (Cambridge, Mass.: MIT Press, 2002), 110–11.
63. DZDY, no. 5 (1952): 4–6; DYFYZL, no. 7 (1954): 30–31; DYFY, no. 4 (1957): 4, 7–9; no. 5 (1957): 7–8; no. 4 (1958): 20; no. 12 (1958): 1; no. 5 (1958): 13.
64. Balguy Yuan Ye, "Xiao kanke" (Little spectator), *Jintian* (Today) (2010), https://www.jintian.net/today/?action-viewnews-itemid-27056.
65. Sun Jian, *Chun zai wuren chu* (Spring is where nobody is) (Zhenjiang: Jiangsu University Press, 2014).
66. DYFY, no. 5 (1958): 7; no. 8 (1958): 23; no. 9 (1958): 5–6; no. 10 (1958): 17; no. 10 (1959): 18–19; *Guangdongsheng* 3:159–71.
67. DYFY, no. 4 (1964): 1–6.
68. Robert Jay Lifton, *Revolutionary Immortality: Mao Tse-tung and the Chinese Cultural Revolution* (New York: Random House, 1968), 50; Elizabeth J. Perry, *Anyuan: Mining China's Revolutionary Tradition* (Berkeley: University of California Press, 2012), 242; Lee, "The Charisma of Power," 406–10.
69. China Film Distribution and Exhibition Company, ed., *Dianying xuanchuan faxing fangying gongzuo qingkuang jianbao* (Briefing on the work of film propaganda, distribution, and projection), no. 5 (1971): 1–3.
70. Stuart R. Schram, "Mao Tse-tung and the Theory of the Permanent Revolution, 1958–69," *China Quarterly*, no. 46 (1971): 221–44.
71. DZDY, no. 8/9 (1952): 52; no. 3 (1952): 38; no. 7 (1952): 28–29. Also see DYFYZL, no. 7 (1954): 32–35; no. 10 (1955): 16–17; no. 11 (1955): 37; no. 2 (1956): 32.
72. Mao Zedong, "Speech at the Second Session of the Eighth Party Congress," May 23, 1958, https://www.marxists.org/reference/archive/mao/selected-works/volume-8/mswv8_10.htm.

73. DYFY, no. 1 (1959): 15; no. 5 (1960): 17–18.
74. DYFY, no. 3 (1957): 10–11; no. 10 (1965): 7–8; *Guangxi*, 60–66, 153–55; *Qinghai*, 45; DZDY, no. 15 (1952): 32–33; DYFYZL, no. 8 (1956): 24–25; DYFY, no. 4 (1957): 20–22.
75. James C. Scott, *The Art of Not Being Governed: An Anarchist History of Upland Southeast Asia* (New Haven, Conn.: Yale University Press, 2009).
76. *Qinghai*, 102; *Yunnansheng* 17, 43; *Guangxi*, 197–206.
77. See, for example, *Yunnansheng*, 16, 24, 92; *Shaanxi*, 94; *Henan*, 1–3; *Anhuisheng*, 123–24; *Fujiansheng*, 4–5, 31, 53; *Qinghai*, 42.
78. Li Qingyue, *Ningxia dianying shihua* (Ningxia film chronicles) (Yinchuan: Ningxia People's Press, 2009), 13–15.
79. Interview with Mr. Yang (1924–), Harbin, 2017.
80. DYFY, no. 10 (1958): 2; no. 11 (1958): 15; no. 4 (1960): 1.
81. *Yunnansheng*, 31.
82. DYFY, no. 7 (1964): 7–10; no. 10 (1965): 5.
83. Hubei Provincial Archives, sz120-4-235, 110.
84. China Film Distribution and Exhibition Company, ed., *Dianying xuanchuan faxing*, no. 5 (1971): 22–27.
85. With a high density of religious sites, Wenzhou also saw a revival of religious and lineage activities since the 1980s. Xiaoxuan Wang, *Maoism and Grassroots Religion: The Communist Revolution and the Reinvention of Religious Life in China* (Oxford: Oxford University Press, 2020), 15.
86. Interview with Mr. Xu (1932–), Zhejiang, 2017. According to Bao Jinting, He Bingwu, and Chen Guoxiong, *Wenzhou dianying jishi 1918–2008* (Wenzhou cinema chronicle 1918–2008) (Wenzhou: Wenzhoushi dianying faxing fangyang gongsi, 1994), 10, three films—*The Passion of Jesus Christ*, *Chaplin*, and *The Birth of Moses*—were shown in the Fenglin Catholic Church in May 1944.
87. For the plight of Christians in Wenzhou, see Wang, *Maoism and Grassroots Religion*, chaps. 4–5.
88. Interviews with Mr. Xu (1932–) and with anonymous villagers Zhejiang, 2017.
89. Interview with anonymous villagers, Zhejiang, 2017.
90. Interview with Mr. Xu (1970–), Zhejiang, 2017.
91. Rebecca Nedostup, *Superstitious Regimes: Religion and the Politics of Chinese Modernity* (Cambridge, Mass.: Asia Center, Harvard University, 2010); Prasenjit Duara, *Rescuing History from the Nation: Questioning Narratives of Modern China* (Chicago: University of Chicago Press, 1996), 85–86, 96–97; Mayfair Yang, "Spatial Struggles: Postcolonial Complex, State Disenchantment, and Popular Reappropriation of Space in Rural Southeast China," *Journal of Asian Studies* 63, no. 3 (2004): 726, 747.

92. Li Aidong, ed., *Dianying: Women gongtong de jiyi* (Cinema: Our common memories) (Beijing: Zhongguo dianying chubanshe, 2007), 3:153; interview with Mr. Lei (1931–), Hubei, 2015.
93. I owe the notion of "ritual competition" to Nedostup, *Superstitious Regimes*, chap. 7.

2. MOBILE PROJECTIONISTS AND THE THINGS THEY CARRIED

1. *Dianying fangying ziliao* (Film projection materials) (hereafter DYFYZL), no. 2 (1953): 38–39, 47; *Guangdongsheng dianying faxing fangying gongzuo shiliao* (Historical materials concerning film distribution and exhibition in Guangdong), 3 vols. (Guangzhou: Guangdong wenhuaju, 1991), 3:166; *Yunnansheng dianying faxing fangying gongzuo jinian tekan* (Commemorative publication on film distribution and exhibition work in Yunnan province) (Internal publication, 1984), 14, 55.
2. Li Daoxin, "Xin Zhongguo dianying faxing fangying wang: Yige lishi de kaocha" (Film distribution and exhibition network in New China: A historical perspective), *Zhejiang chuanmei xueyuan xuebao* (Zhejiang University journal of communications), no. 3 (2017): 2–19.
3. Richard Allen, "Psychoanalytic Film Theory," in *A Companion to Film Theory*, ed. Toby Miller and Robert Stam (Malden, Mass: Blackwell, 1999): 123-45.
4. Francesco Casetti, *The Lumière Galaxy: Seven Key Words for the Cinema to Come* (New York: Columbia University Press, 2015), 10, 69–81.
5. For a concise summary of the generations of filmmakers in China, see Ying Zhu, *Chinese Cinema During the Era of Reform: The Ingenuity of the System* (Westport, Conn.: Greenwood, 2003), 5–6.
6. For English-language studies of early film exhibition in China, see Xuelei Huang and Zhiwei Xiao, "Shadow Magic and the Early History of Film Exhibition in China," in *The Chinese Cinema Book*, ed. Song Hwee Lim and Julian Ward (New York: Palgrave Macmillan, 2011), 47–55; Ramona Curry, "Benjamin Brodsky (1877–1960): The Trans-Pacific American Film Entrepreneur—Part One, Making a Trip Thru China," *Journal of American-East Asian Relations* 18, no. 1 (2011): 58–94.
7. See, for example, Li Qingyue, *Ningxia dianying shihua* (Ningxia film chronicles) (Yinchuan: Ningxia renmin chubanshe, 2009), 13–15; *Yunnansheng*, 125–28.
8. Li Qingyue, *Ningxia dianying shihua*, 1–9.
9. Weihong Bao, *Fiery Cinema: The Emergence of an Affective Medium in China, 1915–1945* (Minneapolis: University of Minnesota Press, 2015), chap. 5; Jie Li, "Phantasmagoric Manchukuo: Documentaries Produced by the South

Manchurian Railway Company, 1932–1940," *positions: east asia cultures critique* 22, no. 2 (2014): 334–36; Jie Li, "A National Cinema for a Puppet State: The Manchurian Motion Picture Association," in *Oxford Handbook of Chinese Cinemas*, ed. Eileen Cheng-yin Chow and Carlos Rojas (Oxford: Oxford University Press, 2013), 82.

10. Wu Zhuqing and Zhang Dai, *Zhongguo dianying de fengbei: Yan'an dianying tuan gushi* (Monument of Chinese cinema: The story of the Yan'an Film Group) (Beijing: Renmin daxue chubanshe, 2008), 116–17.
11. Xi Zhen, "Zai Yanhebian de riri yeye—Ji Yan'an dianyingtuan fangyingdui de huodong" (Days and nights at the Yan riverbank—memories of the activities of the Yan'an Film Group's projection team), December 29, 2008, http://www.cndfilm.com/20081229/105479.shtm.
12. Xi Zhen, "Yan'an dianyingtuan de fangyingdui yu guanzhong" (The projection team and audiences of Yan'an Film Group," *Dianying yishu*, no. 1 (1960): 83–84.
13. Wu and Zhang, *Zhongguo dianying de fengbei*, 119.
14. Xi Zhen, "Zai Yanhebian de riri yeye."
15. *Guangdongsheng* 3:160.
16. Jiang Donghao, ed., *Ha'erbin dianying zhi* (Harbin film chronicles) (Harbin: Ha'erbin chubanshe, 2003), 111, 227, 346.
17. Much of what we know about Zhu Andong comes from his confession on May 22, 1951, purportedly archived at the Harbin Public Security Bureau Archives, vol. 2, no. 44, and transcribed by Zheng Wenfa, who contributed to Jiang Donghao, ed., *Ha'erbin dianying zhi*, 112, 227–28; Zhu Andong's case is also mentioned in Yang Zhihuai, *Fengyu jingxingqu: Dongbei gong'an chuangye zongheng lu* (The march of the wind and rain: A longitudinal record of public security entrepreneurship in Northeast China) (Beijing: Qunzhong chubanshe, 2003), 113.
18. *Dianying fangying* (Film projection) (hereafter DYFY), no. 9 (1957): 29; for a similar narrative, see DYFY no. 1 (1963): 18–19.
19. *Fujiansheng dianying fangying dadui chengli wushi zhounian jinian ce* (Commemorative volume for the fiftieth anniversary of the founding of the Fujian Film Projection Brigade) (Fuzhou, 2001), 12–13; *Guangdongsheng* 3:159–71.
20. *Guangdongsheng* 3: 159–71; Wang Baoyi and Wang Xuqing, *Wangshi ruyan: Yesanpo de tuohuangzhe—Wang Baoyi koushu shilu* (The past is like smoke: Yesanpo's pioneer—Wang Baoyi's oral history) (Beijing: Xinhua chubanshe, 2011), 63; Chen Mo, *Huaji fangying: Shaanxi nüzi fangyingren* (Blooming projection: Shaanxi's female projectionists) (Beijing: Zhongguo dianying chubanshe, 2014), 74–80; interview with Ms. Dai (1934–), Suzhou, 2017.
21. DYFY, no. 2 (1958): 26.

22. *Yunnansheng*, 3, 7, 63, 75.
23. *Fujiansheng*, 29–56, 194–95; *Qinghai dianying zhi* (Qinghai film gazetteer) (Xining: Qinghaisheng wenhuating, 1989), 196–98; *Dazhong dianying* (Mass cinema) (hereafter DZDY), no. 14 (1952): 28–29. Also see DYFY, no. 2 (1956): 2.
24. Interviews with Mr. Lei (1931–), Hubei, 2015; and Mr. Chen (1974–) and Mr. Jin (1934–), Zhejiang, 2015.
25. *Guangxi dianying faxing fangying shi* (History of film distribution and exhibition in Guangxi) (hereafter *Guangxi*) (Guilin: Guangxi dianying faxing fangying gongsi, 1995), 108. I heard variations of the doggerel from projectionists in Zhejiang and Hubei as well.
26. DYFY, no. 8 (1957): 13; also see no. 1 (1957): 12, 26–27; no. 2 (1957): 7–8; no. 6 (1957): 3.
27. DYFY, no. 12 (1960): 8–10.
28. Interviews with Mr. Ye (1945–) and Mr. Zeng (1934–), Hubei, 2015.
29. Interview with Mr. Xia (1947–) and Ms. Gong (1944–), Hubei, 2015.
30. *Yunnansheng*, 14–15, 25, 48–49; Wang Baoyi and Wang Xuaqing, *Wangshi ruyan*, 96–120.
31. *Guangxi*, 185.
32. *Shaanxi sheng dianying faxing fangying gongsi dianying gongzuo jianbao* (Briefing on the film work of Shaanxi Film Distribution and Projection Company), no. 1 (1972): 1–8.
33. For a brief account of the 8.75mm format with images, see super8 database, http://www.filmkorn.org/super8data/database/articles_list/8-75mm_format.htm.
34. Hubei province, Huanggang Prefecture Archives, 82-3-20 (1970), 81.
35. Interview with Mr. Zhou (1956–), Mr. Zhang (1955–), and Mr. Xu (1954–), Hubei, 2015.
36. Interview with Mr. Zhu (1952–), Mr. Liang (1952–), Mr. Xu (1954–), and Ms. Duan (1957–), Hubei, 2015.
37. Interview with Mr. Xia (1974–), Hubei, 2015.
38. Interview with Mr. Liu (1961–) and Mr. Xu (1954–), Hubei, 2015.
39. China Film Distribution and Exhibition Company, ed., *Dianying xuanchuan faxing fangying gongzuo qingkuang jianbao* (Briefing on the work of film propaganda, distribution, and projection), no. 5 (1971): 28–38; Heilongjiang Film Distribution and Projection, *Dianying gongzuo jianbao* (Briefings on film work), no. 4 (1973): 16–19; Hubei Provincial Archives, sz120-4-235, 110–18.
40. Interviews with Mr. Peng (1950–), Mr. Zhou (1956–), and Mr. Liu (1961–), Hubei, 2015.
41. Interviews conducted in Shanghai with former projectionists in Heilongjiang: Mr. Lu (1950–), 2012; Mr. Pan (1948–), 2012; Mr. Qin (1952–), 2013; and Mr. Lou (1953–), 2016.

42. Chen Mo, *Huaji fangying*, 22–25; Also see DYFYZL, no. 3 (1954): 54; no. 4 (1954): 30–41; no. 5 (1954): 18–38; no. 6 (1954): 30–36.
43. This was the general consensus of the former projectionists and audiences whom I interviewed from 2012 to 2019.
44. DYFYZL, no. 6: 21–27; no. 2 (1963): 10–11.
45. Chen Mo, *Huaji fangying*, 23–24; DYFY, no. 2 (1963): 18–9; no. 4 (1963): 8; DZDY, no. 1 (1953): 18–19.
46. DYFY, no. 2 (1957): 22–23.
47. Interview with Mr. Lei (1931–), Hubei, 2015; Hu Guizhen, "Yige nongcun dianyingdui lao fangyingyuan de huiyi" (Memories of an old rural film projectionist on a rural film team), *Shenzhou xinwen wang*, April 1, 2012, http://sznews.zjol.com.cn/sznews/system/2012/04/01/014894278.shtml; also see DYFY, no. 18 (1959): 1–8.
48. DYFY, no. 4 (1963): 27; no. 6 (1956): 6–7.
49. DYFY, no. 2 (1963): 12–13; interview with Mr. Qin (1952–), Shanghai, 2013.
50. Wang Baoyi and Wang Xuqing, *Wangshi ruyan*; Chenshu Zhou, *Cinema Off Screen: Moviegoing in Socialist China* (Berkeley: University of California Press, 2021), 62.
51. Brian Larkin, *Signal and Noise: Media, Infrastructure, and Urban Culture in Nigeria* (Durham, N.C.: Duke University Press, 2008), 218–19.
52. Yu Liang, *Naxie nian naxie shi: Yige nongmin de jiyi* (Those years: A peasant's memories) (Beijing: Haichao chubanshe, 2014), 219; Wang Xinpeng, *Women xin sanjie* (We three new classes) (Beijing: Zuojia chubanshe, 2008), 149.
53. Ge Fei, "Xiangcun dianying" (Village cinema), in *Yigeren de dianying* (An individual's cinema), Ge Fei, Jia Zhangke, et al. (Beijing: Zhongxin chubanshe, 2008), 1–22.
54. Rostislav Berëzkin, *Many Faces of Mulian: The Precious Scrolls of Late Imperial China* (Seattle: University of Washington Press, 2017), 3–5; Wilt L. Idema, *The Immortal Maiden Equal to Heaven and Other Precious Scrolls from Western Gansu* (Amherst, N.Y.: Cambria Press, 2015), 1–2.
55. Berëzkin, *Many Faces of Mulian*, 3–5; Idema, *The Immortal Maiden*, 1–2.
56. Lü Yihuan, ed., *Minjian shuochang wenyi duben* (Folk spoken-singing literature and art reader) (Shenyang: Shenyang chubanshe, 2013), 17–174.
57. Chen Mo, *Huaji fangying*, 16.
58. DZDY, no. 17 (1954): 33.
59. Interview with Mr. Zheng (1930s–), Zhejiang, 2019; Bei Yan, *Shan de nayibian* (The other side of the mountain) (Guangzhou: Ji'nan daxue chubanshe, 2012), 102.
60. *Guangdongsheng* 1:184; DYFYZL, no. 5 (1954): 54.
61. Richard Abel and Rick Altman, eds., *The Sounds of Early Cinema* (Bloomington: Indiana University Press, 2001); Hideaki Fujiki, "Benshi as Stars: The Irony

of the Popularity and Respectability of Voice Performers in Japanese Cinema," *Cinema Journal* 45, no. 2 (2006): 68–84; Kuei-Fen Chiu, "The Question of Translation in Taiwanese Colonial Cinematic Space," *Journal of Asian Studies* 70, no. 1 (2011): 77–97.

62. DYFYZL, no. 7 (1954): 66; DYFY, no. 1 (1963): 22–23; no. 3 (1963): 12.
63. Qing Sun, "The Early Slide Projector and Slide Shows in China from the Late Seventeenth to the Early Twentieth Century," *Journal of Modern Chinese History* 12, no. 2 (2018): 203–26.
64. Frank Dikötter, *Exotic Commodities: Modern Objects and Everyday Life in China* (New York: Columbia University Press, 2006), 251–52.
65. See Zhou, *Cinema Off Screen*, chap. 3, for an extensive account of the slide projector in China.
66. DYFYZL, no. 5 (1954): 62.
67. DYFY, no. 5 (1958): 34; no. 7 (1965): 2–3.
68. Hu Zhiren, "Shezhi gengduo huandeng pian" (Producing more lantern slides), *Dazhong sheying* (Mass photography), no. 1 (1960): 13.
69. Liu Guangyu, *Xin Zhongguo chengli yilai nongcun dianying fangying yanjiu* (Study of rural film exhibitions since the founding of New China) (Beijing: Wenhua yishu chubanshe, 2015), 197; *Guangxi*, 97–98.
70. Wang Baoyi and Wang Xuqing, *Wangshi ruyan*, 48; interview with Mr. Wang (1955–), Hebei, 2017.
71. DYFY, no. 5 (1958): 7; no. 8 (1958): 23; no. 9 (1958): 5–6; interviews with former projectionists in Hubei and Zhejiang, 2015 and 2017.
72. Interviews with Mr. Yan (1940–), Hebei, 2017; Mr. Pan (1948–) and my father Li Bin (1949–), Shanghai, 2012; Mr. Zhou, Hubei, 2015.
73. *Guangdongsheng* 2:68; 1:185.
74. DYFY, no. 9 (1958): 1–5; no. 3 (1959): 11; no. 5 (1960): 10.
75. Hu Zhiren, "Shezhi gengduo huandeng pian," 13.
76. "Huandeng xuanchuan shige hua," DYFY, no. 6 (1959): 15–16; no. 5 (1959): 10–13; no. 9 (1958): 1–4; no. 1 (1959): 1–13.
77. DZDY, no. 10 (1952): 26–27; no. 1 (1953): 18–20. For other all-female movie team stories, see DYFYZL, no. 5 (1954): 16–17; DZDY, no. 18 (1955): 42–44; no. 9 (1963): 24–25.
78. DYFY, no. 16 (1958): 16–17; also no. 6 (1958): 29–30; no. 12 (1958): 13.
79. DYFY, no. 11 (1958): 15; no. 16 (1958): 16–17; no. 17 (1958): 4, 6.
80. Interviews with former rural projectionists in Hubei, Zhejiang, Heilongjiang, and Ningxia provinces, 2015–2019.
81. DZDY, no. 5 (1964): 22.
82. Henrietta Harrison, *The Missionary's Curse and Other Tales from a Chinese Catholic Village* (Berkeley: University of California Press, 2013), 145–46.

83. China Film Distribution and Exhibition Company, ed., *Dianying xuanchuan faxing fangying gongzuo qingkuang jianbao* (Briefing on the work of film propaganda, distribution, and projection), no. 5 (1971): 22–27; interviews with Mr. Pan (1948–), 2012, and Mr. Qin (1952–), Shanghai, 2013.
84. Chen Mo, *Huaji fangying*, 30–31, 85–86.
85. Xu Dongqing, ed., *Jiangyin yu Zhongguo dianying* (Jiangyin and Chinese cinema) (Beijing: Zhongguo dianying chubanshe, 2010), 194; *Guangdongsheng* 1:182–83.
86. Shi Sanfu, *Qiao shui lazhu qu* (Knocking water candles) (Shanghai: Shanghai renmin chubanshe, 2013), 91; interview by Peng Hai with Ms. Zhou (1960–), Ningxia, 2017.
87. Interview with Mr. Lu (1950–), Shanghai, 2012.
88. *Guangdongsheng* 1:187; Chen Mo, *Huaji fangying*, 29, 86; interviews with Mr. Chen (1937–) and Mr. Jin (1937–), Zhejiang, 2015; Mr. Zheng (1930s–), Zhejiang, 2019.
89. Poem published in DZDY, no. 7 (1965): 23.
90. Chen Mo, *Huaji fangying*, 16, 32, 95.
91. *Yunnansheng*, 81. Also see DYFY, no. 2 (1957): 17; no. 4 (1957): 40.
92. Interview by Peng Hai with Ms. Li (1962–), Ningxia, 2017.
93. Interview by Peng Hai with Ms. Li (1961–) who grew up in Gansu and moved to Ningxia for work, 2017.
94. Meir Shahar and Robert P. Weller, eds., *Unruly Gods: Divinity and Society in China* (Honolulu: University of Hawai'i Press, 1996), 22–30.
95. *Guangdongsheng* 2:31–32.
96. China Film Distribution and Exhibition Company, ed., *Dianying xuanchuan faxing*, no. 5 (1971): 41–43, 51.

3. THE THREE SISTERS MOVIE TEAM

1. Zhang Pu, "San duo honghua xiangyang kai: Ji sanjiemei dianying fangyingdui" (Three red flowers facing the sun: On the Three Sisters Movie Team), originally published in *Hebei wenxue* (Hebei literature), no. 1 (1966); reprinted in *Hebei baogao wenxue xuan* (Collected reportage from Hebei) (Shijiazhuang: Hebei renmin chubanshe, 1979), 187–207.
2. Among reports on the Three Sisters Movie Team in the national media are *Dazhong dianying* (Mass cinema) (hereafter DZDY), no. 10/11 (1964): 54–56; and "Nongye zhanxian shang de wenhua jianbing" (Cultural vanguards on the agricultural front), *Zhongguo funü* (Women of China), no. 1/2 (1965): 21–23. The 1966 newsreel was also incorporated into a made-for-TV documentary on the Three Sisters by Baoding television station in 2012.

3. Poem composed by a model projection team in 1974, Hubei Provincial Archives, sz120-4-235, 86–95.
4. Gail Hershatter, *The Gender of Memory: Rural Women and China's Collective Past* (Berkeley: University of California Press, 2011), 212. Donald Munro, "The Chinese View of Modeling," *Human Development* 18, no. 5 (1975): 333–52.
5. For example, see Harriet Evans and Stephanie Donald, *Picturing Power in the People's Republic of China: Posters of the Cultural Revolution* (Lanham, Md.: Rowman & Littlefield, 1999); Laikwan Pang, *The Art of Cloning: Creative Production During China's Cultural Revolution* (New York: Verso, 2017).
6. Brian Winston, *Claiming the Real: The Griersonian Documentary and Its Legitimations* (London: British Film Institute, 1995); Bill Nichols, *Representing Reality: Issues and Concepts in Documentary* (Bloomington: Indiana University Press, 1991); André Bazin, *What Is Cinema?* (Berkeley: University of California Press, 2005).
7. Here I paraphrase a compelling question asked by Jane Gaines, "Did documentary films ever produce social change?," which she derives in part from a National Film Board of Canada poll in 1995 to produce a list of "the 10 documentaries that changed the world." See Gaines, "Political Mimesis," in *Collecting Visible Evidence*, ed. Jane Gaines and Michael Renov (Minneapolis: University of Minnesota Press, 1999), 84–102.
8. Rey Chow, *Primitive Passions: Visuality, Sexuality, Ethnography, and Contemporary Chinese Cinema* (New York: Columbia University Press, 1995), 33.
9. Mao Zedong, "China Is Poor and Blank" and "The Question of Agricultural Cooperation," in *The Political Thought of Mao Tse-tung*, ed. Stuart R. Schram (New York: Praeger, 1963), 252–53, 247–49; *Dianying fangying* (Film projection) (hereafter DYFY), no. 10 (1960): 17.
10. This reading is indebted to William Schaefer, "Poor and Blank: History's Marks and the Photographs of Displacement," *Representations* 109, no. 1 (2010): 5–6.
11. DYFY, no. 2 (1959): 19; no. 18 (1959): 1; no. 9 (1960): 22.
12. DYFY, no. 13 (1958): 22.
13. DYFY, no. 18 (1959): 1; no. 2 (1959): 19.
14. DYFY, no. 18 (1959): 1–6; no. 3 (1960): 12–13; no. 12 (1960): 10–11; no. 3 (1959): 11; no. 12 (1959): 17–18.
15. DYFY, no. 18 (1959): 1.
16. Weihong Bao, *Fiery Cinema: The Emergence of an Affective Medium in China, 1915–1945* (Minneapolis: University of Minnesota Press, 2015), 8–11.
17. Bernard Siegert, *Cultural Techniques: Grids, Filters, Doors, and Other Articulations of the Real* (New York: Fordham University Press, 2015), 56–57.

18. Quoted in Brian Larkin, "The Politics and Poetics of Infrastructure," *Annual Review of Anthropology* 42, no. 1 (2013): 335.
19. Debashree Mukherjee, *Bombay Hustle: Making Movies in a Colonial City* (New York: Columbia University Press, 2020), 40; Thomas Elsaesser, *Film History as Media Archeology: Tracking Digital Cinema* (Amsterdam: Amsterdam University Press, 2016), chap. 5.
20. DYFY, no. 3 (1960): 12–13.
21. Pang, *The Art of Cloning*, 91.
22. Sigrid Schmalzer, *Red Revolution, Green Revolution: Scientific Farming in Socialist China* (Chicago: University of Chicago Press, 2016), 41–42, 136–37.
23. Pang, *The Art of Cloning*, 84.
24. China Film Distribution and Exhibition Company, ed., *Dianying xuanchuan faxing fangying gongzuo qingkuang jianbao* (Briefing on the work of film propaganda, distribution, and projection), no. 5 (1971): 56–59.
25. Hubei Provincial Archives, sz120-4-235, 106–7.
26. Heilongjiang Province Film Distribution and Production, ed., *Dianying gongzuo tongxun* (Film work correspondence), no. 1 (1972): 17.
27. Hubei Provincial Archives, sz120-4-235, 86–95, 110–119.
28. For a comprehensive list, see Liu Guangyu, *Xin Zhongguo chengli yilai nongcun dianying fangying yanjiu* (Study of rural film exhibitions since the founding of New China) (Beijing: Wenhua yishu chubanshe, 2015), 161.
29. Hubei Provincial Archives, sz120-4-235, 86–95, 134–41.
30. Liu Guangyu, *Xin Zhongguo*, 162.
31. *Dianying gongzuo jianbao* (Film work briefings), no. 4 (1973): 7–10, 28–29. On "Iron Girls," see Zheng Wang, *Finding Women in the State: A Socialist Feminist Revolution in the People's Republic of China 1949–1964* (Berkeley: University of California Press, 2017), 221–28.
32. Interview with Mr. Mu (1949–) and Mr. Ma (1949–), Ningxia, 2017.
33. *Dianying gongzuo jianbao*, no. 4 (1973): 7–10; DYFY, no. 1 (1976): 5.
34. *Dianying gongzuo jianbao*, no. 4 (1973): 36–38.
35. DYFY, no. 1 (1978).
36. Interview with Mr. Jin (1934–), Zhejiang, 2015.
37. Interviews with villagers in Zhejiang, 2015.
38. James A. Flath, *The Cult of Happiness: Nianhua, Art, and History in Rural North China* (Seattle: University of Washington Press, 2004), 114–16; Wang Baoyi and Wang Xuying, *Wangshi ruyan* (The past is like smoke) (Beijing: Xinhua chubanshe, 2011), 30–36.
39. Wang Baoyi and Wang Xuying, *Wangshi ruyan*, 28–49; interview with Mr. Liu (1935–), Hebei, 2017.

40. Wang Baoyi and Wang Xuying, *Wangshi ruyan*, 48–49; DYFY, no. 3 (1957): 1; no. 4 (1957): 1; no. 5 (1957): 28–33.
41. *Dianying fangying ziliao* (Film projection materials) (hereafter DYFYZL), no. 8 (1954): 31; DYFY, no. 2 (1957): 22–23; no. 12 (1960): 22–25; no. 13 (1960): 7–8.
42. Wang Baoyi and Wang Xuying, *Wangshi ruyan*, 63.
43. Daisy Yan Du, "Socialist Modernity in the Wasteland: Changing Representations of the Female Tractor Driver in China, 1949–1964," *Modern Chinese Literature and Culture* 29, no. 1 (2017): 67–69.
44. DZDY, no. 10 (1952): 26–27; no. 1 (1953): 18–20. For other all-female movie team stories, see DYFYZL, no. 5 (1954):16–17; DZDY, no. 18 (1955): 42–44; no. 9 (1963): 24–25.
45. Xu Ruzhong, "Cong muyang gunian dao dianying fangyingyuan" (From shepherdess to film projectionist), DYFY, no. 9 (1957): 26–27.
46. DYFY, no. 1 (1959): 8–10.
47. DYFYZL, no. 12 (1955): 29–30.
48. Hebei Film Distribution and Exhibition Company, *Duojingtou huandengji de zhizuo yu shiyong* (Making and using multilens slide projectors) (Beijing: Zhongguo dianying chubanshe, 1965), 1–3; Wang Baoyi and Wang Xuying, *Wangshi ruyan*, 77–79.
49. "Nongye zhanxian shang de wenhua jianbing," 21–23; DZDY, no. 1 (1980): 692.
50. Thomas Lamarre, "Magic Lantern, Dark Precursor of Animation," *Animation: An Interdisciplonary Journal* 6, no. 2 (2011): 143.
51. *Guangdongsheng* 1:226–27; 3: 166; DYFY, no. 3 (1966): 12–16; interviews with Mr. Jin (1937–) and Dai (1934–), Zhejiang, 2015; interview with Mr. Ye (1945–), Hubei, 2015; DZDY, no. 4 (1964): 22–23; DZDY, no. 2/3 (1965): 44; *Guangxi dianying*, 141–42.
52. DYFY, no. 5 (1960): 8–16; no. 10 (1960): 10–11.
53. Zheng Yizhen, "Maozhuxi zhuzuo gei women wuqiong de zhihui he liliang" (Chairman Mao gave us infinite wisdom and power), *Dianying yishu*, no. 1 (1964): 21–26.
54. The accounts of their colleagues are corroborated by frequent mentions of the Three Sisters in other provincial film histories such as *Guangxi dianying*, 99, 143; *Anhuisheng dianying zhi*, 55, 252–53.
55. Interview with Mr. Yan (1940–) and Mr. Han (1938–), Hebei, 2017.
56. Interview with Mr. Yan (1940–), Hebei, 2017.
57. Interviews with Mr. Han (1938–) and Mr. Guo (1937–), Hebei, 2017.
58. Interview with Mr. Liu (1935–), Hebei, 2017.
59. Interview with Mr. Liu (1935–) and Mr. Han (1938–), Hebei, 2017.
60. Interview with Wang Xuying (1955–), Hebei, 2017.
61. Wang Baoyi and Wang Xuying, *Wangshi ruyan*, 95–110.

62. Wang Baoyi and Wang Xuying, 91–93; interview with Mr. Yan (1940–), Hebei, 2017.
63. Interview with Wang Xuying and villagers from the hometown of two of the Three Sisters, Hebei, 2017.
64. Interviews with Mr. Yan (1940–) and Mr. Han (1938–), Hebei, 2017.
65. Interview with Mr. Han (1938–), Hebei 2017.
66. Interview with Ms. Yu (1961–), Hebei, 2017.
67. Interview with Ms. Yu (1961–), Hebei, 2017.
68. *Yunnansheng*, 23.
69. *Guangdongsheng* 1:187; Chen Mo, *Huaji fangying: Shaanxi nüzi fangyingren* (Blooming projection: Shaanxi's female projectionists) (Beijing: Zhongguo dianying chubanshe, 2014), 86; *Fujiansheng*, 44–45. Interviews with Mr. Lei (1931–) and Mr. Zeng (1934–), Hubei, 2015; interview with Mr. Chen (1964–), Zhejiang, 2015.
70. *Guangdongsheng* 1:182–83; Chen Mo, *Huaji fangying*, 16, 53, 96; *Fujiansheng*, 71–73; interview with Ms. Zhou (1960–), Ningxia, 2017.
71. Chen Mo, *Huaji fangying*, 16–17, 23, 34, 38–39, 52–54, 92–96, 221–22, 284.
72. Guo Yanping, "Nongcun xingbie guannian de xiandaixing gaizao: Yi 20 shiji 50 niandai Shaanxi diqu liudong fangying weili" (The modernization of rural gender perception: A case study of Shaanxi mobile projection teams in the 1950s), *Funü yanjiu luncong* (Women's studies), no. 6 (2016), 28–41.
73. The team size was reduced in the next few years and became a mixed-gender team when a male member joined in 1957. Chen Mo, *Huaji fangying*, 16–17, 23, 34, 38–39, 52–54, 92–96, 221–22, 284.
74. Interview with Ms. Dai (1934–), Suzhou, 2017.
75. Interview with Ms. Gong (1944–), Hubei, 2015.
76. Interview with Ms. Duan (1957–) and Mr. Duan (1956–), Hubei, 2015.
77. Interview by Peng Hai with Ms. Zhou (1960–), Ningxia, 2017.
78. Interview with Ms. Chen (1969–), Zhejiang, 2017.
79. Tina Mai Chen, "Female Icons, Feminist Iconography? Socialist Rhetoric and Women's Agency in 1950s China," *Gender and History* 15, no. 2 (2003): 268–95; Xiaobing Tang, *Visual Culture in Contemporary China: Paradigms and Shifts* (Cambridge: Cambridge University Press, 2015); Lingzhen Wang, *Revisiting Women's Cinema: Feminism, Socialism, and Mainstream Culture in Modern China* (Durham, N.C.: Duke University Press, 2020); Wang, *Finding Women in the State*; Hershatter, *The Gender of Memory*, 266.
80. DYFY, no. 1 (1959): 8–10; no. 1 (1976): 17; Chen Mo, *Huaji fangying*, 88.
81. For more on photography during the Great Leap Forward, see chapter 3 of my book *Utopian Ruins: A Memorial Museum of the Mao Era* (Durham, N.C.: Duke University Press, 2020).

4. THE COST OF SPIRITUAL FOOD

1. Annual total cinema attendance numbers are recorded in Chen Bo, ed., *Zhongguo dianying biannian jishi—Faxing fangyingjuan* (Chronicle of Chinese cinema—on distribution and exhibition) (Beijing: Zhongguo wenxian chubanshe, 2005) 1, no. 1. The later statistics come from Statista, "The Number of Movie Tickets Sold in China from 2010 to 2022," https://www.statista.com/statistics/476794/china-cinema-audience-size/; Sina, "Xie Fei: The 3-Year Tranformation of Chinese Films," http://ent.sina.com.cn/r/m/2009-01-07/10552331780.shtml.
2. Ying Zhu, *Chinese Cinema During the Era of Reform: The Ingenuity of the System* (Westport, Conn.: Greenwood, 2003), 211. Other brief mentions of the socialist box office can be found in Paul Clark, *Chinese Cinema: Culture and Politics since 1949* (Cambridge: Cambridge University Press, 1987), 37–40, 74; Chris Berry, *Postsocialist Cinema in Post-Mao China: The Cultural Revolution After the Cultural Revolution* (New York: Routledge, 2004), 22–26; Emilie Yueh-yu Yeh and Darrell William Davis, "Re-nationalizing China's Film Industry: Case Study on the China Film Group and Film Marketization," *Journal of Chinese Cinemas* 2, no. 1 (2008): 37–38.
3. *Dianying fangying* (Film projection) (hereafter DYFY), no. 8 (1957): 17–18.
4. For an argument on socialist cinema facilitating consumerism, see Karl Gerth, *Unending Capitalism: How Consumerism Negated China's Communist Revolution* (Cambridge: Cambridge University Press, 2020), chap. 4.
5. See DYFY, no. 8 (1957): 1–3. For other debates on the socialist box office, see DYFY, no. 6 (1957): 27–30; no. 8 (1957): 12; *Guangxi dianying faxing fangying shi* (History of film distribution and exhibition in Guangxi) (Guilin: Guangxi dianying faxing fangying gongsi, 1995), 68.
6. *Jilinsheng wenhua gongzuo wenjian xuanbian: Dianying faxing fangying 1951–1966* (Jilin cultural work documents: Film distribution and exhibition, 1951–1966) (Changchun: Jilin wenhuaju, 1988), 8–11.
7. *Dianying fangying ziliao* (Film projection materials) (hereafter DYFYZL), no. 2 (1953): 4–5.
8. DYFYZL, no. 2 (1953): 40–41.
9. DYFYZL, no. 5 (1954): 42–50.
10. DYFY, no. 6 (1957): 3; no. 5 (1957): 30–33.
11. DYFY, no. 9 (1957): 13–14.
12. DYFY, no. 2 (1958): 14–21; no. 8 (1957): 13–14; 40–42.
13. *Yunnansheng dianying faxing fangying gongzuo jinian tekan* (Commemorative publication on film distribution and exhibition work in Yunnan province)

(Internal publication, 1984), 58; DYFYZL, no. 3 (1954): 80; no. 5 (1954): 54–57; no. 7 (1954): 7; DYFY, no. 6 (1956): 22–23; no. 1 (1957): 13–16.
14. DYFY, no. 1 (1958): 10; *Guangxi*, 67–73; interview conducted by Li Bingbing and Wang Sisi with Mr. Chen (1937–), Zhejiang, 2015.
15. DYFY, no. 2 (1957): 14–16; no. 8 (1957): 17; no. 5 (1963): 5–8.
16. DYFY, no. 2 (1957): 16; no. 4 (1957): 38–39.
17. DYFY, no. 2 (1957): 16–17.
18. DYFY, no. 2 (1957): 9, 12–14; no. 1 (1958): 2–3.
19. DYFY, no. 2 (1957): 17; no. 4 (1957): 40; no. 6 (1957): 22–23.
20. DYFY, no. 1 (1957): 20.
21. DYFY, no. 2 (1957): 21; no. 3 (1956): 36.
22. DYFY, no. 6 (1956): 24–25.
23. DYFY, no. 6 (1957): 6–7; no. 6 (1958): 14.
24. DYFY, no. 8 (1957): 25.
25. DYFY, no. 8 (1957): 17–18; no. 2 (1957): 9–11; no. 1 (1958): 8; no. 7 (1958): 17–18; no. 6 (1958): 32.
26. DYFY, no. 2 (1958): 18; *Jilinsheng*, 66.
27. DFYFZL, no. 9: 21–22; no. 5 (1971): 12–21 (quotation on 14).
28. DYFY, no. 1 (1957): 12, 26–27; no. 2 (1957): 7–8; no. 6 (1957): 3.
29. DYFY, no. 4 (1960): 3; also see no. 12 (1960), a special issue on heroes and models.
30. DYFY, no. 12 (1958): 1; no. 13 (1958): 16–17; no. 14 (1958): 32; no. 15 (1958): 1.
31. DYFY, no. 9 (1958): 1–4; no. 15 (1958): 17; no. 1 (1959): 14; no. 3 (1959): 13.
32. DYFY, no. 1 (1959): 14; no. 13 (1959): 7.
33. DYFY, no. 8 (1958): 4–5.
34. DYFY, no. 6 (1957): 27–30; no. 15 (1958): 7–8.
35. DYFY, no. 7 (1958): 15; no. 1 (1959): 1; no. 9 (1958): 14–15; no. 9 (1960): 1–7.
36. DYFY, no. 17 (1958): 8; no. 18 (1958): 2–3; no. 1 (1959): 1–7.
37. Interview with Mr. Lei (1931–), Hubei, 2015; *Guangxi*, 73; DYFY, no. 1 (1963): 13–15.
38. DYFY, no. 13 (1959): 5.
39. Lu Xun, *Lu Xun zawenji* (Lu Xun's miscellaneous essays) (Shenyang: Wanjuan chubanshe, 2013), 107
40. DYFY, no. 15 (1958): 17.
41. DYFY, no. 9 (1960): 22.
42. Hu Guizhen, "Yige nongcun dianyingdui lao fangyingyuan de huiyi" (Memories of an old rural film projectionist on a rural film team), *Shenzhou xinwen wang*, April 1, 2012, http://sznews.zjol.com.cn/sznews/system/2012/04/01/014894278.shtml; DYFY, no. 18 (1959): 1–8.

43. *Guangxi*, 108–9, 113, 121; DYFY, no. 13 (1959): 9–10; no. 1 (1963): 5–8; Matthew D. Johnson, "Beneath the Propaganda State: Official and Unofficial Cultural Landscapes in Shanghai, 1949–1965," in *Maoism at the Grassroots*, ed. Jeremy Brown and Matthew D. Johnson (Cambridge, Mass.: Harvard University Press, 2015), 199–229.
44. This principle is mentioned in multiple articles in the July 1963 issue of DYFY.
45. DYFY, no. 1 (1963): 13–15. Also see *Guangxi*, 129.
46. DYFY, no. 7 (1963): 9–17.
47. DYFY, no. 7 (1963): 9–13.
48. DYFY, no. 7 (1963): 9–13; no. 10 (1963): 1–3; no. 2 (1963): 2.
49. DYFY, no. 1 (1963): 11–12; no. 3 (1964): 4–9; no. 4 (1963): 17–19; no. 1 (1965): 7–12, 15.
50. Steve Neale and Sheldon Hall, *Epics, Spectacles, and Blockbusters: A Hollywood History* (Detroit, Mich.: Wayne State University Press, 2010), 139.
51. Chris Berry, "What's Big About the Big Film? 'De-Westernizing' the Blockbuster in Korea and China," in *Movie Blockbusters*, ed. Julian Stringer (New York: Routledge, 2003), 217–18; Ying Zhu, "Feng Xiaogang and Chinese New Year Films," *Asian Cinema* 18, no. 1 (2007): 43–63; Xiaobing Tang, *Visual Culture in Contemporary China: Paradigms and Shifts* (Cambridge: Cambridge University Press, 2015), 180–84; Stanley Rosen, "Film and Society in China: The Logic of the Market," in *A Companion to Chinese Cinema*, ed. Zhang Yingjin (Malden, Mass.: Wiley-Blackwell, 2012), 197–217.
52. *Liaoning dianying faxing fangying jishi* (1906–1994) (Liaoning film distribution and exhibition chronicles [1906–1994]) (Shenyang: Liaoning Film Distribution and Exhibition Company, 1994), 76–73, 92–95, 100–102, 109–10, 121; *Qinghai dianying zhi* (Qinghai film gazetteer) (Xining: Qinghaisheng wenhuating, 1989), 44; *Guangdongsheng dianying faxing fangying gongzuo shiliao* (Historical materials concerning film distribution and exhibition in Guangdong), 3 vols. (Guangzhou: Guangdong wenhuaju, 1991) 2:10–12; 3:22; 1:140–42; *Guangxi*, 37–38.
53. *Guangxi*, 137–138; interview with Mr. Dai (1934–), Zhejiang, 2015.
54. Chen Bo, ed., *Zhongguo dianying*, 806, 1296; Liu Guangyu, *Xin Zhongguo chengli yilai nongcun dianying fangying yanjiu* (Study of rural film exhibitions since the founding of New China) (Beijing: Wenhua yishu chubanshe, 2015), 152–53; DYFY, no. 11 (1963): 4.
55. DYFY, no. 11 (1963): 5.
56. DYFY, no. 9 (1964): 5; Liu Guangyu, *Xin Zhongguo*, 151; interview with Mr. Dai (1934–), Zhejiang, 2015.
57. DYFY, no. 1 (1963): 20–22; no. 8 (1963): 15–16; no. 10 (1964): 4; no. 10 (1965): 15.
58. DYFY, no. 9 (1964): 5; no. 11 (1965): 5; *Guangxi*, 140–41; Liu Guangyu, *Xin Zhongguo*, 154, 207–8.

59. DYFY, no. 1 (1963): 2–3; interview with Mr. Dai (1934–), Zhejiang, 2015.
60. DYFY, no. 7 (1964): 11; Liu Guangyu, *Xin Zhongguo*, 151.
61. Interviews with Mr. Liu (1931–), Hebei, 2017; Ms. Ma (1957–), Ningxia, 2017.
62. *Hunan dianying shiye: (1949–1990)* (Hunan film enterprise: [1949–1990]) (Beijing: Wenhua yishu chubanshe, 1992), 658; Liu Dongchu, *Henan dianying zhi 1909–1987* (Henan film gazetteer 1909–1987) (Zhengzhou: Henan dianying gongsi, 2000), 48.
63. Liu Guangyu, *Xin Zhongguo*, 155.
64. *Liaoning*, 208–13.
65. *Dianying gongzuo qingkuang jianbao* (Film work briefings), no. 1 (1972): 11–15.
66. China Film Distribution and Exhibition Company, ed., *Dianying xuanchuan faxing fangying gongzuo qingkuang jianbao* (Briefing on the work of film propaganda, distribution, and projection), no. 5 (1971): 12–21.
67. Li Daoxin, "Xin Zhongguo dianying dianying faxing fangying wang: Yige lishi de kaocha" (Film distribution and exhibition network in New China: A historical perspective), *Zhejiang chuanmei xueyuan xuebao* (Zhejiang University journal of communications), no. 3 (2017), 2–19.
68. Zhuang Zhijuan, "Sanci teshu de kan dianying jingli" (Three special film-viewing experiences), *Shiji*, no. 2 (2012): 44–45.
69. *Guangxi*, 190; *Guangdongsheng* 3, 167–68.
70. *Liaoning*, 222, 227; interviews with Mr. Qin (1952–), Shanghai, 2013, and Mr. Lou (1953–), Shanghai, 2016.
71. *Guangxi*, 191; Liu Guangyu, *Xin Zhongguo*, 151.
72. Luo Xuepeng, "'Maihua guniang' yu 15 tiao Zhongguo ren de shengping" (Luo Xuepeng's "Flower Girl" and 15 Chinese lives), http://mjlsh.usc.cuhk.edu.hk/Book.aspx?cid=4&tid=3455.
73. For example, see *Guangxi*, 52, 54. Also see Bian Zhenhu, *Ai zai Dunhuang* (Love in Dunhuang) (Beijing: Zuojia chubanshe, 2007), 34.
74. Interviews with Mr. Zeng (1934–), Mr. Duan (1934–), Mr. Xu (1954–), Hubei, 2015; Mr. Zhan (1950–), Zhejiang, 2015.
75. Ge Fei, "Xiangcun dianying" (Village cinema), in *Yigeren de dianying* (An individual's cinema), Ge Fei, Jia Zhangke, et al. (Beijing: Zhongxin chubanshe, 2008), 1–22.
76. Roman Lobato, *Shadow Economies of Cinema: Mapping Informal Film Distribution* (London: Palgrave Macmillan, 2012), 7; Brian Larkin, *Signal and Noise: Media, Infrastructure, and Urban Culture in Nigeria* (Durham, N.C.: Duke University Press, 2008), 225.
77. Mayfair Mei-hui Yang, *Gifts, Favors, and Banquets: The Art of Social Relationships in China* (Ithaca, N.Y.: Cornell University Press, 1994), chap. 5.

78. Interview with Mr. Zhan (1950–), Zhejiang, 2015.
79. *Yunnansheng*, 81.
80. Interview with Mr. Xu (1954–), Hubei, 2015.
81. Interviews with Mr. Zhang (1955–) and Mr. Xu (1954–), Hubei, 2015.
82. DYFY, no. 6 (1978): 14–20.
83. Interview with Mr. Ye (1945–), Hubei, 2015.
84. Interviews with Mr. Chen (1937–), Zhejiang, 2015 and Mr. Zheng (1930–), Zhejiang, 2019.
85. Cui Jizhe, *Zuihou de lang* (The last wolf) (Taiyuan: Sanjin chubanshe, 2014), 98.
86. DYFY, no. 3 (1977): 7–15.
87. DYFY, no. 5 (1977): 10–20, on Heilongjiang movie theaters. Also see Kuang Chen, ed., *Women de qishi niandai* (Our 1970s) (Nanning: Guangxi renmin chubanshe, 2004), 252
88. DYFY, no. 5 (1977): 27–38, 50–55.
89. Wang Xinpeng, *Women xin sanjie* (We three new classes) (Beijing: Zuojia chubanshe, 2008), 155–56.
90. DYFY, no. 3 (1977): 7–15; no. 4 (1978): 13.
91. Prasenjit Duara, *Culture, Power, and the State: Rural North China, 1900–1942* (Stanford, Calif.: Stanford University Press, 1991), 42–56.
92. *Dianying gongzuo jianbao*, no. 4 (1973): 3–5; interview with Mr. Zheng (1947–), Hubei, 2015.
93. Ding Qizhen, "Xiangcun lutian dianying" (Rural open-air cinema), http://blog.sina.com.cn/s/blog_4900fe270100ezl6.html; interview with Mr. Yang (1955—), Zhejiang, 2012.
94. Interview with Mr. Jin (1934–), Zhejiang, 2015.
95. Pang, *The Art of Cloning*, chap. 2.
96. Mayfair Mei-hui Yang, *Re-enchanting Modernity: Ritual Economy and Society in Wenzhou, China* (Durham, N.C.: Duke University Press, 2020), 281; Mayfair Mei-hui Yang, "Putting Global Capitalism in Its Place: Economic Hybridity, Bataille, and Ritual Expenditure," *Current Anthropology* 41, no. 4 (2000): 486.
97. Kenneth Dean, "Local Communal Religion in Contemporary South-east China," *China Quarterly*, no. 174 (2003): 338–58. David Johnson, *Spectacle and Sacrifice: The Ritual Foundations of Village Life in North China* (Cambridge, Mass.: Asia Center, Harvard University, 2010).
98. Johnson, *Spectacle and Sacrifice*, 15.
99. China Film Distribution and Exhibition Company, ed., *Dianying xuanchuan faxing*, no. 5 (1971): 50.

5. THE HOT NOISE OF OPEN-AIR CINEMA

1. Adam Chau, *Miraculous Response: Doing Popular Religion in Contemporary China* (Stanford, Calif.: Stanford University Press, 2005), chap. 8; Shuenn-Der Yu, "Hot and Noisy: Taiwan's Night Market Culture," in *The Minor Arts of Daily Life: Popular Culture in Taiwan*, ed. David K. Jordan, Andrew D. Morris, and Marc L. Moskowitz (Honolulu: University of Hawai'i Press, 2004), 138–39.
2. Robert P. Weller, *Resistance, Chaos, and Control in China: Taipei Rebels, Taiwanese Ghosts, and Tiananmen* (Seattle: University of Washington Press, 1994), 118.
3. Yu, "Hot and Noisy," 138–40.
4. Joshua Goldstein, *Drama Kings: Players and Publics in the Re-creation of Peking Opera, 1870–1937* (Berkeley: University of California Press, 2007), 72.
5. Svetlana Boym, *Common Places: Mythologies of Everyday Life in Russia* (Cambridge, Mass.: Harvard University Press, 1994), 3.
6. Jacques Attali, *Noise: The Political Economy of Music* (Manchester, UK: Manchester University Press, 1985), 27.
7. Mikhail Bakhtin, *Rabelais and His World*, tr. Hélène Iswolsky (Bloomington: Indiana University Press, 1984).
8. Siegfried Kracauer and Thomas Y. Levin, "Cult of Distraction: On Berlin's Picture Palaces," *New German Critique*, no. 40 (Winter 1987): 91–96; Walter Benjamin, *The Work of Art in the Age of Its Technological Reproducibility, and Other Writings on Media* (Cambridge, Mass.: Harvard University Press, 2008); Miriam Hansen, "The Mass Production of the Senses: Classical Cinema as Vernacular Modernism," in *Reinventing Film Studies*, ed. Christine Gledhill and Linda Williams (Oxford: Oxford University Press, 2000), 332–50; Zhen Zhang, *An Amorous History of the Silver Screen: Shanghai Cinema, 1896–1937* (Chicago: University of Chicago Press, 2005), 4; Leo Ou-Fan Lee, *Shanghai Modern: The Flowering of a New Urban Culture in China, 1930–1945* (Cambridge, Mass.: Harvard University Press, 1999), chap. 3; Weihong Bao, *Fiery Cinema: The Emergence of an Affective Medium in China, 1915–1945* (Minneapolis: University of Minnesota Press, 2015), introduction.
9. Zhiwei Xiao, "Movie House Etiquette Reform in Early-Twentieth-Century China," *Modern China* 32, no. 4 (2006): 513–14.
10. Sun Jianwei, *Heilongjiang dianying bainian* (One hundred years of cinema in Heilongjiang) (Ha'erbin: Heilongjiang daxue chubanshe, 2012), 55; Jiang Zequan, *Dianyingyuan jianzhu* (Cinema architecture) (Beijing: Zhongguo gongye chubanshe, 1964), 2–4, 85–148.

11. *Dianyingyuan sheji* (Cinema design) (Nanjing: Nanjing Institute of Technology Pedagogy and Research Group, 1963), 33, 36–38, 72.
12. *Yunnansheng dianying faxing fangying gongzuo jinian tekan* (Commemorative publication on film distribution and exhibition work in Yunnan province) (internal publication, 1984), 14, 121–22; *Guangxi dianying faxing fangying shi* (History of film distribution and exhibition in Guangxi) (hereafter *Guangxi*) (Guilin: Guangxi dianying faxing fangying gongsi, 1995), 26–27; Li Gexin, *Jiangshu Qingdao de gushi* (Telling Qingdao's story) (Ji'nan: Shandongsheng ditu, 2013), 90; Yu Dongxing, *Ma la huoche de difang* (A place of horse-drawn locomotives) (Beijing: Wenlian chubanshe, 2012), 253–58; *Dazhong dianying* (Mass cinema) (hereafter DZDY), no. 1 (1955): 36–37.
13. *Guangxi dianying*, 58.
14. Ge Fei, "Xiangcun dianying" (Village cinema), in *Yigeren de dianying* (An individual's cinema) (Beijing: Zhongxin chubanshe, 2008), 2; interview by Peng Hai with Mr. Li (1959–), Ningxia, 2017.
15. *Guangxi dianying*, 51.
16. John Durham Peters, *The Marvelous Clouds: Toward a Philosophy of Elemental Media* (Chicago: University of Chicago Press, 2015), chap. 4.
17. *Dianying fangying ziliao* (Film projection materials) (hereafter DYFYZL), no. 10 (1955): 31.
18. Chen Mo, *Huaji fangying: Shaanxi nüzi fangyingren* (Blooming projection: Shaanxi's female projectionists) (Beijing: Zhongguo dianying chubanshe, 2014), 13; Mu Xiaoli, *Yigeren de xingzou* (One person's journey) (Ningbo: Ningbo chubanshe, 2011), 146–47.
19. *Qinghai dianying zhi* (Qinghai film gazetteer) (Xining: Qinghaisheng wenhuating, 1989), 194–95; Guo Wenlian, *Yili wangshi* (Memories of Ili) (Hefei: Anhui wenyi chubanshe, 2013), 117.
20. Fan Xiufeng, *Cun shang de shi* (Village matters) (Shijiazhuang: Huashan wenyi chubanshe, 2010), 264; Yu Liang, *Naxie nian naxie shi: Yige nongmin de jiyi* (Those years: A peasant's memories) (Beijing: Haichao chubanshe, 2014), 29; Lian Xiaohua, *Ge'ermu de tiankong* (The sky of Golmud) (Beijing: Zhongguo wenlian, 2005), 157.
21. Wang Anyi, *Wenge yishi* (A tale from the Cultural Revolution) (Shanghai: Shanghai wenyi chubanshe, 2013).
22. Noam M. Elcott, *Artificial Darkness: An Obscure History of Modern Art and Media* (Chicago: University of Chicago Press, 2016), 6.
23. Zhuang Zhijuan, "Sanci teshu de kan dianying jingli" (Three special film-viewing experiences), *Shiji*, no. 2 (2012), 44–45.
24. Qi Yujiang, *Hongdu qingshen* (Deep sentiments for the red capital) (Xi'an: Shaanxi renmin chubanshe, 2011), 117; Bei Yan, *Shan de nayibian* (The other

side of the mountain) (Guangzhou: Ji'nan daxue chubanshe, 2012), 102; Yao Juntao, ed., *Yilingba tuan zhi (1958–2003)* (108th regiment gazetteer [1958–2003]) (Wulumuqi: Xinjiang dianzi chubanshe, 2005), 378.

25. Tang Hongxiang, *Lengnuan rensheng* (Life's vicissitudes) (Beijing: Zhongguo minzu sheying yishu chubanshe, 2005), 10.
26. Interviews by Peng Hai with female villagers in Ningxia, 2017.
27. Tom Gunning, "The Cinema of Attraction[s]: Early Film, Its Spectator, and the Avant-Garde," in *The Cinema of Attractions Reloaded*, ed. Wanda Strauven (Amsterdam: Amsterdam University Press, 2006), 383.
28. Xiao, "Movie House Etiquette Reform," 516–27; Liu Yingying, "Tiantang dianyingyuan" (Cinema paradiso), *Baihuazhou*, no. 3 (2010): 131.
29. DZDY, nos. 2–3 (1965): 47.
30. DYFY, no. 16 (1958): 16–17; no. 2 (1959): 21.
31. Sun Jian, *Chun zai wuren chu* (Spring is where nobody is) (Zhenjiang: Jiangsu daxue chubanshe, 2014), 184; interview with Mr. Qin (1952–), Shanghai, 2013.
32. Interview by Peng Hai with Ms. Li (1961–), Ningxia, 2017; interviews with former projectionists in Hubei, 2015.
33. Mu Xiaoli, *Yigeren de xingzou*, 146–47; Li Yanlin, *Chuntian zhu zai wo de cunzhuang* (Spring lives in my village) (Ji'nan: Shandong jiaoyu chubanshe, 2011), 58; interviews by Peng Hai with villagers, Ningxia, 2017.
34. Chen Jiarui, *Ren zai Chang'an diji qiao* (On which bridge of Chang'an) (Xi'an: Xi'an chubanshe, 2010), 270; Ge Fei, "Xiangcun dianying," 12.
35. Li Yanlin, *Chuntian zhu zai wo de cunzhuang*, 56–57; Qi Yujiang, *Hongdu*, 116; interviews with former rural projectionists in Hubei and Zhejiang provinces, August 2015.
36. Interview with Mr. Qin (1952–), Shanghai, July 21, 2013.
37. Ah Cheng, *The King of Trees: Three Stories by Ah Cheng*, tr. Bonnie S. McDougall (New York: New Directions, 2010), 173.
38. Li Jiantong, *Na nian na ye* (Those years, those nights) (Shijiazhuang: Huashan wenyi chubanshe, 2013), 33; Xia Lei, *Qiu yi wei qi* (Due in autumn) (Tianjin: Baihua wenyi chubanshe, 2009), 159.
39. Michel Chion, *Audio-Vision: Sound on Screen*, tr. Claudia Gorbman (New York: Columbia University Press, 1994), 25–34.
40. Dong Zhi, "Lao dianyingyuan" (Old cinema), *Junma*, no. 3 (2012): 53–57; Nicole Huang, "Listening to Films: Politics of the Auditory in 1970s China," *Journal of Chinese Cinemas* 7, no. 3 (2013): 187–206.
41. Interview by Peng Hai with Mr. Mu (1949–), Ningxia, 2017.
42. Friedrich Kittler, *Discourse Networks, 1800/1900*, tr. Michael Metteer and Chris Cullens (Stanford, Calif.: Stanford University Press, 1990), 116, 229–30.

43. Laura W. Marks, *The Skin of the Film: Intercultural Cinema, Embodiment, and the Senses* (Durham, N.C.: Duke University Press, 2000), 144, 204–5; Vinzenz Hediger and Alexandra Schneider, "The Deferral of Smell: Cinema, Modernity and the Reconfiguration of the Olfactory Experience," in *The Five Senses of Cinema: XI International Film Studies Conference*, ed. Valentina Re et al. (Udine, Italy: Forum, 2005), 243–52.
44. Li Xiaojun, *Hou geming niandai de tongnian* (Postrevolutionary childhood) (Nanchang: Baihuazhou wenyi chubanshe, 2015); Luo Haibo, *Yongyuan de xiangshou* (Forever together) (Hainan: Hainan chubanshe, 2007), 157–58.
45. Xiao, "Movie House Etiquette Reform," 521; Li Aidong, ed., *Dianying: Women gongtong de jiyi* (Cinema: Our common memories) (Beijing: Zhongguo dianying chubanshe, 2007), 3:103–4.
46. Liu Dacheng, *Xiangxi tongnian* (West Hunan childhood) (Hefei: Anhui wenyi chubanshe, 2016), 126–28; Qi Yujiang, *Hongdu*, 116.
47. Cui Jizhe, *Zuihou de lang* (The last wolf) (Taiyuan: Sanjin chubanshe, 2014), 98.
48. Zhang Daquan, "Diyici zai shuixiang fangying" (Showing film in a water town), DYFY, no. 11 (1959): 21–22.
49. Qi Yujiang, *Hongdu*, 116.
50. Maurice Bloch, "Commensality and Poisoning," *Social Research* 66, no. 1 (Spring 1999): 133–49.
51. James L. Watson, "Feeding the Revolution: Public Mess Halls and Coercive Commensality in Maoist China," in *Governance of Life in Chinese Moral Experience: The Quest for an Adequate Life*, ed. Everett Zhang, Arthur Kleinman, and Tu Weiming (New York: Routledge, 2011), 33–46.
52. Wang Liu'er, "Hebin dianyingyuan" (Hebin cinema), *Guiyang wenshi* (Guiyang literature and history), no. 1 (2012): 18–19; Li Aidong, ed., *Dianying*, 1:214; 4:8–9; Mu Xiaoli, *Yigeren de xingzou*, 146–47; He'ergou, "Zuori zhi ri buke zhui, chuntian niannian dao renjian" (We cannot catch yesterday, spring comes every year) (blog), February 26, 2016, https://read01.com/NoADQa.html.
53. Li Aidong, ed., *Dianying* 4:136; Lian Xiaohua, *Ge'ermu de tiankong*, 157–58; Shi Sanfu, *Qiao shui lazhu qu*, 91.
54. Mei Haijun, *Wo ge Jiangbei* (I sing of Jiangbei) (Ningbo: Ningbo chubanshe, 2016), 165.
55. Li Yanlin, *Chuntian zhu zai wo de cunzhuang*, 58; Yu Dongxing, *Ma la huoche de difang*, 253–58.
56. Interview with Mr. Zheng (1930s–), Zhejiang, 2019.
57. DYFY, no. 2 (1957): 17; no. 4 (1957): 40; Wang Xinpeng, *Women xin sanjie* (We three new classes) (Beijing: Zuojia chubanshe, 2008), 149.
58. Tang Hongxiang, *Lengnuan rensheng*, 11.
59. Marks, *Skin of the Film*, 162.

60. Vivian Carol Sobchack, *Carnal Thoughts: Embodiment and Moving Image Culture* (Berkeley: University of California Press, 2004), 56, 84.
61. Guan Wenjie, "Yi Beidahuang" (Remembering the "Great Northern Wilderness"), blogpost, December 2013, http://www.360doc.com/content/13/1203/21/9159788_334249881.shtml.
62. Interviews by Peng Hai with Mr. Hai (1962–) and Mr. Hai (1969–), Ningxia, 2017.
63. Interview by Peng Hai with a Mr. Li (1969–), Ningxia, 2017. For another tale of moviegoing without a movie, see Ding Qizhen, "Zui fengguang dianying guanzhong" (The craziest moviegoers), http://blog.sina.com.cn/s/blog_4900fe270100ez8d.html.
64. Wang Xinpeng, *Women xin sanjie*, 149; Lian Xiaohua, *Ge'ermu de tiankong*, 157–58.
65. Interview via questionnaire with Ms. Xu Xiaoli (1953–), Beijing, 2016.
66. Wang Xinpeng, *Women xin sanjie*, 145–48.
67. Cao Xiu, *You yizhong qianshou jiao wennuan* (A kind of handholding called warmth) (Hohhot: Neimenggu renmin chubanshe, 2009), 48.
68. Wang Xinpeng, *Women xin sanjie*, 145.
69. Yu Liang, *Naxie nian naxie shi*, 219.
70. Tang Hongxiang, *Lengnuan rensheng*, 11; interviews by Peng Hai with villagers in Ningxia, 2017.
71. Bei Yan, *Shan de nayibian*, 102.

6. GUERRILLA CINEMA AND GUERRILLA RECEPTION

1. Xiaoning Lu, *Moulding the Socialist Subject: Cinema and Chinese Modernity (1949–1966)* (Leiden: Brill, 2020), 4.
2. Ban Wang, "Art, Politics and Internationalism: Korean War Films in Chinese Cinema," *The Oxford Handbook of Chinese Cinemas*, ed. Carlos Rojas and Eileen Cheng-yin Chow (Oxford: Oxford University Press, 2013), 251.
3. On guerrilla filmmaking in Latin America, see Fernando Solanas, and Octavio Getino, "Toward a Third Cinema," *Cineaste* 4, no. 3 (1970): 1–10.
4. The idea of industrial military genre is inspired by Alexander Zahlten's notion of industrial genres in Japanese cinema to map "shifting textual constellations of industrial structures and practices, media texts, spaces of circulation, and spectatorships." See Zahlten, *The End of Japanese Cinema: Industrial Genres, National Times, and Media Ecologies* (Durham, N.C.: Duke University Press, 2017), 6.
5. Chen Mo, *Huaji fangying: Shaanxi nüzi fangyingren* (Blooming projection: Shaanxi's female projectionists) (Beijing: Zhongguo dianying chubanshe, 2014),

34–35; *Dianying fangying* (Film projection) (hereafter DYFY), no. 8 (1963): 15; Liu Guangyu, *Xin Zhongguo chengli yilai nongcun dianying fangying yanjiu* (Study of rural film exhibitions since the founding of New China) (Beijing: Wenhua yishu chubanshe, 2015), 222–23.

6. Among the most classic and popular titles of guerrilla war films are *Letter with Feathers* (鸡毛信) (1954), *Guerrillas on the Plain* (平原游击队) (1955), *Railroad Guerrillas* (铁道游击队) (1956), *Heroes on Langya Mountain* (狼牙山五壮士) (1958), *Landmine Warfare* (地雷战) (1962), *Little Soldier Zhang Ga* (小兵张嘎) (1963), *Tunnel Warfare* (地道战) (1965), *The Red Lantern* (红灯记) (1970), *Taking Tiger Mountain by Strategy* (智取威虎山) (1971) and *Sparkling Red Star* (闪闪的红星) (1974).

7. Paul Virilio, *War and Cinema: The Logistics of Perception* (London: Verso, 1989).

8. *Yunnansheng dianying faxing fangying gongzuo jinian tekan* (Commemorative publication on film distribution and exhibition work in Yunnan province) (internal publication, 1984), 14, 121–22; *Guangxi dianying faxing fangying shi* (History of film distribution and exhibition in Guangxi) (Guilin: Guangxi dianying faxing fangying gongsi, 1995), 26–27.

9. *Dianying fangying ziliao* (Film projection materials) (hereafter DYFYZL), no. 10 (1955): 34–37.

10. DYFYZL, no. 6 (1954): 84–85.

11. *Dianying fangying* (Film projection) (hereafter DYFY), no. 1 (1958): 14–15; no. 9 (1958): 8.

12. DYFY, no. 4 (1957): 42–43; no. 10 (1960): 17–19; Guobin Yang, *The Red Guard Generation and Political Activism in China* (New York: Columbia University Press, 2016), 48–68; Shi Tiesheng, "Kan dianying" (Watching movies), in *Jiyi yu yinxiang* (Memories and impressions) (Changsha: Hunan wenyi chubanshe, 2012), 79–86; Li Aidong, ed., *Dianying: Women gongtong de jiyi* (Cinema: Our common memories) (Beijing: Zhongguo dianying chubanshe, 2007), 2:56, 64, 108; 3:55, 220, 232–34.

13. Li Aidong, ed., *Dianying* 2:56, 120, 132; 3:197–98; 4:17–18, 50, 108–13.

14. Interview with Mr. Yuan (1953–), Ningxia, 2017.

15. Zhang Jiantian, *Wo shi Datian ren: Xiangei shangshiji wuliushi niandai chusheng de ren* (I am from Datian: Dedicated to the generation born in the 1950s and the 1960s) (Beijing: Jiefangjun chubanshe, 2013), 143; Liu Hui and Sun Shanyu, *Lao Beijing naxie shi'er* (Miscellanies from old Beijing) (Beijing: Dangdai Zhongguo chubanshe, 2013), 181.

16. *Dianying gongzuo jianbao* (Film work briefings), no. 4 (1973): 7–10.

17. Rui Gao, "Cacophonous Memories of the War: Revision of the Official Narrative on the War of Resistance Against Japan in Post-Mao China and Its

Limitations," in *Routledge Handbook of Memory and Reconciliation in East Asia*, ed. Mikyoung Kim (New York: Routledge, 2015), 37.
18. Donald H. McMillen, "Civil Defence in the People's Republic of China," *Australian Journal of Chinese Affairs*, no. 8 (1982): 35–50.
19. Huang Jingsong, "1969, shen wa didong de niandai" (1969, the era of deep digging), *Putian wanbao*, September 24, 2013; interview by Peng Hai with Ms. Guo (1950–), Ningxia, 2017.
20. Yomi Braester, *Witness Against History: Literature, Film, and Public Discourse in Twentieth-Century China* (Stanford, Calif.: Stanford University Press, 2003), 106–27.
21. Cui Jizhe, *Ye kan fengjing ye dushu* (Viewing the landscape as well as reading a book) (Chengdu: Sichuan wenyi chubanshe, 2016), chap. 5.
22. Mei Xingwu, "Maque zhan, dilei zhan, didao zhan de youlai" (The origin of sparrow warfare, mine warfare, and tunnel warfare), *Hongyan chunqiu* (Hongyan spring and autumn), no. 7 (1991): 54–59.
23. Mao Zedong, "Zai Zhongguo gongchandang diqici quanguo daibiao dahuishang de koutou zhengzhi baogao" (Oral political report at the Seventh National Congress of the Communist Party of China), April 24, 1945, https://www.marxistphilosophy.org/maozedong/mx3/065.htm.
24. Michel Foucault, *Security, Territory, Population: Lectures at the Collège de France, 1977–78* (New York: Palgrave Macmillan, 2007), 125–30.
25. Mao Zedong, "Some Experiences in Our Party's History," September 25, 1956, https://www.marxists.org/reference/archive/mao/selected-works/volume-5/mswv5_54.htm.
26. Xue Pangao, "Lishi jiaoxun juece jingjian: Wei maque fan'an de jiannan licheng" (History lessons, decision mirrors: The arduous path of rehabilitating sparrows), *Yanhuang chunqiu*, no. 12 (1998): 9–15.
27. "1958 nian weijiao maque de 'renmin zhanzheng' shi ruhe fadong de" (How was the "people's war" against sparrows launched in 1958?), https://zhuanlan.zhihu.com/p/426894503.
28. Jiankang bao bianji bu (Editorial Department, Health News), ed., *Zenyang chu sihai* (How to eliminate the four pests) (Beijing: Kexue puji chubanshe, 1958), 19–21; Zheng Guanglu, *Sichuan jiushi* (Stories from Sichuan) (Chengdu: Sichuan renmin chubanshe, 2007), 193–95.
29. Zheng Guanglu, *Sichuan jiushi*, 208.
30. Jiang Yanyan, and Yan Yonghe, "Ye Shengtao riji zhong de 1958" (Ye Shengtao's 1958 diary), *Yanhuang chunqiu*, no. 6 (2010): 55–61.
31. Jiang and Yan. Also see Sheldon Lou, *Sparrows, Bedbugs, and Body Shadows: A Memoir* (Honolulu: University of Hawai'i Press, 2005).
32. Guo Moruo, "Zhou maque" (To curse sparrows), *Beijing wanbao*, April 21, 1958.

33. Fei Jianjun, *Tongji rensheng zhilu* (Counting life's paths) (Shijiazhuang: Hebei renmin chubanshe, 2015), 96–97.
34. Xue Panguo, "Lishi jiaoxun juece jingjian," 9–15.
35. Sally Wen Mao, "On Sparrows," *Kenyon Review* 41, no. 5 (2019): 77–93.
36. Xiaosheng Liang, *Confessions of a Red Guard*, tr. Howard Goldblatt (Portland, Maine: MerwinAsia, 2018), 8–31.
37. Jie Li, "Revolutionary Echoes: Radios and Loudspeakers in the Mao Era," *Twentieth-Century China* 45, no. 1 (2020): 32–33.
38. Dai Jinhua, *After the Post–Cold War: The Future of Chinese History* (Durham, N.C.: Duke University Press, 2018), 109–26; Haiyan Lee, *A Certain Justice: Toward an Ecology of the Chinese Legal Imagination* (Chicago: University of Chicago Press, 2023), chap. 1.
39. Lu, *Moulding the Socialist Subject*, chap.1.
40. Li Aidong, ed., *Dianying* 2: 63.
41. Shi Tiesheng, *Jiyi yu yinxiang* (Memories and impressions) (Beijing: Beijing Press, 2004), 79–86.
42. Li Aidong, ed., *Dianying* 1: 97.
43. Zhou Guandong, ed., *Xin shiqi Jiading zuojia qun (ziliao juan)* (New era Jiading Writing Group [Materials]) (Shanghai: Shanghai wenyi chubanshe, 2010), 493–94.
44. Pan Qiaonan, "Wo zai yuanzhengjun zhong de yiduan jingli" (My experience in the expeditionary force), http://www.hnqz.net/80th/show.php?id=1086.
45. Yang Jichun, *Luobupo zhi ge* (Song of Lop Nur) (Guangzhou: Zhongshan daxue chubanshe, 2013), 230.
46. Chen Zhuo, "Na ge chuanhongxie de yaofan de lao taitai shi tewu" (The old beggar woman in red shoes is a spy), in *Chanhui haishi bu chanhui* / (To repent or not to repent), ed. Yu Kaiwei (Beijing: Zhongguo gongren chubanshe, 2004), 289.
47. Group interview with former sent-down youths, Shanghai, 2016; Fu Sanfeng, *Tingqu washeng yipian* (Listening to frogs) (Ningbo: Ningbo chubanshe, 2013).
48. Qi Wang, "Those Who Lived in a Wallpapered Home: The Historical Space of the Socialist Chinese Counter-Espionage Film," *Journal of Chinese Cinemas* 5, no. 1 (2011): 57; Li Aidong, ed., *Dianying* 4: 128.
49. Carma Hinton, Geremie Barmé, and Richard Gordon, *Morning Sun: A Documentary Film About the Cultural Revolution in China* (Long Bow Group, 2003). *Morning Sun*, and Ge Fei, "Xiangcun dianying," 14–16.
50. Bao Zuojun, *Ni shi Huanghe wo shi sha* (You are the Yellow River, and I am its sand) (Yinchuan: Ningxia renmin jiaoyu chubanshe, 2012), 105; Fu Sanfeng, *Tingqu washeng yipian*, 160; interview with Mr. Lou (1953–) and other sent-down youths, Shanghai, 2016.

51. Tian Huiming, and Zhong Cheng, *Wo de jiu ni de ba* (My wine, your bar) (Beijing: Wenhua yishu chubanshe, 2002), 3; Bao Zuojun, *Ni shi huanghe wo shi sha*, 137–38.
52. E. Ann Kaplan, ed. *Women in Film Noir* (London: British Film Institute, 2019), 10.
53. "Jiang Qing Critiques Old Films," *Morning Sun*, http://www.morningsun.org/smash/jq_films.html.
54. Zhai Jiannong, *Hongse wangshi: 1966–1976 nian de Zhongguo dianying* (The red past: Chinese cinema 1966–1976) (Beijing: Taihai chubanshe, 1998), 92.
55. Yuan Chengliang, "Hua'er weishenme zheyang hong—Dianying *Bingshan shang de laike* dansheng ji" (Why are the flowers so red—the birth of the film *Visitors on Ice Mountain*), *Dangshi zongheng* (Party history), no. 2 (2006): 48–50.
56. Zhang Yiwei, *Kongjian yu jiyi: Zhongguo yingyuan wenhua yanjiu* (Space and memory: Cultural studies of Chinese cinemas) (Beijing: Zhongguo chuanmei Daxue chubanshe, 2015), 193; interview by Peng Hai with Mr. Yuan (1953–), Ningxia, 2017; Liu Haoyuan, *Fengqiao yemu* (A Fengqiao night) (Nanchang: Baihuazhou wenyi chubanshe, 2006), 500.
57. Liang, *Confessions of a Red Guard*, 13–14; interviews with Mr. Lu (1948–), Shanghai, 2016, and Mr. Luo (1960–), Ningxia, 2017.
58. He Dacao, *Shimian shu: Yuye yu lütu suibiji* (Insomnia notes: Essays on rainy nights and journeys) (Wuhan: Huazhong shifan daxue chubanshe, 2012), 37–38.
59. Li Quanmin, "Yao shi ren nie jin quantou, buyao shi ren da la xia naodai: Tan dianying gequ chuangzuo" (Make people clench their fists rather than droop their heads: On film songwriting), *Renmin yinyue* (People's music), no. Z1 (1964): 51–52; Song Yang, "Chengzhe dianying de chibang, ba geming gesheng song dao guangda qunzhong zhong qu" (Riding the wings of movies, sending revolutionary songs to the masses), *Renmin yinyue* (People's music), no. 5 (1964): 32–33.
60. "'Hua er weishenme zheyang hong' de gequ xuanyang de doushi zichanjieji sixiang ganqing" (The song "Why Are the Flowers so Red" promotes bourgeois thoughts and feelings), *Zhongguo qingnian bao* (China youth newspaper), October 13, 1964; "Zhongguo qingnian bao zhankai 'women yao chang shenme yang de gequ' taolun qingkuang zongshu" (China Youth Daily launches "What kind of song do we want to sing" summary discussion), December 1964.
61. Chen Gang, "Cong fante xinpian suo xiangdao de yixie wenti: Jianping 'genzong zhuiji' yu 'bingshan shang de laike'" (Questions inspired by recent counterespionage films: Comments about *On the Trail* and *Visitors on Ice Mountain*), *Dianying yishu* (Film art), no. 6 (1963): 37–44, 75.
62. "Jiang Qing zai quanjun chuangzuo huiyishang fan guanyu dianying de wenti" (Jiang Qing talks about films at the All-Army Creation Conference), April 1966, http://prchistory.org/wp-content/uploads/2014/05/REMEMBRANCE-No-32

-2009%E5%B9%B49%E6%9C%887%E6%97%A5.pdf; http://www.cnd.org/CR/ChuanXinLu_.pdf.

63. Zhou Yinan, *Zhou Yinan wenji* (Zhou Yinan's collected works) (Wuhan: Wuhan daxue chubanshe, 2019), 3:912.
64. Yue Meng, "Female Images and National Myth," in *Gender Politics in Modern China: Writing and Feminism*, ed. Tani Barlow (Durham, N.C.: Duke University Press, 1993), 118–36; Di Bai "Feminism in the Revolutionary Model Ballets: *The White-Haired Girl* and *The Red Detachment of Women*," in *Art in Turmoil: The Chinese Cultural Revolution 1966–1976*, ed. Richard King (Hong Kong: Hong Kong University Press, 2010), 188–202.
65. Haiyan Lee, *The Stranger and the Chinese Moral Imagination* (Stanford, Calif.: Stanford University Press, 2014), 45–52; Lu, *Moulding the Socialist Subject*, 121–41.
66. Xiaofei Kang, "Revisiting White-Haired Girl: Women, Gender, and Religion in Communist Revolutionary Propaganda," in *Gendering Chinese Religions: Subject, Identity, and Body*, ed. Jianhua Jia, Xiaofei Kang, and Ping Yao (Albany: State University of New York Press, 2014), 122–56.
67. Brian DeMare, *Mao's Cultural Army: Drama Troupes in China's Rural Revolution* (Cambridge: Cambridge University Press, 2015), 114–18; Wang Binbin, "'Bai mao nü' yu suku chuantong de xingcheng" ("The White-Haired Girl" and the formation of the tradition of speaking bitterness), *Yangzi jiang pinglun* (Yangzi River review), no. 1 (2016): 22–29.
68. *Dazhong dianying* (Mass cinema) (hereafter DZDY), no. 4 (1952): 37.
69. Xiangshan zhengxie wenshi ziliao weiyuanhui (Xiangshan CPPCC Literature and History Information Committee), ed., *Xiangshan wenshi ziliao*, no. 6 (1992): 64.
70. *Yunnansheng*, 83.
71. *Guangdongsheng dianying faxing fangying gongzuo shiliao* (Historical materials concerning film distribution and exhibition in Guangdong), 3 vols. (Guangzhou: Guangdong wenhuaju, 1991), 1:175–76; 2: 30.
72. DYFYZL, no. 5 (1954): 58–60.
73. The total number of screenings of *The White-Haired Girl* in 1963 alone constituted 21 percent of all screenings of the film since its release. See DYFY, no. 7 (1964): 11.
74. DYFY, no. 11 (1965): 5.
75. DZDY, no. 5 (1964): 22.
76. *Ting yibai ge xiaoshanren hua guoqu de shiqing* (Listen to 100 Xiaoshan people tell stories about the past) (Beijing: Zuojia chubanshe, 2007), 443–47.
77. DYFY, no. 2 (1976): 24–26.
78. *Guangdongsheng* 2:30.
79. DZDY, no. 3 (1952): 37–38.
80. DZDY, no. 4 (1952): 30.

81. For a succinct summary, see Robert Barnett, "What Were the Conditions Regarding Human Rights in Tibet Before Democratic Reform?" in *Authenticating Tibet: Answers to China's 100 Questions*, ed. Anne-Marie Blondeau, Katia Buffetrille, and Wei Jing (Berkeley: University of California Press, 2008), 81–84.
82. White Paper, "Democratic Reform in Tibet," 2019, https://www.chinadaily.com.cn/a/201903/28/WS5c9c0869a3104842260b2f7e.html.
83. Xia Chuan, "Guanyu 'Nongnu' de dianying wenxue juben ji yingpian de zhuyao chengjiu he wenti," in *Nongnu—Cong juben dao yingpian*, ed. Huang Zongjiang (Serf—from script to film) (Beijing: Zhongguo dianying chubanshe, 1965), 288–303.
84. Xie Jiguang, *Chumo touming de yangguang: Xizang shouji* (Touching the transparent sunshine: Notes from Tibet) (Fuzhou: Haifeng chubanshe, 2003), 3–4; Jian Mo, "Zong you yishuang yanjing zai kanzhe ni" (There is always a pair of eyes watching you), *Xizang wenxue* (Tibetan literature), no. 2 (2015): 52–62; interview with Mr. Zhang (1953–), Shanghai, 2016.
85. Zhang Fan, *Chuanyue zhufeng* (Crossing Mt. Everest) (Shanghai: Wenhui chubanshe, 2017), 98.
86. Fengguo lundun ke, "Si menkou de haizimen" (Children at the gate), blogpost, https://www.wenxuecity.com/blog/202101/73045/29284.html.
87. Li Li, *Xunchao wenhua shenfen: Yige Jiarong Zangzu cunluo de zongjiao minzu zhi* (Searching for cultural identity: A religious ethnography of a Tibetan village in Jiarong) (Kunming: Yunnan daxue chubanshe, 2007), 68–69.
88. Interviews with former sent-down youths in Shanghai, 2016.
89. Peng Yiling, "Xizang dianying faxing fangying shiye sishi nian" (Forty years of Tibetan film distribution and screening), *Xizang yishu yanjiu* (Tibetan art studies), no. 2 (1991): 33–38.
90. "Fanshen nongnu tan 'Nongnu'" (Emancipated serfs discuss *Serf*), in Huang Zongjiang, *Nongnu: Cong juben dao yingpian* (Serf: From script to film) (Beijing: Zhongguo dianying, 1979), 363–89.
91. Tsering Shakya, "Tibet and China: The Past in the Present," blogpost, *Open Democracy*, March 28, 2009, https://www.opendemocracy.net/en/tibet-and-china-the-past-in-the-present/.
92. Shakya, "Tibet and China."
93. Linda Williams, "Film Bodies: Gender, Genre, and Excess," *Film Quarterly* 44, no. 4 (1991): 2–13; Haiyan Lee, *Revolution of the Heart: A Genealogy of Love in China, 1900–1950* (Stanford, Calif.: Stanford University Press, 2007), 295.
94. Tsering Woeser [Weise], *Forbidden Memory: Tibet During the Cultural Revolution* (Lincoln: University of Nebraska Press, 2020), 202.
95. Woeser, *Forbidden Memory*, 326.

7. TRANSCULTURAL GUERRILLAS

1. Zhiwei Xiao, "The Expulsion of American Films from China, 1949–1950," *Twentieth-Century China* 30, no. 1 (2004): 64–81; Du Weijia, "Beyond the Ideology Principle: The Two Faces of Dubbed Foreign Films in the PRC, 1949–1966," *Journal of Chinese Cinemas* 9, no. 2 (2015): 141–58; Lanjun Xu, "The Southern Film Corporation, Opera Films, and the PRC's Cultural Diplomacy in Cold War Asia, 1950s and 1960s," *Modern Chinese Literature and Culture* 29, no. 1 (2017): 239–82.
2. Tina Mai Chen, "Internationalism and Cultural Experience: Soviet Films and Popular Chinese Understandings of the Future in the 1950s," *Cultural Critique*, no. 58 (2004): 82–114; Ran Ma, "A Genealogy of Film Festivals in the People's Republic of China: 'Film Weeks' During the 'Seventeen Years' (1949–1966)," *New Review of Film and Television Studies* 14, no. 1 (2016): 40–58; Paul Clark, "Closely Watched Viewers: A Taxonomy of Chinese Film Audiences from 1949 to the Cultural Revolution Seen from Hunan," *Journal of Chinese Cinemas* 5, no. 1 (2011): 73–89.
3. Other projectionists whom I interviewed also mentioned Indian films as full of singing and dancing, whereas Yugoslav films featured thieves and bandits; interviews with Mr. Zheng (1956–), Hubei, 2015, and Mr. Qin (1952–), Shanghai, 2013.
4. Salman Rushdie, *Imaginary Homelands: Essays and Criticism 1981–1991* (New York: Random House, 2012), 17.
5. See, for example, David MacDougall, *Transcultural Cinema*, ed. Lucien Taylor (Princeton, N.J.: Princeton University Press, 1998); Laura W. Marks, *The Skin of the Film: Intercultural Cinema, Embodiment, and the Senses* (Durham, N.C.: Duke University Press, 2000).
6. This definition comes from Silvia Spitta, *Between Two Waters: Narratives of Transculturation in Latin America* (Houston: Rice University Press, 1995), quoted by Karen Thornber, *Empire of Texts in Motion: Chinese, Korean, and Taiwanese Transculturations of Japanese Literature* (Cambridge, Mass.: Asia Center, Harvard University), 1–11, in a discussion of transculturation in East Asian literature.
7. David Bordwell, *Making Meaning: Inference and Rhetoric in the Interpretation of Cinema* (Cambridge, Mass.: Harvard University Press, 1989), 8–9.
8. Zhang Wei, *Tan ying xiao ji: Zhongguo xiandai yingtan de chenfeng yiyu* (Chats about cinema: A dusty corner of China's modern cinema) (Taipei: Xiuwei zixun keji gufen youxian gongsi, 2009), 291–311.
9. Zhen Zhang, *An Amorous History of the Silver Screen: Shanghai Cinema, 1896–1937* (Chicago: University of Chicago Press, 2005), 313–14; Zhiwei Xiao, "American Films in China prior to 1950," in *Art, Politics, and Commerce in Chinese*

Cinema, ed. Ying Zhu, and Stanley Rosen (Hong Kong: Hong Kong University Press, 2010), 61–66.
10. Xuelei Huang, "The Heroic and the Banal: Consuming Soviet Movies in Pre-Socialist China, 1920s–1940s," *Twentieth-Century China* 39, no. 2 (2014): 93–117.
11. Frank S. Nugent, "The Russians Continue Their Biography of a Revolutionist with 'Lenin in 1918' at the Cameo," *New York Times*, June 27, 1939.
12. Wu Zhuqing and Zhang Dai, eds., *Zhongguo dianying de fengbei: Yan'an dianying tuan gushi* (Monument of Chinese cinema: The story of the Yan'an Film Group) (Beijing: Renmin daxue chubanshe, 2008), 119; Ye Yonglie, Zhu Dan, and Shen Yaoyi, "Zhou Enlai fang dianying" (Zhou Enlai shows a movie), *Lianhuan huabao* (Pictorial), no. 2 (2012): 3.
13. *Guangdongsheng dianying faxing fangying gongzuo shiliao* (Historical materials concerning film distribution and exhibition in Guangdong), 3 vols. (Guangzhou: Guangdong wenhuaju, 1991), 2:7–9.
14. Chen, "Internationalism and Cultural Experience," 82; "Zuohao yingpian de xuanchuan jieshi gongzuo—Duzhe laixin zongshu" (Take care to publicize and explain films—A summary of letters from readers), *Renmin ribao*, January 16, 1953, 2.
15. *Guangdongsheng* 3:22. On the dubbing of Soviet films, see Nan Hu, "Familiar Strangers: Images and Voices of Soviet Allies in Dubbed Films in 1950s China," *China Perspectives*, no. 1 (2020), 25–31.
16. Chen, "Internationalism and Cultural Experience," 104.
17. Chen Huan, ed., *Jilin dianying faxing fangying jishi, 1907–1992* (Jilin film distribution and exhibition chronicles, 1907–1992) (Changchun: Jilin Film Distribution and Exhibition Company, 1994), 155.
18. Shi Tiesheng, "Kan dianying" (Watching movies), in *Jiyi yu yinxiang* (Memories and impressions) (Changsha: Hunan wenyi chubanshe, 2012), 79–86.
19. Lu Gusun, "'Wenge' zhong kan dianying" (Watching movies during the "Cultural Revolution"), *Nanfang zhoumo* (Southern weekend), October 15, 2008, www.infzm.com/content/18469; interview with Mr. Qin (1952–), Shanghai, 2013.
20. Wu Hehu, "Liening zai yijiuyiba: Zhifeng zhong de dianying" (Lenin in 1918: Movie between the fingers), in *Liushi niandai jiyi* (Memories of the 1960s), ed. Zhu Yong (Beijing: Zhongguo wenlian chubanshe, 2002), 127–29.
21. Li Aidong, ed., *Dianying: Women gongtong de jiyi* (Cinema: Our common memories) (Beijing: Zhongguo dianying chubanshe, 2007), 2:182.
22. Xie Chunchi, ed., *Gaosu houdai: Xiamen laosanjie zhiqing ren sheng jishi* (For posterity: Documenting the lives of Xiamen's sent-down youth) (Xiamen: Xiamen University Press, 1999), 441–42; Liu Hui and Sun Shanyu, *Lao Beijing naxie shi'er* (Miscellanies from old Beijing) (Beijing: Dangdai Zhongguo chubanshe, 2013), 180.

23. Sun Shijie, "Mo Yan de tongnian yishi" (Childhood stories from Mo Yan), *Shandong jiaoyu bao* (Shandong education news), November 8, 2012, http://sdjys.org/index.php/News/view/id/13233.html.
24. Tan Hui, *Zhongguo yizhi dianying shi* (History of translated cinema in China) (Beijing: Zhongguo dianying chubanshe, 2014), 61.
25. As melodramas in the classical sense of *melos* (music) plus drama, many imported North Korean films were also a type of "body genre" generating emotional excess from the audience. See Linda Williams, "Film Bodies: Gender, Genre, and Excess," *Film Quarterly* 44, no. 4 (1991): 2-13.
26. Li Yiming, "Yi qing dongren de Chaoxian dianying" (North Korean cinema that moved us), *Dazhong dianying* (Popular cinema), no. 16 (2007): 46–47.
27. Anonymous blogpost on watching North Korean films, February 26, 2015, https://read01.com/NoADQa.html#.ZGgoFuzMJBZ.
28. Rensheng ru meng, "'Zhongshen nanwang chang' de xinfu shenghuo" (Happy life at "Unforgettable Factory"), blogpost, June 17, 2012, collected by *Minjian lishi* (Folk history), http://mjlsh.usc.cuhk.edu.hk/book.aspx?cid=2&tid=3012&pid=7257.
29. Richard Dyer, "Entertainment and Utopia," in *Only Entertainment*, 2nd ed. (New York: Routledge, 2002), 19–35.
30. Kim Jong-il, *Kim Chŏng-il chŏnjip* (The works of Kim Jong-il) (Pyongyang: Chosŏn Nodongdang Ch'ulp'ansa, 2016), 15:171–89.
31. Bradley K. Martin, *Under the Loving Care of the Fatherly Leader: North Korea and the Kim Dynasty* (New York: Thomas Dunne Books, 2004), 272.
32. Yi Yang-il, *Yŏnghwa ch'waryŏng* (Filmmaking) (Pyongyang: Munhak Yesul Chonghap, 2003), 163–64.
33. Bai Andan, ed., *Beijingshi dianying faxing fangying danwei shi* (History of Beijing municipal film distribution and exhibition) (Beijing: Beijingshi dianying gongsi wenhuaju, 1995–1996), 82–83.
34. Interview with Mr. Lou (1953–), Shanghai, 2016.
35. *Hangzhou shi dianying zhi* (Hangzhou city film gazetteer) (Hangzhou: Hangzhou chubanshe, 1997), 30; Wang Hong, "Yibu beiju dianying yinfa de beiju" (The tragedy triggered by a tragic film), *Wenzhou dushi bao* (Wenzhou metropolitan daily), December 7, 2006, http://news.sina.com.cn/c/2006-12-07/101210706292s.shtml.
36. Williams, "Film Bodies," 2–13.
37. Ben Singer, *Melodrama and Modernity: Early Sensational Cinema and Its Contexts* (New York: Columbia University Press, 2001), 40.
38. Li Aidong, ed., *Dianying* 3:13.
39. Luo Haibo, *Yongyuan de xiangshou* (Forever together) (Hainan: Hainan chubanshe, 2007), 159.

40. Wang Lichun, "Dadi dianyingyuan" (Big earth cinema), *Haiyan wenxue yuekani* (Haiyan literary monthly), no. 6 (2014): 64–70.
41. Li Baowen, "Xiri lutian dianying de gushi—kann *Maihua guniang*" (Reminiscences of open-air cinema—watching *The Flower Girl*). *Shanxi wanbao*, December 6, 2013, http://www.szhgh.com/Article/wsds/wenyi/201312/38762.html.
42. Jing Fang, "Woshi liulinghou" (I was born in the sixties), *Minjian lishi* (Folk history). http://mjlsh.usc.cuhk.edu.hk/book.aspx?cid=6&tid=173&pid=1302.
43. Mo Yan, "Kan 'Maihua guniang'" (Watching *The Flower Girl*), in *Sanwen xinbian* (New collection of essays) (Beijing: Wenhua yishu chubanshe, 2010), 220–24.
44. Laomalasong, "*Maihua guniang* ye wu qing" (*The Flower Girl* elicits no feelings), *Hunan zhiqing wang*, November 1, 2013, http://2013.hnzqw.com/forum.php?mod=viewthread&action=printable&tid=75517.
45. Li Aidong, ed., *Dianying*, 1:166–67.
46. Wusi adu2, "Dianying 'Maihua Guniang'" (The film *The Flower Girl*), Shanghai zhiqing wang. January 6, 2016; interview with Ms. Xu (1956–), Beijing, 2016.
47. Interview with Wang Yaqing (1952–), Shanghai, 2018.
48. Tan Hui, *Zhongguo yizhi dianying shi*, 61–65.
49. Liu Jialing, *Jiyi xianhong: Guanyu hongse xiju, hongse dianying he wenyi xuanchuandui de wangshi* (Vivid red memories: On red theater, red movies, and the history of the Art Promotion Team) (Beijing: Zhongguo qingnian chubanshe, 2002), 198–199.
50. Tan Hui, *Zhongguo yizhi dianying shi*, 65.
51. Wang Liu'er, "Hebin dianyingyuan" (Hebin cinema), *Guiyang wenshi* (Guiyang literature and history), no. 1 (2012): 18–19.
52. Liu Jialing, *Jiyi xianhong*, 198–99.
53. Regina M. Longo, "The Albanian Cinema Project: Saving and Projecting Albanian Film Heritage for Global Audiences," *KinoKultura*, special issue 16 (2016), http://www.kinokultura.com/specials/16/longo.shtml.
54. Cheng Xiaoyin, *Yu qingchun youguan de nüren* (Women of my youth) (Shanghai: Wenhui chubanshe, 2012), 135–45.
55. Quoted in Zhao Ning, *Qingrenjie de wuhui* (Dancing on Valentine's Day) (Beijing: Zuojia chubanshe, 1997), 80.
56. "Di ba ge shi tongxiang" (The eighth is bronze), blogpost, June 9, 2014, http://www.laobingyuan.com/junshiyingshi/201406/31094.html.
57. Cheng Naishan, *Haishang sakesifeng* (Shanghai saxophone) (Shanghai: Wenhui Press, 2004), 87–89.
58. Chris Berry and Zhang Shujuan, "Film and Fashion in Shanghai: What (Not) to Wear During the Cultural Revolution," *Journal of Chinese Cinemas* 13, no. 1 (2019): 1–25.

59. Zhou Shifen and Xiang Dong, *Ningbo lao qiangmen* (Ningbo's old city gate) (Ningbo: Ningbo chubanshe, 2008), 181; Liu Weixin, *Du die* (Reading discs) (Shanghai: Wenhui chubanshe, 2013), 279; Learning fashion from the movies dates back to the Republican era, when barbers reportedly watched the hairstyles of Hollywood stars because their customers often asked for a specific hairstyle from a given film. See Yao Xiaoou, "Wo kan dianying de jingli" (My experience of watching movies), https://blog.sciencenet.cn/blog-531888-888286.html.
60. Interview with Ms. Li Rong (1960–), Shanghai, 2016.
61. Clarence Tsui, "Why Albanian Films Are Big in China: Cultural Revolution Nostalgia," *South China Morning Post*, March 24, 2017, https://www.scmp.com/culture/film-tv/article/2081841/why-albanian-films-are-big-china-cultural-revolution-nostalgia.
62. Sudha Rajagopalan, *Indian Films in Soviet Cinemas: The Culture of Moviegoing After Stalin* (Bloomington: Indiana University Press, 2008); also see https://www.e-ir.info/2017/01/23/raj-kapoor-and-indias-foremost-cinematic-soft-power-breakthrough/.
63. Brian Larkin, "Indian Films and Nigerian Lovers: Media and the Creation of Parallel Modernities," *Africa* 67, no. 3 (1997): 406–40.
64. Dina Iordanova, "Indian Cinema's Global Reach: Historiography Through Testimonies," *South Asian Popular Culture* 4, no. 2 (2006): 113–40.
65. Quoted in Krista Van Fleit Hang, "'The Law Has No Conscience': The Cultural Construction of Justice and the Reception of Awara in China," *Asian Cinema* 24, no. 2 (2013): 146.
66. Van Fleit Hang, "The Law Has No Conscience," 141–46.
67. Cai Chusheng, "Wei youyi yu heping huanhu: Huanying Yindu dianying zhou de juxing he Yindu dianying gongzuozhe de guanglin" (Hurray for friendship and peace: Welcome to Indian Film Week and the arrival of Indian film workers), in *Cai Chusheng wenji* (Collected works of Cai Chusheng) (Beijing: Zhongguo guangbo dianshi chubanshe, 2006), 2: 220.
68. Chen Baiming, "Yindu yinyue wudao zai Zhongguo de chuanbao he yingxiang" (The spread and influence of Indian music and dancing in China), in *Tan Yunshan xianxiang yu 21 shiji ZhongYin wenhua jiaoliu* (The Tan Yunshan phenomenon and Sino-Indian cultural exchanges in the twenty-first century), ed. Niu Genfu (Beijing: Wenhua yishu chubanshe, 2015), 181.
69. Hu Deping, "Fuqin de yisheng hen zhi" (Father's life was very worthwhile), *Nanfang renwu zhoukan* (Southern people weekly), April 29, 2011, http://news.sina.com.cn/c/sd/2011-04-29/114522381400_2.shtml.
70. Yuan Shuipai, "Dianying gequ qingnian" (Film, song, youth), *Renmin ribao*, December 27, 1956, 8; Zai Yaomu, "'Daochu liulang' tai duo le" (Too much

"wandering everywhere"), *Jiefang ribao* (Liberation daily), November 8, 1956.
71. Gao Ying, *Wo he Ai Qing* (Ai Qing and I) (Beijing: Renmin wenxue, 2012), 77–79.
72. Yu Luowen, *Wojia: Wo de gege Yu Luoke* (My family: My brother Yu Luoke) (New York: World Chinese Publishing, 2016).
73. Interview with Mr. Gong (1949–), Shanghai, 2016.
74. An Guchen, "Liulangzhe de mingyun" (Fate of the vagabond), in *Quyi zhuanji* (Special collection of folk performance art) (Dalian: Dalian Workers Palace, 1979), 101–3.
75. Tom Gold, "Back to the City: The Return of Shanghai's Educated Youth," *China Quarterly*, no. 84 (1980): 755–70.
76. Hu Jian, "Jia Zhangke huo Yindu Mengmai guoji dianying jie jiechu yishu chengjiu jiang" (Jia Zhangke wins excellence in cinema award at Mumbai International Film Festival), *China News Net*, October 21, 2016, http://www.chinanews.com/yl/2016/10-21/8039491.shtml.
77. Stefania Parigi, "The Screen in the Mirror: Thematic and Textual Reflexivity in Italian Cinema," in *A Companion to Italian Cinema*, ed. Frank Burke (Chichester: Wiley, 2017), 513.
78. Andrew Higson, "The Concept of National Cinema," *Screen* 30, no. 4 (1989): 36–47.
79. Will Higbee and Song Hwee Lim, "Concepts of Transnational Cinema: Towards a Critical Transnationalism in Film Studies," *Transnational Cinemas* 1, no. 1 (2010): 7–21.
80. This distinction is inspired by Larkin's *Signal and Noise*, which discusses "cinema in Africa" as opposed to "African cinema" in its conclusion, 253–55.
81. Nicolai Volland, *Socialist Cosmopolitanism: The Chinese Literary Universe, 1945–1965* (New York: Columbia University Press, 2017), 12–14.
82. Ye Zhiguang, "1962 nian: Yige Shanghai yingmi de meihao shidai" (1962: A Shanghai cinephile's golden age), *Dongfang zaobao* (Oriental morning post), February 23, 2011, https://www.douban.com/group/topic/17818768/?_i=0211098K6UF5qf.
83. *Dianying fangying* (Film projection), no. 9 (1960): 1–7; no. 1 (1963): 7; Liu Guangyu, *Xin Zhongguo chengli yilai nongcun dianying fangying yanjiu* (Study of rural film exhibitions since the founding of New China) (Beijing: Wenhua yishu chubanshe, 2015), 147–57.
84. Interviews with Mr. Yuan (1953–) and Ms. Li (1961–), Ningxia, 2017.
85. Interviews with Mr. Ye (1945–), Hubei, 2015; Mr. Li (1959–) and Mr. Luo (1960–), Ningxia, 2017.

8. POISONOUS WEEDS AND CENSORSHIP AS EXORCISM

1. Chen Sihe, "Kan pipan dianying qu" (Going to watch criticized films), https://www.chinesepen.org/blog/archives/166732; Chen Sihe, "Zoulu de huiyi" (Memories of walking), https://www.chinesepen.org/blog/archives/166734.
2. Gao Ju, "Yingpian *Bing lin cheng xia* shi yike xuanyang xiuzheng zhuyi sixiang de ducao" (The film "Army on the City" is a poisonous weed that promotes revisionist ideology), *Renmin ribao*, April 24, 1966, 6.
3. Chen Sihe, "Kan pipan dianying qu."
4. Jacques Derrida, *Dissemination*, tr. Barbara Johnson (London: Bloomsbury, 2016).
5. Michael A. Rinella, *Pharmakon: Plato, Drug Culture, and Identity in Ancient Athens* (Lanham, Md.: Lexington Books, 2010), xvii, 74.
6. Rinella, *Pharmakon*, xxii.
7. Derrida, "Plato's Pharmacy," in *Dissemination*; Bernard Stiegler, *What Makes Life Worth Living: On Pharmacology*, tr. Daniel Ross (Malden, Mass.: Polity, 2013).
8. Yan Liu, *Healing with Poisons: Potent Medicines in Medieval China* (Seattle: University of Washington Press, 2021), introduction and chaps. 1–3.
9. Carla Nappi, *The Monkey, and the Inkpot: Natural History and Its Transformations in Early Modern China* (Cambridge, Mass.: Harvard University Press, 2010), 62–63.
10. Mao Zedong, "Chunjie tanhua jiyao" (Notes on conversations during Spring Festival), February 13, 1964, https://www.marxists.org/chinese/maozedong/1968/5-063.htm; "Dui weisheng gongzuo de zhishi" (Directives on hygiene), June 26, 1965, https://www.marxists.org/chinese/maozedong/1968/5-152.htm.
11. For a thoughtful analysis of the film *Li Shizhen*, see Mia Yinxing Liu, *Literati Lenses: Wenren Landscape in Chinese Cinema of the Mao Era* (Honolulu: University of Hawai'i Press, 2019), chap. 1.
12. Mao Zedong, "On the Correct Handling of Contradictions Among the People," February 27, 1957, https://www.marxists.org/reference/archive/mao/selected-works/volume-5/mswv5_58.htm.
13. Zygmunt Bauman, *Modernity and the Holocaust* (Ithaca, N.Y.: Cornell University Press, 2000), 70. Quoted in Geremie R. Barmé, "Beijing, a Garden of Violence," *Inter-Asia Cultural Studies* 9, no. 4 (2008): 612–13.
14. Barmé, "Beijing, a Garden of Violence," 614–15.
15. Barmé, 635.
16. Mao Zedong, "Things Are Beginning to Change," May 15, 1957, https://www.marxists.org/reference/archive/mao/selected-works/volume-5/mswv5_61.htm.

17. Mao Zedong, "Wenhuibao de zichanjieji fanxiang yingdang pipan" (*Wenhui Daily*'s bourgeois orientation should be criticized), editorial in *Renmin ribao*, July 1, 1957, 1.
18. Cai Chusheng, "You ducao jiude jinxing douzheng: Zai 'Meiyou wancheng de xiju' taolun dahuishang de zongjie fayan" (Poisonous weeds must be fought: Concluding speech at the discussion conference on "Unfinished Comedy"), *Zhongguo dianying*, no. 1 (1958): 30–42.
19. Vera Schwarcz, "A Brimming Darkness: The Voice of Memory / The Silence of Pain in China After the Cultural Revolution," *Bulletin of Concerned Asian Scholars* 30, no. 1 (1998): 48.
20. Du Mu, "Li He ji xu" (Preface to Li He's collection), in *Du Mu quanji* (Complete works of Du Mu) (Shanghai: Shanghai shuji chubanshe, 1997), 94–95.
21. Mao Zedong, "Tong wenyijie daibiao de tanhua" (Talk with representatives of the cultural realm), March 8, 1957, http://marxistphilosophy.org/maozedong/mx7/032.htm; Mao Zedong, "Speech at the Chinese Communist Party's National Conference on Propaganda Work," March 12, 1957, https://www.marxists.org/reference/archive/mao/selected-works/volume-5/mswv5_59.htm.
22. Laikwang Pang, *The Art of Cloning: Creative Production During China's Cultural Revolution* (New York: Verso, 2017), 225.
23. Siegfried Kracauer, *The Mass Ornament: Weimar Essays*, tr. and ed. Thomas Y. Levin (Cambridge, Mass.: Harvard University Press, 1995), 291, 328.
24. Maggie Greene, "A Ghostly Bodhisattva and the Price of Vengeance: Meng Chao, *Li Huiniang*, and the Politics of Drama, 1959–1979," *Modern Chinese Literature and Culture* 24, no. 1 (2012): 154–59.
25. Geremie R. Barmé, "Mao Zedong's Monsters and Demons," *China Heritage* https://chinaheritage.net/journal/essays/sub-essays/mao-zedongs-monsters-and-demons/.
26. Peng Zhen, "Makesi Lieningzhuyi zai Zhongguo de shengli" (The victory of Marxism-Leninism in China), *Renmin ribao*, July 1, 1951, 4.
27. He Xiangning, "Jianjue suqing Hu Feng jituan he yiqie ancang de fangeming fenzi" (Resolutely eliminate the Hu Feng clique and all hidden counterrevolutionaries), *Renmin ribao*, June 24, 1955, 5; "Fan youpai de tiantou shi" (Anti-rightist poems written on farmfields), *Renmin ribao*, August 16, 1957, 3; "Women de jieji fenxi fangfa shi zhao yaojing" (Our class analysis method is a demon-reflecting mirror), *Renmin ribao*, September 4, 1957.
28. Derrida, *Dissemination*, 129–30.
29. Mao Zedong, "Zai Shanghai ju Hangzhou hui shang de jianghua" (Speech at the Hangzhou meeting of the Shanghai bureau), April 1957, https://www.marxists.org/chinese/maozedong/1968/3-109.htm.

30. Mao Zedong, "Things Are Beginning to Change," May 15, 1957; Mao Zedong, "Wenhuibao de zichanjieji fangxiang yingdang pipan" (The bourgeois direction of *Wenhui* newspaper should be criticized), *Renmin ribao*, July 1, 1957, 1.
31. Zhi Fei, "Shi niugui sheshen" (Ox-demons and snake-spirits explained), *Renmin ribao*, April 8, 1958. 8.
32. Wang Yi, "Mao Zedong de dagui celue" (Mao Zedong's ghostbusting strategy), *Yanhuang chungqiu*, no. 5 (1995), 15–19.
33. Steve A. Smith, "Talking Toads and Chinless Ghosts: The Politics of 'Superstitious' Rumors in the People's Republic of China, 1961–1965," *American Historical Review* 111, no. 2 (2006): 417.
34. Maggie Greene, *Resisting Spirits: Drama Reform and Cultural Transformation in the People's Republic of China* (Ann Arbor: University of Michigan Press, 2019), chap. 5.
35. Mao Zedong, "Guanyu nongcun shehuizhuyi jiaoyu deng wenti de zhishi" (Instructions on issues such as rural socialist education, etc.), May 1963, https://www.marxists.org/chinese/maozedong/1968/5-033.htm.
36. Laikwan Pang, "The State Against Ghosts: A Genealogy of China's Film Censorship Policy," *Screen* 52, no. 4 (2011): 467–68.
37. For discussions of socialist horror and *Rent Collection Courtyard*, see Lee, *The Stranger and the Chinese Moral Imagination*, chap. 5; Denise Y. Ho and Jie Li, "From Landlord Manor to Red Memorabilia: Reincarnations of a Chinese Museum Town," *Modern China* 42, no. 1 (2016): 3–37.
38. Wang Yi, "Wenhua da geming yu wushu wenhua" (The Cultural Revolution and witchcraft), *Shehuixue yanjiu* (Sociological studies), no. 3 (1993): 69–78; Wang Yi, "'Da pipan' yu zuzhou wushu" ("Great criticism" and incantation witchcraft), *Renmin bao*, October 6, 2000, https://m.renminbao.com/rmb/articles/2000/10/6/39900m.html.
39. Barend J. Ter Haar, "China's Inner Demons: The Political Impact of the Demonological Paradigm," *China Information* 11, no. 2–3 (1996)," 83. Also see Donald S. Sutton, "Consuming Counterrevolution: The Ritual and Culture of Cannibalism in Wuxuan, Guangxi, China, May to July 1968," *Comparative Studies in Society and History* 37, no. 1 (1995): 144–45; Michael Schoenhals, "Demonising Discourse in Mao Zedong's China: People vs. Non-People," *Totalitarian Movements and Political Religions* 8, no. 3–4 (2007): 465–82.
40. Yan Liu, "Words, Demons, and Illness: Incantatory Healing in Medieval China," *Asian Medicine* 14, no. 1 (2019): 6, 23–24; Liu, *Healing with Poisons*, 65–68.
41. Wang Yi, "'Da pipan' yu zuzhou wushu."
42. See, for example, Yao Wenyuan, "Ping 'Sanjiacun'" (On "Three Family Village"), *Wenhui bao* (Shanghai), May 10, 1966.

43. Lu Xun, "Preface, to *Call to Arms*" in *Selected Stories of Lu Hsun*, tr. Yang Hsien-yi and Gladys Yang (Beijing: Foreign Languages Press, 1978), 2–3.
44. Rinella, *Pharmakon*, xxii, 241.
45. Kracauer, *The Mass Ornament*, 332.
46. Dziga Vertov, *Kino-Eye: The Writings of Dziga Vertov* (Berkeley: University of California Press, 1984), 60, 61, 68, 71.
47. Writer Liu Na'ou did translate and introduce some of Vertov's theoretical writings into Chinese in 1930. See Zhu Yankun, "Lun Jijia Wei'ertuofu dui Zhongguo dianying lilun de yingxiang" (On Dziga Vertov's influence on Chinese film theory), *Hainan shifan daxue xuebao*, no. 3 (2020): 91–98. Also see Jessica Ka Yee Chan, *Chinese Revolutionary Cinema: Propaganda, Aesthetics, and Internationalism* (London: Tauris, 2019), 87–118.
48. *Ma Jiliang (Tang Na) wenji* (Collected works of Ma Jiliang [Tang Na]) (Shanghai: East China Normal University Press, 1993), 367.
49. Bertolt Brecht, *Bertolt Brecht Journals 1934–1955* (New York, Routledge, 1993), 249; Wang Chenwu, "Dadao yique miyao he duyao, dianying ying zuo dazhong de shiliang" (Down with all drugs and poisons, movies should be the food of the people), in *Wang Chenwu dianying pinglun xuanji* (Wang Chenwu's collection of film critiques) (Beijing: Zhongguo dianying chubanshe, 1994), 223–24.
50. Zhiwei Xiao, "The Expulsion of American Films from China, 1949–1950," *Twentieth-Century China* 30, no. 1 (2004): 64–81; Ding Huichuan, "KangMei yuanChao, buyan Meidi yingpian!" (Resist U.S., aid Korea, no screening of American imperialist films!), *Guangming ribao*, December 6, 1950, 2.
51. You Gu, "Meiguo dianying limian youxie shenme dongxi?" (What are the ingredients of American cinema?), *Guangming ribao*, November 18, 1949, 3.
52. Miao Langshan, "Lun Meiguo de wenming yu wenhua" (On American civilization and culture), *Guangming ribao*, December 15, 1950, 4.
53. Vertov, *Kino-Eye*, 61; Peng Ding'an, "Fazhan renmin de dianying shiye" (Develop the people's film industry), *Guangming ribao*, January 12, 1950, 3.
54. Mao Zedong, "Yingdang zhongshi 'Wu Xun zhuan' de taolun" (We should pay attention to discussion of the film *The Life of Wu Xun*), *Renmin ribao*, May 20, 1951, 1.
55. Noël Carroll, *Interpreting the Moving Image* (Cambridge: Cambridge University Press, 1998), 10–13.
56. Zhuoyi Wang, *Revolutionary Cycles in Chinese Cinema, 1951–1979* (New York: Palgrave Macmillan, 2014), 35. Qi Xiaoping, *Xianghua ducao: Hongse niandai de dianying mingyun* (Fragrant flowers and poisonous weeds: The destiny of cinema in the red age) (Beijing: Dangdai Zhongguo chubanshe, 2006), chap.1.
57. Li Zhisui, *The Private Life of Chairman Mao: The Memoirs of Mao's Personal Physician* (New York: Random House, 2011), 141–44.

58. Li Zhisui, 255–57.
59. Liu, *Healing with Poisons*, 79; Paul U. Unschuld, "Traditional Chinese Medicine: Some Historical and Epistemological Reflections," *Social Science & Medicine* 24, no. 12 (1987): 1023–29.
60. Yang Yinlu, *Tingyuan shen Diaoyutai: Wo gei Jiang Qing dang mishu* (In Diaoyutai's deepest courtyard: I worked as Jiang Qing's secretary) (Beijing: Dangdai Zhongguo chubanshe, 2013), 53–59, 206–12.
61. Jiang Qing, "Revolutionizing Peking Opera," speech given at a cultural conference on November 28, 1966, in *Chinese Theories of Theater and Performance from Confucius to the Present*, ed. and tr. Faye Chunfang Fei (Ann Arbor: University of Michigan Press, 1999), 166–69.
62. Francesco Casetti, "Why Fears Matter. Cinephobia in Early Film Culture," *Screen* 59, no. 2 (2018): 154.
63. Jiang Qing, "Revolutionizing Peking Opera," 166–69.
64. Derrida, *Dissemination*, 142; Rinella, *Pharmakon*, 238.
65. Yomi Braester, *Painting the City Red: Chinese Cinema and the Urban Contract* (Durham, N.C.: Duke University Press, 2010), chap. 2.
66. Paul Clark, *The Chinese Cultural Revolution: A History* (Cambridge: Cambridge University Press, 2008), 111, 113.
67. Jiang Qing, "On the Revolution in Peking Opera (Tan Jingju geming)," speech from July 1964, tr. Jessica Ka Yee Chan, *Opera Quarterly* 26, no. 2 (2010): 455–56.
68. Yi Fan and Zi Hui, "'Jinying yingpian' de jinying neimu" (Behind the scenes of "banned films"), *Dang'an chunqiu* (Spring and autumn archives), no. 3 (2006): 26.
69. Yi Fan and Zi Hui, "'Jinying yingpian' de jinying neimu," 26.
70. Qi Zhi, *Mao Zedong shidai de renmin dianying, 1949–1966 nian* (People's cinema during Mao's era, 1949–1966) (Taipei: Xiuwei zixun keji gufen youxian gongsi, 2010), 487; *Guangxi dianying faxing fangying shi* (History of film distribution and exhibition in Guangxi) (Guilin: Guangxi dianying faxing fangying gongsi, 1995), 139.
71. Yi Fan and Zi Hui, "'Jinying yingpian' de jinying neimu," 26.
72. *Jiang Qing tongzhi lun wenyi geming* (Comrade Jiang Qing on the Cultural Revolution) (Kunming, Yunnan: Kunming chubanshe, 1969), 12.
73. *Jiang Qing tongzhi lun wenyi geming*, 301–5.
74. Yu Xin, "Yong bizi xiu yi xiu" (Use your nose to take a sniff), in *Qingchun jiyu* (Messages for youth) (Shanghai: Shanghai renmin chubanshe, 1965), 20–23. The English translation of the Lu Xun quote is from Gloria Davis, *Lu Xun's Revolution: Writing in a Time of Violence* (Cambridge, Mass.: Harvard University Press, 2013), 61.
75. Ruan Yuan, "Xuehui duli bianbie xianghua ducao de benling" (Learn the ability to identify fragrant flowers and poisonous weeds), *Renmin ribao*, April 16, 1965, 6.

76. Jiang Qing, "Lin Biao tongzhi weituo Jiang Qing tongzhi zhaokai de budui wenyi gongzuo zuotanhui jiyao" (Summary of the Forum on Artistic Work in the Armed Forces with which Comrade Lin Biao entrusted Comrade Jiang Qing), *Hongqi*, no. 4 (May 1967): 6–11.
77. "Jiang Qing zai quanjun chuangzuo huiyi shang tan guanyu dianying de wenti" (Jiang Qing discusses cinema at the All-Army Creation Conference), April 1966, http://www.cnd.org/CR/ChuanXinLu_1.pdf.
78. "Jiang Qing zai quanjun chuangzuo."
79. Gao Ju, "Yingpian 'Binglin cheng xi' shi yike xuanyang xiuzheng zhuyi sixiang de ducao" (The film "Beseiged City" is a poisonous weed that promotes revisionist ideology), *Renmin ribao*, April 24, 1966, 6.
80. Wen Siye, "Chedi jielu yingpian *Taohua shan* de fangeming yinmou" (Thoroughly expose the counterrevolutionary conspiracy of the film *Peach Blossom Fan*), *Guangming ribao*, July 12, 1966, 4; Yao Weidou, "Nucai zhexue he 'xunfu gongju' lun" (Lackey philosophy and a theory of "taming tools"), *Renmin ribao*, May 26, 1967, 8.
81. Gao Ju, "Yingpian 'Binglin cheng xia.'"
82. Chen Bo, ed., *Zhongguo dianying biannian jishi—Faxing fangyingjuan* (Chronicle of Chinese cinema—on distribution and exhibition) (Beijing: Zhongguo wenxian chubanshe), 1, no. 1 (2005): 62–64; Bai Andan, ed., *Beijingshi dianying faxing fangying danwei shi* (History of film distribution and exhibition in Beijing municipality) (Beijing: Beijing wenhuaju, 1995), 75–78.
83. Gao Ju, "Yingpian 'Binglin cheng xia.'"
84. Chen Sihe, "Kan pipan dianying qu"; Lu Gusun, "'Wenge' zhong kan dianying" (Watching movies during the "Cultural Revolution"), *Nanfang zhoumo* (Southern weekend), October 15, 2008.
85. Luo Lingshan, "Shanghai shiwei xiezuo banzi de lailong qumai" (The ins and outs of the Shanghai Municipal Committee Writing Groups), *Bainian chao* (Hundred year tide), no. 12 (2005): 12–17.
86. Quoted in Qi Zhi, *Jiemi Zhongguo dianying: Jiedu wenge yingpian* (Unmasking Chinese cinema: Reading Cultural Revolution films) (Taipei: Xinrui wenchuang, 2013), 121.
87. Interview with former sent-down youths, Shanghai, 2016.
88. For an annotated bibliography of such publications, see Hu Zhuangzi, "Wenge zaofanpai dianying 'dapipan' ziliao shulue" (Cultural Revolution rebel faction film "great criticism" materials), *Jiyi* (Remembrances), no. 65 (2014), http://prchistory.org/wp-content/uploads/2014/05/REMEMBRANCE-No-65-2010%E5%B9%B412%E6%9C%8830%E6%97%A5.pdf.
89. Lu Gusun, "'Wenge' zhong kan dianying."

90. "Wenge zhong *Nuchao* zuowei 'ducao yingpian' fangyingshi de pipan chahua" (During the Cultural Revolution, *Indignant Tide* was a critical interjection when it was shown as a "poisonous-weed film"), reprinted in *Jiyi* (Remembrances), no. 65 (2014): 69, http://prchistory.org/wp-content/uploads/2014/05/REMEMBRANCE-No-65-2010%E5%B9%B412%E6%9C%8830%E6%97%A5.pdf.
91. Interview with Wang Yaqing (1952–), Shanghai, 2018.
92. Alicui, "Wo dai nimen zoujin sanshi nianqian de dianyingyuan" (I take you into the cinema from three decades ago), blogpost, http://zhenren.com/action-blogdetail-uid-3-id-841.htm.
93. Lu Zhonghui, "Kan dianying zayi" (Miscellaneous memories of watching films), http://tieba.baidu.com/p/3659977066.
94. Bai Andan, ed., *Beijingshi dianying*, 76–77.
95. Zhuang Zhijuan, "Sanci teshu de kan dianying jingli." (Three special film-viewing experiences), *Shiji*, no. 2 (2012), 44–45.
96. Chen Sihe, "Kan pipan dianying qu."
97. Interview with Ms. Xu Xiaoli (1953–); also with Shanghai's sent-down youth focus group in 2016.
98. Yan Jiaqi, and Gao Gao, *Turbulent Decade: A History of the Cultural Revolution*, tr. D.W.Y. Kwok (Honolulu: University of Hawai'i Press, 1996), 205–14; "Wenge zhong *Nuchao* zuowei 'ducao yingpian' fangyingshi de pipan chahua"; interview with Mr. Qian, a former sent-down youth from Shanghai, 2016.
99. An Na, "'Wenge' yinmu huaijiu" (Screen nostalgia from the Cultural Revolution), http://www.xys.org/xys/ebooks/others/history/contemporary/culture_revolution/yinmu.txt.
100. Interviews with Mr. Zhang (1953–) and Mr. Sun (1954–), Shanghai, 2016.
101. Xinhuashe tongxunyuan, "Geming da pipan de xin zhanchang: Mudanjiang huoche zhan zuzhi lüke kaizhan geming da pipan sanji" (A new battlefield of revolutionary criticism: An essay on the organization of passengers at Mudanjiang Railway Station to carry out revolutionary criticism), *Renmin ribao*, June 15, 1968, 4. For a feminist rereading of *The Story of Liubao*, see Lingzhen Wang, *Revisiting Women's Cinema: Feminism, Socialism, and Mainstream Culture in Modern China* (Durham, N.C.: Duke University Press, 2020), chap. 2.
102. Ximeng zhengxie wenshi ziliao weiyuanhui (Ximeng Political Consultative Conference Literature and History Information Committee), "Suiyue ruge: Jinian zhiqing shangshan xiaxiang 40 zhounian" (The times are like songs: Collected works to commemorate the fortieth anniversary of educated youth going up to the mountains and going down to the countryside), *Wenshi ziliao*, no. 7 (2009): 137–38.
103. Da Yu, *Qiaodianyun chuan* (The legend of Qiaodianyun) (Beijing: Zhongguo qingnian chubanshe, 2011), 138–39

104. Zhang Jiantian, *Wo shi Datian ren*, 144–45.
105. "Hefei guanyu neibu fangying sanbu riben fandong yingpian de tongzhi" (Notice on internal screenings of three Japanese reactionary films), February 16, 1971, http://communistchinadoc.blogspot.com/2015/02/1971216.html.
106. Wu Di, ed., *Zhongguo dianying yanjiu ziliao, 1949–1976* (Source documents for the study of Chinese cinema, 1949–1976) (Beijing: Wenhua yishu chubanshe, 2006), 3:268–69.
107. Luan Zhe, "Wo de 'wenge' yule shenghuo" (My leisure life in the "Cultural Revolution"), *Lishi xuejia chazuo* (Historians' tea forum), no. 4 (2009), https://www.chinesepen.org/blog/archives/23587.
108. Cao Lei, *Yuanqu de huixiang: Liushi bu yizhipian peiyin biji* (Faraway echoes: Notes on the dubbing of sixty films) (Shanghai: Shanghai cishu chubanshe, 2006), 3–5.
109. *Dianying biaoyan yishu tansuo* (Exploration of film performing arts) (Beijing: Zhongguo dianying chubanshe, 1984), 81.
110. Francesco Casetti, *The Lumière Galaxy: Seven Key Words for the Cinema to Come* (New York: Columbia University Press, 2015), 79.

EPILOGUE

1. The film crew included such renowned figures as director Xie Jin and writer Ru Shoujuan, whose daughter, the famous contemporary writer Wang Anyi, also visited Yongjia, Zhejiang, several years later retrace to retrace the footsteps of her mother. See Wang Anyi, "Kuocang shan, Nanxi jiang" (Kuocang mountain, Nanxi river), *Wenhui bao*, October 8, 2012.
2. Vivian Sobchack, "What Is Film History? Or the Riddle of the Sphinxes," *Spectator* 20, no. 1 (1999): 8-22.
3. *Yunnansheng dianying faxing fangying gongzuo jinian tekan* (Commemorative publication on film distribution and exhibition work in Yunnan Province) (internal publication, 1984), 14–15.
4. Interviews with Mr. Zhou (1956–) and Mr. Hu (1956–), Hubei, 2015.
5. Interview with Mr. Duan (1956–) and Mr. Tan (1942–), Hubei, 2015.
6. Interviews with Mr. Xu (1954–) and Mr. Duan (1956–), Hubei, 2015.
7. Liu Guangyu, *Xin Zhongguo chengli yilai nongcun dianying fangying yanjiu* (Study of rural film exhibitions since the founding of New China) (Beijing: Wenhua yishu chubanshe, 2015).
8. Yu Ji et al., *Quxian dianying shichang tianye diaocha* (District and county film market fieldwork investigation) (Beijing: Communication University of China Press, 2009).
9. Interviews with Mr. Zhu (1952–), Hubei, 2015; Ms. Zhou (1960), Ningxia, 2017.

10. Radio Free Asia, https://www.rfa.org/cantonese/news/petitioner-09182017094438.html, and New Tang Dynasty Television, https://www.ntdtv.com/gb/2017/09/19/a1343001.html, both reported on the petitioning by Hunan's former projectionists.
11. Such media outlets include Radio Free Asia, Epoch Times, and Aboluo Net.
12. Debashree Mukherjee, *Bombay Hustle: Making Movies in a Colonial City* (New York: Columbia University Press, 2020), 11.
13. Francesco Cassetti, *The Lumière Galaxy: Seven Key Words for the Cinema to Come* (New York: Columbia University Press, 2015), 79.
14. *Yunnansheng*, 12.
15. *Yunnansheng*, 72–73, 82–84, 103.
16. "Zhongxuanbu, guojia jiaowei, guangbo dianying dianshi bu, wenhua bu guanyu yunyong youxiu yingshi pian zai quanguo zhong xiaoxue kaizhan aiguo zhuyi jiaoyu de tongzhi" (Circular of the Central Propaganda Department, the State Education Commission, the Ministry of Radio, Film, and Television, and the Ministry of Culture on using excellent films and TV films to carry out patriotic education in primary and secondary schools), 1993, http://www.elinklaw.com/zsglmobile/lawView.Aspx?Id=41266./
17. Suisheng Zhao, "A State-Led Nationalism: The Patriotic Education Campaign in Post-Tiananmen China," *Communist and Post-Communist Studies* 31, no. 3 (1998): 287–302; "Zhongguo zhong xiaoxue yingshi jiaoyu gaige kaifang sishinian sougou de fazhan jieduan" (Forty years of reform and opening up in the development of China's primary and secondary school film and television education), *Xiju zhijia* (Home drama), no. 20 (2020): 115–16.
18. Julian Ward, "'The One and the Eight' and Cultural Production in Modern China: How a Poem About the Anti-Japanese War Written in the 1950s Was Transformed as a Film in the 1980s and for Television in 2015," *Screening the Past*, no. 45 (December 2020).
19. "Ba wenming xiangfeng zhong jin nongmin xintian, Zhejiang wenhua litang jihuo zheng nengliang" (Planting civilized rural customs into the hearts of farmers, Zhejiang cultural auditorium activates positive energy), *Renmin ribao*, February 24, 2014, http://politics.people.com.cn/n/2014/0224/c1001-24440980.html.
20. "Rang geng duo de nongmin kanshang dianying" (Let more peasants see movies), Sina.com.cn, http://news.sina.com.cn/o/2005-11-24/06147523140s.shtml. According to the first "lama-projectionist," a monastic movie team could choose films appropriate for monks to avoid the embarrassment of uncensored films that were available to the general public. See http://news.sina.com.cn/c/2003-11-30/09351217617s.shtml; https://news.sina.cn/sa/2005-02-06/detail-ikknscsi5750876.d.html.

21. See http://xj.xinhuanet.com/fangtan/69/. For examples of showing films inside mosques, see http://www.xjsmgq.gov.cn/gk/gongzuodongtai/14603.htm; http://mzzjw.beijing.gov.cn/zwgk/mzdt/201905/t20190522_1077632.html; "Xinjiang Weiwu'er zizhiqu kashen diqu diyi pi guojia gonggong wenhua shifan qu jizhong pingyi huibao cailiao" (The first batch of national public cultural demonstration zones in Kashgar, Xinjiang Uyghur Autonomous Region, the first batch of centralized evaluation report materials), September 16, 2013, https://www.mct.gov.cn/whzx/bnsj/ggwhs/201903/t20190329_841126.htm.
22. "Xizangqu Songxian kaizhan song aiguo zhuyi jiaoyu yingpian jin simiao huodong" (Tibet's Qusong county launches campaign to send patriotic educational videos to temples), *Zhongguo Xizang xinwenwang*, February 29, 2012, http://zcfj.fjnet.com/zcfjxw/xwnr/201202/t20120229_190746.htm. For other news items on "cinema entering temples and monasteries," see http://theory.people.com.cn/n/2014/0404/c359404-24829973.html; https://www.sohu.com/a/161794699_160909.
23. See https://jyj.lasa.gov.cn/lasa/sgdj/201911/77f3e20c60b8458d930a8a9cbe1fc1ba.shtml; http://tibet.news.cn/2020-04/24/c_139004333.htm.
24. For example, see "San dai ren gongyi chuxin—dianying dangke rang dangshi xuexi jiaoyu 'huo' qilai" (Three generations remember our original aspirations—cinematic party lessons bring party history education to life"): http://www.sznews.com/content/mb/2021-12/12/content_24806856.htm. Also see https://www.12371.cn/special/dydk/; http://www.ningbo.gov.cn/art/2021/4/3/art_1229099763_59027085.html.
25. Zhen Zhang, Angela Zito, and Sheldon H. Lu, eds., *DV-Made China: Digital Subjects and Social Transformations after Independent Film* (Honolulu: University of Hawai'i Press, 2015); Paul G. Pickowicz, and Yingjin Zhang, eds., *Filming the Everyday: Independent Documentaries in Twenty-first-century China* (Lanham, Md.: Rowman & Littlefield, 2016).
26. See http://news.sina.com.cn/o/2010-11-07/142318338429s.shtml.
27. Geremie R. Barmé, "A Voice from Old Shanghai Under COVID Lockdown," *China Project*, April 6, 2022.
28. Paul Mozur, Muyi Xiao and John Liu, "'Breach of the Big Silence': Protests Stretch China's Censorship to Its Limits," *New York Times*, November 30, 2022.

Index

access to cinema, 119, 134–36, 138, 166, 213
Admiral Yamamoto (*Isoroku Yamamoto*), 237, 238–39
Adolescence in the Flames of War, 231
Adventures in the Bandit's Den, 179–80, 179
agricultural production groups, 57, 58, 85, 128–29
agriculture: collectivization, 100, 123–25; films on, 95, 96, 97, 200; films shown near fields, 57; insecticides, 84; model fields, 97–98, 115, 120; in North Korea, 200; in Soviet Union, 24; Sputnik rice paddy, 115, 120. *See also* Four Pests Campaign
Ah Cheng, 154
Ai Qing, 210
Albanian films, 193, 204–7
All-China Federation of Trade Unions, 56. *See also* workers
Althusser, Louis, 95
animated slideshows. *See* lantern slides

anti-Japanese mythic dramas, 246
Anti-Rightist Campaign, 127, 218, 219, 220–21
antisuperstition films, 14, 22, 183, 184, 187–89
apparatus theory, 9, 67, 95
Attali, Jacques, 147
audience reception: applause, 154; of bitter films, 183–87, 189–90; at criticism screenings, 234–35, 240; of documentary newsreels, 56, 63, 96, 98–100, 115–16, 127–28, 139, 174, 233; expectations, 164, 185; of foreign films, 193–94, 196–205, 206–7, 208–11, 212–14; guerrilla tactics, 3, 13–14, 163, 179, 191–92, 234–36, 240; of guerrilla war films, 13, 154, 164, 165–70, 191; of images of Mao, 23, 51–52, 54, 151, 154; listening modes, 155; of melodramas, 169, 201; mistaking films for reality, 23, 149, 184; performative responses, 13, 14, 25, 55, 154, 164, 190, 202; of poisonous weed films, 234–36, 242;

audience reception (*continued*)
  potential for mobilization, 50, 56–57; of propaganda films, 163, 179–80; of revolutionary spirit mediumship, 170, 191; of revolutionary spy thrillers, 177–80, 181–82, 183; of *Serf*, 14, 189–90; of socialist education films, 9, 13; of war films, 13, 57; of *The White-Haired Girl*, 149, 183–87
audiences: behaviors and sounds, 153, 154; of cadres, 57; clothing, 152, 159; comprehension of films, 81; during Cultural Revolution, 133, 134; discussions after screenings, 69, 71, 81, 153; diversity, 28; fatal accidents, 134–35; female, 51, 98, 102, 118–19, 186–87, 201, 207; first-time film viewers, 23, 149; oral-history interviews, 32; in postsocialist era, 242; preferences, 9, 132–33; responses to arrival of projection teams, 52–53, 149–50; revolutionary energy, 97; rural, 9, 13–14, 149–50; socializing by, 160–61; soldiers, 57–58, 59–60, 69, 81, 119, 134, 166; students, 246; as transcultural guerrillas, 194, 197, 199, 204, 212–13, 214; travel to screenings, 13, 149, 159; unequal access to cinema, 119, 134–36, 138, 166, 213; workers, 55–56, 75, 100, 114–15, 129, 166. *See also* hot noise; screenings
August First Film Studio, 164, 167, 187–88
Awaara, 207–11

Bakhtin, Mikhail, 147
Balzac and the Little Chinese Seamstress (*Xiao caifeng*), 204, 211
bamboo clappers, 79, 80–81, 91

Bao, Weihong, 21, 26
baojuan (precious scrolls), 80
barefoot projectionists, 73–77, 137. *See also* projectionists
Battle of the Japan Sea (*Nihonkai daikaisen*), 237
Bazin, André, 50
Beijing: "bridge man" protest, 250; criticism screenings, 234, 236; film screenings for students, 246; internal reference screenings, 238; sparrow extermination campaign, 174–76
The Bell Rings at the Old Temple (*Gusha zhongsheng*), 189
Benjamin, Walter, 7, 21, 50, 52
Besieged City (*Binglin chengxia*), 232
Besieging Sparrows (*Weijiao maque*), 96, 172–74, *173*
bitter films, 116, 117. *See also Serf*; speaking bitterness; *The White-Haired Girl*
blockbusters, 131–32. *See also* villagebusters
bloodline theory, 210, 211
bodies: of audience members, 147, 156; of projectionists, 9, 67, 78, 89, 102–3, 244. *See also* embodiment
Bordwell, David, 194
Boym, Svetlana, 146
Brecht, Bertolt, 225
Buck-Morss, Susan, 57
Buddhism: antisuperstition films, 184, 187–89; *baojuan*, 80; monks, 189–90, 249; ox-demons and snake-spirits, 219, 222; pilgrimage sites, 245–46; Tibetan, 187–90. *See also* ritual spaces
The Butterfly Lovers (*Liang shanbo yu Zhu Yingtai*), 125–26

cadres: food provided to mobile projection units, 158; local, 57, 75, 85, 88, 154–55; purges, 73; speeches, 154–55

The Case of Xu Qiuying (*Xu Qiuying anjian*), 177

Casetti, Francesco, 67

Catholic Church: churches in China, 62, 63, 85–86; propaganda, 19

CCP. *See* Chinese Communist Party

censorship: as exorcism, 215–16, 220–23, 239; of films, 226; internal reference films, 236–39, 240; by masses, 219; online, 250; by projectionists of foreign films, 197–98; screenings, 209; self-, 219

Chau, Adam, 145

Chen Bo'er, 46

Chen Huangmei, 50

Chen Sihe, 215, 235

Chiang Kai-shek (Jiang Jieshi), 18, 178

children: acting as surveillance agents, 177, 178–79; of female projectionists, 113, 114; film screenings for, 246; Four Pests Campaign and, 176; in guerrilla war films, 1–3, 2; labor of, 127; of military families, 166, 237; role-playing inspired by war films, 166; in war films, 166–67, 169

China Pictorial, 105, 106–8, 110

Chinese cinema: attendance rates, 121, 133; foreign films and, 211–12; golden ages, 27; history, 26, 27, 68, 195; patriotic films, 131; publicity, 131; red economy, 136–37; villagebusters, 131, 132–36. *See also* Maoist cinema

Chinese Cinema Yearbook, 46

Chinese Communist Party (CCP): film production, 46; guerrilla governance style, 44–45; photographers, 7–8; Propaganda Department, 18–19, 229; treatment of critics, 220; use of media, 1, 43–44, 45; Yan'an Film Group, 7, 46, 69. *See also* media infrastructure; propaganda

Chinese Communist Revolution, 1, 43–44

Chion, Michel, 155

Chongqing: female projectionists, 102–3; film screenings, 99, 134, 187

Christian churches, 60, 62, 63, 85–86, 245–46, 249

cinema of conscription, 57, 78, 161, 167, 191

cinematic cult of Mao, 23, 50–55

cinematic extraction, 122, 129, 140

cinematic guerrillas: audiences as, 13–14, 165, 183, 191–92; economic, 122; filmmakers as, 14, 249; meanings, 3, 8–9, 13–16; onscreen guerrillas, 3, 8, 14, 163–70, 191; in postsocialist era, 242–50. *See also* guerrilla reception; projectionists

cinematic liturgy, 14–15, 19, 82, 84, 89, 90

cinematic mediumship, 20–21. *See also* revolutionary spirit mediumship

cinematic nation-building, 49–59, 60, 64

City Without Night (*Bu ye cheng*), 230, 233

Civil War, Chinese, 4–5, 165, 246

clapper-talk, 80–81, 91. *See also* bamboo clappers

Clark, Paul, 14, 229

class enemies: demonization, 86; denunciations, 178; exorcisms, 24–25, 185; in films, 157, 184, 185; landlords and rich peasants, 90, 103, 139, 153, 157, 184, 185, 186–87. *See also* struggle sessions

Index 325

clothing: of audience members, 152, 159; fashion inspired by films, 207, 311–12n59; of projectionists, 86, 88
commune-based movie teams, 47, 68, 73–77, 74, 98, 128, 136–37, 242–44
Communist Youth League, 71
copy-runners, 79, 133, 150, 154, 159–60
corruption, 130, 133, 136, 137–38
counterespionage films. *See* revolutionary spy thrillers
COVID pandemic, 250
criticism screenings: as exorcism, 216; guerrilla reception, 234–36, 240; as inoculation, 215, 232, 239–40; Mao on, 229; publications related to, 233, 234; purpose, 215, 216, 230, 232; Red Guard preparations, 232–33; in schools, 233; voiceovers, 233–34
crosstalk (*xiangsheng*), 84, 199, 210
Cultural Revolution: attacks on projectionists, 73; audiences during, 133, 134; audiovisual media, 223, 240; banned films, 63, 223; bloodline theory, 210, 211; compared to religious revival, 20; demon metaphors, 222–23; denunciations of enemies, 178; extra-filmic propaganda, 86; film exhibition network, 73, 98, 133–34; foreign films screened during, 193, 196–97, 202–4, 205; goals, 240; Great Criticism, 222–23, 240; Jiang Qing and, 228–29, 230–32; mass rallies, 78; paramilitary organizations, 59; purges, 73; radio broadcasts, 76; red treasure films, 53, 133; revolutionary model opera films, 62, 133–34, 229; revolutionary model works, 14, 73, 94, 98, 180–81; screenings during, 14, 27, 58, 78, 86, 111, 134–35; songs, 191; struggle sessions, 24–25, 62, 110, 111, 222–23, 233, 240; Three Sisters Movie Team and, 110–11. *See also* criticism screenings; Red Guards; sent-down youths
cultural ritual halls, 248–49

Dai Sijie, *Balzac and the Little Chinese Seamstress*, 204, 211
Daoism, 5, 60, 218, 222
Dazhai, 17, 98–100, 99, 120, 137, 139, 200
Dazhong dianying. *See Mass Cinema*
demon-deflecting mirror, 220, 221, 222, 239
demon metaphors, 86, 222–23. *See also* exorcisms; ox-demons and snake-spirits
Derrida, Jacques, 216, 229, 239
Dianying fangying. *See Film Projection*
digital projectionists, 112–13, 246–47
The Disclosed Identity (*Sumgil su ŏmnŭn chŏngch'e*), 178
Doctor Bethune (*Baiqiu'en daifu*), 214
documentaries: on agricultural techniques, 95–97, 129, 200; on Dazhai, 98–100, 139; educational mission, 125, 128, 139; internal reference screenings, 237; on Mao's funeral, 63, 116; screening of, 56, 115, 125, 128, 139; on The Three Sisters Movie Team, 91, 101. *See also Besieging Sparrows*; *Liu Shaoqi Visits Indonesia*; newsreels; *Rent Collection Courtyard*
drama troupes, 48, 75, 76–77
The Dream of the Red Chamber (*Honglou meng*), 63, 135–36, 218
Du Mu, 219

326 *Index*

Early Spring in February (*Zaochun eryue*), 229, 230
Echo on the Seaside (*Oshëtime në bregdet*), 204–5
economic practices: extraction of labor and grain, 129, 140; private profits, 139; sustainability, 9, 128–30. *See also* screening fees
The Eighth Is Bronze (*I teti në bronx*), 206–7
Eighth Route Army, 9, 69
electricity, 2, 78, 147, 149. *See also* power generators
Electric Shadows (*Mengying tongnian*), 205, 206, 211–12
Elsaesser, Thomas, 97
embodiment: in Maoist media networks, 21; of propaganda by projectionists, 9, 29, 30; of revolutionary spirit, 170. *See also* bodies
emphasis films, 132, 185. *See also* socialist education films; villagebusters
ethnic minorities: film audiences, 51, 60; in films, 181–82; Hui, 117; indigenous religions, 25, 61; projectionists, 60, 71, 72, 117, 249; Tajiks, 181–82; Uyghurs, 249. *See also* Tibet
The Everlasting Radio Signals (*Yongbu xiaoshi de dianbo*), 4–5, *4*, 170, 178
exorcisms: censorship as, 215–16, 220–23, 239; of class enemies, 24–25, 185; criticism screenings as, 216; incantations, 222; Maoist cinema as exorcist medium, 62

female projectionists: acceptance, 120; backgrounds, 102, 114, 115, 116, 120; bodies, 102–3; challenges, 113, 114; clothing, 88; as entrepreneurs, 112–13, 118; at factories, 114–15; lodging, 119–20; as models, 102–5, 119–20; oral-history interviews, 93, 113–18; ordinary, 93, 113–18, 120; performances, 112; physical training, 102, 112; pregnancies and children, 102–3, 113, 114; recruitment, 72; revolutionary spirit mediumship, 119–20; transportation, 86–87. *See also* Three Sisters Movie Team
Feng Xiaocai, 32, 92
Feng Xiaogang, 63
Fighting South and North (*Nanzheng beizhan*), 165
Film Bureau, 47, 49, 50, 52, 123, 131, 227, 229
film exhibition network: blank spots, 9, 60, 130–31; during Cultural Revolution, 73, 98, 133–34; economic targets, 123–24, 125; expansion, 1, 9, 28, 46–48, 49–50, 60, 98, 133; gray economy, 136–39; military, 47, 164, 166; participants, 47–48; Soviet, 45–46; trade union, 55–56, 75, 100, 114–15. *See also* mobile projection units; movie theaters; projectionists
Film Guidance Committee, 226
film noir, 180
Film Projection (*Dianying fangying*): articles, 79, 83–84, 121, 127, 131, 137, 151; audiences, 128; covers, *10*, *11*; editorials, 102, 132–33; projectionists reports, 51, 72, 122, 127; years of publication, 129
film projectionists. *See* projectionists

film reels: copy-runners, 79, 133, 150, 154, 159–60; as precious scrolls, 79–80; protecting, 79–80; technical issues, 79

film studies: alternative origin stories, 89; questions, 26–28, 122, 244–45. *See also* media theory

Fiske, John, 13

Five Heroes on Langya Mountain (Langya shan wu zhuangshi), 129, 231

The Flourishing Village (Kkot p'inŭn maŭl), 200

The Flower Girl (Kkot p'anŭn ch'ŏnyŏ), 134, 200–204, 203, 245

Flowers of the Motherland (Zuguo de huaduo), 218

food: commensality, 157; consumed at screenings, 156, 157–58; Great Leap famine, 115–16, 129, 157, 221, 249; for mobile projection teams, 86, 87–89, 137, 158; peddlers, 87, 137, 156, 157; production, 156–57; in socialist cinema, 157; spiritual, 156–57, 158. *See also* agriculture

foreign films: Albanian, 193, 204–7; countries of origin, 193, 213; diversity, 193; dubbed, 196, 237–38; extra-filmic meanings, 194, 209–10, 211; Hollywood, 131, 193, 195, 225–26, 227, 241–42; Indian, 207–11; internal reference screenings, 237–39, 240; Japanese, 237, 238–39; metacinematic references, 197, 204, 205, 211–12; as poisonous weed films, 225–26, 231; popular, 134, 138; in postsocialist era, 212, 214, 242; reception, 193–94, 201–2, 204–5, 206–7, 208–11, 212–14; Romanian, 134, 193; transcultural interpretation, 193–94, 199, 204–5,

206–7, 212; transnational, 212; Yugoslav, 138. *See also* North Korean films; Soviet films

Foucault, Michel, 171, 177

Four Cleanups campaign, 110, 185

Four Pests Campaign, 96, 172–76

Gansu, mobile projection units, 88, 95

Gao Ying, 210

gardening analogies, 218–19. *See also* poisonous weeds

Gateway to Glory (Ah, Kaigun), 237

Ge Fei, 135–36, 145, 156

gender: norms, 92, 102, 114, 118; patriarchy, 116, 132. *See also* female projectionists; women

generators. *See* power generators

Getino, Octavio, 14–15

ghost plays and stories, 219–20, 221–22, 228. *See also* ox-demons and snake-spirits

Gods and Ghosts Are Inefficacious (Shengui bu ling), 22

Goldstein, Joshua, 146

Gone with the Wind, 227

Great Criticism, 222–23, 240

Great Leap Forward: famine, 115–16, 129, 157, 221, 249; film screenings during, 101, 129–30, 153; mass rallies, 78, 127; model workers, 72; oral histories, 249; propaganda, 95, 115, 129; public canteens, 157; slogans, 60, 129, 241, 242; songs, 48; steel production, 129

Great Sparrow Massacre. *See* sparrow extermination campaign

Guangdong, film screenings, 133, 184–85, 186

Guangxi: agricultural production brigades, 128–29; film screenings,

53, 60, 132, 133, 149, 186–87; screening fee collection, 121
guerrilla cinema, 14–15, 163–65. *See also* cinematic guerrillas; guerrilla war films
guerrilla governance style, 44–45
Guerrilla on the Plains (*Pingyuan youjidui*), 166–67
guerrilla media networks, 44, 45, 64
guerrilla reception, 3, 13–14, 163, 179, 191–92, 234–36, 240. *See also* audience reception
guerrilla research methods, 31–34
guerrillas: Chinese term, 5; Mao Zedong on, 5–6, 18, 44–45; networks, 7; propaganda units, 6–7; tactics, 5–6, 167–69; transcultural, 194, 197, 199, 204, 212–13, 214; youth as, 1–3. *See also* cinematic guerrillas; sparrow tactic
guerrilla war films: Albanian, 204–7; anti-Japanese mythic dramas, 246; children in, 1–3, 2; embodied mediation, 170; heroes, 3, 8, 165, 166, 180, 191; human communication networks, 169; Jiang Qing on, 231; messages, 8, 191; military pedagogical films, 167, 170; popularity, 164; in postsocialist era, 246; produced by PLA, 167; propaganda messages, 129, 164; reception, 13, 154, 164, 165–70, 191; as red classics, 8, 191; revolutionary spirit mediumship, 4–5, 164; screenings, 8, 56, 116, 129, 191, 246, 249; televisual broadcasts, 8
Guizhou, mobile projection unit reports, 51
Gunning, Tom, 152–53
Guo Degang, 199
Guo Moruo, "To Curse Sparrows," 175

Harbin: film screenings, 53, *54–55*, 195; movie theaters, 27, 70
Harrison, Henrietta, 85–86
Hebei: clapper-talks, 80; Laishui County, 92–93, 101, 112; mobile projection units, 103, 109; research trips, 32–33, 92–93, 105, 109–10, 112–13, 161. *See also* Three Sisters Movie Team
Heilmann, Sebastian, 44–45
Heilongjiang, film screenings, 27, 32, 70, 87, 99, 159, 201. *See also* Harbin; Manchuria
Henan: film screenings, 236; mobile projection units, 121; spirit mediums, 25
The Heroic Little Guerrillas (*Yingxiong xiao balu*), 1–3, *2*, 250
hidden transcripts, 14, 183, 191
Higson, Andrew, 212
Hollywood films, 131, 193, 195, 225–26, 227, 241–42
Hong Kong: films, 130; screenings, 27
horror, 165, 183, 189, 201, 222
hot noise (*renao*): auditory, 152–55; gustatory and olfactory, 155–58; in postsocialist era, 161; socialist, 147–48, 162; tactile and haptic, 158–61; use of term, 26, 119, 145–47, 214; visual, 148–51. *See also* open-air screenings
Hu Jie, 249
Hu Yaobang, 209
Huang Baomei, 96
Huang, Xuelei, 195
Hubei: commune-run cinema, 73–74; female projectionists, 102, 113, 115–17; film screenings, 54, 61–62, 99, 156, 214, 247; mobile projection units, 93–94, 102, 125, 137, 247;

Hubei (*continued*)
    projectionists, 185–86, 244; research trips, 32–33, 187, 247
Hubei Sino-Soviet Movie Team, 85
Hunan: film screenings, 129–130, 165; projectionist petition movement, 244, *244*
Hundred Flowers Movement, 218

Independent Brigade (*Duli dadui*), 231
Indian films: filmmakers' visit to China, 208, *209*; global reach, 208; reception, 208–11; shown in China, 207–11
Indignant Tide (*Nuchao*), 233, 235
industrialization of populace, 50, 55–56, 64, 245
information trees, 169, *169*
Inner Mongolia, film screenings, 159–60, 236
insects, 84, 176. *See also* Four Pests Campaign
internal reference films, 236–39, 240
In the Heat of the Sun (*Yangguang canlan de rizi*), 197, *198*, 211, 237
Ivens, Joris, 7

Japan: colonial rule of Manchuria, 46, 69; films, 237, 238–39; storytellers at silent film screenings, 81–82
Jia Zhangke, 211
Jiang Qing: censorship campaigns, 223, 226; on cinema as opium, 223, 224, 225; condemnation of poisonous weed films, 215, 225, 229–30, 239; cultural criticism, 228–29; Cultural Revolution and, 228–29, 230–32; film criticism, 180–81, 182–83, 231–32; on film music, 231; film project in Zhejiang, 100, 241; films watched by, 227–28, 229–30; illnesses, 227–28; internal reference screenings, 237; propaganda poster, 223; revolutionary model works and, 73, 98; sensory sensitivities, 227, 229, 231; speeches, 224, 228, 229; three prominences theory, 180
Jiang Wen, 197, 211, 237
Jiangnan in the North (*Beiguo Jiangnan*), 229
Jiangsu: audience reactions to films, 50; mobile projection units, 87, 122, 125–26
Jiangsu Provincial Mass Education Center, 46
Jilin, mobile projection units, 123
Johnson, David, 25

Kang Sheng, 229
Kang, Xiaofei, 184
Kapoor, Prithviraj, 208
Kapoor, Raj, 208; *Awaara* (*The Vagabond*), 207–11
Kim Il-sung, 200
Kim Jong-il, 200, 201
Kittler, Friedrich, 15–16, 29
KMT. *See* Nationalist Party
Korean films. *See* North Korean films
Korean War, 59, 225–26
Kracauer, Siegfried, 220, 225

Laishui County, Hebei: projectionists, 91, 101–13; research trip, 92–93, 105. *See also* Three Sisters Movie Team
Landmine Warfare (*Didao zhan*), 116, 167
land reform, 24, 48, 184
lantern slides: animated slideshows, 91, 101, 103, *104*, 109, 112; on local models, 83, 84–85, 96; producing,

84–85, 109; slideshows, 80, 82–86, 83, 89–90, 95
Larkin, Brian, 23, 27
The Last Roman (*Kampf um Rom*), 237–38
Latin America, guerrilla cinema, 14–15
Lee, Haiyan, 177, 190
Lenin, Vladimir, 7, 45–46
Lenin in 1918 (*Lenin v 1918 godu*), 194, 195–99, *198*
Lenin in October (*Lenin v oktyabre*), 194, 195–97
Letter with Feather (*Jimao xin*), 169, *169*, 170
Li Jun, 206
Li Shizhen, 217–18, 231
Li Shuangshuang, 132
Li Zhensheng, 53
Li Zhisui, 227
Liang Xiaosheng, 176
Liaoning: agricultural production brigades, 128–29; film screenings, 62
The Life of Wu Xun (*Wu Xun zhuan*), 226, 232, 235
Lifton, Robert Jay, 20
Lin Biao, 54–55, 230
The Lin Family Shop (*Lin jia puzi*), 230
literature and arts work groups, 8
Little Soldier Zhang Ga (*Xiao bing Zhang Ga*), 166
Liu Shaoqi, 111, 133, 233–34, 236
Liu Shaoqi Visits Indonesia, 233–34, 236
Liu Xiaobo, 18
Liu Zhenzhong, 71
Lu Gusun, 197
Lu Shukun, 114
Lu, Xiaoning, 177
Lu Xun, 129, 224–25, 230
Lu Zailiang, "Commune member by day, projectionist by night," 74

Madame Mao. *See* Jiang Qing
magic lantern slides. *See* lantern slides
Manchuria: film screenings, 46, 69, 70, 87, 201; Manchurian Motion Picture Association, 46, 69
Mao Zedong: on criticism screenings, 229; death and funeral, 63, 116, 241, 242; films criticized by, 226; gardening analogies, 218–19; on guerrilla warfare, 5–6, 18, 44–45; Indian filmmakers and, 208, *209*; little red book, 77; as media theorist, 4–6, *On Protracted Warfare*, 167; on ox-demons and snake-spirits, 219–21; personality cult, 23, 25, 50, 51–55, 151, 245; on poisonous weeds, 216, 218–19; projectionists and, 101; on propaganda, 6–7, 95; quotations, 22; on red flag, 60; on revolution, 43; on Socialist Education Movement, 221; on sparrows, 170–72; at Tiananmen Red Guard rallies, 23, 53, 133
Mao Zedong, images of: audience reception, 23, 51–52, *54*, 151, 154; in lantern slides, 101; in newsreels, 23, 52, 53–55, *55*, 151; power, 222; religious aura, 20
Maoist cinema: climate-changing power, 30, 94, 97–100; defined, 15; economic goals and value, 123, 128, 139; educational mission, 121, 128; as exorcist medium, 62; as guerrilla media network, 26, 163–65; heroes and villains, 180–81; mass character, 50; mediumship, 20–21; messages, 50, 56–57, 80; as physical and spirit medium, 90; propaganda value, 45–46, 121, 123, 163; revolutionary roles, 49–50, 80, 119; socialist distant horizon education, 24, 50,

Maoist cinema (*continued*)
123; socialist education films, 9, 13, 22, 56, 132–33, 221–22; as spiritual food, 26, 156–57; state sponsorship, 15. *See also* guerrilla war films

Maoist cultural economy, 140–41

Marks, Laura W., 158

Marxism-Leninism, 43, 220, 224

Mass Cinema (*Dazhong dianying*), 16–17, 102, 208

materiality, 29, 30, 67, 79, 86–89, 90

McLuhan, Marshall, 3, 53

media infrastructure: human constitution of, 3, 43–45, 48–49, 64, 67, 80, 89; revolutionary role, 1, 43–44. *See also* film exhibition network; propaganda; radio; television

media revolution, 1, 43–44, 64, 250

media theory: apparatus theory, 9, 67, 95; assemblages, 67; Chinese, 5–7; defining media, 20; human spirit in, 29–31, 250; Latin American, 14–15; Marxist, 7; mediation as mediumship, 20–26; prescriptive theories, 26, 34, 216, 239; warfare and, 15–16. *See also* film studies

medicine, poisonous weeds and, 217–18. *See also* pharmakon

mediumship, 20–26. *See also* revolutionary spirit mediumship; spirit mediums

melodramas, 119, 134, 183–191, 200–2. *See also* bitter films

militarization of populace: cinema and, 5–9, 15–16, 55–59, 64, 148, 164, 166–70, 245; projectionist training and, 71; propaganda networks and, 44; role of mobile projection units, 49–50; shock battalions, 57, 129.

See also guerrilla cinema, People's Liberation Army

military pedagogical films, 167, *168*, 170

militias, local, 167, 179

Mo Yan, 199, 202

mobile projection units: copy-runners, 79, 133, 150, 154, 159–60; costs, 122, 123, 133; equipment, 67, 73, 77–78, 88, 89, 201; food, 86, 87–89, 137, 158; generator operators, 78; itineraries, 9, 47–48, *47*, 72, 131; of KMT, 46; local problem solving, 90; members, 66; model teams, 93–94; number of, 1, 46, 128; organization, 47; for PLA, 59–60; in postsocialist era, 243, 246–49; responsibilities, 8–9, 66; seen as privileged, 88; shelter, 72, 87; songs, 42–43; transportation, 8–9, 86–87, *88*; welcomed by residents, 52–53, 149–50. *See also* projectionists; screenings; Three Sisters Movie Team

model projectionists, 72, 101, 102, 103, 105, 119, 161, 247–49. *See also* Three Sisters Movie Team

models: agricultural, 97–98; emulation of, 94, 95, 99–100; labor, 83, 84–85, 96; Maoist, 94; projection of, 93–100; relationship to reality, 94–95; towns, 98–100; *yangban*, 97–98. *See also* revolutionary model works

The Monkey King Thrice Defeats the White-Boned Demon (*Sun Wukong san da Baigujing*), 63, 132–33

movie theaters: architecture, 148–49; conditions in 1970s, 137–38; current status, 32–33; early, 27, 70, 195; employees, 137–38; at factories, 56, 115; number of, 1, 46; renovated

332 *Index*

ritual spaces, 60–61, 63; state-run, 47; township, 63; widescreen films shown, 201. *See also* film exhibition network; screenings

Mukherjee, Debashree, 97, 244–45

Mulvey, Laura, 180

music. *See* songs; *Swan Lake*

Muslims: audiences, 185; female projectionists, 117

Nanjing, projectionist training, 42, 49, 71

National Academy of Chinese Theatre Arts, 218

National Agricultural Science Committee, 97–98

Nationalist Party (KMT): Civil War, 4, 165, 246; former officer, 178; government film screenings, 7, 46, 69; mobile projection units, 46; slogans, 18; in Taiwan, 1–2

nation-building, cinematic, 49–59, 60, 64

networks: cultural, 48; guerrilla, 7; human communication, 169; patriarchal, 116; propaganda, 3, 8, 44, 45, 48–49, 64. *See also* film exhibition network

newsreels: *Besieging Sparrows*, 96, 172–74, *173*; internal reference screenings, 237; Mao's image in, 23, 52, 53–55, *55*, 151; reception, 96; screenings, 128; Three Sisters Movie Team in, 91, 101. *See also* documentaries

Ningxia: female projectionists, 113, 117–18; film screenings, 54–55, 99–100, 166–67, 213–14; first projectionist, 68–69; mobile projection unit itineraries, *47*; People's Cinema, 60; travel to screenings, 159

noise. *See* hot noise; sparrow tactic

Northeast Film Studio, 46, 196

Northeast provinces, research trips, 32–33. *See also* Heilongjiang; Manchuria

North Korean films: comedies, 200; genres, 199; musical melodramas, 134, 200–1; reception, 199–204; screenings in China, 125, 132, 134, 157, 193, 199–204; spy thrillers, 178

Old Wounds (*Plagë të vjetra*), 207

On the Docks (*Haigang*), 134

On the Long March (*Wanshui qianshan*), 57

open-air screenings: accidents, 134–35, 201; fee collection, 124; poetic description, 16–17; in postsocialist era, 161; screens, 9, 25, 30, 112, 150–52; seating, 159–60; sites, 9, 57; as socialist hot noise, 147–48; sounds, 152–55; as spectacles, 145–46, 147–48, 152, 161, 162; weather, 159–60. *See also* hot noise; mobile projection units; screening fees; screening locations

opera: ghost plays, 219–20, 228; Peking, 68, 134, 146, 229; Ping, 199; revolutionary model, 62, 98, 170, 210; ritual, 25

opera films, 25, 63, 118, 125–26, 127, 132–33, 135–36. *See also* revolutionary model opera films

opium: cinema as, 223, 224, 225–26; religion as, 224; spiritual, 26, 216, 232, 239

Our Leaders Work with Us (*Lingxiu he women tong laodong*), 52

ox-demons and snake-spirits, 111, 136, 215, 216, 219–21, 222, 229, 232, 239. *See also* demon metaphors

Index 333

Pang, Laikwan, 97, 140, 222
participatory surveillance, 177–79
Partisan Girl (*Ppalch'isan ch'ŏnyŏ*), 125
Path to Dazhai (*Dazhai zhilu*), 17, 99
patriotism: patriotic education films, 131, 246, 249; sentiments, 166, 182
Peach Blossom Fan (*Taohua shan*), 232
peasants. *See* agricultural production groups; rural areas
Peking opera, 68, 134, 146, 229. *See also* opera
Peng Dehuai, 235
People's Daily, 218–19, 221, 222, 226, 230
People's Liberation Army (PLA): children of soldiers, 166; Civil War, 165, 246; cultural clubs, 60–61, *61*; cultural conferences, 230–31; emulation of, 58–59; film exhibition network, 47, 164; film screenings for soldiers, 57–58, 59–60, 81, 119, 134, 166; film studio, 164, 167, 187–88; internal reference screenings, 237–38; Korean War, 59, 225–26; shelling of Taiwan Strait islands, 1–2; in Tibet, 188
Perry, Elizabeth J., 20, 44–45
Peters, John Durham, 21, 149–50
pharmakon, 216, 220, 229, 239
Photography Net, 7–8
Pickpocket (*Xiao Wu*), 211
Ping opera, 199
PLA. *See* People's Liberation Army
PLA Daily, 232
Platform (*Zhantai*), 211
Plato, 225, 229
poisonous weed films: advice for audiences, 230; criticism of, 232; foreign films as, 225–26, 231; internal reference screenings, 236–39, 240; Jiang Qing's condemnation of, 215, 225, 229–30, 239; reception, 215, 234–36, 242; screenings after Mao's death, 135–36, 242; use of term, 215, 216, 239. *See also* criticism screenings
poisonous weeds, 128, 216, 217–19, 225
postsocialist era: audiences, 242; cinematic guerrillas, 249–50; foreign films, 212, 214, 242; guerrilla war films, 246; hot noise, 161; legacies of cinematic guerrillas, 242–45; mobile projection units, 243, 246–49; open-air screenings, 161; projectionists, 112–13, 242–44, 246–49; ritual economy, 140–41
power generators, 23, 77–78, 116, 118, 154
precious scrolls: *baojuan*, 80; film reels as, 79–80
prescriptive theories, 26, 34, 216, 239
projectionists: activities before and after screenings, 8–9, 29, 57, 80–85, *81*; backgrounds, 71–72, 75–76; barefoot, 73–77, 137; bodies, 9, 67, 78, 89, 102–3, 244; as bureaucratic intermediaries, 139–40; challenges, 72–73, 75, 78, 79–80, 87, 89, 127, 151; clothing, 86, 88; commune-based (third generation), 47, 68, 73–77, *74*, 98, 128, 136–37, 242–44; competitions, 75; complaints, 72, 127; digital, 112–13, 246–47; diversity, 28, 66, 71; economic priorities, 9, 64, 127; as entrepreneurs, 139; at factories, 56; generations, 66–67, 68–77; as guerrillas, 3, 8–9, 13, 14–15, 132, 138–39; illustrations, *10–12*; marriage, 72, 114–17; materiality of everyday life, 86–89; mediating roles, 3, 17–18; model, 72, 101, 102, 103, 105, 119, 161, 247–49; narrating

334 *Index*

films, 81, 82–83, 149, 185; number of, 66; oral-history interviews, 32, 33–34; performances, 76–77, 81–86, 89–90; periodicals, 31, 51, 122; petition movement, 243–44, *244*; poetry, 16–17, 156–57; in postsocialist era, 32–34, 112–13, 242–44, 246–49; pre-1949 pioneers (first generation), 68–70; propaganda activities, 8–9, 29, 30, 245; recruitment, 71–72, 75; reminiscences, 31–32; reports and records, 31, 33, 50, 51, 72; retirement, 33, 110, 243; revolutionary energy, 89, 94, 96; revolutionary roles, 49–50, 60, 64, 71; revolutionary spirit mediumship, 3–4, 17–18, 21, 64, 67, 119, 245; as ritual specialists, 19, 20, 22, 80; songs by, 41–43, 49; as spirit mediums, 90; state employees (second generation), 68, 71–73; training, 49, 71, 75, 112, 117. *See also* female projectionists; lantern slides; mobile projection units; screenings

propaganda: actions of mobile projectionists, 8–9, 29, 30, 245; artworks, 8, 20, 222; attacks on religion, 187–89; CCP system, 18–19, 229, 245–46; Chinese term (*xuanchuan*), 6, 19, 29; during Cultural Revolution, 86; documentaries, 95–97, 129; economics of, 140; during Great Leap Forward, 95, 115, 129; literature and arts work groups, 8; Mao on, 6–7, 95; masses as media, 3, 6–7, 147; media, 1, 7–8; networks, 3, 8, 44, 45, 48–49, 64; origins of term, 19; radio broadcasts, 1, 8; revolutionary spirit mediumship, 3–5, 17–26, 95–100, 245; spiritual framing, 19; villagebusters, 131, 132–36; wartime, 6–8. *See also* lantern slides; Maoist cinema

propagandists: as cinematic guerrillas, 16; as human media network, 44, 48, 64, 245; indigenous religions of audiences and, 22; on mobile projection teams, 82; on models, 94; pensions, 244; rural youths as, 115–16, 127

Qin Xianglian, 126
Qinghai, film screenings, 23, 60, 132, 185

radio, 1, 4–5, 8, 45, 76. *See also* media infrastructure
radio receptionists, 45
red classics, 8, 191
Red Crag (*Hong yan*), 178
The Red Detachment of Women (*Hongse niangzijun*), 58, 247
Red Guards: criticism screenings and, 232–33; as exorcists, 222; response to Lenin biopics, 197; slogans and art, 222; sparrow warfare, 176; suspected spies and, 178; Tiananmen rally films, 23, 53–55, *54*, *55*, 63, 133; violence, 235. *See also* Cultural Revolution
The Red Lantern (*Hongdeng ji*), 62, 98, 170, 210
Red Propagandist (*Pulgŭn sŏndongwŏn*), 132
red treasure films, 53, 133
religion: analogies to revolution, 19–20, 24; antisuperstition films, 14, 22, 183, 184, 187–89; campaigns against, 18–19, 22–23, 63, 221–22, 245–46, 249; competition from cinema, 61–62, 63–64, 141; indigenous,

Index   335

religion (*continued*)
22–23, 61, 183; as opium of the people, 224; popular, 25, 60, 63, 145–46, 183, 184; shamanism, 22, 185–86, 240. *See also* Buddhism; Catholic Church; Christian churches; Muslims; ritual spaces

renao. *See* hot noise

Rent Collection Courtyard (*Shouzuyuan*), 90, 222

revolutionary cinema. *See* Maoist cinema

revolutionary cultural economy, 140–41

revolutionary energy, 89, 94, 96, 97, 119

revolutionary horror and redemption, 183. *See also Serf; The White-Haired Girl*

revolutionary model opera films, 14, 62, 133–34, 229

revolutionary model operas, 98, 170, 210

revolutionary model works, 14, 73, 94, 98, 180–81

revolutionary spirit, 3, 17, 18, 93–100, 170

revolutionary spirit mediumship: audience reception, 170, 191; dimensions, 3–4, 17–18; by female projectionists, 119–20; of guerrilla war films, 4–5, 164; legacies, 245, 249–50; by projectionists, 3–4, 17–18, 21, 64, 67, 119, 245; propaganda as, 3–5, 17–26, 95–100, 245; socialist hot noise and, 147

revolutionary spy thrillers, 177–81, 182–83, 194, 199, 231

revolutionary war films. *See* guerrilla war films

ritual economy, 140–41, 245

ritual efficacy, 22, 25

ritual spaces: ancestral halls, 60–61, *61*, 62–63, 130, 247–49; Christian churches, 60, 62, 63, 85–86, 245–46; converting into theaters, 60–61, *61*, 63; films shown in, 22, 60–61, 62–63, 130, 247–49, *248*; temples, 60, 62, 63, 141, 245–46

ritual specialists: projectionists as, 19, 20, 22, 80; spirit mediums, 22, 25–26

Romm, Mikhail: *Lenin in 1918*, 194, 195–99, *198*; *Lenin in October*, 194, 195–97

Rooster Crows at Midnight (*Banye ji jiao*), 90

rural areas: cultural networks, 48; film screenings, 131, 132–36, 246–47; gender norms, 114; infrastructure construction, 100; poverty, 13, 158, 159; social hierarchies, 160. *See also* agriculture; mobile projection units; open-air screenings

Rushdie, Salman, 193

rustic cinema. *See* lantern slides

schools: criticism screenings, 233; patriotic education films, 246

science education films, 96, 155, 157, 237

screening fees: bartering for, 122, 127, 130; collecting, 121–22, 123, 124, 127, 128–29, 130, 139; criticism of, 125; during Cultural Revolution, 133; flat, 124, 125, 130; levels, 123–24, 131, 137; paid by communes, 121, 125, 128; revenues, 118, 125; seen as taxes, 26, 125, 129, 139; sneaking in without paying, 13, 124, 130, 137, 138; subsidized, 130–31; ticket sales, 118, 124–25, 127, 130–31 screening locations: enclosed spaces, 13, 63, 124–25, 130, 134; memories of, 33; schools, 233, 246; selection of, 123, 126–27; as spiritual battlegrounds, 60–64. *See also* movie theaters; open-air screenings; ritual spaces

screenings: audio issues, 81, 152; collective singing before, 58, *59*, 84; during Cultural Revolution, 14, 27, 58, 78, 86, 111, 134–35; delayed, 125–26, *126*; double bills, 125; internal reference, 236–39, 240; number of, 128; schedules, 126–27, 128, 141, 152; seating, 80–81, 159–60; at workers' clubs, 55–56, 119. *See also* audiences; criticism screenings; lantern slides; mobile projection units; movie theaters; open-air screenings; projectionists

screens: effects of wind, 151–52; meanings, 30; raising, 9, 25, 112, 150–52; sizes, 152

Secret Drawings (*Mimi tuzhi*), 177

Secret Post in Canton (*Yangcheng anshao*), 177

semiotic guerrilla warfare, 13, 250

sensorium, 148, 161

sensory experiences. *See* hot noise

sent-down youths: as film audiences, 32, 137, 154, 156, 159, 203–5, 213; military uniforms, 59; projectionists, 75–76, *76*, *77*, 87, 89; returns to cities, 210–11

Serf: attacks on Tibetan Buddhism, 187–89; audience reactions, 14, 189–90; messages, 183; music, 190–91; plot, 187, 188–89; screenings, 14, 117, 249; stills, *188*

Shaanxi: female projectionists, 114; indigenous religions, 22; mobile projection units, 86–87

shamanism, 22, 185–86, 240

Shanggan Ridge (*Shanggan ling*), 62, 166, 214

Shanghai: criticism screenings, 215, 230, 233, 234–36; film critics of 1930s, 225; film screenings, 27, 53, 189, 207, 210, 213; films made in, 46, 208; movie theaters, 56, 215; sparrow extermination campaign, 176

Shanghai Dubbing Studio, 238

Shanghai Film Studio, 115, 217–18

Shangzhi County Movie Station, *Film Work Correspondence*, 81, 83

Shanxi, 50, 85–86, 121, 130, 137

Shen Yaoyi, *Lianhuan huabao*, 7

Shi Tiesheng, 177, 196–97, 238

shock battalions, 57, 129

Sichuan: Emei Film Studio, 172–74; film screenings, 185; Four Pests Campaign, 172–74

silent films, 62, 81–82, 149, 152–53

Sino-Japanese War, Second, 18, 46, 62, 170–71

sky media, 149–50

slideshows. *See* lantern slides

Smith, Steve A., 22

snake-spirits. *See* ox-demons and snake-spirits

Snow in the Forest (*Linhai xueyuan*), 231

Sobchack, Vivian Carol, 158, 241–42

socialist cosmopolitanism, 28, 212

socialist distant horizon education, 24, 50, 123

socialist education films, 9, 13, 22, 56, 132–33, 221–22. *See also* emphasis films; Maoist cinema

Socialist Education Movement, 85–86, 103, 116, 132, 185, 221–22

socialist hot noise, 147–48, 162. *See also* hot noise

Index 337

Solanas, Fernando, 14–15
songs: collective singing before screenings, 58, 59, 84; during Cultural Revolution, 191; in films, 2, 153–54, 181–82, 183, 190–91; folk songs, 84, 182, 184; in foreign films, 203, 205, 208, 209–11; during Great Leap Forward, 48; in poisonous weed films, 235–36; by projectionists, 41–43, 49, 184; revolutionary, 82, 84, 153, 190–91; "Sunny Sky in Autumn," 236; "We Are the Heirs of Communism," 2; "Why Are the Flowers So Red," 181–82
Sorrows of the Forbidden City (Qinggong mishi), 234, 235
sounds. *See* hot noise; songs
Soviet films: dubbed, 196; exhibition network, 45–46; Lenin biopics, 194, 195–99; reception, 196–99; shown by Zhou Enlai, 7, *7*, 69–70, 195–96; shown in China, 193, 195–99, 226; war films, 81
Soviet Union: collective farms, 24; Indian films shown in, 208; mobile film units, 45; shock work, 57
Sparks Amid the Reeds (Shajiabang), 98
sparrow extermination campaign, 172–76. *See also* Four Pests Campaign
sparrow tactic, 164–65, 170–71, 176
speaking bitterness, 24–25, 29, 85, 132, 165, 183, 184–85. *See also* bitter films; struggle sessions
spectacles, 145–46, 147–48, 152, 161, 162. *See also* hot noise
spirit mediums, 22, 25–26. *See also* revolutionary spirit mediumship
spiritual battlegrounds, screening locations as, 60–64

spiritual opium, 26, 216, 232, 239
A Spring River Flows East (Yijiang chunshui xiang dong liu), 115
spy thrillers. *See* revolutionary spy thrillers
Stalin, Joseph, 46
Stewart, Jacqueline N., 31–32
The Storm on South Island (Nandao Fengyun), 166
The Story of Liubao (Liubao de gushi), 231, 236
storytellers and storytelling, 48–49, 81–82, 137, 149, 204
struggle sessions, 24–25, 62, 110, 111, 222–23, 233, 240
Sun Daolin, 233
Sun Yat-sen, 18
Suzhou Steel Factory, 56, 113, 114–15
Swan Lake (Tchaikovsky), 197–98

Taiwan: films, 245; night markets, 146
Taiwan Strait islands, shelling of, 1–2
Taking Tiger Mountain by Strategy (Zhiqu Weihushan), 133, 180
Tang Na, 225
Tao Yanling, "Commune member by day, projectionist by night," *74*
Tao Yuanming, "Peach Blossom Spring," 17
Taussig, Michael, 23
television: competition with mobile projection units, 243, 247; films shown on, 8, 191
Ter Haar, Barend J., 222
theaters. *See* movie theaters
Third Cinema, 14–15, 28, 249
Three Sisters Memorial Hall, 33, 92, 112
Three Sisters Movie Team: animated slideshows, 91, 103, *104*, 109; downfall, 110–11; fame, 91, 100–1,

338 *Index*

103–5, 109–10; leader, 109, 110, 111; male team members, 109–10; media coverage, 91–92, 100–1, 103–5, 109–10, 120; as models, 91–92, 100–1, 103–5, 120; nationwide tours, 109; in newsreels, 91, 101; performances, 91; photographic images of, 105, *106–8*, 109; propaganda posters, 91, *92*; recruitment, 91, 101, 103; as role models, 91; successors, 112, 247

thrillers. *See* revolutionary spy thrillers

Tiananmen Red Guard rally films, 23, 53–55, *54, 55*, 63, 133

Tibet: audiences at film screenings, 14, 23, 189–90; Chinese accounts of conditions, 187; film screenings at monasteries, 249; mobile projection units, 249; model female projectionist, 102; PLA occupation, 188. *See also Serf*

Tibetan Buddhism, 187–89

ticket sales. *See* screening fees

township movie theaters, 63

tractors: drivers, 75, 102, 116–18; in North Korean films, 200; on Soviet collective farms, 24, *24*, 50; transportation by, 8, 87, 118

transcultural cinema, 193–94. *See also* foreign films

transcultural guerrillas, 194, 197, 199, 204, 212–13, 214

Tsering Shakya, 14, 190

Tseten Drolma, 190–91

Tsivian, Yuri, 32

Tunnel Warfare (*Didao zhan*), 116, 167–69, *168*

2131 project, 246–47

Two Stage Sisters (*Wutai jiemei*), 234–35

United States: Chinatown video stores, 205; Hollywood films, 131, 193, 195, 225–26, 227, 241–42; Soviet films shown in, 195

urban areas: movie theaters, 47, 130, 148–49; radio sets, 45; screenings of foreign films, 193, 208, 213; ticket sales, 124–25. *See also* specific cities

Uyghur projectionist, 249

Van Fleit Hang, Krista, 208

Vertov, Dziga, 225, 226

Victory Over Death (*Ngadhënjim mbi vdekjen*), 205–6, *206*, 207

villagebusters: popular, 131, 132–33, 134–36; state-led, 131, 132, 133–34

Virilio, Paul, 15

Visitors on Ice Mountain (*Bingshan shang de laike*), 181–83, *181*, 231

Volland, Nicolai, 212

Wang Anyi, 151–52

Wang Baoyi, 101, 103, 105, 109, 111

Wang Guangmei, 111, 233–34, 236

Wang Mingqi, "Projection Team on the Lake," *146*

Wang Xinpeng, 138

Wang Yaqing, 203, *203*

war films: Chinese, 115; heroes, 129; Japanese, 237; popularity, 126, 127, 132; Soviet, 81. *See also* guerrilla war films

Waves of the Danube (*Valurile Dunării*), 134

Wei Binhai, 178

Weller, Robert P., 145–46

Wenzhou, Zhejiang, 100, 140, 161, *248*

When We Pick Apples (*Sagwa ttal ttae*), 200

The White-Haired Girl (*Bai mao nü*): ballet, 184, 185–86; messages, 183; opera, 184; reception, 149, 183–87; rerelease in 1960s, 132, 185; screenings, 17, 62, 116, 151–52, 183–85; villain, 184, 245
"Why Are the Flowers So Red," 181–82
Williams, Linda, 190
Woeser, 190–91
women: agents in spy thrillers, 179–80; as audiences, 51, 98, 102, 118–19, 186–87, 201, 207; clothing and hairstyles inspired by films, 207; film exhibition jobs, 113; films seen by, 118–19; gender norms, 92, 102, 114, 118; patriarchal networks and, 116; responses to *The White-Haired Girl*, 186–87. *See also* female projectionists
workers: agricultural, 57, 85, 128–29; construction, 56, 75; at criticism screenings, 234–35; film screenings for, 55–56, 75, 100, 114–15, 129, 166; model, 83, 84–85, 96; railway, 236; shock battalions, 57, 129
workers' clubs and cultural palaces, 55–56
Wu Baixin, 182–83
Wu Desheng, *Tractor Comes to Our Village*, 24
Wu Qingxun, woodcut of projectionist, 12
Wu Wenguang, 249
Wu Xun, 226. *See also The Life of Wu Xun*

Xi Zhen, 69
Xia Chuan, 187–89
Xiao Jiang, 205, 211–12
Xie Jin: *Huang Baomei*, 96; *Two Stage Sisters*, 234–35

Xinjiang: exiles in, 210; film set in, 181–83; screenings in, 195, 249

Yan'an: films shown in, 69–70, 195–96; pagoda, 4
Yan'an Film Group, 7, 46, 69
Yan'an Xinhua Radio, 8
Yang, Mayfair Mei-hui, 136, 140
Yang Yinlu, 227–28
Ye Qingrui, "Poor and Lower-Middle Peasants Watch Movies," 16–17
Ye Shengtao, 174–75
Ye Zhiguang, 213
Yi Sha, 206–7
You Jingu, woodcut of projectionist, *12*
Young Pioneers, 2
Yu Luoke, "On Family Background," 210
Yuan Muzhi, 46
Yuan Xiuying, 114
Yugoslav films, 138
Yunnan: film screenings, 60, 61, 154; mobile projection units, 88, 136; rural filmmakers, 249; Yi community, 25

Zhan Juying, 249
Zhang Heming, *Tractor Comes to Our Village*, 24
Zhang Wanbao, 68–69
Zhang Xiliao, "The Battle Hymn of Red Projectionists," 42–43
Zhang Zhen, 26, 27
Zhang Zhentao, "Happy at Cinema's Return," *150*
Zhang Zhuoya, 177
Zhejiang: female projectionists, 113, 118; film screenings, 100, 161, 185, 213, 214, 247; mobile projection units, 125, 137, 247; projectionist pensions, 243–44; religious sites, 62,

248; research trips, 32–33, 161, 187, 241, 247; rural ecotourism, 241; screening locations, 62–63; Wenzhou, 100, 140, 161, *248*

Zheng Junli, *A Spring River Flows East*, 115

Zheng Yizhen, 105

Zhongshan Film and Slide Propaganda Team, 42

Zhou, Chenshu, 27, 56

Zhou Enlai: film praised by, 226; films shown by, 7, *7*, 69–70, 195–96; Indian filmmakers and, 208, *209*; Japanese films and, 237; newsreel of funeral, 116

Zhou Xuan, 235

Zhu Andong (Tanaka Taro), 70

Zhuang Ping, *Tractor Comes to Our Village*, 24

Zhu De, 226

GPSR Authorized Representative: Easy Access System Europe, Mustamäe tee 50, 10621 Tallinn, Estonia, gpsr.requests@easproject.com

www.ingramcontent.com/pod-product-compliance
Lightning Source LLC
Chambersburg PA
CBHW022028290426
44109CB00014B/792